2nd EDITION

Ventures

TEACHER'S EDITION

BASIC

Gretchen Bitterlin Dennis Johnson Donna Price Sylvia Ramirez
K. Lynn Savage (Series Editor)
with Becky Tarver Chase
Lois Miller

CAMBRIDGE UNIVERSITY PRESS

CAMBRIDGE
UNIVERSITY PRESS

32 Avenue of the Americas, New York, NY 10013-2473, USA

Cambridge University Press is part of the University of Cambridge.

It furthers the University's mission by disseminating knowledge in the pursuit of education, learning and research at the highest international levels of excellence.

www.cambridge.org
Information on this title: www.cambridge.org/9781107676084

First published 2008
4th printing 2014

Printed in Mexico by Editorial Impresora Apolo, S.A. de C.V.

A catalog record for this publication is available from the British Library.

ISBN 978-1-107-64102-0 Student's Book with Audio CD
ISBN 978-1-107-69108-7 Workbook with Audio CD
ISBN 978-1-139-88532-4 Online Workbook
ISBN 978-1-107-67608-4 Teacher's Edition with Assessment Audio CD / CD-ROM
ISBN 978-1-107-66806-5 Class Audio CDs
ISBN 978-1-107-61622-6 Presentation Plus

Additional resources for this publication at www.cambridge.org/ventures

Art direction, book design, photo research, and layout services: Q2A / Bill Smith
Audio production: CityVox, LLC

Contents

Introduction

Teaching Notes

Additional Resources

To the teacher

What is *Ventures*?

Ventures is a six-level, four-skills, standards-based, integrated-skills series that empowers students to achieve their academic and career goals.

- This most complete program with a wealth of resources provides instructors with the tools for any teaching situation.
- The new Online Workbook keeps students learning outside the classroom.
- Easy-to-teach materials make for a more productive classroom.

What components does *Ventures* have?

Student's Book with Audio CD

Each of the core **Student's Books** contains ten topic-focused units, interspersed with five review units. The main units feature six skill-focused lessons.

- **Lessons** in the Student's Book are self-contained, allowing for completion within a one-hour class period.
- **Review lessons** recycle and reinforce the listening, vocabulary, and grammar skills developed in the two prior units and include a pronunciation activity.
- **Self-assessments** in the back of the book give students an opportunity to reflect on their learning. They support learner persistence and help determine whether students are ready for the unit test.
- **Reference charts**, also in the back of the book, provide grammar paradigms; rules for spelling, punctuation, and grammar; and lists of ordinal numbers, cardinal numbers, countries, and nationalities.
- References to the **Self-study audio CD** that accompanies the Student's Book are indicated in the Student's Book by an icon and track number: STUDENT TK 10 CLASS CD1 TK 14 Look for the audio icon and track number to find activities with self-study audio. "STUDENT" refers to the self-study audio, and "CLASS" refers to the class audio. A full class audio is available separately.
- A **Student Arcade,** available online at www.cambridge.org/venturesarcade, allows students to practice their skills with interactive activities and download self-study audio.

Teacher's Edition with Assessment Audio CD / CD-ROM

The interleaved **Teacher's Edition** includes easy-to-follow lesson plans for every unit.

- Tips and suggestions address common areas of difficulty for students and provide suggestions for expansion activities and improving learner persistence.
- A **More Ventures** chart at the end of each lesson indicates where to find additional practice material in other *Ventures* components such as the Workbook, Online Teacher's Resource Room (see below), and Student Arcade.
- Unit, midterm, and final tests, which include listening, vocabulary, grammar, reading, and writing sections, are found in the back of the Teacher's Edition.
- The **Assessment Audio CD / CD-ROM** that accompanies the Teacher's Edition contains the audio for each unit, midterm, and final test. It also features all the tests in customizable format so teachers can customize them to suit their needs.

Online Teacher's Resource Room (www.cambridge.org/myresourceroom)

Ventures 2nd Edition offers a free Online Teacher's Resource Room where teachers can download hundreds of additional worksheets and classroom materials including:

- A *placement test* that helps place students into appropriate levels of *Ventures.*
- A *Career and Educational Pathways* solution that helps students identify their educational and career goals.
- *Collaborative activities* for each lesson in Levels 1–4 that develop cooperative learning and community building within the classroom.
- *Writing worksheets* that help Literacy-level students recognize and write shapes, letters, and numbers, while alphabet and number cards promote partner and group work.
- *Picture dictionary cards and worksheets* that reinforce vocabulary learned in Levels Basic, 1, and 2.
- *Extended readings and worksheets* that provide added reading skills development for Levels 3 and 4.
- ***Add Ventures*** *worksheets* that were designed for use in multilevel classrooms and in leveled classes where the proficiency level of students differs.

Log on to www.cambridge.org/myresourceroom to explore these and hundreds of other free resources.

Workbook with Audio CD

The **Workbook** provides two pages of activities for each lesson in the Student's Book and includes an audio CD.

- If used in class, the Workbook can extend classroom instructional time by 30 minutes per lesson.
- The exercises are designed so learners can complete them in class or independently. Students can check

their answers with the answer key in the back of the Workbook. Workbook exercises can be assigned in class, for homework, or as student support when a class is missed.

- Grammar charts at the back of the Workbook allow students to use the Workbook for self-study.

Literacy Workbook

The **Literacy Workbook** develops reading and writing readiness skills by focusing on letter formation, the conventions of writing in English, and the connection between written and spoken language. For each lesson in the Basic Student's Book, the Literacy Workbook has two pages of activities focusing on key words and sentences.

- The left-hand page is for students who are pre-, non-, or semiliterate in their own languages.
- The right-hand page is for students who are literate in their first languages, but unfamiliar with the Roman alphabet used in English. When appropriate, students who complete the left-hand page with confidence can move to the right-hand page.
- Students who begin with the right-hand page, but require remediation, can move to the left.

Online Workbooks

The self-grading **Online Workbooks** offer programs the flexibility of introducing blended learning.

- They provide the same high-quality practice opportunities as the print Workbooks and give students instant feedback.
- They allow teachers and programs to track student progress and time on task.

Unit organization

Each unit has six skill-focused lessons:

LESSON A Listening focuses students on the unit topic. The initial exercise, ***Before you listen***, creates student interest with visuals that help the teacher assess what learners already know and serve as a prompt for the unit's key vocabulary. Next is ***Listen***, which is based on conversations. Students relate vocabulary to meaning and relate the spoken and written forms of new theme-related vocabulary. ***After you listen*** concludes the lesson by practicing language related to the theme in a communicative activity, either orally with a partner or individually in a writing activity.

LESSONS B AND C focus on grammar. The lessons move from a ***Grammar focus*** that presents the grammar point in chart form; to ***Practice*** exercises that check comprehension of the grammar point and provide guided practice; and, finally, to ***Communicate*** exercises that guide learners as they generate original answers and conversations. These lessons often include a *Culture note*, which provides information directly related to the conversation practice (such as the use of titles with last names), or a *Useful language* note, which introduces useful expressions and functional language.

LESSON D Reading develops reading skills and expands vocabulary. The lesson opens with a ***Before you read*** exercise, designed to activate prior knowledge and encourage learners to make predictions. A *Reading tip*, which focuses on a specific reading skill, accompanies the ***Read*** exercise. The reading section of the lesson concludes with ***After you read*** exercises that check comprehension. In Levels Basic, 1, and 2, the vocabulary expansion portion of the lesson is a ***Picture dictionary***. It includes a *word bank*, pictures to identify, and a conversation for practicing the new words. The words expand vocabulary related to the unit topic. In Books 3 and 4, the vocabulary expansion portion of the lesson uses new vocabulary from the reading to build skills such as recognizing word families, selecting definitions based on the context of the reading, and using clues in the reading to guess meaning.

LESSON E Writing provides practice with process writing within the context of the unit. ***Before you write*** exercises provide warm-up activities to activate the language needed for the writing assignment, followed by one or more exercises that provide a model for students to follow when they write. A *Writing tip* presents information about punctuation or paragraph organization directly related to the writing assignment. The ***Write*** exercise sets goals for the student writing. In the ***After you write*** exercise, students share with a partner.

LESSON F Another view has three sections. ***Life-skills reading*** develops the scanning and skimming skills used with documents such as forms, charts, schedules, announcements, and ads. Multiple-choice questions (modeled on CASAS[1] and BEST[2]) develop test-taking skills. ***Fun with vocabulary*** provides interactive activities that review and expand the vocabulary of the unit. Finally, ***Wrap up*** refers students to the self-assessment page in the back of the book, where they can check their knowledge and evaluate their progress.

---

1 The Comprehensive Adult Student Assessment System. For more information, see www.casas.org.
2 The Basic English Skills Test. For more information, see www.cal.org/BEST.

Scope and sequence

UNIT TITLE TOPIC	FUNCTIONS	LISTENING AND SPEAKING	VOCABULARY	GRAMMAR FOCUS
Welcome pages 2–5	▪ Identifying the letters of the alphabet ▪ Spelling names ▪ Identifying classroom directions ▪ Identifying numbers	▪ Saying classroom directions ▪ Saying the alphabet ▪ Saying numbers	▪ Classroom directions ▪ The alphabet with capital and lowercase letters ▪ Numbers	
Unit 1 **Personal information** pages 6–17 Topic: **Describing people**	▪ Identifying names ▪ Identifying area codes and phone numbers ▪ Identifying countries of origin ▪ Exchanging personal information	▪ Asking and answering questions about personal information	▪ Personal information ▪ Countries ▪ Months of the year	▪ Possessive adjectives (*my*, *your*, *his*, *her*)
Unit 2 **At school** pages 18–29 Topic: **The classroom**	▪ Identifying classroom objects ▪ Describing location ▪ Finding out location	▪ Asking what someone needs ▪ Asking about and giving the location of things	▪ Classroom furniture ▪ Classroom objects ▪ Days of the week	▪ Prepositions of location (*in*, *on*, *under*)
Review: Units 1 and 2 pages 30–31		▪ Understanding conversations		
Unit 3 **Friends and family** pages 32–43 Topic: **Family**	▪ Identifying family relationships ▪ Describing a family picture	▪ Asking and answering questions about family relationships	▪ Family relationships ▪ Family members ▪ People	▪ *Yes / No* questions with *have*
Unit 4 **Health** pages 44–55 Topic: **Health problems**	▪ Describing health problems	▪ Asking and answering questions about health problems	▪ The doctor's office ▪ Body parts ▪ Health problems	▪ Singular and plural nouns
Review: Units 3 and 4 pages 56–57		▪ Understanding conversations		
Unit 5 **Around town** pages 58–69 Topic: **Places and locations**	▪ Identifying buildings and places ▪ Describing location	▪ Asking and answering questions about where someone is ▪ Asking and answering questions about the location of buildings and places ▪ Describing your neighborhood	▪ Buildings and places ▪ Transportation	▪ Prepositions of location (*on*, *next to*, *across from*, *between*) ▪ *Where* questions

READING	WRITING	LIFE SKILLS	PRONUNCIATION
▪ Reading classroom directions ▪ Reading the alphabet ▪ Reading numbers	▪ Writing the alphabet ▪ Writing numbers	▪ Understanding classroom directions	▪ Pronouncing the alphabet ▪ Pronouncing numbers
▪ Reading a paragraph about a new student	▪ Completing sentences giving personal information ▪ Completing an ID card	▪ Reading an ID card	▪ Pronouncing key vocabulary ▪ Pronouncing area codes and phone numbers
▪ Reading a note about school supplies ▪ Reading a memo about class information	▪ Completing sentences about class information	▪ Reading a class schedule	▪ Pronouncing key vocabulary
			▪ Pronouncing *a* as in *name* and *o* as in *phone*
▪ Reading a paragraph about a family	▪ Completing sentences about a family ▪ Completing sentences about your family	▪ Reading a housing application	▪ Pronouncing key vocabulary
▪ Reading a paragraph about a visit to the doctor's office	▪ Completing a sign-in sheet at the doctor's office	▪ Reading a label on a box of medicine	▪ Pronouncing key vocabulary
			▪ Pronouncing *e* as in *read, i* as in *five*, and *u* as in June
▪ Reading a notice about a library opening ▪ Reading a description of someone's street	▪ Completing sentences describing your street	▪ Reading a map	▪ Pronouncing key vocabulary

UNIT TITLE TOPIC	FUNCTIONS	LISTENING AND SPEAKING	VOCABULARY	GRAMMAR FOCUS
Unit 6 **Time** pages 70–81 Topic: **Daily activities and time**	▪ Asking the time ▪ Asking for and giving information about the days and times of events	▪ Asking and answering questions about the time ▪ Asking and answering questions about events	▪ Clock time ▪ Activities and events ▪ Times of the day	▪ *Yes / No* questions with *be*
Review: Units 5 and 6 pages 82–83		▪ Understanding conversations		
Unit 7 **Shopping** pages 84–95 Topic: **Clothes and prices**	▪ Identifying clothing items ▪ Reading prices ▪ Identifying colors	▪ Asking and answering questions about prices ▪ Identifying the colors of clothing	▪ Clothing ▪ Prices ▪ Colors	▪ *How much is? / How much are?*
Unit 8 **Work** pages 96–107 Topic: **Jobs and skills**	▪ Identifying jobs ▪ Identifying job duties	▪ Asking and answering questions about jobs ▪ Asking and answering questions about job duties	▪ Names of jobs ▪ Job duties	▪ *Yes / No* questions with simple present ▪ Short answers with *does* and *doesn't*
Review: Units 7 and 8 pages 108–109		▪ Understanding conversations		
Unit 9 **Daily living** pages 110–121 Topic: **Home responsibilities**	▪ Identifying family chores	▪ Asking and answering questions about family chores ▪ Asking and answering questions about people's activities	▪ Chores ▪ Rooms of a house	▪ *What* questions with the present continuous
Unit 10 **Free time** pages 122–133 Topic: **Free-time activities**	▪ Identifying free-time activities ▪ Describe what people like to do	▪ Asking and answering questions about free-time activities	▪ Free-time activities	▪ *like to* + verb ▪ *What* questions with *like to* + verb
Review: Units 9 and 10 pages 134–135		▪ Understanding conversations		

READING	WRITING	LIFE SKILLS	PRONUNCIATION
▪ Reading a paragraph about a person's schedule ▪ Reading someone's daily schedule	▪ Completing a schedule ▪ Completing sentences about a schedule	▪ Reading an invitation	▪ Pronouncing key vocabulary ▪ Pronouncing times
			▪ Pronouncing *a* as in *at* and *o* as in *on*

READING	WRITING	LIFE SKILLS	PRONUNCIATION
▪ Reading an e-mail about a shopping trip	▪ Completing a shopping list	▪ Reading a store receipt	▪ Pronouncing key vocabulary ▪ Pronouncing prices
▪ Reading an article about the employee of the month ▪ Reading a letter about people's jobs	▪ Completing sentences about people's jobs	▪ Reading help-wanted ads	▪ Pronouncing key vocabulary
			▪ Pronouncing *e* as in *red*, *i* as in *six*, and *u* as in *bus*

READING	WRITING	LIFE SKILLS	PRONUNCIATION
▪ Reading an e-mail about problems with family chores ▪ Reading a chart of family chores	▪ Completing a chart about family chores ▪ Completing sentences about family chores	▪ Reading a work order	▪ Pronouncing key vocabulary
▪ Reading an e-mail to a friend	▪ Completing sentences about free-time activities	▪ Reading a course description	▪ Pronouncing key vocabulary
			▪ Reviewing pronunciation of *a*, *e*, *i*, *o*, and *u* in key vocabulary

Correlations

UNIT	CASAS Competencies	NRS Educational Functioning Level Descriptors *Oral BEST: 0–15 (SPL 0–1)* *BEST Plus: 400 and below (SPL 0–1)* *BEST Literacy: 0–7 (SPL 0–1)*
Unit 1 **Personal information** Pages 6–17	0.1.2, 0.1.4, 0.1.5, 0.2.1, 2.3.2, 4.8.1, 6.0.1, 7.4.1, 7.4.2, 7.4.3, 7.5.1	▪ Speaking and understanding isolated words ▪ Speaking and understanding isolated phrases ▪ Connecting print to spoken language ▪ Practicing using a writing instrument ▪ Practicing basic reading and writing skills ▪ Communicating through gestures and isolated words ▪ Recognizing common signs and symbols
Unit 2 **At school** Pages 18–29	0.1.2, 0.1.5, 1.4.1, 2.3.2, 4.5.1, 4.8.1, 7.4.1, 7.4.2, 7.4.3, 7.5.1	▪ Speaking and understanding isolated words ▪ Speaking and understanding isolated phrases ▪ Practicing using a writing instrument ▪ Practicing basic reading and writing skills ▪ Communicating through gestures and isolated words ▪ Recognizing common signs and symbols ▪ Exposure to computers or technology
Unit 3 **Friends and family** Pages 32–43	0.1.2, 0.1.4, 0.1.5, 0.2.1, 4.8.1, 7.4.1, 7.4.2, 7.4.3, 7.5.1, 8.3.1	▪ Speaking and understanding isolated words ▪ Speaking and understanding isolated phrases ▪ Connecting print to spoken language ▪ Practicing using a writing instrument ▪ Practicing basic reading and writing skills ▪ Communicating through gestures and isolated words ▪ Exposure to computers or technology
Unit 4 **Health** Pages 44–55	0.1.2, 0.1.4, 0.1.5, 0.2.1, 3.1.1, 3.1.3, 3.3.1, 3.3.2, 3.4.1, 4.8.1, 7.4.1, 7.4.2, 7.4.3, 7.5.1, 8.3.2	▪ Speaking and understanding isolated words ▪ Speaking and understanding isolated phrases ▪ Connecting print to spoken language ▪ Practicing using a writing instrument ▪ Practicing basic reading and writing skills ▪ Communicating through gestures and isolated words ▪ Recognizing common signs and symbols
Unit 5 **Around town** Pages 58–69	0.1.2, 0.1.4, 0.1.5, 0.2.1, 1.1.3, 2.2.1, 2.2.3, 2.2.5, 2.5.4, 4.8.1, 7.1.1, 7.4.1, 7.4.2, 7.4.3, 7.4.8, 7.5.1, 7.5.6	▪ Speaking and understanding isolated words ▪ Speaking and understanding isolated phrases ▪ Connecting print to spoken language ▪ Practicing using a writing instrument ▪ Practicing basic reading and writing skills ▪ Communicating through gestures and isolated words ▪ Recognizing common signs and symbols

All units of *Ventures 2nd Edition* meet most of the EFF content standards and provide overall BEST test preparation. The chart above lists areas of particular focus.

For more details and correlations to other state standards, go to: www.cambridge.org/myresourceroom

EFF	Florida Adult ESOL	LAUSD ESL Beginning Literacy Competencies
▪ Conveying ideas in writing ▪ Cooperating with others ▪ Listening actively ▪ Reading with understanding ▪ Reflecting and evaluating ▪ Speaking so others can understand ▪ Taking responsibility for learning	1.01.01, 1.01.02, 1.01.03, 1.01.04, 1.01.05, 1.01.06, 1.01.10, 1.03.12, 1.04.01	I. 1a, 1b, 1c, 2, 3, 4 II. 5m III. 8, 9
▪ Assessing what one knows already ▪ Organizing and presenting information ▪ Paying attention to the conventions of spoken English ▪ Seeking feedback and revising accordingly ▪ Working with pictures and numbers ▪ Cooperating with others ▪ Speaking so others can understand	1.01.02, 1.01.04, 1.01.05, 1.03.10, 1.03.12, 1.03.16, 1.04.09	I. 3 II. 6b III. 8, 9, 11
▪ Conveying ideas in writing ▪ Cooperating with others ▪ Listening actively ▪ Monitoring comprehension and adjusting reading strategies ▪ Offering clear input on own interests and attitudes ▪ Organizing and presenting information ▪ Speaking so others can understand	1.01.03, 1.02.07, 1.03.12, 1.04.04, 1.05.01	I. 1d, 3 III. 9
▪ Anticipating and identifying problems ▪ Attending to oral information ▪ Interacting with others in ways that are friendly, courteous, and tactful ▪ Solving problems and making decisions ▪ Speaking so others can understand ▪ Using strategies appropriate to goals ▪ Cooperating with others	1.01.04, 1.02.07, 1.03.12, 1.03.16, 1.05.01, 1.05.02, 1.05.03, 1.05.04, 1.07.03	I. 3 II. 7 III. 9
▪ Seeking feedback and revising accordingly ▪ Seeking input from others ▪ Selecting appropriate reading strategies ▪ Speaking so others can understand ▪ Taking responsibility for learning ▪ Cooperating with others	1.01.03, 1.02.01, 1.02.02, 1.02.10, 1.03.12, 1.04.09, 1.06.01, 1.06.02, 1.06.03	I. 3 II. 5k III. 10

UNIT	CASAS Competencies	NRS Educational Functioning Level Descriptors *Oral BEST: 0–15 (SPL 0–1)* *BEST Plus: 400 and below (SPL 0–1)* *BEST Literacy: 0–7 (SPL 0–1)*
Unit 6 **Time** Pages 70–81	0.1.2, 0.1.4, 0.1.5, 0.2.1, 2.3.1, 2.3.2, 4.5.3, 4.8.1, 6.0.1, 7.1.1, 7.1.4, 7.4.1, 7.4.2, 7.4.3, 7.5.1	▪ Speaking and understanding isolated words ▪ Speaking and understanding isolated phrases ▪ Connecting print to spoken language ▪ Practicing using a writing instrument ▪ Practicing basic reading and writing skills ▪ Communicating through gestures and isolated words ▪ Recognizing common signs and symbols
Unit 7 **Shopping** Pages 84–95	0.1.2, 0.1.4, 0.1.5, 0.2.1, 1.1.6, 1.2.1, 1.2.2, 1.3.9, 1.6.3, 4.8.1, 6.0.1, 7.1.1, 7.4.1, 7.4.2, 7.4.3, 7.5.1, 8.1.4	▪ Speaking and understanding isolated words ▪ Speaking and understanding isolated phrases ▪ Connecting print to spoken language ▪ Practicing using a writing instrument ▪ Practicing basic reading and writing skills ▪ Communicating through gestures and isolated words ▪ Exposure to computers or technology
Unit 8 **Work** Pages 96–107	0.1.2, 0.1.4, 0.1.5, 0.2.1, 1.1.6, 2.3.2, 4.1.3, 4.1.6, 4.1.8, 4.8.1, 4.8.2, 6.0.1, 7.1.1, 7.1.4, 7.4.1, 7.4.2, 7.5.1	▪ Speaking and understanding isolated words ▪ Speaking and understanding isolated phrases ▪ Practicing using a writing instrument ▪ Practicing basic reading and writing skills ▪ Communicating name and other personal information ▪ Practicing entry-level job-related writing ▪ Practicing entry-level job-related speaking
Unit 9 **Daily living** Pages 110–121	0.1.2, 0.1.5, 0.2.1, 0.2.4, 1.4.1, 1.7.4, 4.1.8, 4.7.3, 4.7.4, 4.8.1, 7.1.1, 7.4.1, 7.4.2, 7.4.3, 7.5.6, 8.1.4, 8.2.1, 8.2.2, 8.2.3, 8.2.4, 8.2.5	▪ Speaking and understanding isolated words ▪ Speaking and understanding isolated phrases ▪ Connecting print to spoken language ▪ Practicing using a writing instrument ▪ Practicing basic reading and writing skills ▪ Recognizing common signs and symbols ▪ Exposure to computers or technology
Unit 10 **Free time** Pages 122–133	0.1.1, 0.1.2, 0.1.4, 0.1.5, 0.2.1, 0.2.4, 2.3.1, 2.3.2, 4.8.1, 7.1.1, 7.4.1, 7.4.2, 7.4.3, 7.5.1, 7.5.6	▪ Speaking and understanding isolated words ▪ Connecting print to spoken language ▪ Practicing using a writing instrument ▪ Practicing basic reading and writing skills ▪ Communicating through gestures and isolated words ▪ Recognizing common signs and symbols ▪ Exposure to computers or technology

All units of *Ventures 2nd Edition* meet most of the EFF content standards and provide overall BEST test preparation. The chart above lists areas of particular focus.

For more details and correlations to other state standards, go to: www.cambridge.org/myresourceroom

EFF	Florida Adult ESOL	LAUSD ESL Beginning Literacy Competencies
▪ Attending to oral information ▪ Identifying own strengths and weaknesses as a learner ▪ Interacting with others in ways that are friendly, courteous, and tactful ▪ Monitoring comprehension and adjusting reading strategies ▪ Organizing and presenting information ▪ Cooperating with others ▪ Speaking so others can understand	1.01.03, 1.01.05, 1.02.02, 1.03.09, 1.03.12, 1.03.16, 1.04.01	I. 3 II. 6a, 6c
▪ Cooperating with others ▪ Listening actively ▪ Reading with understanding ▪ Reflecting and evaluating ▪ Speaking so others can understand ▪ Taking responsibility for learning	1.01.03, 1.03.12, 1.03.16, 1.04.01, 1.04.02, 1.04.06	I. 3 III. 13, 14
▪ Attending to oral information ▪ Listening actively ▪ Monitoring comprehension and adjusting reading strategies ▪ Reading with understanding ▪ Reflecting and evaluating ▪ Speaking so others can understand ▪ Cooperating with others	1.01.03, 1.03.01, 1.03.02, 1.03.12, 1.03.14	I. 3 III. 8, 13
▪ Identifying own strengths and weaknesses as a learner ▪ Interacting with others in ways that are friendly, courteous, and tactful ▪ Monitoring progress toward goals ▪ Offering clear input on own interests and attitudes ▪ Organizing and presenting information ▪ Reading with understanding ▪ Cooperating with others ▪ Speaking so others can understand	1.01.03, 1.01.04, 1.03.12	I. 3 II. 7 III. 8
▪ Conveying ideas in writing ▪ Cooperating with others ▪ Listening actively ▪ Reading with understanding ▪ Reflecting and evaluating ▪ Speaking so others can understand ▪ Taking responsibility for learning	1.01.02, 1.01.03, 1.01.04, 1.03.12	I. 3 II. 5

Features of the Student's Book

The Most Complete Course for Student Success

Ventures empowers students to achieve their academic and career goals.

- The most complete program with a wealth of resources provides instructors with the tools for any teaching situation.
- The new Online Workbook keeps students learning outside the classroom.
- Easy-to-teach materials make for a more productive classroom.

The Big Picture

- Introduces the unit topic and provides rich opportunities for classroom discussion.
- Activates students' prior knowledge and previews the unit vocabulary.

Unit Goals

- Explicit unit goals ensure student involvement in the learning process.

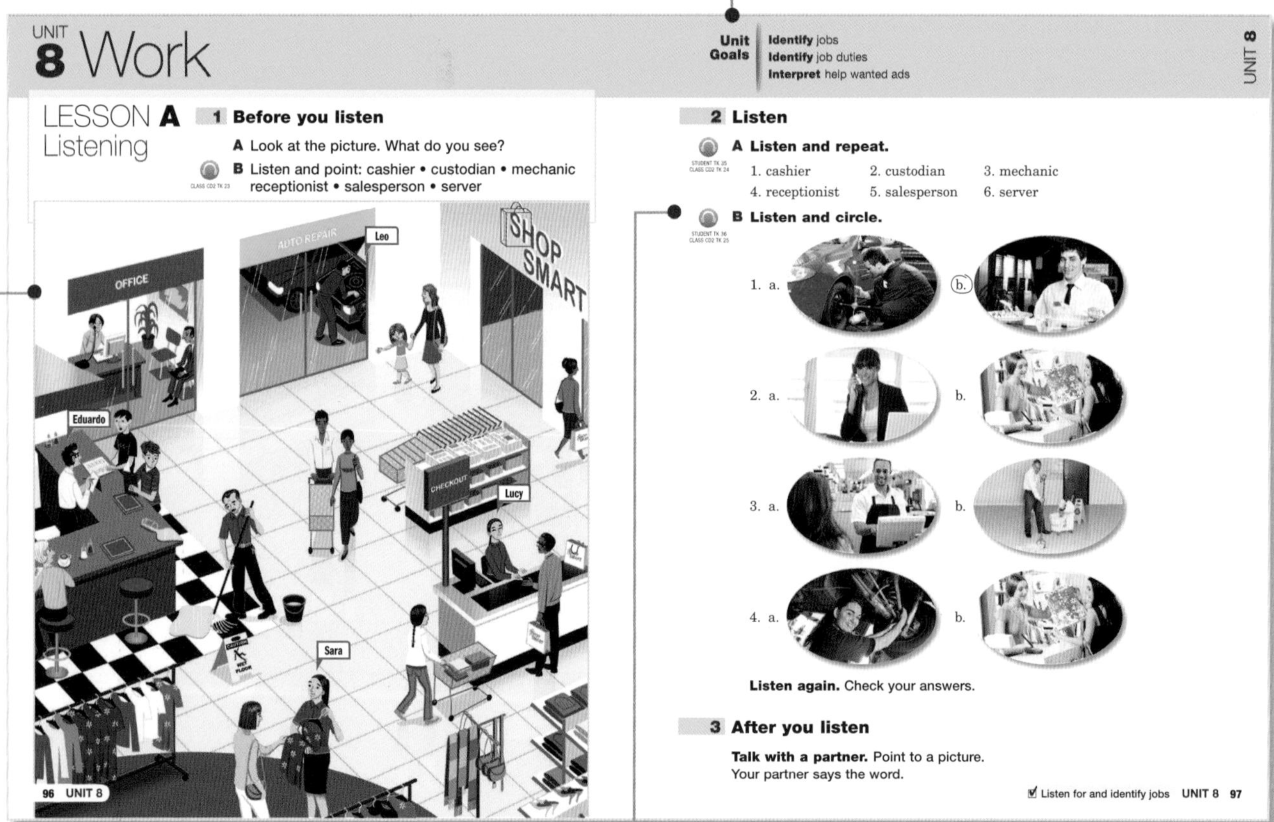
UNIT 8 Work

Unit Goals: **Identify** jobs; **Identify** job duties; **Interpret** help wanted ads

UNIT 8

LESSON A Listening

1 Before you listen

A Look at the picture. What do you see?

B Listen and point: cashier • custodian • mechanic receptionist • salesperson • server

96 UNIT 8

2 Listen

A Listen and repeat.

1. cashier 2. custodian 3. mechanic
4. receptionist 5. salesperson 6. server

B Listen and circle.

1. a. (b.)
2. a. b.
3. a. b.
4. a. b.

Listen again. Check your answers.

3 After you listen

Talk with a partner. Point to a picture. Your partner says the word.

Listen for and identify jobs UNIT 8 97

Two Different Audio Programs

- Class audio features over two hours of listening practice to improve listening comprehension.
- Self-study audio encourages learner persistence and autonomy.
- Easy navigation between the two with clear track listings.

Vocabulary Practice

- Explicit vocabulary practice with accompanying audio equips students with the tools necessary to succeed outside the classroom.

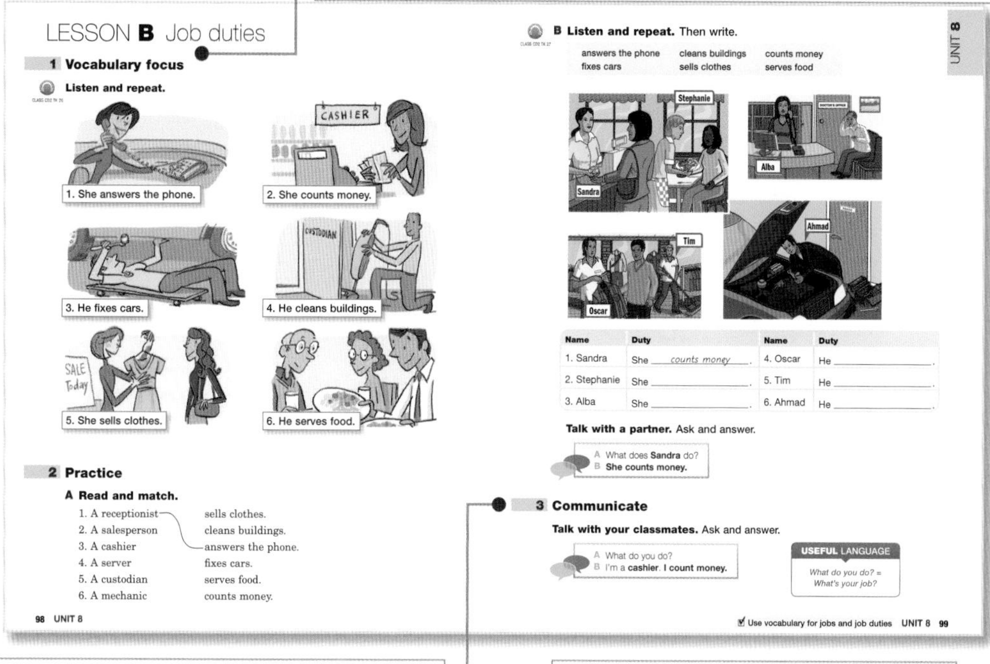

LESSON **B** Job duties

1 Vocabulary focus

Listen and repeat.

1. She answers the phone.
2. She counts money.
3. He fixes cars.
4. He cleans buildings.
5. She sells clothes.
6. He serves food.

2 Practice

A Read and match.

1. A receptionist — sells clothes.
2. A salesperson — cleans buildings.
3. A cashier — answers the phone.
4. A server — fixes cars.
5. A custodian — serves food.
6. A mechanic — counts money.

98 UNIT 8

B Listen and repeat. Then write.

answers the phone, cleans buildings, counts money, fixes cars, sells clothes, serves food

Name	Duty	Name	Duty
1. Sandra	She counts money.	4. Oscar	He ______.
2. Stephanie	She ______.	5. Tim	He ______.
3. Alba	She ______.	6. Ahmad	He ______.

Talk with a partner. Ask and answer.

A What does Sandra do?
B She counts money.

3 Communicate

Talk with your classmates. Ask and answer.

A What do you do?
B I'm a cashier. I count money.

USEFUL LANGUAGE
What do you do? = *What's your job?*

Use vocabulary for jobs and job duties UNIT 8 99

Natural Progression

- Students gain fluency and confidence by moving from guided practice to communicative activities.

Real-life Practice

- Meaningful application of the grammar allows for better student engagement.

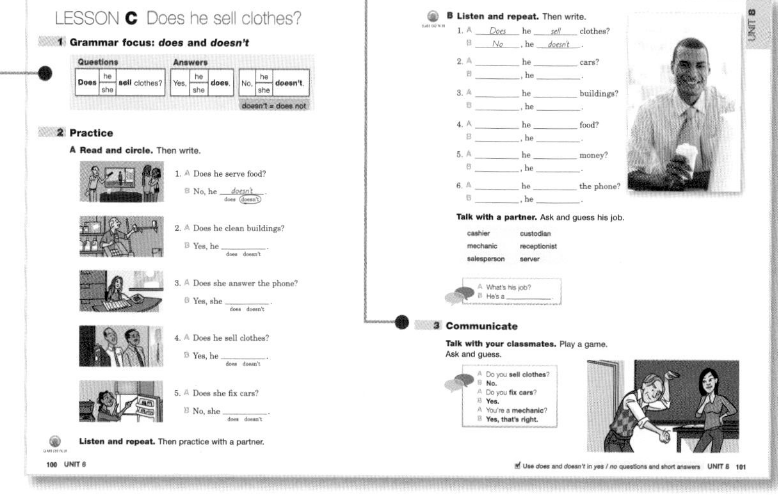

LESSON **C** Does he sell clothes?

1 Grammar focus: *does* and *doesn't*

Questions	Answers	
Does he/she sell clothes?	Yes, he/she does.	No, he/she doesn't.

doesn't = does not

2 Practice

A Read and circle. Then write.

1. A Does he serve food? B No, he doesn't. (does / doesn't)
2. A Does he clean buildings? B Yes, he ______. (does / doesn't)
3. A Does she answer the phone? B Yes, she ______. (does / doesn't)
4. A Does he sell clothes? B Yes, he ______. (does / doesn't)
5. A Does she fix cars? B No, she ______. (does / doesn't)

Listen and repeat. Then practice with a partner.

100 UNIT 8

B Listen and repeat. Then write.

1. A Does he sell clothes? B No, he doesn't.
2. A ______ he ______ cars? B ______, he ______.
3. A ______ he ______ buildings? B ______, he ______.
4. A ______ he ______ food? B ______, he ______.
5. A ______ he ______ money? B ______, he ______.
6. A ______ he ______ the phone? B ______, he ______.

Talk with a partner. Ask and guess his job.

cashier, custodian, mechanic, receptionist, salesperson, server

A What's his job?
B He's a ______.

3 Communicate

Talk with your classmates. Play a game. Ask and guess.

A Do you sell clothes?
B No.
A Do you fix cars?
B Yes.
A You're a mechanic?
B Yes, that's right.

Use *does* and *doesn't* in *yes / no* questions and short answers UNIT 8 101

Grammar Chart

- Clear grammar charts with additional grammar reference in the back of the book allow for greater teacher flexibility.

Reading

- *Ventures* features a three-step reading approach that highlights reading strategies and skills needed for success: **Before you read**, **Read**, **After you read**.

Picture Dictionary

- This visual page expands unit vocabulary and works on pronunciation for richer understanding of the topic.

Integrated-skills Approach

- Reading is combined with writing and listening for an integrated approach that ensures better comprehension.

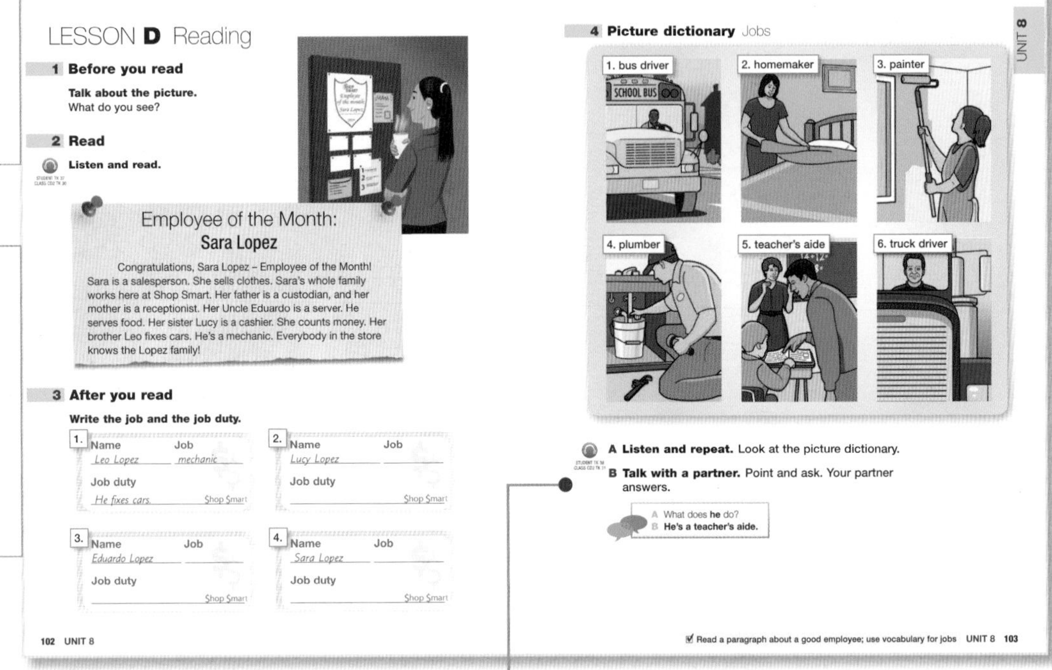

LESSON **D** Reading

1 Before you read

Talk about the picture. What do you see?

2 Read

Listen and read.

Employee of the Month:
Sara Lopez

Congratulations, Sara Lopez – Employee of the Month! Sara is a salesperson. She sells clothes. Sara's whole family works here at Shop Smart. Her father is a custodian, and her mother is a receptionist. Her Uncle Eduardo is a server. He serves food. Her sister Lucy is a cashier. She counts money. Her brother Leo fixes cars. He's a mechanic. Everybody in the store knows the Lopez family!

3 After you read

Write the job and the job duty.

1. Name *Leo Lopez* Job *mechanic* Job duty *He fixes cars.* Shop Smart
2. Name *Lucy Lopez* Job ____ Job duty ____ Shop Smart
3. Name *Eduardo Lopez* Job ____ Job duty ____ Shop Smart
4. Name *Sara Lopez* Job ____ Job duty ____ Shop Smart

102 UNIT 8

4 Picture dictionary Jobs

A Listen and repeat. Look at the picture dictionary.

B Talk with a partner. Point and ask. Your partner answers.

A What does **he** do?
B **He's a teacher's aide.**

Read a paragraph about a good employee; use vocabulary for jobs UNIT 8 103

Talk with a Partner

- Spoken practice helps students internalize the vocabulary and relate it to their lives.

Process Writing

- *Ventures* includes a robust process-writing approach: prewriting, writing, and peer review.

Writing for Success

- *Ventures* writing lessons are academic and purposeful, which moves students toward work and educational goals.

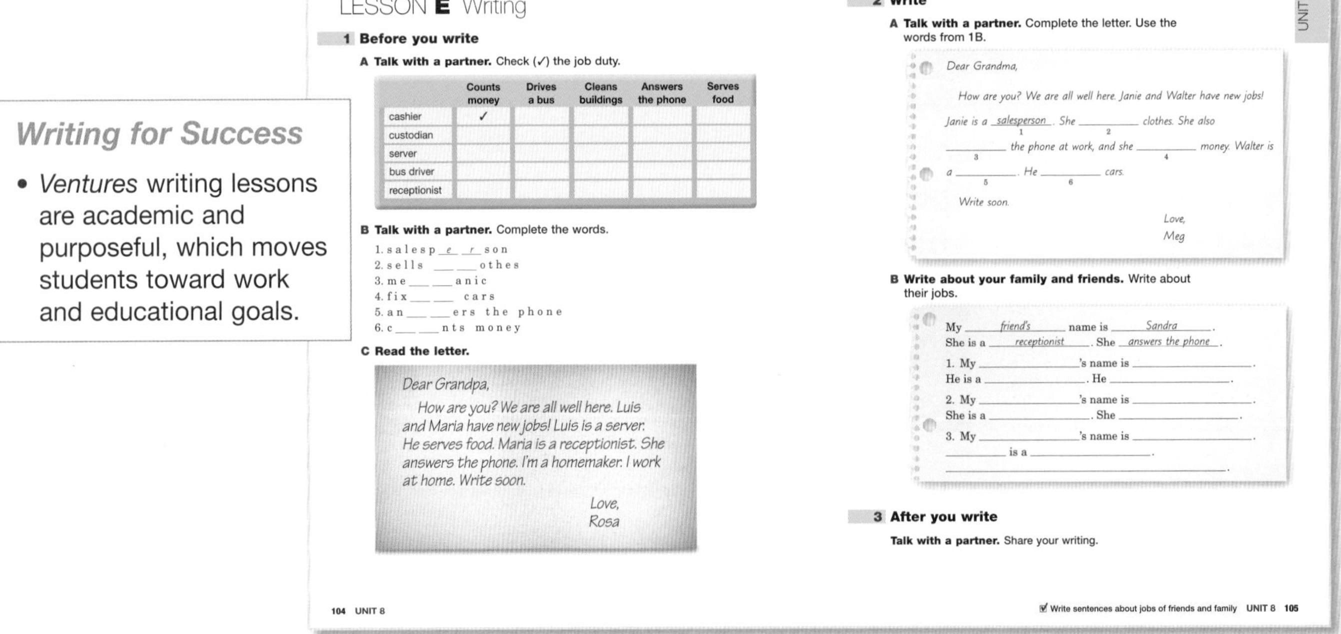

LESSON **E** Writing

1 Before you write

A Talk with a partner. Check (✓) the job duty.

	Counts money	Drives a bus	Cleans buildings	Answers the phone	Serves food
cashier	✓				
custodian					
server					
bus driver					
receptionist					

B Talk with a partner. Complete the words.

1. salesp *e* *r* son
2. sells ___ ___ othes
3. me ___ ___ anic
4. fix ___ ___ cars
5. an ___ ___ ers the phone
6. c ___ ___ nts money

C Read the letter.

Dear Grandpa,
How are you? We are all well here. Luis and Maria have new jobs! Luis is a server. He serves food. Maria is a receptionist. She answers the phone. I'm a homemaker. I work at home. Write soon.
Love,
Rosa

104 UNIT 8

2 Write

A Talk with a partner. Complete the letter. Use the words from 1B.

Dear Grandma,
How are you? We are all well here. Janie and Walter have new jobs!
Janie is a *salesperson* (1). She ____ (2) clothes. She also ____ (3) the phone at work, and she ____ (4) money. Walter is a ____ (5). He ____ (6) cars.
Write soon.
Love,
Meg

B Write about your family and friends. Write about their jobs.

My *friend's* name is *Sandra*.
She is a *receptionist*. She *answers the phone*.
1. My ____'s name is ____.
He is a ____. He ____.
2. My ____'s name is ____.
She is a ____. She ____.
3. My ____'s name is ____.
____ is a ____.
____.

3 After you write

Talk with a partner. Share your writing.

Write sentences about jobs of friends and family UNIT 8 105

Document Literacy

- Explicit practice with authentic-type documents builds real-life skills.

Fun with Vocabulary

- Interactive activities provide review and expand the vocabulary of the unit.

LESSON **F** Another view

1 Life-skills reading

Help Wanted

JOB A
Salesperson
$15.00 an hour
Monday and Wednesday
Call 555-1188

JOB B
Painter
Acme Paint Company
Call 555-8491
Part-time work

JOB C
Cashier
$12.00 an hour
Shop Smart
E-mail: ShopSmart@cup.org

JOB D
Bus Driver
City Bus Company
Work mornings
Call evenings
555-7654

A Read the sentences. Look at the ads. Fill in the answer.

1. Job A is for a ___.
   - Ⓐ cashier
   - Ⓑ receptionist
   - Ⓒ salesperson
2. Job B is for a ___.
   - Ⓐ driver
   - Ⓑ painter
   - Ⓒ plumber
3. For Job C, ___.
   - Ⓐ write to Shop Smart
   - Ⓑ go to Shop Smart
   - Ⓒ call Shop Smart
4. Call City Bus Company ___.
   - Ⓐ in the morning
   - Ⓑ in the afternoon
   - Ⓒ in the evening

B Talk with a partner.

What job do you want?

106 UNIT 8

2 Fun with vocabulary

A Read and match.

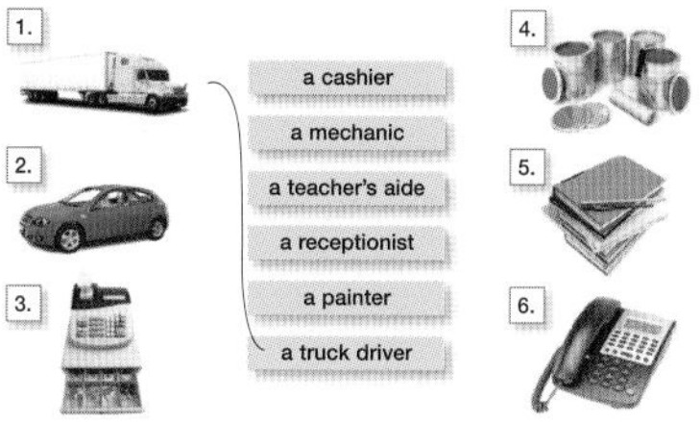

1. 2. 3. 4. 5. 6.

a cashier
a mechanic
a teacher's aide
a receptionist
a painter
a truck driver

Talk with a partner. Check your answers.

B Circle the words in the puzzle.

answer cashier clean count custodian fix mechanic sell server

t	f	i	x	a	b	c	o	u	n	t	q
f	g	m	e	c	h	a	n	i	c	r	o
s	e	r	v	e	r	c	c	l	e	a	n
d	s	e	a	n	s	w	e	r	u	b	a
s	e	l	l	l	c	a	s	h	i	e	r
t	r	c	u	s	t	o	d	i	a	n	r

3 Wrap up

Complete the **Self-assessment** on page 143.

UNIT 8

UNIT 8 Work

A Vocabulary Check (✓) the words you know.

☐ answer the phone ☐ custodian ☐ salesperson
☐ cashier ☐ fix cars ☐ sell clothes
☐ clean buildings ☐ mechanic ☐ serve food
☐ count money ☐ receptionist ☐ server

B Skills Check (✓) *Yes* or *No*.

	Yes	No
I can ask and answer questions with *does*: *Does he sell clothes? Yes, he does. No, he doesn't.*		
I can read an article about an employee.		
I can write about jobs.		
I can read a help-wanted ad.		

C What's next? Choose one.

☐ I am ready for the unit test.
☐ I need more practice with ___.

SELF-ASSESSMENTS 143

Test-taking Skills

- Bubble answers prepare students for standardized tests like the CASAS.

Self-assessment

- Students log the vocabulary, skills, and functions they have learned for greater learner autonomy.

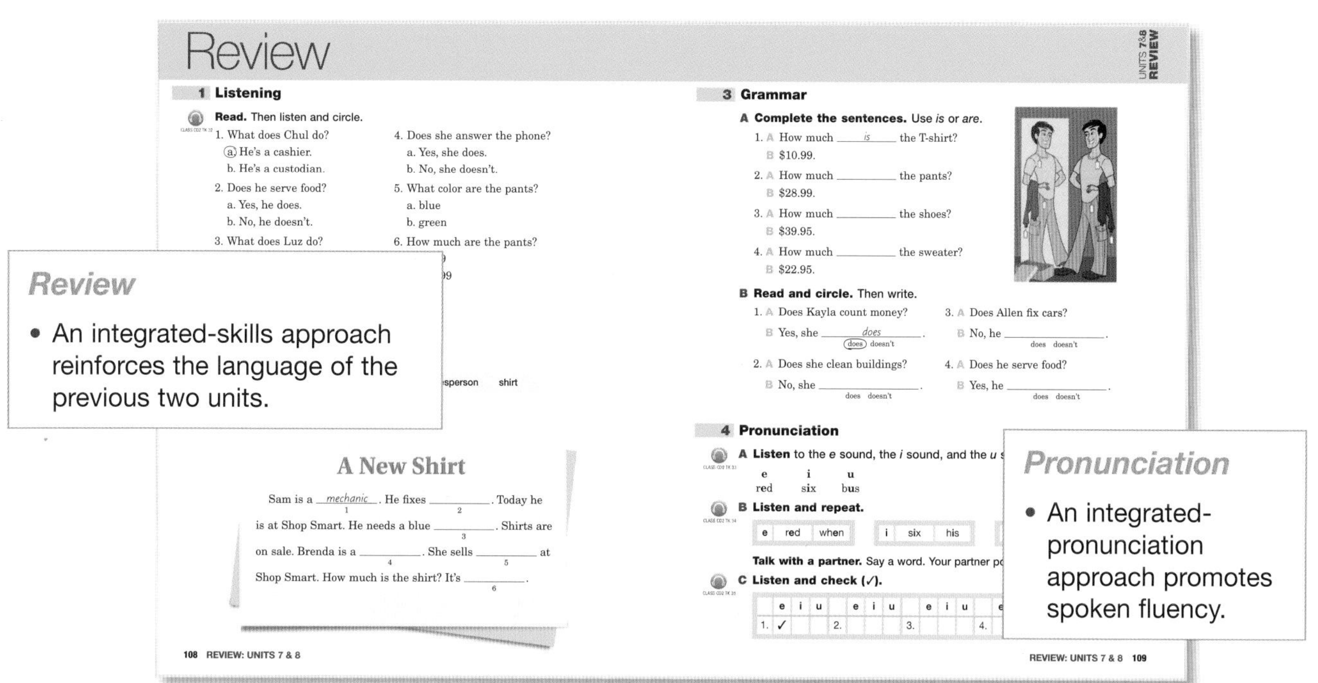

Review

- An integrated-skills approach reinforces the language of the previous two units.

Pronunciation

- An integrated-pronunciation approach promotes spoken fluency.

Features of the Teacher's Edition

Introduction

Ventures Teacher's Edition includes step-by-step teaching notes for each lesson. The teaching notes divide the lesson into six stages. Each lesson begins with a warm-up and review followed by a presentation stage. The practice, comprehension, application, and evaluation stages do not follow a strict sequence in the Teacher's Edition. They vary depending on the content of the lesson being presented.

Stages of a lesson

Warm-up and review Each lesson begins with a review of previous material and connects that material to the present lesson. Quick review activities prompt students' memories. Warm-up activities at the beginning of class introduce the new lesson. These activities may take many forms, but they are quick, focused, and connected to the new material to be introduced. A warm-up also helps teachers ascertain what students already know about the topic and what they are able to say.

Presentation During this stage of the lesson, the teacher presents new information, but it should not be a one-way delivery. Rather, it is a dynamic process of student input and interaction – a give-and-take between the teacher and students as well as students and students. The teacher may give examples rather than rules, model rather than tell, and relate the material to students' experiences.

Practice It is important that students have enough time to practice. A comfortable classroom environment needs to be created so that students are not afraid to take risks. The practice needs to be varied and interesting. There should be a progression from guided to independent practice. In the *Ventures* grammar lessons, for example, practice begins with mechanical aspects such as form, moves to a focus on meaning, and ends with communicative interactions.

Comprehension check Asking, "Do you understand?" is not enough to ascertain whether students are following the lesson. The teacher must ask concrete questions and have students demonstrate that they understand. In this stage, students are asked to repeat information in their own words. Students are also invited to come to the board or to interact with other students in some way.

Application A teacher must provide opportunities for students to practice newly-acquired language in realistic situations. These situations could be in class or out of class. The important point is that students use what they have learned in new ways. In the grammar lessons, for example, the Communicate section asks students to role-play, interview, share information, or ask questions.

Evaluation An ongoing part of the lesson is to determine whether students are meeting the lesson objectives. This can be done formally at the end of a unit by giving the unit test and having students complete the self-assessment, but it can also be done informally toward the end of the lesson. Each lesson in the Teacher's Edition ends with a review and verification of understanding of the lesson objectives. Any in-class assignment or task can serve as an evaluation tool as long as it assesses the objectives. Having students complete Workbook pages can also serve as an informal evaluation to gauge where students may be having difficulty.

The following chart presents the most common order of stages and suggests how long each stage could take within a one-hour class period.

Stages of the lesson	Approximate time range
Warm-up and review	5–10 minutes
Presentation	10–20 minutes
Practice	15–20 minutes
Comprehension check	5–10 minutes
Application	15–20 minutes
Evaluation	10–15 minutes

The Teacher's Edition includes:

- Interleaved Student's Book pages with answers
- Lesson objectives and step-by-step teaching instructions
- Expansion activities, extra teaching tips, and culture notes
- Activities to encourage learner persistence and community building
- Tests, games, self-assessments, and projects
- Ideas for multilevel classroom management
- Class audio listening scripts
- An assessment CD-ROM with test audio and customizable tests.

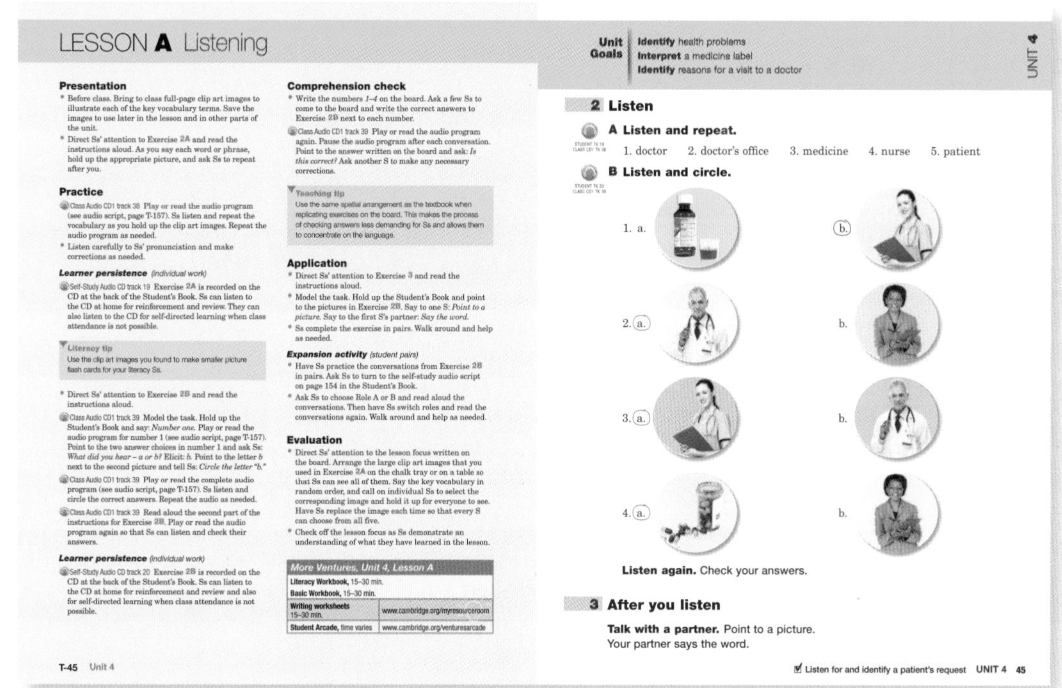

LESSON **A** Listening

Presentation

- Before class. Bring to class full-page clip art images to illustrate each of the key vocabulary terms. Save the images to use later in the lesson and in other parts of the unit.
- Direct Ss' attention to Exercise 2A and read the instructions aloud. As you say each word or phrase, hold up the appropriate picture, and ask Ss to repeat after you.

Practice

Class Audio CD1 track 38 Play or read the audio program (see audio script, page T-157). Ss listen and repeat the vocabulary as you hold up the clip art images. Repeat the audio program as needed.

- Listen carefully to Ss' pronunciation and make corrections as needed.

Learner persistence *(individual work)*

Self-Study Audio CD track 19 Exercise 2A is recorded on the CD at the back of the Student's Book. Ss can listen to the CD at home for reinforcement and review. They can also listen to the CD for self-directed learning when class attendance is not possible.

Literacy tip
Use the clip art images you found to make smaller picture flash cards for your literacy Ss.

- Direct Ss' attention to Exercise 2B and read the instructions aloud.

Class Audio CD1 track 39 Model the task. Hold up the Student's Book and say: *Number one.* Play or read the audio program for number 1 (see audio script, page T-157). Point to the two answer choices in number 1 and ask Ss: *What did you hear – a or b?* Elicit: *b.* Point to the letter *b* next to the second picture and tell Ss: *Circle the letter "b."*

Class Audio CD1 track 39 Play or read the complete audio program (see audio script, page T-157). Ss listen and circle the correct answers. Repeat the audio as needed.

Class Audio CD1 track 39 Read aloud the second part of the instructions for Exercise 2B. Play or read the audio program again so that Ss can listen and check their answers.

Learner persistence *(individual work)*

Self-Study Audio CD track 20 Exercise 2B is recorded on the CD at the back of the Student's Book. Ss can listen to the CD at home for reinforcement and review and also for self-directed learning when class attendance is not possible.

Comprehension check

- Write the numbers *1–4* on the board. Ask a few Ss to come to the board and write the correct answers to Exercise 2B next to each number.

Class Audio CD1 track 39 Play or read the audio program again. Pause the audio program after each conversation. Point to the answer written on the board and ask: *Is this correct?* Ask another S to make any necessary corrections.

Teaching tip
Use the same spatial arrangement as the textbook when replicating exercises on the board. This makes the process of checking answers less demanding for Ss and allows them to concentrate on the language.

Application

- Direct Ss' attention to Exercise 3 and read the instructions aloud.
- Model the task. Hold up the Student's Book and point to the pictures in Exercise 2B. Say to one S: *Point to a picture.* Say to the first S's partner: *Say the word.*
- Ss complete the exercise in pairs. Walk around and help as needed.

Expansion activity *(student pairs)*

- Have Ss practice the conversations from Exercise 2B in pairs. Ask Ss to turn to the self-study audio script on page 154 in the Student's Book.
- Ask Ss to choose Role A or B and read aloud the conversations. Then have Ss switch roles and read the conversations again. Walk around and help as needed.

Evaluation

- Direct Ss' attention to the lesson focus written on the board. Arrange the large clip art images that you used in Exercise 2A on the chalk tray or on a table so that Ss can see all of them. Say the key vocabulary in random order, and call on individual Ss to select the corresponding image and hold it up for everyone to see. Have Ss replace the image each time so that every S can choose from all five.
- Check off the lesson focus as Ss demonstrate an understanding of what they have learned in the lesson.

More Ventures, Unit 4, Lesson A	
Literacy Workbook, 15–30 min. **Basic Workbook,** 15–30 min.	
Writing worksheets 15–30 min.	www.cambridge.org/myresourceroom
Student Arcade, time varies	www.cambridge.org/venturesarcade

T-45 Unit 4

Unit Goals
Identify health problems
Interpret a medicine label
Identify reasons for a visit to a doctor

UNIT 4

2 Listen

A Listen and repeat.

1. doctor 2. doctor's office 3. medicine 4. nurse 5. patient

B Listen and circle.

1. a. (b.)
2. (a.) b.
3. (a.) b.
4. (a.) b.

Listen again. Check your answers.

3 After you listen

Talk with a partner. Point to a picture. Your partner says the word.

☑ Listen for and identify a patient's request UNIT 4 45

End-of-unit activities

Ventures provides several resources to help wrap up a unit:

The **Self-assessment** referenced at the end of Lesson F and available in the Online Teacher's Resource Room www.cambridge.org/myresourceroom as well as in the back of the Student's Book can be used in several ways:

- To identify any needs for additional practice before the unit test.
- For portfolio assessment. Print out copies for each student and keep completed self-assessments in a folder.
- For pre- and post-assessment. Print out two self-assessments for each student. Have students complete one before beginning and another after finishing the unit.

The **Projects** are another useful tool and a fun way to wrap up a unit. They are in the back of the Teacher's Edition and can be found on the Online Teacher's Resource Room.

The **Unit Tests** are a third end-of-unit activity. They are available at the back of this book. In addition, customizable unit tests can be found on the Assessment Audio CD / CD-ROM included in the back of this book.

Class time guidelines

Ventures is designed to be flexible enough for use with one-, two-, and three-hour classes.

Component	One-hour class	Two-hour class	Three-hour class
Student's Book	Follow lesson plan in Teacher's Edition		
Workbook	Assign as homework		Use in class
Student Arcade	Assign for lab or homework		
Online Teacher's Resource Room		Use Picture Dictionary Worksheets and Extended Reading Worksheets in class	

Meet the *Ventures* author team

Gretchen Bitterlin has been an ESL teacher and an ESL department chair. She is currently the ESL coordinator for the Continuing Education Program at San Diego Community College District. Under Gretchen's leadership, the ESL program has developed several products – for example, an ESL oral interview placement test and writing rubrics for assessing writing for level exit – now used by other agencies. She is a co-author of *English for Adult Competency*, has been an item writer for CASAS tests, and chaired the task force that developed the TESOL *Adult Education Program Standards*. She is a recipient of her district's award, Outstanding Contract Faculty. Gretchen holds an MA in TESOL from the University of Arizona.

Dennis Johnson had his first language-teaching experience as a Peace Corps volunteer in South Korea. Following that teaching experience, he became an in-country ESL trainer. After returning to the United States, he became an ESL trainer and began teaching credit and non-credit ESL at City College of San Francisco. As ESL site coordinator, he has provided guidance to faculty in selecting textbooks. He is the author of *Get Up and Go* and co-author of *The Immigrant Experience*. Dennis is the demonstration teacher on the *Ventures Professional Development DVD*. Dennis holds an MA in music from Stanford University.

Donna Price began her ESL career teaching EFL in Madagascar. She is currently associate professor of ESL and vocational ESL / technology resource instructor for the Continuing Education Program, San Diego Community College District. She has served as an author and a trainer for CALPRO, the California Adult Literacy Professional Development Project, co-authoring training modules on contextualizing and integrating workforce skills into the ESL classroom. She is a recipient of the TESOL Newbury House Award for Excellence in Teaching, and she is author of *Skills for Success*. Donna holds an MA in linguistics from San Diego State University.

Sylvia Ramirez started as an instructional aide in ESL. Since then she has been a part-time teacher, a full-time teacher, and a program coordinator. As program coordinator at Mira Costa College, she provided leadership in establishing Managed Enrollment, Student Learning Outcomes, and Transitioning Adults to Academic and Career Preparation. Her more than forty years in adult ESL includes multilevel ESL, vocational ESL, family literacy, and distance learning. She has also provided technical assistance to local ESL programs for the California State Department of Education. In 2011 she received the Hayward Award in education. Her MA is in education / counseling from Point Loma University, and she has certificates in TESOL and in online teaching.

K. Lynn Savage first taught English in Japan. She began teaching ESL at City College of San Francisco in 1974, where she has taught all levels of non-credit ESL and has served as vocational ESL resource teacher. She has trained teachers for adult education programs around the country as well as abroad. She chaired the committee that developed *ESL Model Standards for Adult Education Programs* (California, 1992) and is the author, co-author, and editor of many ESL materials including *Crossroads Café, Teacher Training through Video, Parenting for Academic Success, Building Life Skills, Picture Stories, May I Help You?,* and *English That Works*. Lynn holds an MA in TESOL from Teachers College, Columbia University.

Welcome

1 Meet your classmates

Look at the picture. What do you see?

Lesson objectives

- Learn school vocabulary
- Learn the alphabet

Warm-up

- Before class. Write today's lesson focus on the board.
  Welcome unit:
  School vocabulary
  The alphabet (Aa, Bb, Cc . . .)
- Before class. Prepare a name card for each S. Fold pieces of card stock lengthwise so that they can "stand" like a tent on a desk or table. Use your class roster to write Ss' first and last names in capital letters on both sides of the cards so that the names are easily visible to anyone in the classroom.

Teaching tip

Collect the name cards at the end of class and use them again in later classes to help you and the Ss learn everyone's name.

- Begin class. Books closed. Say: *Welcome to English class!*
- Write your name on the board. Point to it. Say: *My name is* _____. Ask a S: *What's your name?* If the S doesn't answer, ask different Ss until someone can answer you.
- As Ss tell you their names, place the name cards you prepared earlier on Ss' desks or tables. Use any remaining cards to find out the names of Ss who haven't spoken yet.
- Go around the room and ask all the Ss to say their names. After each S speaks, say: *Nice to meet you,* _____.

Teaching tip

Don't expect every S to understand you or be able to respond at this point. Friendly facial expressions and a little extra help from you will reassure the true beginners in your group and allow them to follow along with class activities.

Presentation

- Books open. Set the scene. Hold up the Student's Book. Show Ss the picture on page 2. Ask: *What do you see?* Point to your eyes and then to the picture to illustrate the meaning of *see.* Elicit and write on the board any vocabulary that Ss know, such as: *classroom, cafeteria, computer lab, hallway, students, books, etc.*
- If Ss don't know any English words for what they see in the picture, say to the class: *I see a classroom.* Write the word *classroom* on the board. Repeat the process with *woman, books, hallway, computer lab,* and *students, backpack* or with other words for items in the picture.
- Point to each of the words on the board, and say it aloud. After you say each word, indicate that Ss should repeat after you.
- Hold up the Student's Book. Point to the items in the picture that correspond to the words you and the Ss just said. For example, point to the students. Ask the class: *Are they students?* Nod your head and encourage Ss to say *yes.*
- Repeat the process with each of the words you wrote on the board.

Expansion activity *(whole group)*

- If you have some of the items from the picture in your classroom, walk around and ask the class about the items. For example, pick up a book and ask: *Is this a book?* Nod your head and encourage Ss to say *yes.* Some Ss may be able to name the items.
- Point to the sign that says "101" in the picture. Ask the class: *Do you see the numbers?* Say the word *numbers* and indicate that Ss should repeat the word after you.
- Write the numbers *1–10* across the board. Say each number, and indicate that Ss should repeat after you.
- If this exercise is easy for your group, have Ss say the numbers without your help, or continue with the numbers *11–20.*

Literacy tip

If you have literacy Ss in the class, encourage them to participate actively in this first page of the Welcome unit, which is mostly very communicative in nature.

Welcome

Presentation

- Direct Ss' attention to the lesson focus written on the board (school vocabulary.) Read the second part of the lesson focus aloud (the alphabet), and indicate that Ss should repeat after you. Point to the letters *Aa*, *Bb*, *Cc* . . . and say them aloud.
- Write the alphabet on the board using large capital letters. Ask Ss: *What is this?* Elicit: *the alphabet.*
- Circle one letter on the board. Tell the class: *This is a letter.* Write the word *letter* on the board. Say the word, and ask Ss to repeat after you.
- Circle another letter. Ask Ss: *What is this?* Elicit: *a letter.* Gesture toward all the letters and say to the class: *These are the letters of the English alphabet.*
- To introduce the idea of capital and lowercase letters, write the following on the board: *A* = *a*, *B* = *b*, *C* = *c*. Tell the class: *There are two ways to write letters.* Point to and read aloud the pairs of letters.
- Direct Ss' attention to the chart in Exercise 2A. Point to the capital and lowercase letters written on the board. Read the first pair aloud. Then point to *Aa* in the Student's Book chart, and repeat the letters to help Ss see that each letter is written two ways.

Teaching tip

When you write on the board, be aware that some Ss may recognize only capital letters. You might use only capital letters at first, or else write two versions of a word, one in capitals and one in lowercase.

Practice

Class Audio CD1 track 2 Read the instructions for Exercise 2A aloud. Then play or read the audio program (see audio script, page T-155). Ss listen and point to the letters. Repeat the audio program as needed.

Class Audio CD1 track 2 Read aloud the second part of the instructions for Exercise 2A. Play or read the audio program again (see audio script, page T-155). Ss listen and repeat the letters of the alphabet.

Learner persistence (individual work)

Self-Study Audio CD track 2 Exercise 2A is recorded on the CD at the back of the Student's Book. Ss can listen to the CD at home for reinforcement and review. They can also listen to the CD for self-directed learning when class attendance is not possible.

Literacy tip

Literacy Ss should be able to perform the "Listen and point" exercise in Exercises 2A and 4A. In the other exercises, while the rest of the class is writing, assign pages 2–5 in the *Literacy Workbook.*

Comprehension check

- Direct Ss' attention to Exercise 2B and read the instructions aloud.

Class Audio CD1 track 3 Model the exercise. Hold up the Student's Book and point to number 1. Play or read aloud the first part of the audio program (see audio script, page T-155). Point to the blank in number 1 and ask Ss: *What letter?* Elicit: *A.* Make sure Ss understand the task.

Class Audio CD1 track 3 Play or read the complete audio program (see audio script, page T-155). Ss listen and write the first letter of each name. Repeat the audio program as needed.

- Check answers with the class. Write the numbers *1–8* on the board. Call on individual Ss to write the names from Exercise 2B on the board. Point to each answer and ask Ss: *Is this correct?* Make corrections on the board.

Learner persistence (individual work)

Self-Study Audio CD track 3 Exercise 2B is recorded on the CD at the back of the Student's Book. Ss can listen to the CD at home for reinforcement and review and also for self-directed learning when class attendance is not possible.

Application

- Direct Ss' attention to the first part of Exercise 2C and read the instructions aloud. Have Ss write their first names.
- Read aloud the instructions for the second part of Exercise 2C. Point to the picture and read aloud the example sentence. Make sure Ss understand the task.
- Ss complete the exercise in groups of four. Walk around and help as needed.

Evaluation

- Turn Ss' attention to the first line of the lesson focus written on the board. Elicit some of the school vocabulary from page 2. Write the words on the board, and call on individual Ss to say the words and point to them in the big picture on page 2.
- Focus Ss' attention on the second part of the lesson focus (the alphabet). Ask Ss to say the alphabet aloud as you point to the letters on the board.
- Erase the letters from the board. Invite a S to come up to the board. Hand him / her a marker. Say: *Write the letter "C."* Continue with different Ss writing the remaining letters *A–Z*.
- Check off the lesson focus as Ss demonstrate an understanding of what they have learned in the lesson.

2 The alphabet

STUDENT TK 2
CLASS CD1 TK 2

A Listen and point. Look at the alphabet.

Aa	Bb	Cc	Dd	Ee	Ff	Gg	Hh	Ii
Jj	Kk	Ll	Mm	Nn	Oo	Pp	Qq	Rr
Ss	Tt	Uu	Vv	Ww	Xx	Yy	Zz	

Listen again and repeat.

STUDENT TK 3
CLASS CD1 TK 3

B Listen and write.

1. _A_ nita
2. _D_ aniel
3. _P_ eizhi
4. _Y_ uri
5. _F_ ranco
6. _L_ ee
7. _H_ akim
8. _K_ arla

C Write your name.

(Answers will vary.)

Talk with 3 classmates. Say your name. Spell your name.

3 Classroom directions

STUDENT TK 4
CLASS CD1 TK 4

A Listen and point. Look at the pictures.

1. Look.

2. Listen.

3. Point.

4. Repeat.

5. Talk.

6. Write.

7. Read.

8. Circle.

9. Match.

Listen again and repeat.

B Talk with a partner. Say a word. Your partner points to the picture.

Lesson objectives

- Learn classroom directions
- Learn the numbers 1–20

Warm-up and review

- Before class. Write today's lesson focus on the board.
  Welcome Unit:
  Classroom directions
- Begin class. Books open. Review vocabulary words from the last lesson. Gesture around you. Ask: *What is this room?* (A classroom.) Point to other classroom objects and ask: *What's this?* (book, backpack, student, etc.)

Presentation

- Direct Ss' attention to the lesson focus written on the board. Read the lesson focus aloud, and indicate that Ss should repeat after you.
- Direct Ss' attention to the pictures in Exercise **3A**. Tell Ss: *These are classroom directions.* Point to the corresponding picture as you read each word aloud. Indicate that Ss should repeat each word after you.
- As you go through the classroom directions, use gestures and items in your classroom to further illustrate meaning.

Practice

- Read aloud the instructions for Exercise **3A**. As you say *Listen and point*, cup your hand behind your ear and then point to the pictures in the book.

Class Audio CD1 track 4 Model the exercise. Play or read aloud the first word on the audio program (see audio script, page T-155). Hold up the Student's Book and point to the first picture. Make sure Ss understand the task.

Class Audio CD1 track 4 Play or read the complete audio program (see audio script, page T-155). Ss listen and point to the pictures in the Student's Book. Repeat the audio program as needed.

- Read aloud the second part of the instructions for Exercise **3A**.

Class Audio CD1 track 4 Model the exercise. Play or read aloud the first word on the audio program (see audio script, page T-155). Then repeat the word. Make sure Ss understand the task.

Class Audio CD1 track 4 Play or read the complete audio program (see audio script, page T-155). Ss listen and repeat the words.

Learner persistence *(individual work)*

Self-Study Audio CD track 4 Exercise **3A** is recorded on the CD at the back of the Student's Book. Ss can listen to the CD at home for reinforcement and review and also for self-directed learning when class attendance is not possible.

- Direct Ss' attention to Exercise **3B** and read the instructions aloud.
- Model the exercise. Point to the pictures in Exercise **3A**. Say to a S: *Please say a word.* Indicate all of the exercise to show that the S can choose any word.
- After the first S says a word from the Student's Book page, say to his or her partner: *Point to the picture.* If the S doesn't understand you, point to the appropriate picture yourself to demonstrate.
- Model the formation of pairs with two Ss who are sitting near each other. Say to one S, for example: *Marlene, Yoko is your partner.* Say to the other S, for example: *Yoko, Marlene is your partner.* Use the Ss' names to help everyone in the class find a partner.
- Ss practice saying the words from the Student's Book page and pointing to the corresponding pictures in pairs. Walk around and help with pronunciation as needed.
- When Ss are finished, have them switch roles so that both Ss have a chance to say the words.

Expansion activity *(whole group)*

- Before class. Write the words from Exercise **3A** on cards large enough to be seen easily.
- Arrange the cards in random order along the chalk tray, or tape them to the board or wall.
- Review the vocabulary by eliciting the words from Ss. For example, start writing on the board. Point to the word cards and ask the class: *What word?* Elicit or say: *Write.* Point to or hold up the appropriate word card.
- Continue with the remaining words. For example, circle one of the words in the sentence you wrote on the board. Ask: *What word?* Elicit: *Circle.* You can use gestures to elicit *Look* and *Listen*, and say the same word twice using two different voices to elicit *Repeat.* Write a simple matching exercise on the board, and draw a line between two items to elicit *Match.*
- Finally, gather the cards and show the class one of them. Say the word, and call on a S to perform the action. For the words, *Write*, *Match*, and *Circle*, invite the S to the board to perform the action.

Community building *(whole group)*

- To review Ss' names, write on the board: *My name is* ______. Point to each word as you read it aloud. Then point to and say each word again, and have Ss repeat after you.
- Say to the class: *My name is* ______. Have Ss say their names using the model sentence.

Presentation

- Point to the second part of the lesson focus written on the board. Say the word *numbers* and ask Ss to repeat after you.
- Direct Ss' attention to the chart in Exercise **4A**. Tell the class: *These are numbers.*

Practice

- Read the instructions in Exercise **4A** aloud.

Class Audio CD1 track 5 Play or read the audio program (see audio script, page T-155). Ss listen and point to the numbers in their books. Repeat the audio program as needed.

- Read aloud the second part of the instructions in Exercise **4A**.

Class Audio CD1 track 5 Play or read the audio program again (see audio script, page T-155). Ss listen and repeat the numbers.

Learner persistence (individual work)

Self-Study Audio CD track 5 Exercise **4A** is recorded on the CD at the back of the Student's Book. Ss can listen to the CD at home for reinforcement and review. They can also listen to the CD for self-directed learning when class attendance is not possible.

Teaching tip

Some Ss may have trouble pronouncing the "teen" numbers. You can help by modeling the numbers with two distinct syllables with equal stress and a clearly pronounced /t/ sound. For *seventeen*, stress the first and third syllables.

Comprehension check

- Direct Ss' attention to Exercise **4B** and read the instructions aloud.

Class Audio CD1 track 6 Model the exercise. Play or read aloud the first number on the audio program (see audio script, page T-155). Hold up the Student's Book and point to where *6* has been written for number 1. Make sure Ss understand the task.

Class Audio CD1 track 6 Play or read the complete audio program (see audio script, page T-155). Ss listen and write the numbers they hear. Repeat the audio program as needed.

- Read aloud the second part of the instructions in Exercise **4B**. Ss check their answers in pairs.
- Check answers with the class. Write the numbers *1–8* on the board. Call on individual Ss to write their answers on the board. Point to each answer and ask Ss: *Is this correct?* Make any necessary corrections on the board.

Learner persistence (individual work)

Self-Study Audio CD track 6 Exercise **4B** is recorded on the CD at the back of the Student's Book. Ss can listen to the CD at home for reinforcement and review and also for self-directed learning when class attendance is not possible.

Expansion activity (whole group)

- You can expand on your presentation of numbers by including numbers over 20, a list of which can be found on page 149 of the Student's Book.

Expansion activity (whole group)

- Make sequentially numbered word cards, and give one to each S, trying to keep the numbers more or less in order.
- Ask Ss to "count off," starting with *one.* If you have more than 20 Ss in the class, be prepared to assist Ss who receive the higher numbers. Alternatively, you can divide the class into two or more groups.

  Option 1 Make the activity easier by writing the numeral on one side of the card and the corresponding word on the other side.

  Option 2 Make the activity more challenging by distributing the numbers randomly around the room.
- Collect the numbers and keep them for Ss to use as flashcards.

Evaluation

- Direct Ss' attention to the lesson focus written on the board.
- Write some of the classroom directions from Exercise **3A** on the board. Call on individual Ss to say the words and perform the actions.
- Write the numbers *1–20* on the board one at a time, and call on Ss to say the numbers.
- Erase the numbers from the board. Invite a S to come up to the board. Say, for example: *Write the number "4."* Continue with different Ss writing the remaining numbers *1–20.*
- Check off each part of the lesson focus as Ss demonstrate an understanding of what they have learned in the lesson.

4 Numbers

STUDENT TK 5
CLASS CD1 TK 5

A Listen and point. Look at the numbers.

1 one	2 two	3 three	4 four	5 five
6 six	7 seven	8 eight	9 nine	10 ten
11 eleven	12 twelve	13 thirteen	14 fourteen	15 fifteen
16 sixteen	17 seventeen	18 eighteen	19 nineteen	20 twenty

Listen again and repeat.

STUDENT TK 6
CLASS CD1 TK 6

B Listen and write the number.

1. 6 2. 18 3. 5 4. 3
5. 12 6. 11 7. 15 8. 9

Talk with a partner. Check your answers.

UNIT
1 Personal information

LESSON A Listening

1 Before you listen

A Look at the picture. What do you see?

CLASS CD1 TK 7

B Listen and point: area code • country • first name ID card • last name • phone number

Lesson objectives

- Introduce Ss to the topic
- Find out what Ss know about the topic
- Preview the unit by talking about the picture
- Practice key vocabulary
- Practice listening skills

UNIT **1**

Warm-up and review

- Before class. Write today's lesson focus on the board.
  Lesson A:
  Personal information
- Begin class. Books closed. Review vocabulary for classroom directions from the Welcome unit. Write the following words on the board: *Look*, *Listen*, *Point*, *Repeat*, *Talk*, *Write*, *Read*, *Circle*, *Match*.
- Point to each word as you say it aloud. After each word, say to Ss: *Please repeat.*
- Use gestures, classroom items, and the board to review the meanings of the words. For example, gesture with your hand from your eyes to something or someone you are looking at. Say: *Look.* Ask Ss to repeat after you, using the same gestures.
- Continue in this manner with all the words for classroom directions.
- Point to the words *Personal information* written on the board. Say each word aloud. After each word, say to Ss: *Please repeat. Point to yourself when you say "personal."*
- Say to Ss: *Personal information is about you – for example, your name and your telephone number.*

Literacy tip

If you have literacy Ss in your class, it might be helpful to spend time at the beginning of any activity that contains art or photos talking about the pictures before focusing Ss' attention on the printed words in the exercise. Have Ss work in pairs. Tell them to ask each other: *What do you see?* Encourage Ss to describe the pictures to each other. Consider pairing literacy Ss with Ss who can help them read the text in the exercise. This will help preview the exercise for literacy Ss and make them more confident as the exercise continues.

Presentation

- Books open. Set the scene. Hold up the Student's Book. Show Ss the picture on page 6. Ask: *What do you see?* Elicit and write on the board any vocabulary that Ss know, such as: *classroom*, *student*, *backpack*, *clock*, *ID card*, *cell phone.* Point to similar items in the classroom as you go over each vocabulary word.

Practice

- Direct Ss' attention to the key vocabulary in Exercise **1B**. Read aloud each word or phrase while pointing to the corresponding part of the picture. Ask Ss to repeat and point.

Class Audio CD1 track 7 Play or read the audio program (see audio script, page T-155). Tell Ss: *Listen and point to the picture.* As Ss hear the key vocabulary, check to see that they are pointing to the correct part of the picture. Repeat the audio program as needed.

Comprehension check

- Ask Ss *Yes / No* questions about the picture. Cup your hand behind your ear and tell the class: *Listen. Say "yes" or "no."* Nod or shake your head to illustrate the meanings of *yes* and *no*.

  Point to the picture. Ask: *Is this a classroom?* (Yes.)
  Point to Mexico on the map. Ask: *Is this a country?* (Yes.)
  Point to the ID card. Ask: *Is this an ID card?* (Yes.)
  Point to the name Ernesto on the ID card. Ask: *Is this a last name?* (No.)
  Point to the phone number on the ID card. Ask: *Is this a phone number?* (Yes.)
  Point to the area code. Ask: *Is this a last name?* (No.)

Teaching tip

Do not expect Ss to answer with responses longer than *yes* and *no*. The purpose of these questions is to show whether or not Ss understand what you are asking them.

Expansion activity *(whole group)*

- Hold up the Student's Book, and point to the *I ♥ Mexico* T-shirt in the picture on page 6. Write on the board: *I love Mexico*. Say the sentence again and have Ss repeat it.
- Circle the word *Mexico*.
- If you have a map in the classroom, point to Mexico and say the name aloud. Point to where you are from on the map, and say the name of the country. Ask S volunteers to stand up and say the names of their countries. Point to the countries on the map as they say them.

Literacy tip

For an alternative activity, refer literacy Ss to pages 6–7 in the *Literacy Workbook* at any time during the lesson.

LESSON A Listening

Presentation

- Draw on the board a simple version of the ID card on page 6. Point to and say each piece of information and the corresponding key vocabulary term.
- Direct Ss' attention to Exercise **2A**. Tell Ss: *This is personal information.*
- Point to the lesson focus on the board. Say *personal information* and ask Ss to repeat after you.
- Read the instructions for Exercise **2A** aloud.

Practice

Class Audio CD1 track 8 Play or read the audio program (see audio script, page T-155). Repeat the vocabulary with Ss. Repeat the audio and correct Ss' pronunciation as needed.

- Draw a picture of an ID card on the board using your information. Point to your first name. Ask: *First name?* Elicit: *Yes*. Continue with last name, phone number, and area code.

Learner persistence (individual work)

Self-Study Audio CD track 7 Exercise **2A** is recorded on the CD at the back of the Student's Book. Ss can listen to the CD at home for reinforcement and review. They can also listen to the CD for self-directed learning when class attendance is not possible.

Expansion activity (whole group)

- Write the vocabulary from Exercise **2A** on the board in random order in a numbered column. To the right, make a lettered column with examples of each term in random order.
- Point to the two columns and say: *Please match the number with the letter.* Write on the board: *Match.* Point to the word as you say it aloud and have Ss repeat.
- Model the task. Draw a line from a word in the left-hand column to the correct item on the right.
- Ask for volunteers to match the remaining items.

Comprehension check

- Erase the lines drawn between the columns. Ask a volunteer to come to the board. Gesture to the left-hand column and say: *Listen and point.*

Class Audio CD1 track 8 Play or read the audio program again. Pause the audio program after each word or phrase. Have the S point to the word and ask the class: *Yes? Is this correct?*

- Direct Ss' attention to Exercise **2B** and read the instructions aloud.

Class Audio CD1 track 9 Model the task. Hold up the Student's Book and say: *Number one.* Play or read the audio program for number 1 (see audio script, page T-155). Elicit: *a.* Point to the *a* next to the first picture and tell Ss: *Circle the letter "a."*

Class Audio CD1 track 9 Play or read the complete audio program (see audio script, page T-155). Ss listen and circle the answers. Repeat the audio as needed.

Class Audio CD1 track 9 Read aloud the second part of the instructions for Exercise **2B**. Play or read the audio again so that Ss can check their answers.

Learner persistence (individual work)

Self-Study Audio CD track 8 Exercise **2B** is on the CD at the back of the Student's Book. Ss can listen to the CD when class attendance is not possible.

> **Useful language**
> Read aloud the information in the tip box. Write the numbers *2 0 1* on the board. Say each number aloud and ask Ss to repeat. Write on the board phone numbers with zero and read them with the class.

Comprehension check

- Write the numbers *1–4* on the board. Ask a few Ss to come to the board and write the correct answers to Exercise **2B** next to each number.

Class Audio CD1 track 9 Play or read the audio program again. Pause after each conversation. Point to the answer on the board and ask: *Is this correct?* Ask another S to make any necessary corrections.

Application

- Direct Ss' attention to Exercise **3** and read the instructions aloud.
- Model the task. Hold up the Student's Book and point to the pictures in Exercise **2B**. Say to one S: *Point to a picture.* Say to S1's partner: *Say the word.*
- Ss complete the exercise in pairs. Help as needed.

Evaluation

- Direct Ss' attention to the lesson focus on the board. Check Ss' understanding of the key vocabulary. Ask them to point to items in the picture on page 6 or on the ID card you drew on the board.
- Check off the lesson focus as Ss demonstrate an understanding of what they have learned in the lesson.

More Ventures, Unit 1, Lesson A	
Literacy Workbook, 15–30 min. **Basic Workbook,** 15–30 min.	
Writing worksheets 15–30 min.	www.cambridge.org/myresourceroom
Student Arcade, time varies	www.cambridge.org/venturesarcade

Unit Goals
Recognize names and vocabulary for personal identification
Identify countries of origin
Complete an ID card

2 Listen

STUDENT TK 7
CLASS CD1 TK 8

A Listen and repeat.

1. area code 2. country 3. first name
4. ID card 5. last name 6. phone number

STUDENT TK 8
CLASS CD1 TK 9

B Listen and circle.

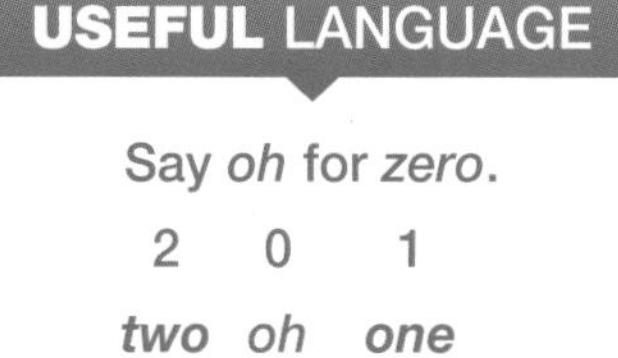
USEFUL LANGUAGE

Say *oh* for *zero*.
2 0 1
two oh one

1. (a.)

b.
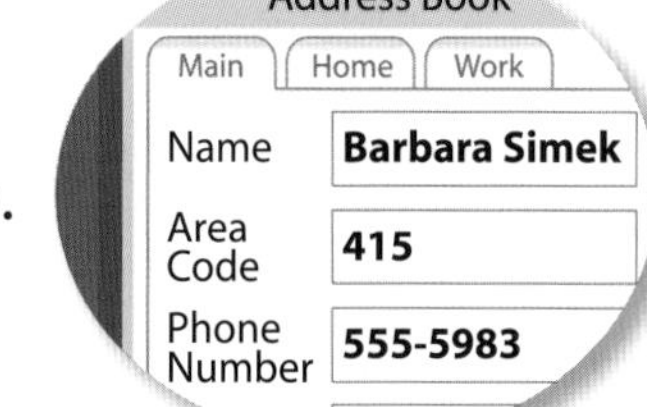

2. (a.)
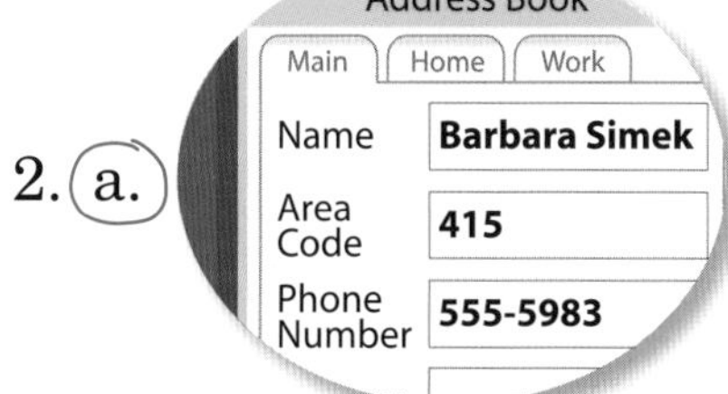

b.

3. (a.)

b.
Class Sign Up
First name Last name
Pilar Mendez

4. a.
Class Sign Up
First name Last name
Pilar Mendez

(b.)

Listen again. Check your answers.

3 After you listen

Talk with a partner. Point to a picture.
Your partner says the words.

LESSON B Countries

1 Vocabulary focus

Listen and repeat.

CLASS CD1 TK 10

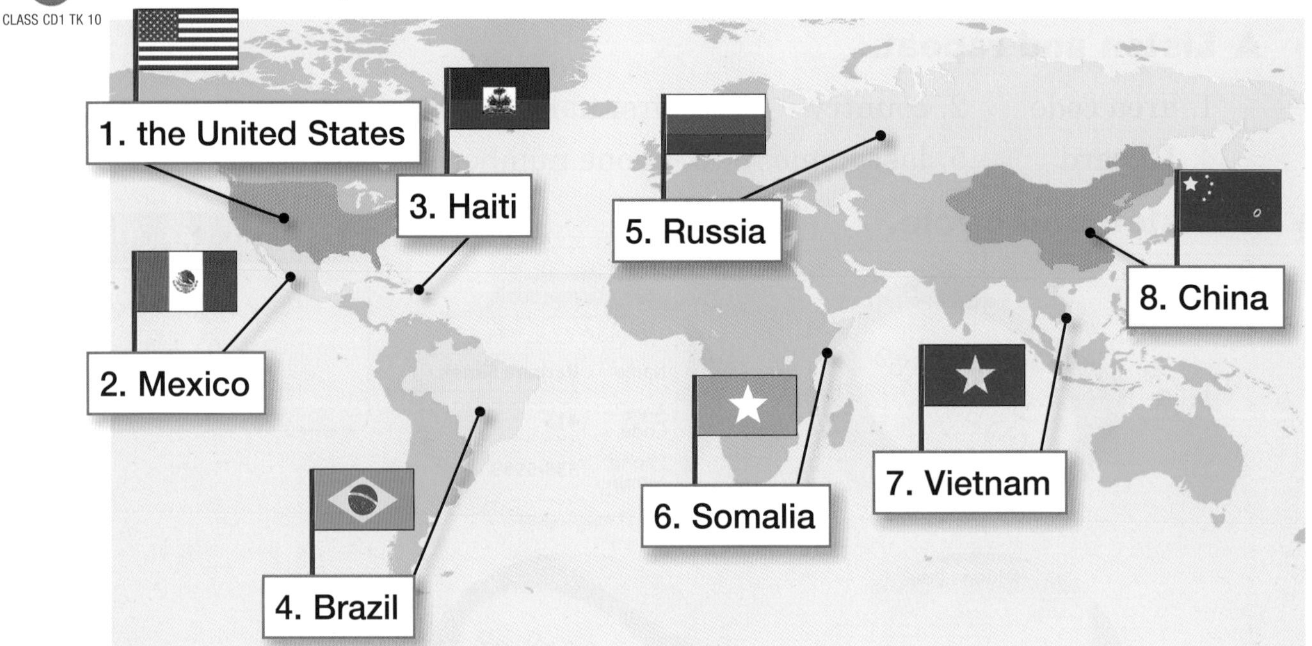

2 Practice

A Read and match.

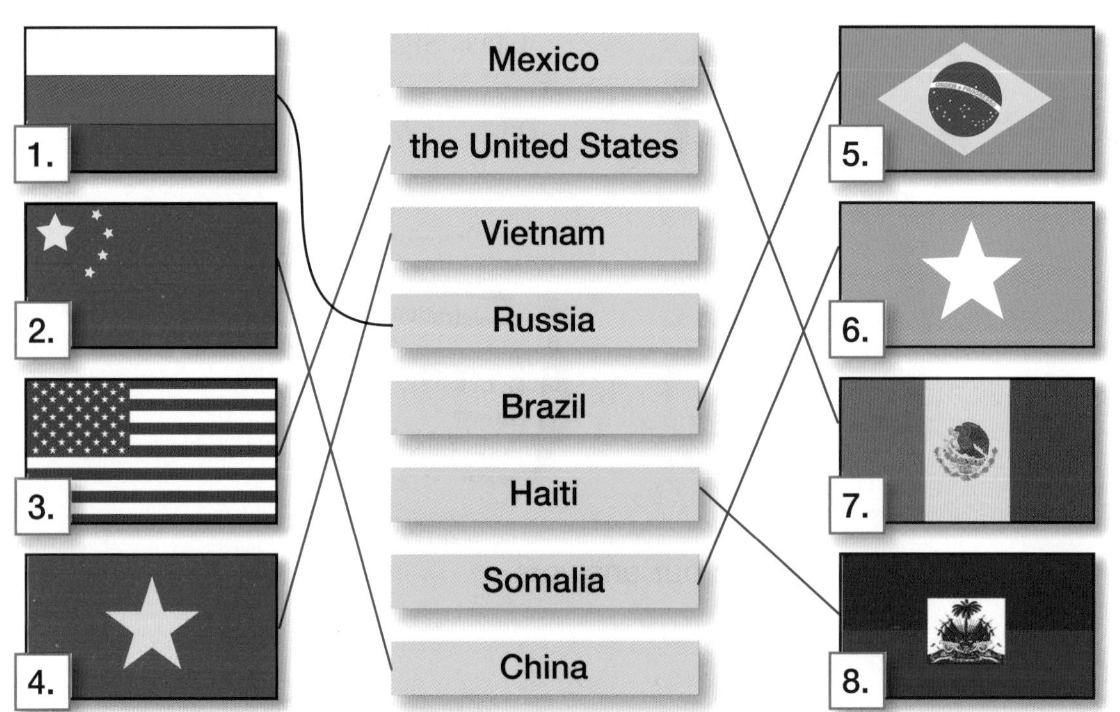

Lesson objectives

- Introduce countries of origin
- Practice exchanging personal information
- Introduce questions with *Where*

Warm-up and review

- Before class. Write today's lesson focus on the board.
  Lesson B:
  Countries
- Begin class. Books open. Direct Ss' attention to the picture on page 6. Review key vocabulary from the unit by asking Ss to point to the following in their books: *area code*, *country*, *first name*, *ID card*, *last name*, *phone number.*
- Walk around and check to see that Ss are pointing to the correct items in the picture.
- Write on the board: *Mexico*. Ask Ss: *What is Mexico?* When a S responds correctly, write on the board: *country*. Say the word aloud and ask Ss to repeat after you. Tell Ss: *Mexico is a country.* If you have a map in the classroom, show where Mexico is located.

Presentation

- Point to the word *Countries* at the top of page 8 in the Student's Book. Say the word aloud and ask Ss to repeat after you. Hold up one finger and say: *One country.* Hold up two fingers and say: *Two countries.*
- Direct Ss' attention to the map in Exercise **1**. Read the instructions aloud.

Practice

Class Audio CD1 track 10 Play or read the audio program (see audio script, page T-155). Listen and repeat along with Ss. Repeat the audio program as needed.

- Listen carefully to Ss' pronunciation and correct as needed.
- Have pairs of Ss practice saying the names of the countries to each other and pointing to the appropriate word and flag in the exercise.
- Model the task. Stand near a S and say, for example: *Somalia*. Indicate the S's own book and say to the S: *Please point to Somalia*. Then ask the same S to say the name of a country. Point to that country in your book for the rest of the class to see.

Teaching tip

There are many ways to divide the class into pairs, but the most transparent way to do this at the beginning level is to say two Ss' names, for example: *Michael and Jorge*, *you are partners*. At the same time, indicate with gestures that the two Ss should work together. With a very large class, using hand gestures alone to identify two Ss as you say the word *partners* can work quickly and almost as well.

Practice

- Direct Ss' attention to Exercise **2A**. As you read aloud the instructions, hold up the Student's Book and indicate that Ss should look at the pictures and draw a line between the pictures and the corresponding words.
- Model the task. Hold up the Student's Book. Point to the first picture. Ask: *What country is this?* (Russia.) Say: *Match the picture with the word.*
- Ss complete the exercise individually. Help as needed.

Comprehension check

- Write the numbers *1–8* on the board. Ask a few Ss to come to the board and write the answers to Exercise **2A** on the board.
- Ask different Ss to read the answers written on the board. After each answer is read, ask: *Is this correct?* Ask another S to make any necessary corrections on the board.

Teaching tip

At the beginning of the course, avoid asking Ss who have difficulty writing to write answers on the board. Instead, ask for volunteers to do the writing so that Ss will not be embarrassed in front of the class.

Teaching tip

To make all your Ss feel involved in the class, add other countries your Ss are from to the examples used in Lesson B. A reference list of countries and nationalities can be found on page 151 of the Student's Book.

Expansion activity *(whole group)*

- Before class, draw or print from the Internet color pictures of the flags from your Ss' countries.
- Tape the pictures across the board, leaving room for Ss to write the names of the countries.
- Point to each flag. Ask for a volunteer from that country to come to the board and write the name of the country under the flag. If you think your Ss will have difficulty with this, write the names of the countries yourself.
- Practice saying the names of the countries with the class.

Literacy tip

For an alternative activity, refer literacy Ss to pages 8–9 in the *Literacy Workbook* at any time during the lesson.

LESSON **B** Countries

Presentation

- Direct Ss' attention to the picture in Exercise **2B**. Read aloud the names and the countries, and ask Ss to repeat after you.
- Divide the board into two columns with *Name* and *Country* as headings.
- Point to the word *Name* on the board. Say the word aloud and have Ss repeat after you.
- Hold up the Student's Book and point to each person in the picture in turn. Ask the class: *What's his / her name?* List the names in the left-hand column of the chart.

Teaching tip
Don't expect Ss to produce questions or sentences themselves at this point. However, they are likely to understand the word *name* and to understand from the context that they should respond with a person's name.

- Point to the word *Country* on the board. Say the word aloud and have Ss repeat after you.
- Point to each person in the picture in turn and ask: *What country?* List the countries in the right-hand column.
- Point to each name on the chart and ask, for example: *Where is Ivan from?* Point to that person's country and have the class say the name of the country as a group, for example: *Russia.*

Practice

- Read aloud the first part of the instructions for Exercise **2B**.
- Class Audio CD1 track 11 Model the task. Say: *Listen and repeat.* Play or read the audio program for number 1 (see audio script, page T-155), and point to Ivan in the picture as you repeat. Say: *Then write.* Point to the word *Russia* written in the chart. Make sure Ss understand the task.
- Class Audio CD1 track 11 Play or read the complete audio program (see audio script, page T-155). Ss listen and repeat. Encourage Ss to point to the people in the picture as they repeat.
- Ss complete the chart individually. Repeat the audio program as needed.
- Check answers with the class. Write the numbers *1–6* on the board, and ask for volunteers to write their answers on the board. Point to each answer and ask the class: *Yes? Is this correct?* Make corrections on the board.
- Read aloud the second part of the instructions for Exercise **2B**. Point to and model the example conversation.
- Call on a pair of volunteers to read the example conversation aloud for the class.
- Point to another person in the picture on page 9. Ask a S: *Where is (name) from?* Elicit the answer. Repeat with different people in the picture. Indicate that Ss should ask and answer questions about all the people.
- Ss complete the exercise in pairs. Walk around and help as needed.

Application

- Direct Ss' attention to Exercise **3** and read the instructions aloud.
- Model the task. Read each line of the example conversation, and ask Ss to repeat after you. Point to where the information has been written in the chart.
- Ss complete the exercise in small groups. Depending on class size, you may want to prepare and distribute larger charts for Ss to fill in or else have Ss write the information in their notebooks.

Teaching tip
Remind Ss to look at the reference list of countries and nationalities on page 151 of the Student's Book.

- When Ss are finished, walk around the room and ask about each person in the class. For example, gesture toward a S and ask his or her group: *Where is ____ from?* Elicit correct responses that the whole class can hear.

Evaluation

- Direct Ss' attention to the lesson focus written on the board.
- Write across the board the names of the people in Exercise **2B**. Point to each person's name and ask: *Where is he / she from?* As Ss respond correctly, invite them to the board to write the country under each name. Alternatively, write the names of the countries yourself.
- Check off the lesson focus as Ss demonstrate an understanding of what they have learned in the lesson.

More Ventures, Unit 1, Lesson B	
Literacy Workbook, 15–30 min. **Basic Workbook,** 15–30 min.	
Writing worksheets, 15–30 min.	www.cambridge.org/myresourceroom
Student Arcade, time varies	www.cambridge.org/venturesarcade

CLASS CD1 TK 11

B Listen and repeat. Then write.

Name	Country	Name	Country
1. Ivan	*Russia*	4. Elsa	*the United States*
2. Asad	*Somalia*	5. Luisa	*Brazil*
3. Eduardo	*Mexico*	6. Jun-Ming	*China*

Talk with a partner. Ask and answer.

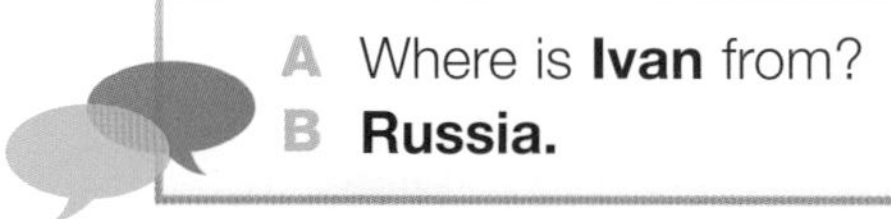

3 Communicate

Talk in a group. Ask and answer. Complete the chart.

Name	Country
Binh	*Vietnam*
(Answers will vary.)	

LESSON C What's your name?

1 Grammar focus: *my, your, his, her*

Questions

What's	**your**	name?
	his	
	her	

Answers

My	name is	Angela.
His		Kevin.
Her		Julia.

What's = What is

2 Practice

A Read and circle. Then write.

1. A What's your name?
   B ___My___ name is Nancy.
   (My) Your

2. A What's his name?
   B ___His___ name is Chin.
   (His) Her

3. A What's her name?
   B ___Her___ name is Alima.
   His (Her)

4. A What's your name?
   B ___My___ name is Vincent.
   (My) Your

CLASS CD1 TK 12

Listen and repeat. Then practice with a partner.

Lesson objectives

- Introduce possessive adjectives (*my*, *your*, *his*, *her*)
- Practice asking and answering questions about personal information

Warm-up and review

- Before class. Write today's lesson focus on the board.
  Lesson C:
  my, your, his, her
  What's ______ name?
- Begin class. Books closed. Review *What's your name?* and *Where are you from?* Ask several Ss in the class the first question. Then call on individual Ss to ask a classmate the question. Ask the second question and list Ss' countries on the board.
- Point to the word *your* written on the board. Ask a S: *What's your name?* Point to the S to emphasize the meaning.
- Point to the word *his* written on the board. Ask about several individual male Ss: *What's his name?*
- Point to the word *her* written on the board. Ask about several individual female Ss: *What's her name?*

Presentation

- Books open. Direct Ss' attention to the grammar chart in Exercise **1**.
- Have Ss ask and answer the questions in the grammar chart in pairs.
- Write the names *Angela*, *Kevin*, and *Julia* on the board. Say them aloud, and ask Ss to repeat after you. Point to *Angela*. Ask: *What's her name?* Elicit: *Her name is Angela.* Continue with *Kevin* and *Julia*. Emphasize the difference between *his* and *her*.

Comprehension check

- Ask Ss the questions in the grammar chart about people in the class. Ss should answer appropriately.

Practice

- Direct Ss' attention to the first picture in Exercise **2A**.
- Ask two Ss to read the example conversation aloud. After Speaker B's line is read, show Ss the two answer choices under the blank and ask: *My or Your?* Elicit: *My.*
- Read aloud the instructions for Exercise **2A**.
- Model the task. Hold up the Student's Book and point to number 1. Say: *Read* as you point to and pretend to read the two speakers' words. Say: *Circle* as you pretend to circle the word *My* under the blank. Say: *Write* as you pretend to write the word *My* in the blank.
- Ss complete the exercise individually. Walk around and help as needed.

Comprehension check

- Read aloud the second part of the instructions for Exercise **2A**.

Class Audio CD1 track 12 Play or read the audio program (see audio script, page T-155). Ss listen and repeat as they check their answers.

- Write the numbers *1–4* on the board. Ask volunteers to come to the board and write the words they circled. Make any necessary corrections on the board.
- Ss in pairs. Ask Ss to choose Role A or B and practice the questions and answers in Exercise **2A**. Then have Ss switch roles and practice again. Walk around and help as needed.
- Ask several pairs to say the questions and answers for the rest of the class.

Expansion activity *(small groups)*

- Divide the class into small groups, making sure to include at least one male S and one female S in each group.
- Have Ss take turns asking one of the questions from the grammar chart about the people in their group.
- To model the activity, sit down with one group and ask a question, for example: *What's her name?* Elicit the name from Ss in the group. If they don't know that S's name yet, ask her: *What's your name?*
- Gesture toward the S next to you and the questions in the chart to indicate that the S should ask the next question.
- If necessary, repeat the procedure with all the small groups so that Ss are sure what to do.

Literacy tip

For an alternative activity, refer literacy Ss to pages 10–11 in the *Literacy Workbook* at any time during the lesson.

LESSON C What's your name?

Presentation

- Direct Ss' attention to one of the ID cards in Exercise **2B**. Ask Ss: *What is this?* Elicit: *ID card.*
- Write on the board the key vocabulary terms as they appear on the ID card.
- Ask a S to write his / her information on the board. Tell the S he / she can invent the phone number they prefer. Point to the first name on the board. Ask: *What's his / her first name? What's his / her last name?* etc.

Learner persistence (whole group)

- Fill out the "ID card" on the board with your office telephone number if you have one. Tell Ss they can call you at your office to talk about the class.

Practice

- Read aloud the first part of the instructions for Exercise **2B**.
- Class Audio CD1 track 13 Model the task. Say: *Listen and repeat*. Play or read the audio program for number 1 (see audio script, page T-155), and point to Jack's first name on his ID card as you repeat. Say: *Then write*. Point to the word *name* written in the chart. Make sure Ss understand the task.
- Class Audio CD1 track 13 Play or read the complete audio program (see audio script, page T-155). Ss listen and repeat. Encourage Ss to point to the items on the ID cards as they repeat.
- Ss complete the chart individually. Repeat the audio program as needed.
- Check answers with the class. Write the numbers *1–8* on the board, and ask for volunteers to write their answers on the board. Point to each answer and ask the class: *Yes? Is this correct?* Make any necessary corrections.
- Read aloud the second part of the instructions for Exercise **2B**. Point to and model the example conversation.
- Call on a pair of volunteers to read the example conversation aloud for the class.
- Point to another item on one of the ID cards. Ask a S: *What's (her last name)?* Elicit the answer. Repeat with different items on the ID cards. Indicate that Ss should ask and answer questions about all the items.
- Ss complete the exercise in pairs. Walk around and help as needed.

Application

- Direct Ss' attention to Exercise **3** and read the instructions and the example conversation aloud. Have Ss repeat each line after you. Point to where *Yuri* has been written in the chart.

Useful language

Read the tip box aloud and ask Ss to repeat after you. Ask several Ss how they spell their first or last names. Encourage Ss to use the useful language as they interview classmates in Exercise **3**.

- Point to each column of the chart. Read the headings aloud and ask Ss to repeat after you.
- Model the task. Draw on the board a simple ID card similar to the ID cards in Exercise **2B**. Use the example first name *Yuri*, and invent the other information.

Teaching tip

Some Ss may not want to give out their real phone numbers. Tell Ss they can use fake phone numbers instead, such as the 555 numbers in Exercise **2B**.

- Ask for a volunteer to come up to the board. Point to the ID card on the board and tell the class: *I am Yuri.* Point to the example conversation in the Student's Book and say: *Talk to me*. Elicit the question from the example conversation: *What's your first name?* Respond with the example answer.
- Encourage the S to ask you the question from the *Useful language* box and then to write *Yuri* on the board.
- Write the four questions necessary to complete the chart on the board. Read each question aloud and ask Ss to repeat after you.
- Ask Ss to stand up, move around the classroom, and interview four classmates. Ss complete the chart.
- Walk around and listen to Ss' interviews. Help with pronunciation, grammar, and spelling as needed.

Evaluation

- Direct Ss' attention to the lesson focus written on the board. Gesture toward different Ss in the class and call on individual Ss to answer questions, such as: *What's her first name? What's my last name? What's your area code? What's his last name?*
- Check off the lesson focus as Ss demonstrate an understanding of what they have learned in the lesson.

More Ventures, Unit 1, Lesson C	
Literacy Workbook, 15–30 min.	
Basic Workbook, 15–30 min.	
Writing worksheets, 15–30 min.	www.cambridge.org/myresourceroom
Student Arcade, time varies	www.cambridge.org/venturesarcade

CLASS CD1 TK 13

B Listen and repeat. Then write.

Tops Adult School

First name: Jack
Last name: Lee
Area code: 203
Phone number: 555-9687

Tops Adult School

First name: Sara
Last name: Garza
Area code: 415
Phone number: 555-3702

What's his . . . ?		What's her . . . ?	
1. first *name*	Jack	5. *area* code	415
2. last *name*	Lee	6. *phone* number	555-3702
3. area *code*	203	7. *last* name	Garza
4. phone *number*	555-9687	8. *first* name	Sara

Talk with a partner. Ask and answer.

A What's **his first name**?
B **Jack.**

3 Communicate

Talk with your classmates. Complete the chart.

A What's your **first name**?
B My **first name** is **Yuri**.

USEFUL LANGUAGE

*How do you spell **Yuri**?*
Y-U-R-I

First name	Last name	Area code	Phone number
Yuri			
(Answers will vary.)			

☑ Use *my, your, his,* and *her* to ask and answer questions about names

LESSON **D** Reading

1 Before you read

Talk about the picture.
What do you see?

2 Read

STUDENT TK 9
CLASS CD1 TK 14

Listen and read.

Meet our new student.

His first name is Ernesto.

His last name is Delgado.

He is from Mexico.

Welcome, Ernesto Delgado!

3 After you read

Read the sentences. Circle *Yes* or *No*.

1. His name is Ernesto Mexico. Yes No
2. His first name is Ernesto. Yes No
3. His last name is Delgado. Yes No
4. He is from Ecuador. Yes No

Lesson objectives

- Introduce and read "Welcome!"
- Introduce the months of the year
- Practice using new topic-related words

Warm-up and review

- Before class. Write today's lesson focus on the board.
  Lesson D:
  Read "Welcome!"
  The months of the year
- Begin class. Books closed. Write on the board:
  What's ______ first name?
  What's ______ last ______?
  Where ______ ______ from?
- Read the questions aloud. Point to the blanks. Fill in the first one as an example. Write *your* in the blank. Ask Ss to fill in the correct words. Write the missing words in the blanks as Ss say them.

Presentation

- Books open. Direct Ss' attention to the picture in Exercise **1** and read the instructions aloud. Ask: *What do you see?* Elicit and write on the board any vocabulary that Ss know, such as: *school*, *student*, *backpack*, *bus*.
- Point to Ernesto in the picture and tell Ss: *His name is Ernesto. He is a new student.*
- Direct Ss' attention to the picture on page 6 of Lesson A. Ask Ss: *Do you see Ernesto?* Have Ss point to the appropriate person.
- Hold up the Student's Book as you point to the word *Welcome* in the picture on page 6. Say the word aloud and ask Ss to repeat after you.

Practice

- Direct Ss' attention to Exercise **2**. Point to the title of the reading and ask Ss: *What word is this?* Elicit or provide: *Welcome.*

Class Audio CD1 track 14 Read aloud the instructions for Exercise **2**. Play or read the audio program and ask Ss to read along (see audio script, page T-155). Repeat the audio program as needed.

- Read aloud each sentence of the reading and ask Ss to repeat after you. Answer any questions Ss have about the reading.
- Ask Ss oral questions about the reading, For example: *What's his last name?*

Learner persistence (individual work)

Self-Study Audio CD track 9 Exercise **2** is recorded on the CD at the back of the Student's Book. Ss can listen to the CD at home for reinforcement and review and also for self-directed learning when class attendance is not possible.

Literacy tip

Literacy Ss should be able to participate in most parts of this lesson. For Exercise **3**, have literacy Ss work with a higher-level partner who can read the questions and answer choices aloud.

Comprehension check

- Read aloud the instructions for Exercise **3**.
- Model the task. Point to and read aloud the first sentence. Then point to the answer choices and ask: *Yes or no?* Elicit: *No.* Tell Ss: *That's right. His name is not Ernesto Mexico.* Point to where *No* has been circled for number 1.
- Ss complete the exercise individually. Walk around and help as needed.
- Go over the answers with the class. Read each sentence aloud and call on Ss to give their answers. For the two false sentences, write on the board the beginning of each sentence, and encourage Ss to supply the correct ending. For example: *His name is Ernesto . . . Delgado. That's right! His name is Ernesto Delgado.*

Expansion activity (whole group)

- Write on the board *Ernesto*, *Delgado*, and *Mexico.*
- Point to each word on the board and ask: *What's the question?* If Ss don't understand you, point to and read the three questions you wrote on the board at the beginning of the class. Elicit the questions necessary to elicit the information in the reading: *What's his first name? / What's his last name? / Where is he from?*

Literacy tip

For an alternative activity, refer literacy Ss to pages 12–13 in the *Literacy Workbook* at any time during the lesson.

LESSON D Reading

Presentation

- Direct Ss' attention to the picture dictionary in Exercise 4. Point to the words *Months of the year*. Read the words aloud and ask Ss to repeat after you.
- If you have a wall calendar in the classroom, show examples of the months as you go through the list. Say, for example: *September. September is a month. October. October is a month.*
- Direct Ss' attention to Exercise 4A and read the instructions aloud.

Class Audio CD1 track 15 Play or read the audio program (see audio script, page T-156). Listen to Ss' pronunciation as they repeat the names of the months. Correct pronunciation as needed.

Teaching tip

To help Ss with the pronunciation of the months, it is a good idea to emphasize stressed syllables clearly when saying the months. You may also want to clap your hands when saying the strongest syllable.

Expansion activity *(individual work)*

- Before class, create handouts with 12 numbered lines. On each line, make blanks for the letters of one of the months of the year with the first blank filled in, starting with January. For example, the first line would be:
  J__ __ __ __ __ __ __ .
- Give each S a handout and ask them to write the names of the months. Ss may use the picture dictionary to help with spelling.
- Practice saying the months in order with the class, or have pairs of Ss take turns saying the months to each other.

Learner persistence *(individual work)*

Self-Study Audio CD track 10 Exercise 4A is recorded on the CD at the back of the Student's Book. Ss can listen to the CD at home for reinforcement and review and also for self-directed learning when class attendance is not possible.

Practice

- Direct Ss to Exercise 4B and read the instructions aloud.
- Ask two Ss to read the example conversation aloud. Point to the information written in the chart.
- Model the task. Ask one or two Ss the questions in the exercise and pretend to write their answers in the chart in your book. Make sure Ss understand the task.
- Ss stand up, walk around the classroom, and talk to at least three classmates. Walk around and help as needed.
- Ask several pairs of Ss to perform the conversation for the rest of the class. As Ss answer, list the months of the year in which they were born on the board. Afterward, point to and say each month aloud, and ask Ss to repeat after you.

Evaluation

- Direct Ss' attention to the lesson focus written on the board. Hold up the Student's Book and point to the picture of Ernesto in Exercise 1. Ask: *What's his first name? What's his last name? Where is he from?* Elicit complete sentences, for example: *His first name is Ernesto.*
- Make a grid with 12 numbered squares on the board. Fill in some of the squares with their corresponding months, and leave some squares empty. Point to and say the names of the months you have written, and ask Ss to repeat after you. Point to each empty square, and call on Ss to supply the missing months.
- Ask several Ss: *When is your birthday?* After each S answers, ask a different S about the first S's answer: *When is his / her birthday?*
- Check off each part of the lesson focus as Ss demonstrate understanding of what they have learned in the lesson.

More Ventures, Unit 1, Lesson D	
Literacy Workbook, 15–30 min. **Basic Workbook,** 15-30 min.	
Picture Dictionary activities, 30–45 min. **Writing worksheets,** 15–30 min.	www.cambridge.org/myresourceroom
Student Arcade, time varies	www.cambridge.org/venturesarcade

4 Picture dictionary Months of the year

1. January

	1	2	3	4	5	6
7	8	9	10	11	12	13
14	15	16	17	18	19	20
21	22	23	24	25	26	27
28	29	30	31			

2. February

				1	2	3
4	5	6	7	8	9	10
11	12	13	14	15	16	17
18	19	20	21	22	23	24
25	26	27	28			

3. March

				1	2	3
4	5	6	7	8	9	10
11	12	13	14	15	16	17
18	19	20	21	22	23	24
25	26	27	28	29	30	31

4. April

1	2	3	4	5	6	7
8	9	10	11	12	13	14
15	16	17	18	19	20	21
22	23	24	25	26	27	28
29	30					

5. May

		1	2	3	4	5
6	7	8	9	10	11	12
13	14	15	16	17	18	19
20	21	22	23	24	25	26
27	28	29	30	31		

6. June

					1	2
3	4	5	6	7	8	9
10	11	12	13	14	15	16
17	18	19	20	21	22	23
24	25	26	27	28	29	30

7. July

1	2	3	4	5	6	7
8	9	10	11	12	13	14
15	16	17	18	19	20	21
22	23	24	25	26	27	28
29	30	31				

8. August

			1	2	3	4
5	6	7	8	9	10	11
12	13	14	15	16	17	18
19	20	21	22	23	24	25
26	27	28	29	30	31	

9. September

						1
2	3	4	5	6	7	8
9	10	11	12	13	14	15
16	17	18	19	20	21	22
23 30	24	25	26	27	28	29

10. October

	1	2	3	4	5	6
7	8	9	10	11	12	13
14	15	16	17	18	19	20
21	22	23	24	25	26	27
28	29	30	31			

11. November

				1	2	3
4	5	6	7	8	9	10
11	12	13	14	15	16	17
18	19	20	21	22	23	24
25	26	27	28	29	30	

12. December

						1
2	3	4	5	6	7	8
9	10	11	12	13	14	15
16	17	18	19	20	21	22
23 30	24 31	25	26	27	28	29

STUDENT TK 10
CLASS CD1 TK 15

A Listen and repeat. Look at the picture dictionary.

B Talk with your classmates. Complete the chart.

A What's your name?
B **Eva.**
A When's your birthday?
B **In April.**

Name	Month
Eva	*April*
(Answers will vary.)	

LESSON E Writing

1 Before you write

A Talk with a partner. Complete the words.

1. f irst
2. l ast
3. n ame
4. area c ode
5. phone n umber

B Read the ID card. Complete the sentences.

CULTURE NOTE

Your signature is how you write your name.

1. Her first name is Linda.
2. Her last name is Wong.
3. Her area code is 916.
4. Her phone number is 555-7834.
5. She is from China.

Lesson objectives
- Complete sentences with personal information
- Complete an ID card

Warm-up and review

- Before class. Write today's lesson focus on the board.
  Lesson E:
  Complete sentences with personal information
  Complete an ID card
- Begin class. Books closed. Review vocabulary and grammar from the unit. Ask as many Ss as possible questions about the names and birth months of people in the class. For example, ask S1: *What's your name?* Elicit answer. Ask S2, indicating S1 or a different S: *What's his / her name?* Elicit answer. Ask S3: *When's your birthday?* Elicit answer. Ask S4, indicating S3: *When's his / her birthday?*

Presentation

- Books open. Direct Ss' attention to Exercise **1A** and read the instructions aloud.
- Write the first item on the board, leaving a blank for the first letter. Point to the blank and ask: *What letter?* Ss should notice the example in the book and answer: *f.* Write the letter *f* in the blank. Then point to the word on the board and ask: *What's the word?* Elicit: *first.*

Practice

- Ss work in pairs to complete the words.
- When Ss are finished, call on different pairs to write their answers on the board. Go over the answers and have Ss make any necessary corrections on the board.

Literacy tip
If your literacy Ss are not able to do the writing in Lesson E, have them practice letter tracing and word recognition on pages 14–15 of the *Literacy Workbook*, or have them practice forming the key vocabulary words using letter cards.

- Direct Ss' attention to the ID card in Exercise **1B**.
- Ask Ss questions about the person pictured on the card, using vocabulary from the unit, for example: *What's her first name? What's her last name?*
- When you get to the word *signature* in Exercise **1B**, ask: *What is a signature*? Ss will probably recognize from the example that a signature is a handwritten name. Write your signature on the board as another example.
- Ask several Ss to write their signatures on the board as examples.

Culture note
Read the tip box aloud. Have Ss practice signing their names.

- Read the instructions for Exercise **1B** aloud.
- Ss complete the sentences individually using information from the ID card. Walk around and help as needed.
- Check answers as a class. Write the numbers *1–5* on the board, and ask for volunteers to write their answers on the board. Point to and say each answer and ask the class: *Yes? Is this correct?* Make any necessary corrections on the board.

Comprehension check

- Ask Ss questions that can be answered using the sentences in Exercise **1B**. For example: *What's her last name?* (Her last name is Wong.) *Where is she from?* (She is from China.)

Expansion activity *(whole group)*

- On the board, draw a large ID card similar to the one in Exercise **1B**. Draw a simple "photo" that is clearly male. Ask Ss: *What is this?* Elicit: *ID card.*
- Fill in the information on the card with the class. Point to different parts of the card and ask Ss, for example: *What goes here? What word?* If Ss don't seem to understand, fill in *last name* yourself. Elicit: *last name, first name, area code, phone number, country, signature.* Invite S volunteers to write the words on the board.
- As a class, invent personal information for the ID card. Ask volunteers to give the man a first and last name, area code and phone number, and country. Have a volunteer write the man's signature.
- Ask Ss to take out a piece of paper and write five sentences about the man similar to the sentences in Exercise **1B** but beginning with *His . . . .*
- If time allows, repeat this activity about a famous celebrity. Ask different Ss to come to the board and invent the celebrity's phone number and signature.

LESSON E Writing

Presentation

- Direct Ss' attention to Exercise 2A and read the instructions aloud. Point to the blank ID card and ask the class: *What is this?* (ID card.) Point to the "photo" on the card and ask: *Who is this?* Elicit *Me* or tell Ss *You*. Say: *This is your ID card.*
- Ask Ss: *What will you write? Will you write your first name?* (Yes.) Elicit and list on the board the other pieces of personal information Ss will include on the ID card: *last name*, *area code*, *phone number*, *country*, *signature*.

Teaching tip
Remind Ss that they do not need to use their real phone numbers in the exercises.

Practice

- Ss complete the ID card individually. Encourage Ss to use the ID card in Exercise 1B as a model.
- Read aloud the instructions for Exercise 2B. Ss complete the sentences individually. Walk around and help as needed.

Comprehension check

- Direct Ss' attention to Exercise 3 and read the instructions aloud.
- Model the task. Show your "ID card" to Ss and say the sentences in Exercise 2B using your own information.
- Ss share their sentences in pairs. Walk around and spot-check Ss' writing.

Teaching tip
While Ss are reading their sentences aloud to each other, listen carefully to their pronunciation. When Ss are finished, list on the board any words Ss had difficulty pronouncing, and practice saying them with the class.

Expansion activity *(student pairs)*

- Have Ss exchange books and then stand up and tell the class about their partners using *His* or *Her*, for example: *His first name is Felix. His last name is Medina.*

Community building *(pairs)*

- If Ss don't mind sharing their personal information with a classmate, have pairs of Ss copy their "ID cards" from Exercise 2A onto paper and exchange them with a classmate. Tell Ss: *You can call your classmate.* Pantomime making a telephone call, and show that Ss can call each other to ask about homework or other issues; for example: *Hi, Sam. This is Steven. What's the homework for English class?*

Evaluation

- Direct Ss' attention to the lesson focus written on the board. Write in various places around the board examples of personal information of the type found in the ID cards. Have Ss label the pieces of information with the key vocabulary: *first name*, *last name*, and so on. (You may want to use celebrity names that Ss will easily recognize.)
- Ask Ss to come up to the board and write sentences. Dictate the beginnings of the sentences from Exercise 2B, and have Ss complete the sentences with their own or invented information.
- Check off each part of the lesson focus as Ss demonstrate an understanding of what they have learned in the lesson.

More Ventures, Unit 1, Lesson E	
Literacy Workbook, 15–30 min.	
Basic Workbook, 15–30 min.	
Writing worksheets, 15–30 min. **Real Life Document,** 15–30 min.	www.cambridge.org/myresourceroom

2 Write

A Complete the ID card. Write about yourself.

Central Adult School Library

(Answers will vary.)
Last name

First name

Area code

Phone number

Country

Signature

B Complete the sentences. Write about yourself.

1. My first name is (Answers will vary.).
2. My last name is ______________.
3. My area code is ______________.
4. My phone number is ______________.
5. My birthday is in ______________.

3 After you write

Talk with a partner. Share your writing.

LESSON **F** Another view

1 Life-skills reading

Midtown Adult School

Name: Samir Ahmed

Address: 1432 Woodrow Street
Tampa, FL 33612

Phone: (813) 555-6978

Birthday: February 8, 1990

Samir Ahmed
SIGNATURE

A Read the sentences. Look at the ID card. Fill in the answer.

1. His first name is ____.
   - Ⓐ Ahmed
   - Ⓑ Woodrow
   - ● Samir

2. His area code is ____.
   - Ⓐ 33612
   - ● 813
   - Ⓒ 555

3. His birthday is in ____.
   - Ⓐ January
   - ● February
   - Ⓒ August

4. His last name is ____.
   - ● Ahmed
   - Ⓑ Woodrow
   - Ⓒ Tampa

B Talk with a partner.

Say two things about Samir.

Lesson objectives
- Practice reading an ID card
- Review vocabulary and grammar from the unit
- Complete the self-assessment

Warm-up and review

- Before class. Write today's lesson focus on the board.
  Lesson F:
  Read an ID card
- Before class. Write in random places on the board examples of the key vocabulary. For example, you might write: *Jennifer*, *555-7924*, *Brazil*, *Clifton*, *(239)*, or draw a picture of an ID card.
- Begin class. Books closed. Review key vocabulary from the unit by calling on Ss to circle the items on the board. For example: *Please circle the country. Country.* (S circles *Brazil* on the board.)
- Ask volunteers to go to the board. Say: *Write a country / phone number / area code / birthday / last name / first name.* Make sure that Ss write correct examples on the board.

Presentation

- Books open. Direct Ss' attention to the ID card in Exercise **1A**. Ask: *What is this?* (ID card.) Tell Ss: *That's right. This is an ID card from Midtown Adult School.* Point to and repeat the name of the school on the card.
- Ask: *What's the first name on the ID card?* (Samir.) Ask: *What is Samir's last name?* (Ahmed.)
- Read aloud the words in the left-hand column of the ID card, and ask Ss to repeat after you.
- When you get to the word *address* on the ID card, ask: *What is an address?* Ss will probably recognize from the example that an address shows where a building is. (In this case, the address shows where Samir lives.)
- Write the street address of your school on the board as another example.

Practice

- Read aloud the instructions for Exercise **1A**. This task helps prepare Ss for standardized-type tests they may have to take.
- Write the first item on the board along with the three answer choices labeled *a*, *b*, and *c*.
- Read the item and the answer choices aloud and then point to the student ID. Ask: *What is his first name?* Show Ss where to look for the information. Elicit: *Samir.*
- Point to the three answer choices on the board. Ask Ss: *a*, *b*, or *c* (c)? Fill in the letter *c* and tell Ss: *Fill in the answer.* Make sure Ss understand the task.
- Have Ss individually scan for and fill in the answers.

Comprehension check

- Go over the answers to Exercise **1A** together. Make sure that Ss followed instructions and filled in their answers. As Ss give their answers, have them point to the part of the ID card where they found the information.

Practice

- Direct Ss' attention to Exercise **1B** and read the instructions aloud. Ss practice saying sentences about Samir in pairs.
- Ask several volunteers to say a sentence about Samir for the rest of the class.

Expansion activity *(whole group)*

- Teach Ss how to write an address on an envelope.
- On the board, draw a rectangle with a "stamp" in the upper right corner, and write Samir's information as you would on an envelope:
  Samir Ahmed
  1432 Woodrow Street
  Tampa, FL 33612
- Bring some envelopes in that were addressed to the school. Point out how the name and address are written on the envelopes.
- Point out that the name is on one line, the street number and name on another line, and the city, state, and zip code on another line. (Explain that every part of the country has a different zip code.)
- Point out the capital letters and the comma between the city and the state.
- Give each S an envelope or ask Ss to take out a piece of paper and write their own name and address. Walk around and help Ss individually. If possible, provide information about the zip codes in the areas where your Ss live. If Ss prefer, they can write the name of the school on their envelopes.

Literacy tip
For an alternative activity, refer literacy Ss to pages 16–17 in the *Literacy Workbook* at any time during the lesson.

LESSON F Another view

Presentation

- Books closed. Write the following list on the board:

  November

  Ernesto (or the name of a S in your class)

  March

  January
- Read aloud each item in the list and ask Ss to repeat. After each item, ask Ss: *What is this?* (month, first name, etc.)
- Point to each word and say to the class: *Month, first name, month, month.* Circle *Ernesto* on the board and say: *Ernesto is a first name. It's not a month. It's different.*
- Write on the board and say the word *different.* Ask Ss to repeat after you.
- Write another similar example on the board and repeat the procedure, but this time, ask for a volunteer to circle the word that is different and, if possible, to explain his or her choice.

Practice

- Books open. Direct Ss' attention to Exercise **2A** and read the instructions aloud. Read aloud the list in number 1 and ask Ss to repeat after you. Ask Ss: *What word is different?* (November.) Point to where *November* has been circled as an example. Make sure Ss understand the task.
- Ss complete the exercise individually.
- Read aloud the second part of the instructions for Exercise **2A**. Have Ss compare their answers in pairs.
- Check answers as a class. Ask volunteer pairs to write the circled words on the board.

Expansion activity (whole group)

- Ask Ss to work individually or in pairs to create a new list similar to the lists in Exercise **2A**.
- Have each S or pair of Ss write their list on the board. Ask a volunteer from the class to go to the board and circle the word that is different.

Presentation

- Books closed. Demonstrate the process of writing something in order. Draw a large circle on the board and write the numbers *1–12* in a random arrangement inside the circle.
- On a different part of the board, begin to write the sequence *1 – 2 – 3*. Ask a volunteer to come to the board. Say: *Please finish. Write the numbers in order. In order.* The S should continue by writing *4 – 5 – 6* and so on through *12*.

Practice

- Books open. Direct Ss' attention to Exercise **2B** and read the instructions aloud.
- Have Ss work in pairs to write the months in order in the grid.
- Check answers as a class. Draw a large grid on the board similar to the one in Exercise **2B**. Call on individual Ss to come to the board and write one of the months. Then go over the grid and ask the class: *Yes? Is this correct?* Make any necessary corrections on the board. If you have a wall calendar in the room, show each month in turn as you check the correct order.

Expansion activity (whole group)

- Practice saying the months of the year starting at different points in the year. First, do this chorally by saying a month, for example: *March.* Ask Ss to repeat the month after you. Then continue with the rest of the months through February. Do this a few times using different months as starting points.
- Next, say a month, and call on a S to repeat it and say the remaining months. Give as many Ss as possible an opportunity to say the months. Help with pronunciation as needed.

Evaluation

- Before asking Ss to turn to the self-assessment on page 136, do a quick review of the unit. Have Ss turn to Lesson A. Ask the class to talk about what they remember about this lesson. Prompt Ss, if necessary, with questions, for example: *What words are on this page? What do you see in the picture?* Continue in this manner to review each lesson quickly.
- **Self-assessment** Read the instructions for Exercise **3**. Ask Ss to turn to the self-assessment page and complete the unit self-assessment.
- If Ss are ready, administer the unit test on pages T-165–T-167 of this Teacher's Edition (or on the Assessment Audio CD / CD-ROM). The audio and audio script for the tests are on the Assessment Audio CD / CD-ROM.

More Ventures, Unit 1, Lesson F	
Literacy Workbook, 15–30 min.	
Basic Workbook, 15–30 min.	
Writing worksheets, 15–30 min.	www.cambridge.org/myresourceroom

2 Fun with vocabulary

A What word is different? Circle the word.

1. Countries

Mexico	China	November	Somalia

2. Months

April	September	May	Russia

3. Phone numbers

555-4861	555-6978	415	555-7934

4. Area codes

555-6948	813	212	915

5. First names

Linda	Alima	Nasser	Mexico

6. Last names

Cruz	February	Delgado	Lee

Talk with a partner. Check your answers.

B Work with a partner. Write the months in order.

April	August	December	February	January	July
June	March	May	November	October	September

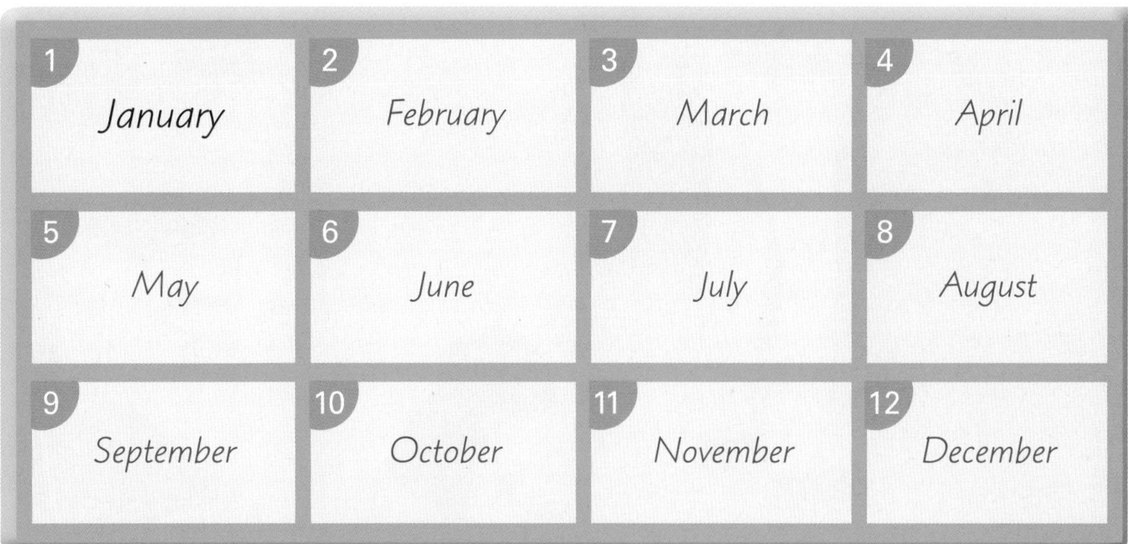

3 Wrap up

Complete the **Self-assessment** on page 136.

At school

LESSON A Listening

1 Before you listen

A Look at the picture. What do you see?

CLASS CD1 TK 16

B Listen and point: a book • a chair • a computer a desk • a notebook • a pencil

Lesson objectives

- Introduce Ss to the topic
- Find out what Ss know about the topic
- Preview the unit by talking about the picture
- Practice key vocabulary
- Practice listening skills

UNIT 2

Warm-up and review

- Before class. Write today's lesson focus on the board.

  Lesson A:
  At school
- Begin class. Books closed. Review the alphabet and the months of the year.
- Draw a grid on the board with two rows and six columns. Write the word *January* in the first square. In each of the other squares, write only the first letter of the corresponding month.
- Point to the word *January*. Circle the letter *J* and ask: *What letter is this?* Elicit: *J*. Point to the word and ask: *What month is this?* Elicit: *January.*
- Circle the letter *F* in the next square and ask Ss: *What letter is this?* Elicit: *F*. Ask: *What month is this?* Elicit: *February*. Call on a higher-level S to complete the word *February* on the board.
- Continue in this manner until Ss have named the first letter of each month and filled in the grid with the months of the year.
- Ask Ss a few questions about the months, for example: *What month is it now? When is your birthday?*
- Point to the lesson focus written on the board. Read the words aloud and ask Ss to repeat after you. Say: *Today, we will talk about things at school. At school.*

Literacy tip

If you have literacy Ss in your class, it might be helpful to spend time at the beginning of any activity that contains art or photos talking about the pictures before focusing Ss' attention on the printed words in the exercise. Have Ss work in pairs. Tell them to ask each other: *What do you see?* Encourage Ss to describe the pictures to each other. Consider pairing literacy Ss with Ss who can help them read the text in the exercise. This will help preview the exercise for literacy Ss and make them more confident as the exercise continues.

Presentation

- Books open. Set the scene. Hold up the Student's Book. Show Ss the picture on page 18. Ask: *What do you see?* Elicit and write on the board any vocabulary that Ss know, such as: *classroom*, *students*, *desk*, *computer*, *clock*.

Teaching tip

If Ss don't know any vocabulary for things they see in the picture, say *OK*, and go on to Exercise **1B**.

Practice

- Direct Ss' attention to the key vocabulary in Exercise **1B**. Read aloud each word or phrase while pointing to the corresponding part of the picture. Ask Ss to repeat and point.
- Point to the woman labeled *Sue* and ask: *What's her name?* Elicit or provide the name *Sue*. Repeat with the other people in the picture.

Class Audio CD1 track 16 Play or read the audio program (see audio script, page T-156). Tell Ss: *Listen and point to the picture*. As Ss hear the key vocabulary, check to see that they are pointing to the correct part of the picture. Repeat the audio program as needed.

Comprehension check

- Ask Ss *Yes / No* questions about the picture. Tell Ss: *Listen. Say "yes" or "no."*

  Point to the picture. Ask: *Is this a classroom? (Yes.)*
  Point to the desk. Ask: *Is this a chair? (No.)*
  Point to the teacher. Ask: *Is she a teacher? (Yes.)*
  Point to the computer. Ask: *Is this a book? (No.)*
  Point to the computer. Ask: *Is this a computer? (Yes.)*
  Point to the chair. Ask: *Is this a chair? (Yes.)*
  Point to the desk. Ask: *Is this a desk? (Yes.)*
  Point to the notebook. Ask: *Is this a pencil? (No.)*

Expansion activity *(whole group)*

- Teach vocabulary for additional classroom objects seen in the picture. Write on the board: *clock*, *map*, *filing cabinet.* Say the words aloud and ask Ss to repeat them after you.
- Ask Ss to point to each object in the picture. Hold up the Student's Book and point to each object for Ss who have not heard the words before.
- Ask follow-up questions about the objects. Ask Ss what time it is in the picture. Draw a large clock on the board to review the numbers *1–12* and assess Ss' knowledge of basic time-telling. Point to the map in the picture and ask: *What country is this?* (The United States.) Elicit and list on the board the names of other countries Ss know. If you have a filing cabinet in your classroom, open a drawer and ask Ss: *What is in a filing cabinet?* (Papers, files.) Show Ss examples of papers and files.
- Ask Ss: *What is in our classroom?* Point to objects in the classroom. Elicit the names of items listed in Exercise **1B** as well as the names of the additional items written on the board for this expansion activity.

LESSON A Listening

Presentation

- Direct Ss' attention to Exercise **2A**. Tell Ss: *These are things at school.*
- Hold up or point to real classroom objects as you read each word aloud. Ask Ss to repeat after you. If you don't have one of the objects in your classroom, draw a quick sketch and label it on the board.
- Read aloud the instructions for Exercise **2A**.

Practice

Class Audio CD1 track 17 Play or read the audio program (see audio script, page T-156). Listen and repeat the vocabulary along with Ss. Repeat the audio program as needed.

- Listen carefully to Ss' pronunciation and make corrections as needed.

Learner persistence (individual work)

Self-Study Audio CD track 11 Exercise **2A** is recorded on the CD at the back of the Student's Book. Ss can listen to the CD at home for reinforcement and review. They can also listen to the CD for self-directed learning when class attendance is not possible.

Expansion activity (whole group)

- Books closed. Write the six key vocabulary words on the board in any order: *a book*, *a chair*, *a computer*, *a desk*, *a notebook*, *a pencil.*
- Ask a S to come to the board. Say the vocabulary words randomly and have the volunteer point to each word.
- Repeat the procedure with other Ss. If you have all the objects available in your classroom, you could also have Ss point to the objects instead of to the words on the board.

> **Literacy tip**
> For an alternative activity, refer literacy Ss to pages 18–19 in the *Literacy Workbook* at any time during the lesson.

Practice

- Direct Ss' attention to Exercise **2B** and read the instructions aloud.

Class Audio CD1 track 18 Model the task. Hold up the Student's Book and say: *Number one.* Play or read the audio program for number 1 (see audio script, page T-156). Point to the two answer choices in number 1 and ask Ss: *What did you hear – a or b?* Elicit: *b.* Point to the letter b next to the second picture and tell Ss: *Circle the letter "b."*

Class Audio CD1 track 18 Play or read the complete audio program (see audio script, page T-156). Ss listen and circle the correct answers. Repeat the audio as needed.

Class Audio CD1 track 18 Read aloud the second part of the instructions for Exercise **2B**. Play or read the audio program again so that Ss can listen and check their answers.

Learner persistence (individual work)

Self-Study Audio CD track 12 Exercise **2B** is recorded on the CD at the back of the Student's Book. Ss can listen to the CD at home for reinforcement and review and also for self-directed learning when class attendance is not possible.

Comprehension check

- Write the numbers *1–4* on the board. Ask a few Ss to come to the board and write the correct answers to Exercise **2B** next to each number.

Class Audio CD1 track 18 Play or read the audio program again. Pause the audio program after each conversation. Point to the answer written on the board and ask: *Is this correct?* Ask another S to make any necessary corrections.

Application

- Direct Ss' attention to Exercise **3** and read the instructions aloud.
- Model the task. Hold up the Student's Book and point to the pictures in Exercise **2B**. Say to one S: *Point to a picture.* Say to the first S's partner: *Say the word.* Indicate that the second S should say the word that the first S pointed to.
- Ss complete the exercise in pairs. Walk around and help as needed.

Evaluation

- Direct Ss' attention to the lesson focus written on the board. Check Ss' understanding of the key vocabulary by asking them to point to the items in the picture on page 18 or to real items in your classroom: *a book, a chair, a computer, a desk, a notebook, a pencil.* Check that Ss are pointing to the correct items.
- Check off the lesson focus as Ss demonstrate an understanding of what they have learned in the lesson.

More Ventures, Unit 2, Lesson A	
Literacy Workbook, 15–30 min.	
Basic Workbook, 15–30 min.	
Writing worksheets, 15–30 min.	www.cambridge.org/myresourceroom
Student Arcade, time varies	www.cambridge.org/venturesarcade

Unit Goals

Identify classroom objects
Name location of classroom objects
Complete school information form

2 Listen

A Listen and repeat.

STUDENT TK 11
CLASS CD1 TK 17

1. a book 2. a chair 3. a computer
4. a desk 5. a notebook 6. a pencil

B Listen and circle.

STUDENT TK 12
CLASS CD1 TK 18

1. a.   (b.) 

2. a.   (b.) 

3. (a.)  b. 

4. (a.)  b. 

Listen again. Check your answers.

3 After you listen

Talk with a partner. Point to a picture.
Your partner says the word.

LESSON B Classroom objects

1 Vocabulary focus

Listen and repeat.

CLASS CD1 TK 19

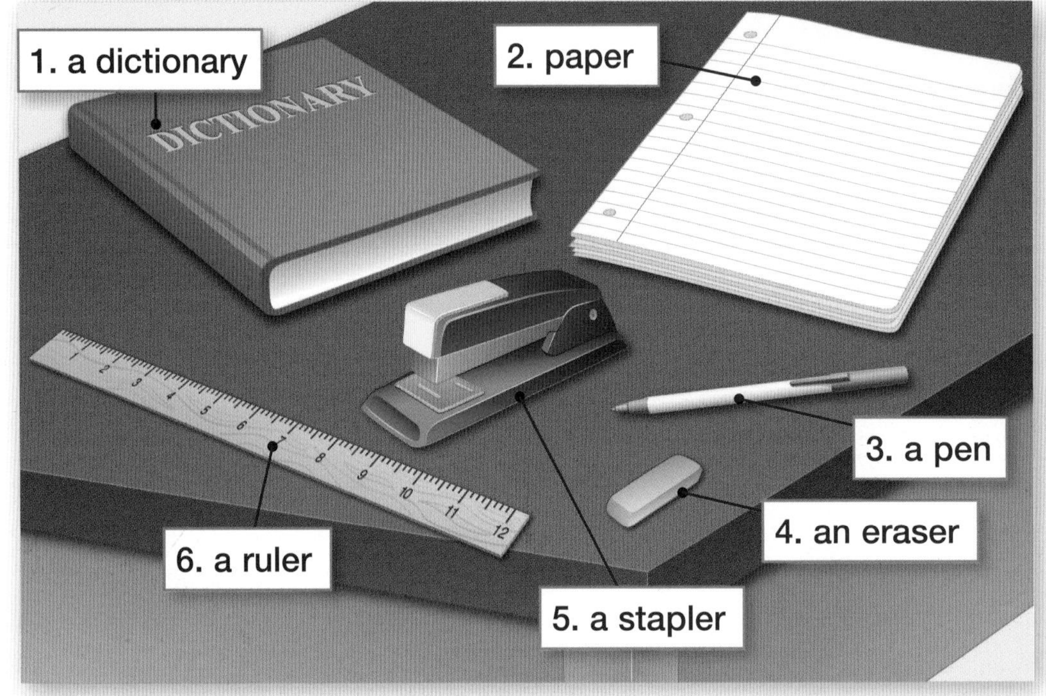

2 Practice

A Read and match.

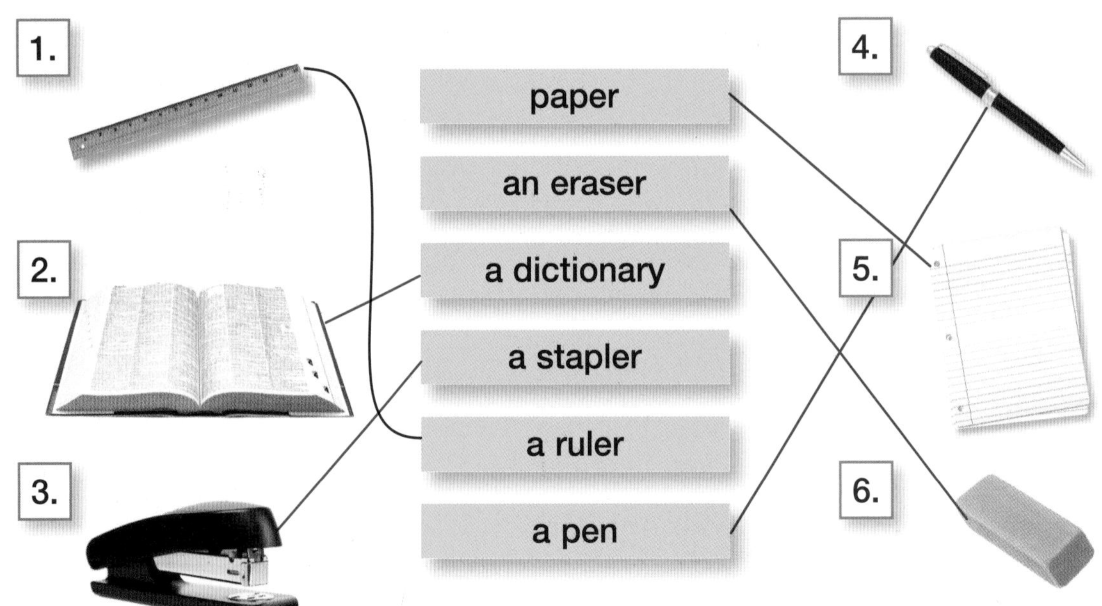

Lesson objectives

- Introduce additional vocabulary for classroom objects
- Practice asking what someone needs

Warm-up and review

- Before class. Write today's lesson focus on the board.
  Lesson B:
  Classroom objects
  What do you need?
- Before class. Write the key vocabulary from Lesson A on the board: *a book, a chair, a computer, a desk, a notebook, a pencil.*
- Point to each word on the board in turn and say: *Point to a book,* etc. Look around and make sure that Ss understand the meanings of the words.
- Begin class. Books open. Point to and say the key vocabulary words from Lesson A. Ask Ss to repeat.

Teaching tip

If you have literacy Ss in the class, you can practice word recognition by calling on Ss to come to the board and point to the key vocabulary words as you say them, either in the order they are written or in random order.

- Direct Ss' attention to the picture on page 18. Say the key vocabulary words again and ask Ss to point to the corresponding parts of the picture. Walk around and check to see that Ss are pointing to the correct items in the picture.

Presentation

- Point to the words *Classroom objects* at the top of page 20 in the Student's Book. Say the words aloud and ask Ss to repeat after you. Tell the class: *Classroom objects are things in the classroom.* Gesture to indicate your own classroom, or hold up the picture on page 18 to help clarify the meaning of the word *classroom.*
- Direct Ss' attention to Exercise **1**. Read the instructions aloud.

Practice

Class Audio CD1 track 19 Play or read the audio program (see audio script, page T-156). Listen and repeat along with Ss. Repeat the audio program as needed.

- Listen carefully to Ss' pronunciation and correct as needed.

Expansion activity (student pairs)

- Have pairs of Ss practice saying the words for classroom objects to each other and pointing to the appropriate part of the picture in the exercise.
- Model the task. Tell one S: *Say a word.* Point to the first vocabulary word in the Student's Book, indicating that he or she should say *a dictionary.* Then, say to his or her partner: *Please point to a dictionary in the picture.*
- Have Ss take turns saying the words and pointing to the picture. Alternatively, pair higher-level Ss with lower-level Ss, and ask the higher-level Ss to say the words while the lower-level Ss point to the picture.

Practice

- Direct Ss' attention to Exercise **2A**. As you read aloud the instructions, hold up the Student's Book and indicate that Ss should read the words and then draw a line between the pictures and the corresponding words.
- Model the task. Hold up the Student's Book. Point to the first picture. Ask: *What is this?* (A ruler.) Say: *Match the picture with the word.* Write the word *match* on the board. Point to it and say the word aloud. Ask Ss to repeat.
- Ss complete the exercise individually. Help as needed.

Comprehension check

- Write the numbers *1–6* on the board. Ask a few Ss to come to the board and write the answers to Exercise **2A**.
- Ask different Ss to read the answers written on the board. After each answer is read, ask: *Is this correct?* Ask another S to make corrections on the board.

Literacy tip

For an alternative activity, refer literacy Ss to pages 20–21 in the *Literacy Workbook* at any time during the lesson.

Expansion activity (small groups)

- Give each group a set of 12 index cards with one vocabulary word from Lessons A and B on each card. Shuffle the cards and place them in a stack facedown.
- Give each group at least 12 pieces of blank scrap paper to draw pictures on.
- Model the activity. Take the top card from one group's stack and read the word, but don't say the word aloud or show it to the Ss. Draw a picture of the classroom object, and show it to the Ss, who try to guess what you drew. When Ss guess correctly, say: *Correct!* and show them the word on your card.
- Have Ss take turns choosing and drawing words until all the words are chosen.

Multilevel tip

Match higher-level Ss with literacy Ss to work together in the expansion activity.

LESSON B Classroom objects

Presentation

- Direct Ss' attention to the word bank in Exercise 2B. Read the words aloud and ask Ss to repeat after you.
- Point to the picture in Exercise 2B. Ask: *What do you see?* Elicit and write on the board any pictured vocabulary that Ss know, including the unit vocabulary for classroom objects.
- Point to each S in the picture and ask: *What's his / her name?* Write the names on the board and practice saying them with the class.
- To help Ss understand the situation, point to Carla's desk in the picture, desk number 1. Ask: *Does Carla have a ruler? A ruler?* (Yes.) Write *a ruler* on the board. Continue in this manner until all the classroom objects on Carla's desk have been listed on the board.
- Then ask Ss: *Does Carla have a dictionary? A dictionary?* (No.) Tell Ss: *Correct. Carla does not have a dictionary.* Write on the board: *Carla needs a dictionary.* Point to where a dictionary has been written for number 1.
- Point to several Ss' desks in the classroom in turns. Ask: *Does* (name of S) *have a dictionary? Does* (name of S) *have a ruler?* etc. Elicit *Yes / No* responses.

Practice

- Read aloud the first part of the instructions for Exercise 2B.
- Class Audio CD1 track 20 Model the task. Say: *Listen and repeat.* Play or read the audio program for number 1 (see audio script, page T-156), and point to the teacher and then Carla in the picture as you repeat. Say: *Then write.* Point to the words *a dictionary* written on the memo. Make sure Ss understand the task.
- Class Audio CD1 track 20 Play or read the complete audio program (see audio script, page T-156). Ss listen and repeat. Encourage Ss to point to the people in the picture as they repeat.
- Ss complete the memo individually. Repeat the audio program as needed.
- Check answers with the class. Write the numbers *1–6* on the board and ask for volunteers to write their answers on the board. Point to each answer and ask the class: *Yes? Is this correct?* Make any necessary corrections on the board.
- Read aloud the second part of the instructions for Exercise 2B. Point to and model the example conversation.
- Call on a pair of volunteers to read the example conversation aloud for the class.
- Point to another person in the picture on page 21. Ask: *What do you need, (name)?* Elicit the answer from a volunteer. Repeat with different people in the picture. Indicate that Ss should ask and answer questions about all the people in the picture.
- Ss complete the exercise in pairs. Walk around and help as needed.
- Ask several S pairs to say their questions and answers to the rest of the class.

Application

- Direct Ss' attention to Exercise 3 and read the instructions aloud.
- Model the task. Read the example question and answer aloud, and ask Ss to repeat after you. Point to where the information has been written in the chart.

> **Teaching tip**
> Look through old magazines, and cut out pictures of the items in Exercise 2A on page 20. Alternatively, write the names of the items on slips of paper. Give each S one of the pictures to represent the item he or she needs in Exercise 3. As you hand out the pictures, tell Ss, for example: *Kara, you need a pen.*

- Ss complete the activity in small groups. Depending on class size, you may want to prepare and distribute larger charts for Ss to fill in, or else have Ss write the information in their notebooks.
- Continue by asking individual Ss what they need. Then check to see that the Ss' group members have written that information in their charts.

Evaluation

- Direct Ss' attention to the lesson focus written on the board.
- Hold up real examples of each classroom item from the lesson or point to the items in the pictures on page 20 and ask: *What is this?* As Ss respond correctly, invite them to the board to write the words.
- Collect the pictures you distributed earlier. Give one picture to a S and ask, for example: *Daisuke, what do you need?* After the S responds with the word for the classroom item in the picture, pretend to offer the item as you say: *Here you are.* Repeat the procedure with as many Ss as possible.
- Check off each part of the lesson focus as Ss demonstrate an understanding of what they have learned in the lesson.

More Ventures, Unit 2, Lesson B	
Literacy Workbook, 15–30 min. **Basic Workbook,** 15–30 min.	
Writing worksheets, 15–30 min.	www.cambridge.org/myresourceroom
Student Arcade, time varies	www.cambridge.org/venturesarcade

CLASS CD1 TK 20

B Listen and repeat. Then write.

a dictionary	an eraser	paper
a pen	a ruler	a stapler

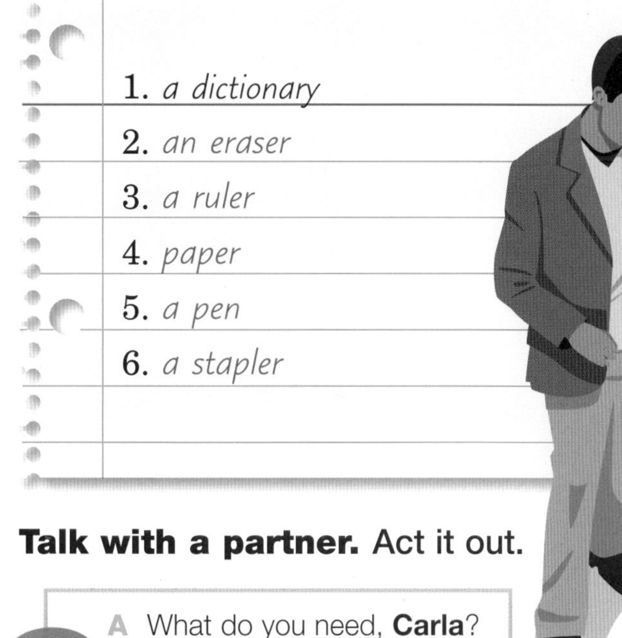

Talk with a partner. Act it out.

A What do you need, **Carla**?
B **A dictionary.**
A Here you are.

3 Communicate

Talk with your classmates. Complete the chart.

A What do you need, **Mahmoud**?
B **An eraser.**

Name	Classroom object
Mahmoud	*an eraser*
(Answers will vary.)	

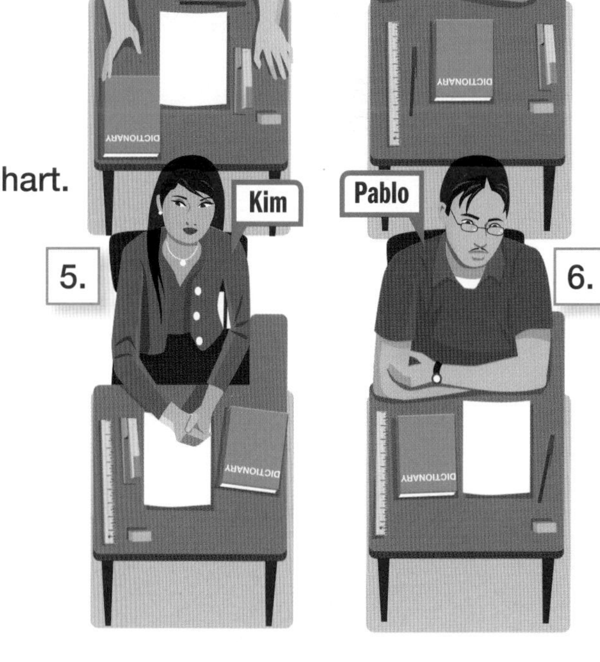

LESSON C Where's my pencil?

1 Grammar focus: *in*, *on*, and *under*

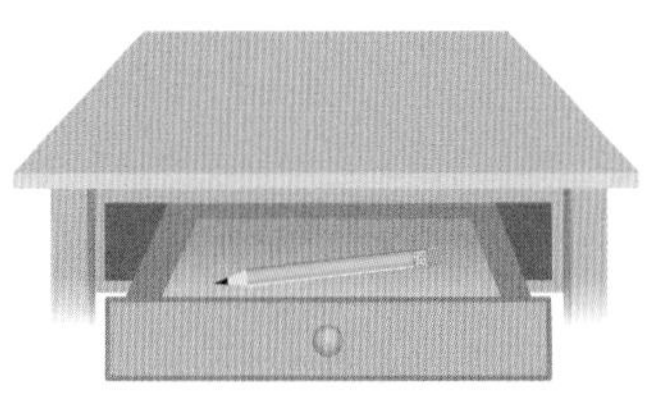
in the desk

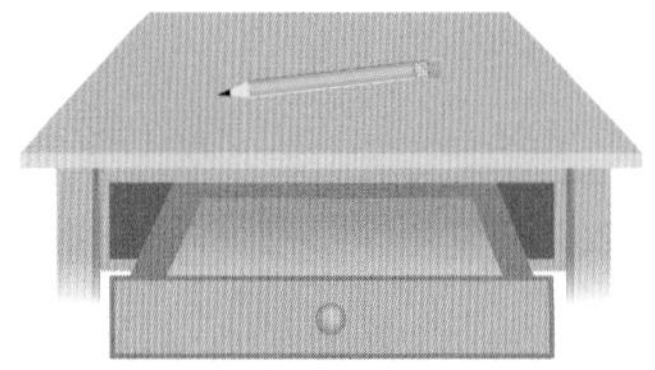
on the desk

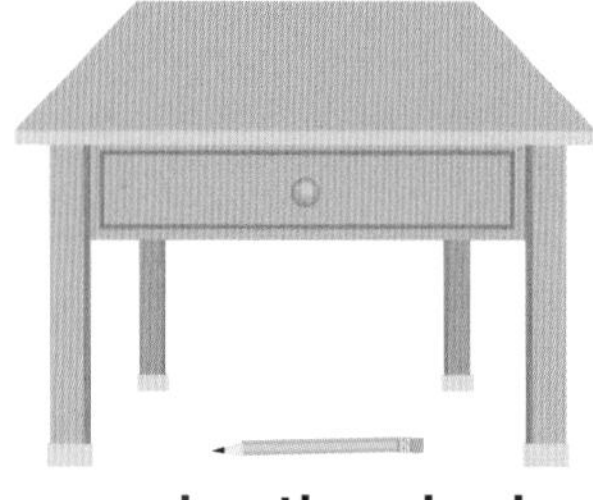
under the desk

2 Practice

A Read and circle. Then write.

1. A Where's my pencil?
   B ___In___ the desk.
   (In) On Under

2. A Where's my notebook?
   B ___On___ the desk.
   In (On) Under

3. A Where's my pen?
   B ___On___ the floor.
   In (On) Under

4. A Where's my dictionary?
   B ___Under___ the table.
   In On (Under)

5. A Where's my ruler?
   B ___On___ the table.
   In (On) Under

6. A Where's my paper?
   B ___Under___ the desk.
   In On (Under)

CLASS CD1 TK 21

Listen and repeat. Then practice with a partner.

Lesson objectives

- Introduce the prepositions of location *in*, *on*, and *under*
- Practice asking about and giving the location of things

Warm-up and review

- Before class. Write today's lesson focus on the board.
  Lesson C:
  in, *on*, and *under*
  Where's my _____?
- Before class. List the following on the board: *a book, a chair, a computer, a desk, a dictionary, an eraser, a notebook, paper, a pen, a pencil, a ruler, a stapler.*
- Begin class. Books closed. Review vocabulary for classroom objects. Point to and say each vocabulary word on the board and ask Ss to repeat after you.
- Hold up or point to as many real examples of the classroom objects as possible and ask Ss: *What is this?* As Ss respond correctly, circle the vocabulary words on the board.

Presentation

- Before class. Bring to class a small cardboard box or other object to place things in, on, and under.
- Point to the first part of the lesson focus written on the board. Tell the class: *Today, we will learn about "in," "on," and "under."* Show Ss an eraser or other classroom object and ask: *What is this?* (An eraser.) Teach Ss *box* or the words for other objects you brought to class.
- Place the eraser inside the box and tell Ss: *The eraser is in the box. In.* Point to the word *in* on the board. Ask Ss to repeat it after you.
- Close the box (or turn it on its side), and place the eraser on top. Tell Ss: *The eraser is on the box. On.* Point to the word *on* written on the board. Ask Ss to repeat it after you. Put the eraser under the box. Tell Ss: *The eraser is under the box. Under.* Point to the word *under* on the board. Ask Ss to repeat it after you. Continue to put the eraser in, on, or under the box as you say the prepositions as many times as necessary. Then place the eraser in, on, or under the box and ask: *In, on, or under?* (Ss respond appropriately.)
- Books open. Direct Ss' attention to the pictures in Exercise **1**. Read each phrase aloud as you point to the corresponding picture. Ask Ss to repeat the phrases after you.
- Point to each of the pictures in Exercise **1** and ask: *Where's the pencil?* Elicit: *in*, *on*, or *under the desk* as appropriate. Repeat with as many Ss as possible.

Practice

- Direct Ss' attention to the picture in Exercise **2A**. Ask two Ss to read the example conversation aloud. When Speaker B's line is read, show Ss the three answer choices under the blank and ask: *In, on, or under?* Elicit: *In.*
- Read aloud the instructions for Exercise **2A**. Point to where *In* has been circled and written for number 1.
- Ss complete the exercise individually. Walk around and help as needed.

Literacy tip

Literacy Ss should be able to do Warm-up and review and Presentation in Lesson C, and in Exercise **2A**, they can work with a higher-level partner who reads aloud the question and answer choices. The second page of this lesson, however, involves a large amount of reading and writing, so you may want to assign pages 22–23 of the *Literacy Workbook* as an alternative activity.

Comprehension check

- Read aloud the second part of the instructions for Exercise **2A**.

Class Audio CD1 track 21 Play or read the audio program (see audio script, page T-156). Ss listen and repeat as they check their answers.

- Write the numbers *1–6* on the board. Ask volunteers to come to the board and write the words they circled. Make any necessary corrections on the board.
- Ss in pairs. Ask Ss to choose Role A or B and practice the questions and answers in Exercise **2A**. Then have Ss switch roles and practice again. Walk around and help as needed.
- Ask several pairs to say the questions and answers for the rest of the class.

Expansion activity *(whole group)*

- Write on the board: *the floor, the filing cabinet, the table, a chair.* Point to and say each word and ask Ss to repeat after you.
- Use your own classroom or the picture on page 18 to practice this vocabulary. Place various items on the floor and on the table (if you have one), and in or on the filing cabinet. Also place some items under the table or a chair. Ask Ss where the items are and elicit prepositional phrases.
- Ask Ss questions about the picture on page 18 if you don't have a filing cabinet or table in your classroom.

LESSON C Where's my pencil?

Practice

- Direct Ss' attention to Exercise **2B** and read the instructions aloud.
- Model the task. Point to number 1 and read aloud: *my book.* Point to the picture and ask: *Where is her book?* Elicit: *in the desk.* Point to the line that has been drawn as an example. Make sure Ss understand the task.
- Ss complete the task individually. Walk around and help as needed.
- Check answers with the class. Duplicate the four columns from the exercise on the board, and ask for volunteers to match the classroom objects to their locations. For each match, ask the class: *Is this correct?* Make any necessary corrections on the board.
- Read aloud the second part of the instructions for Exercise **2B**.
- If you have a desk with a drawer in it, place a book in a desk so that Ss can see it. Point to and model the example conversation, pretending to be the woman in the picture when reading Speaker A's part.
- Read each line of the example conversation aloud and ask Ss to repeat after you.
- Point to the words *my stapler* in number 2 on the board. Call on two higher-level Ss to model the conversation and act it out, putting a stapler on a book. Indicate that Ss should act out conversations for all the items in Exercise **2B**. Make sure Ss understand the task.
- Have Ss practice the conversations in pairs. When Ss are finished, call on several pairs to perform one of the conversations for the class.

Application

- Direct Ss' attention to Exercise **3** and read the instructions aloud. Place a pencil on your desk and read the example conversation aloud. Point to the word *pencil* in the first column of the chart and to the phrase *on the desk* in the second column.
- Ask Ss to take out a pencil, a book, a piece of paper, a pen, a dictionary, and a notebook. Ask Ss to put the objects in, on, and under various places around them, for example: on the desk, in a notebook, under a chair, and on the floor.
- Model the task. Stand near a S, point to his or her piece of paper, and say: *Ask the question "Where's my paper?"* (S1 asks the question.)
- Gesture toward S1's partner to indicate that he or she should answer. Elicit the appropriate prepositional phrase, for example: *on the floor.* Point to S1's chart and say: *Write "on the floor."*
- Have Ss work in pairs to complete their charts. Tell Ss: *Talk about your classroom objects.* Write the words. Walk around and help as needed.

Teaching tip

If you think your Ss need additional help with Exercise **3**, write the necessary questions to complete the chart on the board. Read each question aloud and ask Ss to repeat after you.

Useful language

- Read aloud the sentence in the tip box and ask Ss to repeat after you. Illustrate the meaning of *I don't know* by shrugging your shoulders and shaking your head.
- Ask Ss about the location of a classroom object they cannot see as you pretend to look for it, for example: *Where's my ruler?* Indicate that Ss should answer: *I don't know.*
- Encourage Ss to use the useful language if applicable as they interview classmates in Exercise **3**.

Evaluation

- Direct Ss' attention to the lesson focus written on the board. Place real classroom objects in various places and ask, for example: *Where's my dictionary?* Elicit correct responses with *on*, *in*, and *under*, for example: *It's in the filing cabinet.*
- Call on Ss to ask their classmates questions about their own classroom objects.
- Check off each part of the lesson focus as Ss demonstrate an understanding of what they have learned in the lesson.

More Ventures, Unit 2, Lesson C	
Literacy Workbook, 15–30 min. **Basic Workbook,** 15–30 min.	
Writing worksheets, 15–30 min.	www.cambridge.org/myresourceroom
Student Arcade, time varies	www.cambridge.org/venturesarcade

B Look at the picture. Match the words.

1. my book	under the chair
2. my stapler	on the desk
3. my notebook	in the desk
4. my ruler	on the book

5. my paper	in the notebook
6. my pen	under the desk
7. my pencil	on the paper
8. my dictionary	on the chair

Talk with a partner. Act it out.

A Where's my **book**?
B **In the desk.**
A Thanks.

3 Communicate

Talk with a partner. Complete the chart.

A Where's my **pencil**?
B **On the desk.**

USEFUL LANGUAGE

I don't know.

my pencil	*on the desk*
my book	*(Answers will vary.)*
my paper	
my pen	
my dictionary	
my notebook	

LESSON **D** Reading

1 Before you read

Talk about the picture.
What do you see?

2 Read

STUDENT TK 13
CLASS CD1 TK 22

Listen and read.

Sue,

It's Monday, your first day of English class! You need a pencil, eraser, notebook, and dictionary. The pencil is in the desk. The eraser is on the desk. The notebook is on my computer. And the dictionary is under the chair.

Have fun at school!

Mom

3 After you read

Read and match.

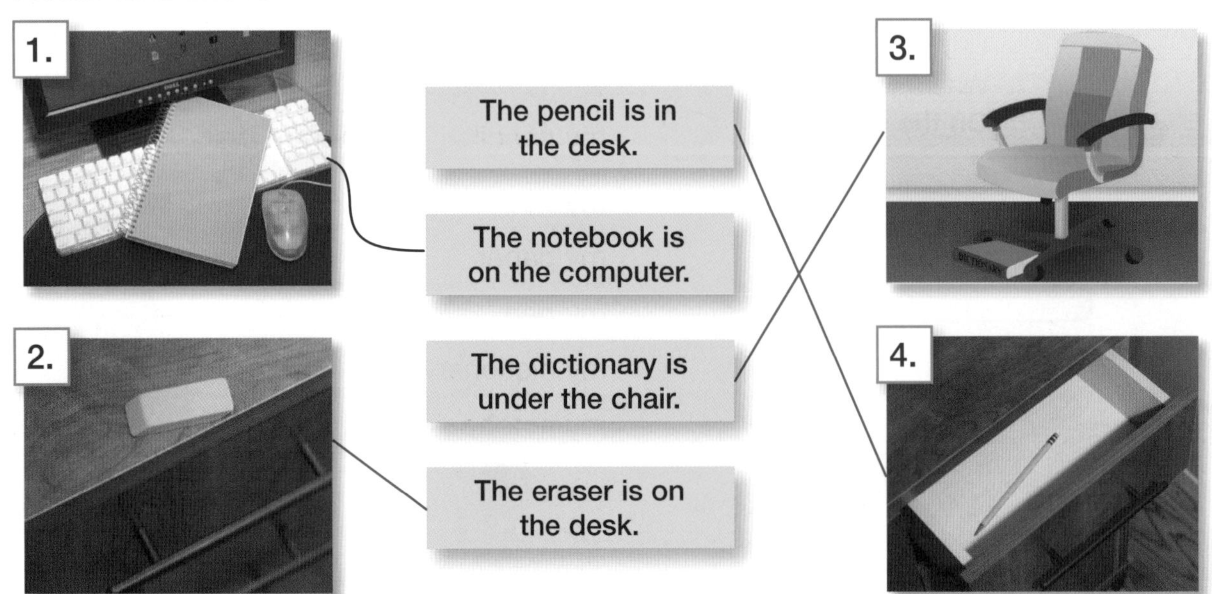

Lesson objectives

- Introduce and read a note about school supplies
- Introduce the days of the week
- Practice using new topic-related words

Warm-up and review

- Before class. Write today's lesson focus on the board.
  Lesson D:
  Read a note
  Days of the week
- Begin class. Books closed. Write on the board:
  What do you need?
  Where's my notebook?
- Read each question aloud and ask Ss to repeat after you.
- Review vocabulary from the unit. Hold up or arrange on a table several classroom objects, for example: a pen, a pencil, a ruler, a dictionary, paper, and a stapler. Ask as many Ss as possible: *What do you need?* As Ss respond with the vocabulary words, hand them the objects and say: *Here you are.*
- Collect the classroom objects you handed out and place them in various places. Ask as many Ss as possible: *Where's my* _____ *?* As Ss respond with prepositional phrases, for example, *on the desk*, say: *Thanks!*

Presentation

- Books open. Direct Ss' attention to the picture in Exercise **1** and read the instructions aloud. Ask: *Who is this? What's her name?* Ss should recognize Sue from the picture on page 18.
- Ask: *What do you see?* Elicit and write on the board any vocabulary about the picture that Ss know, such as: *kitchen*, *refrigerator*, *juice.*
- Point to the note on the refrigerator. Write the word *note* on the board. Say the word and ask Ss to repeat after you. Tell Ss: *Sue is reading a note.*

Practice

- Direct Ss' attention to Exercise **2**. Tell Ss: *This is the note.*

Class Audio CD1 track 22 Read aloud the instructions for Exercise **2**. Play or read the audio program and ask Ss to read along (see audio script, page T-156). Repeat the audio program as needed.

- Read aloud each sentence of the reading and ask Ss to repeat after you. Answer any questions Ss have about the reading.

Teaching tip

You can vary the presentation of the reading by asking Ss to read the note silently before they listen to the audio program or to close their books and just listen before they read.

Literacy tip

If you have literacy Ss in the class, prepare a list of the key vocabulary words from the reading and one or two additional vocabulary words. Use large lowercase letters. While the rest of the class is reading the note, ask the literacy Ss to circle only those words on the list that they also see in the reading.

Learner persistence *(individual work)*

Self-Study Audio CD track 13 Exercise **2** is recorded on the CD at the back of the Student's Book. Ss can listen to the CD at home for reinforcement and review and also for self-directed learning when class attendance is not possible.

Comprehension check

- Read aloud the instructions for Exercise **3**.
- Model the task. Point to the first picture. Then point to the sentences and ask: *Which sentence?* Elicit: *The notebook is on the computer.* Point to the line drawn between the first picture and the second sentence. Say: *Match the picture with the sentence.*
- Ss complete the exercise individually. Walk around and help as needed.
- Go over answers with the class. Write the sentences from Exercise **3** on the board, surrounded by numbered boxes to represent the pictures in the exercise. Read each sentence aloud, ask Ss to repeat after you, and call on Ss to match each sentence to the numbered pictures on the board. For each match, ask the class: *Is this correct?* Make any necessary corrections on the board.

Literacy tip

For an alternative activity, refer literacy Ss to pages 24–25 in the *Literacy Workbook* at any time during the lesson.

LESSON D Reading

Presentation

- Direct Ss' attention to the picture dictionary in Exercise 4. Point to the words *Days of the week.* Read the words aloud and ask Ss to repeat after you.
- Tell the class, for example: *Today is Monday. Monday.* Ask Ss to repeat the day. Tell Ss: *Monday is a day of the week.*
- Read aloud the instructions for Exercise 4A.

Class Audio CD1 track 23 Play or read the audio program (see audio script, page T-156). Listen to Ss' pronunciation as they repeat the days of the week. Correct pronunciation as needed.

Expansion activity (individual work)

- Before class, create handouts with seven numbered lines. On each line, make blanks for the letters of one of the days of the week with the first blank filled in, starting with Monday. For example, the first line would be:
  _M_ _____ _____ _____ _____ _____. Alternatively, write the words with blanks on the board, and ask Ss to copy them down and fill in the blanks.
- Give each S a handout and ask them to write the days of the week. Ss may use the picture dictionary to help with spelling.
- Practice saying the days of the week with the class, or have pairs of Ss take turns saying the days to each other.

Learner persistence (individual work)

Self-Study Audio CD track 14 Exercise 4A is recorded on the CD at the back of the Student's Book. Ss can listen to the CD at home for reinforcement and review and also for self-directed learning when class attendance is not possible.

Practice

- Direct Ss' attention to Exercise 4B and read the instructions aloud. Hold up your Student's Book and point to the iPad. Ask: *What's this?* (It's an iPad). Point to the calendar on the iPad. Ask: *What's this?* (It's a calendar.) Point to *Monday* in the picture dictionary. Ask two Ss to read the example conversation aloud.
- Model the task. Hold up your Student's Book and point to a different day of the week. Ask a S: *What day is it?* Elicit the day you are pointing to.
- Ss complete the activity in pairs. Say to one S: *Point to a day.* Say to his or her partner: *Say the day of the week.* Walk around and help as needed.
- When Ss are finished, write the days of the week in order across the board. Ask Ss to come to the board, point to one of the days, and ask a classmate: *What day is it?*

Evaluation

- Direct Ss' attention to the lesson focus written on the board. Hold up the Student's Book and point to the reading in Exercise 2. Ask: *What does Sue need for school?* List the needed items on the board and for each one, ask: *Where's the _____?* Elicit the locations given in the reading.
- Draw seven long blanks across the board. Point to each blank and ask for volunteers to fill in the blanks with the days of the week.

> **Teaching tip**
> If you have enough Ss in your class, it might be fun to have seven Ss at the board at the same time working out which day each one will write in which blank.

- Ask Ss a few simple questions about days of the week, for example: *Is today Sunday? What day is today? What days do we have English class?*
- Check off each part of the lesson focus as Ss demonstrate an understanding of what they have learned in the lesson.

More Ventures, Unit 2, Lesson D	
Literacy Workbook, 15–30 min. **Basic Workbook,** 15–30 min.	
Picture Dictionary activities, 30–45 min. **Writing worksheets,** 15–30 min. **Real Life Document,** 15–30 min.	www.cambridge.org/myresourceroom
Student Arcade, time varies	www.cambridge.org/venturesarcade

4 **Picture dictionary** Days of the week

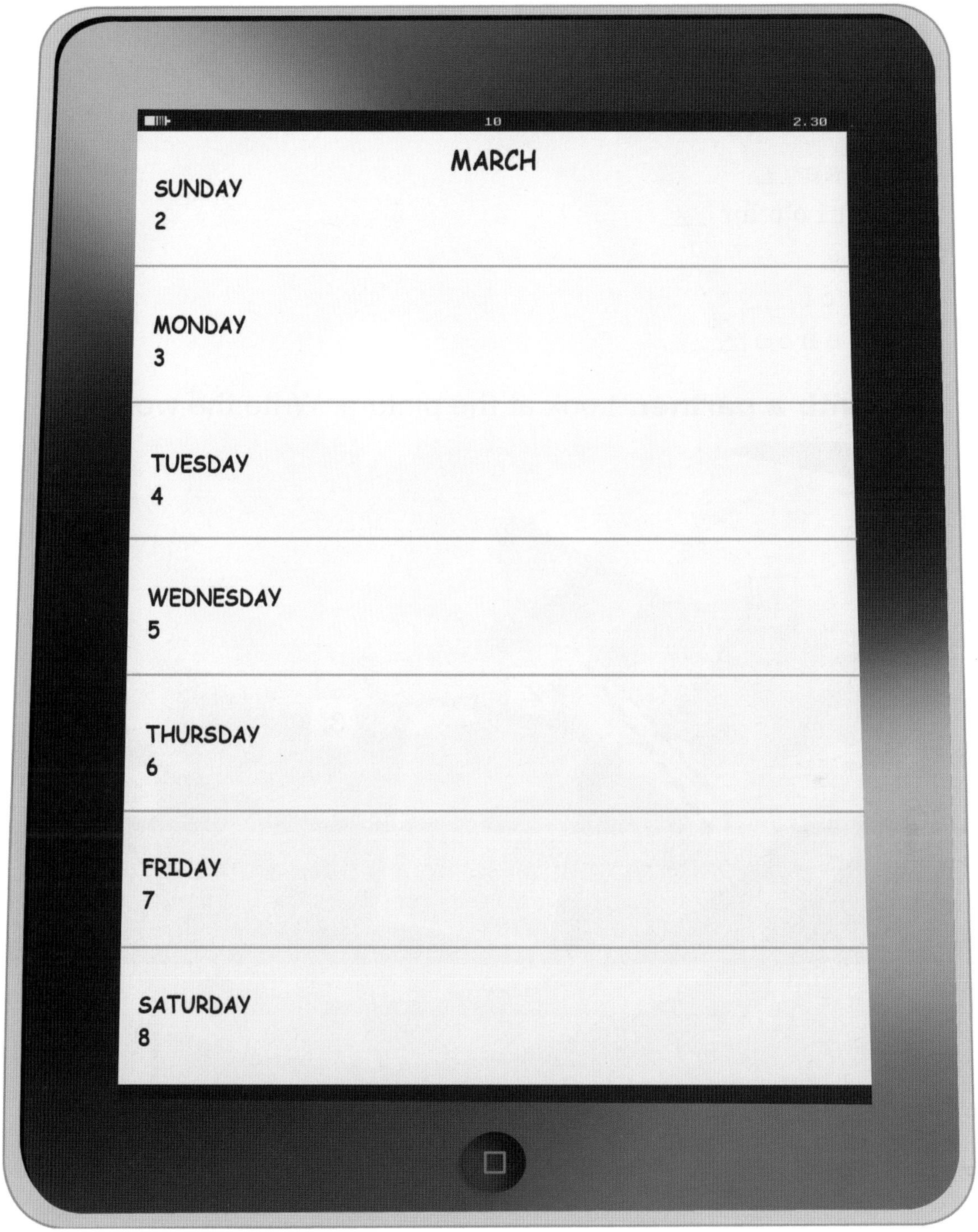

10
2.30
MARCH
SUNDAY
2
MONDAY
3
TUESDAY
4
WEDNESDAY
5
THURSDAY
6
FRIDAY
7
SATURDAY
8

A Listen and repeat. Look at the picture dictionary.

STUDENT TK 14
CLASS CD1 TK 23

B Talk with a partner. Point and ask. Your partner answers.

A What day is it?
B **Monday.**

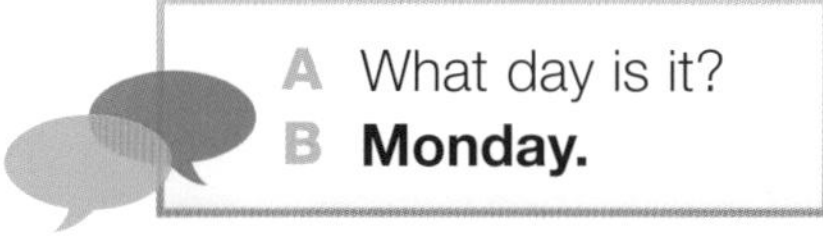

LESSON E Writing

1 Before you write

A Talk with a partner. Complete the words.

1. e r a s e _r_
2. d i c t i o n a r _y_
3. p e _n_
4. p e n c i _l_
5. n o t e b o o _k_

B Talk with a partner. Look at the picture. Write the words.

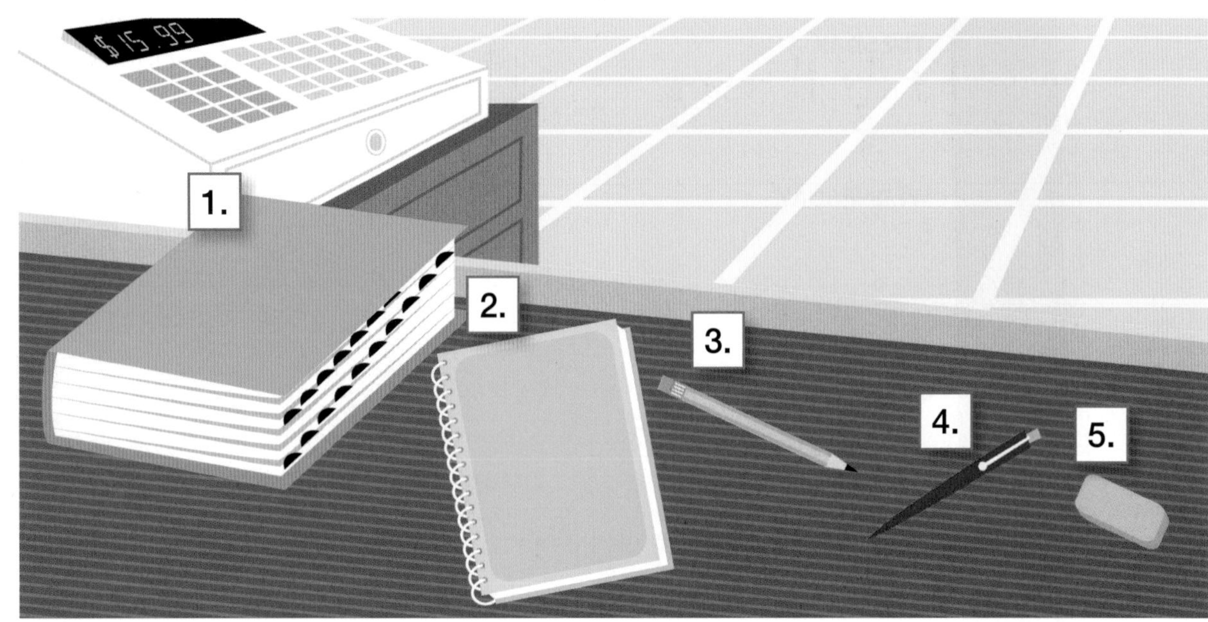

1. *dictionary*
2. *notebook*
3. *pencil*
4. *pen*
5. *eraser*

Lesson objectives

- Practice writing key vocabulary words
- Complete sentences about class information

Warm-up and review

- Before class. Write today's lesson focus on the board.
  Lesson E:
  Write words for classroom objects
  Complete sentences about school
- Begin class. Books closed. Review the meaning of the word *need*. Place a few classroom objects on a desk or table, for example, a ruler, a pen, and some paper. Hold up the ruler and ask Ss: *What's this?* (A ruler.) Tell Ss: *I have a ruler.*
- Look over the objects on the table and say: *Hmm . . . I have a ruler but no dictionary. I need a dictionary*. Write on the board: *I need a dictionary.* Look around the room hopefully, and say the sentence until a S offers you a dictionary. Accept the dictionary and say: *Thanks.*
- Repeat the procedure with the other objects, telling Ss that you have a pen and paper, but you need, for example, a pencil and an eraser. Make sure Ss understand the meaning of *need*.

Presentation

- Books open. Direct Ss' attention to Exercise **1A** and read the instructions aloud. Point to the first item and say to Ss: *Number 1. What's the word?* (Eraser.) Say to Ss: *e-r-a-s-e . . . What letter do we need?* (r) Point to where the letter r has been written for number 1.

Practice

- Ss work in pairs to complete the words.
- When Ss are finished, call on different pairs to write their completed words on the board. Review the alphabet by asking Ss who write answers on the board to say the letters aloud. Have Ss make any necessary corrections on the board.

Expansion activity (small groups)

- Before class. Type out the words *dictionary*, *notebook*, *pencil*, *pen*, and *eraser*, using large letters. Make five copies and cut them into strips so that each strip has one word on it. If you have a larger class, make copies in multiples of five.
- Put the sets of words into five envelopes. Arrange the words so that each envelope is missing one of the five words and has two of the same word.
- Distribute the envelopes to five small groups of Ss. Write the five words on the board and tell Ss: *You do not have all the classroom objects. You need one classroom object. What do you need?*
- Give each group time to look at the words in their envelopes and determine which word is missing. Say: *Talk to your classmates. Ask them what they need.* Write on the board: *What do you need?* and *Here you are.*
- Model the task. Have a volunteer ask you the question you wrote on the board. Tell that S's group, for example: *I need a notebook. Do you have two notebooks?* If the group has only one, ask the other groups: *Do you have two notebooks?* Have the group with two notebooks give you one and say: *Here you are.*
- Have Ss talk to the other groups to get the word they need. Walk around and help as needed.

Practice

- Direct Ss' attention to the picture in Exercise **1B**.
- Read the instructions for Exercise **1B** aloud.
- Ss work in pairs to write the words for the classroom objects in the picture.
- Check answers with the class. Write the numbers *1–5* on the board, and ask for volunteers to write their answers on the board. Point to and say each answer and ask the class: *Is this correct?* Make any necessary corrections on the board.

> **Teaching tip**
> Encourage Ss who did not write on the board in Exercise **1A** to do the writing for Exercise **1B**.

Comprehension check

- Ask Ss to take out a piece of paper. Tell Ss: *Write the words.* Show the class real examples of the classroom objects on page 26. For example, hold up a pen and say: *Write the word.*
- Collect the papers to check Ss' writing, or have Ss compare their writing in pairs.

> **Literary tip**
> For an alternative activity, refer literacy Ss to pages 26–27 in the *Literacy Workbook* at any time during the lesson.

LESSON E Writing

Presentation

- Ask Ss' to turn to page 24 in the Student's Book. Direct their attention to the picture of Sue in Exercise 1. Remind Ss of the note from Sue's mother about things Sue needs for school. Ask questions such as: *Who is this?* (Sue.) *What is Sue reading?* Point to the note. *What is this?* (A note.) *What does Sue need for school?* (A pencil, a notebook, a dictionary, and an eraser.)
- Direct Ss' attention to Exercise 2A on page 27 and read the instructions aloud. Explain that *memo* is another word for *note*. Say *memo* aloud and ask Ss to repeat.
- Give Ss time to read the memo silently. Then read each line of the memo aloud and ask Ss to repeat. Answer any questions Ss have about the memo.

Teaching tip

To help Ss understand the meaning of *first*, write the numbers *1–3* on the board and read them aloud. Ask: *What number is first?* Elicit or point to *1*. Say: *Number one is first.* If you have a calendar, point to the date the class was first held and tell Ss, for example: *The first day of school.*

Practice

- Direct Ss' attention to Exercise 2B and read the instructions aloud.
- Read aloud the first prompt: *The first day of school is . . .* Ask: *What day?* Remind Ss by pointing to the day school started. If Ss still don't understand, tell them, for example: *The first day of school was Tuesday. Tuesday.*
- Ss complete the sentences individually. Walk around and help as needed.

Comprehension check

- Direct Ss' attention to Exercise 3 and read the instructions aloud.
- Model the task. Show your memo to a S and say the sentences in Exercise 2B, using your own information. Ask that S to read and show you his or her sentences.
- Ss share their sentences in pairs. Walk around and spot-check Ss' writing.

Expansion activity *(individual groups)*

- Ask Ss to write their completed sentences on a piece of paper and hand them in.

Literacy tip

If any of the writing exercises are too difficult for your literacy Ss, provide alternative tasks for them to work on at their desks or in self-access centers in the classroom. Appropriate tasks include copying or tracing letters, using letter cards to form words, or matching pairs of vocabulary flashcards.

Community building

- If you have any extra school supplies, for example, pencils, pens, or paper, offer them to Ss. Say, for example: *Do you need a pencil?*
- Ask Ss if they need anything else for the class. If someone needs a notebook, for example, or an eraser, ask if anyone in the class has two of those things. Don't put any pressure on Ss to give away their school supplies, but if they want to help each other in this way, encourage them to do so.

Evaluation

- Direct Ss' attention to the first part of the lesson focus written on the board. Read the phrase aloud and ask Ss to repeat. Show Ss real examples of classroom objects and call on individual Ss to write the corresponding words on the board.
- Direct Ss' attention to the second part of the lesson focus written on the board. Read it aloud and ask Ss to repeat. Write sentence prompts on the board similar to the ones in Exercise 2B. Call on individual Ss to complete the sentences on the board.
- Check off each part of the lesson focus as Ss demonstrate an understanding of what they have learned in the lesson.

More Ventures, Unit 2, Lesson E	
Literacy Workbook, 15–30 min.	
Basic Workbook, 15–30 min.	
Writing worksheets, 15–30 min.	www.cambridge.org/myresourceroom

2 Write

A Read the memo.

Welcome to Miami Adult School! MAS

The first day of school is Monday.
Your teacher is Ms. Moreno.
Your class is in Room 101.
For class, you need:
- a dictionary
- a notebook
- a pencil
- a pen
- an eraser

B Complete the memo. Write about yourself.

The first day of school is *(Answers will vary.)*.
My teacher is ________________.
My class is in Room ______.
For class, I need ________________.
I need ________________.
I need ________________.
I need ________________.
I need ________________.

3 After you write

Talk with a partner. Share your writing.

LESSON F Another view

1 Life-skills reading

MAIN ST Community School

JANUARY CLASS SCHEDULE

English 1	Introduction to Computers
Teacher: **Lynn Jones**	Teacher: **Harry Dawson**
Room: **12**	Room: **Computer Lab A**
Tuesday and Thursday	Monday and Wednesday
10:00 a.m.–12:00 noon	1:00 p.m.–3:00 p.m.

A Read the sentences. Look at the class schedule. Fill in the answer.

1. The English class is on ____.
   - Ⓐ Monday and Wednesday
   - ● Tuesday and Thursday
   - Ⓒ Tuesday and Wednesday

2. The computer class is on ____.
   - ● Monday and Wednesday
   - Ⓑ Tuesday and Thursday
   - Ⓒ Monday and Tuesday

3. The English class is in ____.
   - Ⓐ Room 1
   - ● Room 12
   - Ⓒ Lab A

4. The computer class is in ____.
   - ● Lab A
   - Ⓑ Lab B
   - Ⓒ Room 1

B Talk with a partner.

Talk about your class schedule.

Lesson objectives

- Practice reading a class schedule
- Review vocabulary and grammar from the unit
- Complete the self-assessment

Warm-up and review

- Before class. Write today's lesson focus on the board.
  Lesson F:
  Read a class schedule
- Before class. Write on the board:
  What class?
  What teacher?
  What room?
  What days?
  What time?
- Begin class. Books closed. Review the days of the week by drawing seven long blanks on the board. Ask: *What day is today?* Write the day in the appropriate blank. Point to the next blank and ask Ss: *What day?* Elicit and write the remaining days of the week. Practice saying the days in order chorally.

Presentation

- Books open. Direct Ss' attention to the class schedule in Exercise **1**. Tell Ss: *This is a class schedule.* Point to the words *Class Schedule.* Ask Ss to repeat after you.
- Tell Ss: *A class schedule tells us about classes at a school.* Ask: *What is the name of the school?* Point to and say: *Main Street Community School.* Ask Ss to repeat after you.
- Point to the schedule and ask: *What classes do you see? What classes?* (English 1 and Introduction to Computers.) Write the class titles on the board as the headings for two columns to the right of the questions on the board.
- To help Ss preview the class schedule, point to the questions written on the board. Read each question aloud, have Ss repeat after you, and elicit the answers. Write on the board in two columns the information about the two classes. Alternatively, ask a S volunteer to write the answers that other Ss say aloud.

Practice

- Read the instructions for Exercise **1A** aloud. This task helps prepare Ss for standardized-type tests they may have to take.
- Write the first item on the board along with the three answer choices labeled *a*, *b*, and *c*.
- Read the item and the answer choices aloud and then point to the first class schedule in the exercise. Ask: *Is English class on Monday and Wednesday, Tuesday and Thursday, or Tuesday and Wednesday?* Continue to gesture toward the schedule to show Ss where to look for the information. Elicit: *Tuesday and Thursday.*
- Point to the three answer choices on the board. Ask Ss: *a*, *b*, or *c*? (b) Fill in the letter *b* and tell Ss: *Fill in the answer.* Make sure Ss understand the task.
- Have Ss individually scan for and fill in the answers.

Comprehension check

- Go over the answers to Exercise **1A** together. Make sure that Ss followed instructions and filled in their answers. As Ss give their answers, ask them to point to the information in the class schedule.

Application

- Read the instructions for Exercise **1B** aloud. Ask Ss: *What classes do you have?* Everyone should say they have your English class. Ask Ss: *What other classes do you have? Do you have more classes?* Elicit the titles of any other classes Ss might be taking, and list them on the board.
- Point to the questions written on the board. Tell Ss: *Talk to your partner. Tell your partner about your class schedule.*
- Model the task. Talk about a real or invented class that you are taking, and to give your Ss a model to refer to, write the sentences on the board. Be sure to include all the information needed to answer the questions you wrote earlier, for example: *I have English class. It is on Tuesday and Thursday. The teacher is Mr. Jones. It is in Room 47. The time is 3:00 to 4:15.*
- Ss complete the task in pairs. Walk around and help as needed.
- When Ss are finished, ask them to find new partners to talk to about class schedules.

Expansion activity *(small group)*

- Before class. Bring in a large sheet of poster paper and markers for each group of Ss. Tell Ss: *Please make a class schedule for this class.*
- Walk around and help as needed. Make sure Ss include the class title at the top of the schedule as well as the teacher, the room, the days, and the time.
- When Ss are finished, have them tape their posters to the classroom walls and read the posters aloud for the rest of the class.

Literacy tip

For an alternative activity, refer literacy Ss to pages 28–29 in the *Literacy Workbook* at any time during the lesson.

LESSON **F** Another view

Presentation

- Books closed. Write on the board three classroom objects or pieces of classroom furniture that you have in your classroom and one that you don't. For example, if you have all of these except a computer in your classroom, write:

  a desk
  a stapler
  a computer
  a dictionary
- Read aloud each item in the list and ask Ss to repeat. After each item, gesture around the classroom and ask Ss: *Do we have a ____?* Elicit short answers: *yes* or *no.* Make a check mark next to every item that you have. In the example above, you would not make a check mark next to *a computer.*

Practice

- Books open. Direct Ss' attention to Exercise **2A** and read the instructions aloud.
- Model the task. Read aloud the first item, *a book.* Look around the classroom and ask Ss: *Do we have a book?* If the answer is *yes*, indicate that Ss should make a check mark in the box next to *a book.*
- Ss complete the task in pairs.
- Follow up by asking different pairs about the items in the exercise. For every item Ss checkmarked, ask them to show the rest of the class that item.

Literacy tip
The exercises on this page might be a challenge for literacy Ss, but if they work with a higher-level partner in Exercise **2A**, and if there is no pressure on them to finish Exercise **2B**, they should be able to participate.

Expansion activity *(whole group)*

- Using the words in the list in Exercise **2A**, play a picture-drawing game with the class.
- Model the activity. Look at the words in the list. Then begin to draw the object on the board. As you draw, say to the class: *What classroom object? What is it?* Encourage Ss to guess what you are drawing.
- When a S guesses correctly, invite him or her to the board to draw a different classroom object.

Practice

- Direct Ss' attention to the word puzzle in Exercise **2B**. Ask the class: *What is this? What do you see?* Ss may say that they see letters.
- Read the instructions for Exercise **2B** aloud. Point to and say the first word in the word box: *book.* Point to the puzzle and ask Ss: *Do you see "book" here?* Ss should point to the circled example.
- Ss work individually or in pairs to find the words. When most of the Ss have finished, ask Ss if there are words they can't find in the puzzle. Have other Ss in the class show them where the words are.

Evaluation

- Before asking Ss to turn to the self-assessment on page 137, do a quick review of the unit. Have Ss turn to Lesson A. Ask the class to talk about what they remember about this lesson. Prompt Ss, if necessary, with questions, for example: *What words are on this page? What do you see in the picture?* Continue in this manner to review each lesson quickly.
- **Self-assessment** Read the instructions for Exercise **3**. Ask Ss to turn to the self-assessment page and complete the unit self-assessment.
- If Ss are ready, administer the unit test on pages T-168–T-170 of this Teacher's Edition (or on the Assessment Audio CD / CD-ROM).

More Ventures, Unit 2, Lesson F	
Literacy Workbook, 15–30 min.	
Basic Workbook, 15–30 min.	
Writing worksheets, 15–30 min. **Real Life Document,** 15–30 min.	www.cambridge.org/myresourceroom

2 Fun with vocabulary

A Talk with a partner. What's in your classroom? Check (✓).

☐ a book	☐ a chair	☐ a computer
☐ a desk	☐ a dictionary	☐ an eraser
☐ a notebook	☐ paper	☐ a pen
☐ a pencil	☐ a ruler	☐ a stapler

B Circle the words in the puzzle.

book	chair	computer	desk	dictionary	eraser
notebook	paper	pen	pencil	ruler	stapler

h	s	h	f	e	b	o	o	k	t	z	a
q	u	p	e	n	c	i	l	a	f	r	s
l	i	g	o	w	n	e	r	a	s	e	r
v	y	b	d	e	s	k	a	f	l	k	o
d	i	c	t	i	o	n	a	r	y	o	j
f	e	t	h	s	t	a	p	l	e	r	e
w	r	n	n	o	t	e	b	o	o	k	r
p	e	n	k	v	l	z	o	j	s	y	n
o	t	c	o	m	p	u	t	e	r	m	q
t	r	u	l	e	r	g	a	r	x	z	a
h	o	m	t	c	z	e	c	h	a	i	r
p	a	p	e	r	n	y	i	d	e	m	t

3 Wrap up

Complete the **Self-assessment** on page 137.

Review

1 Listening

CLASS CD1 TK 24

Read. Then listen and circle.

1. What's his first name?
   a. Ali
   (b.) Hassan
2. What's his last name?
   (a.) Ali
   b. Garcia
3. Where is he from?
   a. Mexico
   (b.) Somalia
4. When is his birthday?
   (a.) in August
   b. in October
5. Where's the notebook?
   (a.) on the desk
   b. on the chair
6. Where's the paper?
   (a.) in the notebook
   b. on the chair

Talk with a partner. Ask and answer.

2 Vocabulary

Write. Complete the story.

book Brazil card February name Tuesday

Welcome, Luisa Pinto!

Luisa is a new student. She is from ___Brazil___ (1). Her last ___name___ (2) is Pinto. Her birthday is in ___February___ (3). In fact, her birthday is on ___Tuesday___ (4). Happy birthday! Luisa needs a ___book___ (5) and an ID ___card___ (6).

Welcome, Luisa!

Lesson objectives

- Review vocabulary and grammar from Units 1 and 2
- Introduce the pronunciation of *a* as in *name* and *o* as in *phone*

Warm-up and review

- Before class. Write today's lesson focus on the board.
  Review unit:
  Review vocabulary and grammar from Units 1 and 2.
  Pronounce "a" as in "name" and "o" as in "phone."
- Begin class. Books closed. Direct Ss' attention to the first two items in the lesson focus written on the board. Help Ss understand the idea of review by showing them pages from Units 1 and 2.
- Review vocabulary from Units 1 and 2. Ask individual Ss, for example:
  What's your first name? What's his first name?
  What's your last name? What's her last name?
  Where are you from? (What country?) Where are they from?
  When is your birthday? (What month?)
  Where's the computer? Where's my notebook?

Practice

- Books open. Direct Ss' attention to Exercise **1** and read the instructions aloud. Read the question and answer choices in number 1 aloud.
- Class Audio CD1 track 24 Model the task. Play or read only the first conversation on the audio program (see audio script, page T-156). Point to the two answer choices in number 1 and ask: *Maria or Hassan?* (Hassan.) Point to where the letter b has been circled.
- Read aloud the remaining questions and answer choices. Say: *Now, listen and circle the correct answers.*
- Class Audio CD1 track 24 Play or read the complete audio program (see audio script, page T-156). Ss listen and circle the correct answers. Repeat the audio program as needed.
- Check answers with the class. Read each question aloud and call on different Ss to answer.

> **Teaching tip**
> You may need to play the audio program several times to give Ss a chance to extract the information they need. Then, to check comprehension and to help Ss who may be struggling, play the audio program again, and ask Ss to repeat the parts of the conversation that contain the answers to the questions.

- Read aloud the second part of the instructions for Exercise **1**. Ss practice asking and answering the questions in pairs. Walk around and help as needed.
- Ask several pairs to ask and answer the questions for the rest of the class.

Expansion activity (small groups)

- Divide the class into an even number of small groups, and have each group create an oral quiz using questions similar to the ones in Exercise **1**.
- Ask each group to choose a secretary to write down six questions about the people and classroom objects in their group. Unlike the questions in Exercise **1**, these questions can be about different Ss. For example, one group might ask *What's her first name?* about one S and *What's his last name?* about another. Ss should also ask about the location of their classroom objects, for example: *Where's the dictionary?*
- Ask half of the groups to join another group for the quiz. After the questions are asked and answered, have the groups switch roles.

Practice

- Direct Ss' attention to Exercise **2**. Write the word *title* on the board. Say it aloud and ask Ss to repeat it after you. Point to the title of the story and ask: *What is the title of this story?* (Welcome, Luisa Pinto!) Read the title aloud for them.
- Have Ss read the story silently to get the main idea. When Ss are finished reading, ask: *Who is the story about?* (Luisa Pinto, a new student.)
- Read the instructions for Exercise **2** aloud. Read aloud the first and second sentences and ask Ss to repeat after you. Point to *Brazil* in the word bank so that Ss know where to find the answers.
- Ss read the story and fill in the blanks individually. Walk around and help as needed.
- Write the numbers *1–6* on the board. Ask Ss to come up to the board to write the answers.
- Read the story aloud using Ss' answers. If there is an error, say to Ss: *This is not correct. What is the correct answer?* Make any necessary corrections on the board.

Expansion activity (student pairs)

- Tell Ss: *Today, you are a new student. Welcome!* Ask Ss to ask their partners questions so that they can write a story about their partner like the one in Exercise **2**. Brainstorm the questions they can ask and write them on the board *(Where are you from? When's your birthday? What do you need?)*. Tell Ss to write their stories about their partners in their notebooks.

Review

Warm-up and review

- Write on the board: *in*, *on*, *under*.
- Point to the words. Place a classroom object *in* something in the room and ask Ss, for example: *Where's the ruler?* (In the desk, etc.) Place the object *on* something and ask Ss the same question. Elicit: *on the floor*, *on the chair*, *under the desk*, etc.
- Write on the board: *his*, *her*, *my*, *your.*
- Point to the words *his* / *her* / *my* / *your.* Ask Ss about their classmates' names. Gesture toward appropriate people in the class and ask their names.

Practice

- Direct Ss to Exercise **3A**. Read the instructions aloud.
- Point to the picture in Exercise **3A** and ask Ss: *Where's the pen?* (Under the notebook.)
- Model the task. Read the beginning of the sentence in number 1: *The pen is . . . in, on or under?* Point to where *under* has been written for number 1 and read the complete sentence aloud.
- Ss write their answers individually. Check answers by calling on Ss to read the sentences aloud. As Ss read the sentences, point to either *in*, *on*, or *under* written on the board to make the answer clear.
- Direct Ss to Exercise **3B**. Read the instructions aloud.
- Point to Alberto in the picture in Exercise **3B** and ask: *What's his name?* (Alberto.)
- Read the sentence in number 1 without the first word: _____ *name is Alberto.* Point to the answer choices and ask Ss: *His or Her?* Point to where *His* has been circled and written for number 1. Read the complete sentence aloud.
- Ss write their answers individually. Check answers by calling on Ss to read the sentences aloud. As Ss read the sentences, point to the appropriate possessive adjective written on the board to help make the answer clear.

Presentation

- Direct Ss' attention to the second part of the lesson focus written on the board.
- Write on the board: *name*, *day*, *say.* Point to and say each word and ask Ss to repeat.
- Underline the *a* in each of the words. Say a long *a* (/ei/) sound before repeating each word, for example: /ei/, *name.* Ask Ss to repeat after you.
- Write on the board: *phone*, *code*, *note.* Repeat the procedure, underlining the *o* in the words and pronouncing a long *o* (/ou/) sound.

Practice

Class Audio CD1 track 25 Direct Ss' attention to Exercise **4A** and read the instructions aloud. Play or read the audio program (see audio script, page T-156). Ss listen to examples of the two vowel sounds.

Class Audio CD1 track 26 Direct Ss' attention to Exercise **4B**, and read the instructions aloud. Play or read the audio program (see audio script, page T-156). Ss listen and repeat what they hear.

- Read aloud the second part of the instructions for Exercise **4B**. Model the task. Point to the two charts and tell one S: *Say a word.* After that S says any word in the charts, tell his or her partner: *Point to the word.*
- Ss complete the task in pairs. Walk around and help as needed.

Class Audio CD1 track 27 Direct Ss' attention to Exercise **4C** and read the instructions aloud. Model the task. Play or read the first word on the audio program (see audio script, page T-156). Ask: *Which letter is it? "a"* or *"o"?* Point to where the letter has been checked.

Class Audio CD1 track 27 Play or read the complete audio program (see audio script, page T-156). Ss listen and make a checkmark under the letter they hear.

Class Audio CD1 track 27 Reproduce the chart from Exercise **4C** on the board and play or read the audio program again. Pause after each word and ask a S to check the appropriate letter in the chart on the board.

Community building *(whole group)*

- To help Ss be more comfortable when talking about local places, make a list of names of well-known places and streets in your community that contain the long *a* and / or *o* sounds. Conduct a class discussion of those places and practice pronouncing the names (e.g., *Blain's Market. Who shops at Blain's Market? Raise your hands. Good. Now, repeat:* /ei/, *Blain's*).

Evaluation

- Direct Ss' attention to the lesson focus written on the board.
- Ask individual Ss questions similar to the ones in Exercise **1**. Be sure to use different possessive adjectives and the prepositions *in, on,* and *under* in your questions.
- Write on the board: *name*, *phone.* Call on individual Ss as you point to one of the words and ask the S to say it. Listen to pronunciation and correct as needed.
- Check off each part of the lesson focus as Ss demonstrate an understanding of what they have learned in the lesson.

3 Grammar

A Complete the sentences.

Use *in*, *on*, or *under*.

1. The pen is ___under___ the notebook.
2. The dictionary is ___on___ the desk.
3. The book is ___on___ the chair.
4. The stapler is ___in___ the desk.

B Read and circle. Then write.

1. ___His___ name is Alberto.
   (His) Her
2. ___Her___ name is Layla.
   His (Her)
3. **A** What is ___your___ name?
   his (your)

   B ___My___ name is Kim.
   (My) Your

4 Pronunciation

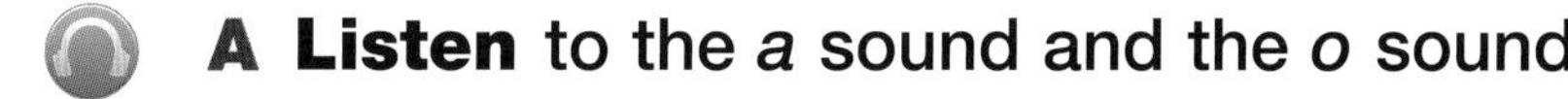

A Listen to the *a* sound and the *o* sound.

CLASS CD1 TK 25

a	o
name	phone

B Listen and repeat.

CLASS CD1 TK 26

a	name	day	say

o	phone	code	note

Talk with a partner. Say a word. Your partner points. Take turns.

C Listen and check (✓).

CLASS CD1 TK 27

	a	o		a	o		a	o		a	o		a	o
1.	✓		2.		✓	3.	✓		4.		✓	5.	✓	

UNIT
3 Friends and family

LESSON A Listening

1 Before you listen

A Look at the picture. What do you see?

CLASS CD1 TK 28

B Listen and point: daughter • father grandfather • grandmother • mother • son

Lesson objectives

- Introduce Ss to the topic
- Find out what Ss know about the topic
- Preview the unit by talking about the picture
- Practice key vocabulary
- Practice listening skills

UNIT
3

Warm-up and review

- Before class. Write today's lesson focus on the board.

  Lesson A:
  Family
- Begin class. Books closed. Review the months of the year from Unit 2. Write the word *January* on the board with 11 long blanks for the other months after it. Point to and say the word. Ask Ss to repeat after you.
- Point to the first blank and ask Ss: *What month is next?* (February.) Continue in this manner until all the months of the year are written on the board. Practice saying the months with the class.
- Ask several different Ss: *When's your birthday?* As Ss answer, checkmark their birth months on the board.

Literacy tip

If you have literacy Ss in your class, it might be helpful to spend time at the beginning of any activity that contains art or photos talking about the pictures before focusing Ss' attention on the printed words in the exercise. Have Ss work in pairs. Tell them to ask each other: *What do you see?* Encourage Ss to describe the pictures to each other. Consider pairing literacy Ss with Ss who can help them read the text in the exercise. This will help preview the exercise for literacy Ss and make them more confident as the exercise continues.

Presentation

- Books open. Set the scene. Hold up the Student's Book. Show Ss the picture on page 32. Tell Ss: *This is a birthday party. Happy birthday!*
- Direct Ss' attention to the lesson focus written on the board. Say the word *family* and ask Ss to repeat after you. Show the class the people in the picture and say: *They are a family. Family.*
- Ask Ss about the picture: *What do you see?* Elicit and write on the board any vocabulary that Ss know, such as: *sofa, table, children, cake.*

Teaching tip

It might be helpful to draw a family-tree diagram on the board with two sets of grandparents, a few children for each set of grandparents, and from two of those children, a son and daughter. Circle the people in the family tree who can be seen in the picture, and use the tree to clarify the meaning of the key vocabulary.

Practice

- Direct Ss' attention to the key vocabulary in Exercise **1B**. Read aloud each word or phrase while pointing to the corresponding part of the picture. Ask Ss to repeat and point.

Class Audio CD1 track 28 Play or read the audio program (see audio script, page T-156). Tell Ss: *Listen and point to the picture.* As Ss hear the key vocabulary, check to see that Ss are pointing to the correct part of the picture. Repeat the audio program as needed.

Comprehension check

- Ask Ss *Yes / No* questions about the picture. Tell Ss: *Listen. Say "yes" or "no."*

  Point to the picture. Ask: *Is this a family?* (Yes.)
  Point to the picture. Ask: *Is this a birthday party?* (Yes.)
  Point to the father. Ask: *Is he a mother?* (No.)
  Point to the mother. Ask: *Is she a mother?* (Yes.)
  Point to the daughter. Ask: *Is she a daughter?* (Yes.)
  Point to the son. Ask: *Is he a daughter?* (No.)
  Point to the son. Ask: *Is he a father?* (No.)
  Point to the grandmother. Ask: *Is she a grandmother?* (Yes.)
  Point to the grandfather. Ask: *Is he a grandmother?* (No.)
- Ask Ss questions about the names of people in the picture.
- For example, point to Gloria. Ask: *What's her name?* (Gloria.)

Expansion activity *(whole group)*

- Teach vocabulary for celebrations. Write on the board: *cake, candles, balloons, presents / gifts, cards.* Point to and say each word aloud and ask Ss to repeat it after you. For each word, point to the corresponding parts of the picture or draw a simple picture of each item on the board.
- Provide Ss with "sticky notes," preferably cut in half to make narrow strips. Have Ss write the new vocabulary on the notes and then label the festive items in the picture on page 32 of the Student's Book.

LESSON A Listening

Presentation

- Direct Ss' attention to Exercise **2A**. Tell Ss: *These are words for people in a family.*
- Point to the family members in the picture on page 32 or in the family tree you drew on the board as you read each word aloud. Ask Ss to repeat the words after you.
- Read aloud the instructions for Exercise **2A**.

Practice

Class Audio CD1 track 29 Play or read the audio program (see audio script, page T-156). Listen and repeat the vocabulary along with Ss. Repeat the audio program as needed.

- Listen carefully to Ss' pronunciation and make corrections as needed.

Learner persistence *(individual work)*

Self-Study Audio CD track 15 Exercise **2A** is recorded on the CD at the back of the Student's Book. Ss can listen to the CD at home for reinforcement and review. They can also listen to the CD for self-directed learning when class attendance is not possible.

Expansion activity *(whole group)*

- Books closed. Write the six key vocabulary words on the board in any order: *daughter*, *father*, *grandfather*, *grandmother*, *mother*, *son.*
- Ask for a volunteer to come to the board. Say each vocabulary word randomly and have the volunteer point to the word you say. Repeat the procedure with other Ss.

> **Literacy tip**
> For an alternative activity, refer literacy Ss to pages 30–31 in the *Literacy Workbook* at any time during the lesson.

Practice

- Direct Ss' attention to Exercise **2B** and read the instructions aloud.

Class Audio CD1 track 30 Model the task. Hold up the Student's Book and say: *Number one.* Play or read the audio program for number 1 (see audio script, page T-157). Point to the two answer choices in number 1 and ask Ss: *What did you hear – a or b?* Elicit: *a.* Point to the letter a next to the first picture and tell Ss: *Circle the letter "a."*

Class Audio CD1 track 30 Play or read the complete audio program (see audio script, page T-157). Ss listen and circle the correct answers. Repeat the audio as needed.

Class Audio CD1 track 30 Read aloud the second part of the instructions for Exercise **2B**. Play or read the audio program again so that Ss can listen and check their answers.

Learner persistence *(individual work)*

Self-Study Audio CD track 16 Exercise **2B** is recorded on the CD at the back of the Student's Book. Ss can listen to the CD at home for reinforcement and review and also for self-directed learning when class attendance is not possible.

Comprehension check

- Write the numbers *1–4* on the board. Ask a few Ss to come to the board and write the correct answers to Exercise **2B** next to each number.

Class Audio CD1 track 30 Play or read the audio program again. Pause the audio program after each conversation. Point to the answer written on the board and ask: *Is this correct?* Ask another S to make any necessary corrections.

Application

- Direct Ss' attention to Exercise **3** and read the instructions aloud.
- Model the task. Hold up the Student's Book and point to the pictures in Exercise **2B**. Say to one S: *Point to a picture.* Say to the first S's partner: *Say the word.*
- Ss complete the exercise in pairs. Walk around and help as needed.

Evaluation

- Direct Ss' attention to the lesson focus written on the board. Check Ss' understanding of the key vocabulary by asking them to point to the family members in the picture on page 32 or in the family tree on the board. Check to see that Ss are pointing to the correct items.
- Check off the lesson focus as Ss demonstrate an understanding of what they have learned in the lesson.

More Ventures, Unit 3, Lesson A	
Literacy workbook, 15–30 min.	
Basic Workbook, 15–30 min.	
Writing worksheets, 15–30 min.	www.cambridge.org/myresourceroom
Student Arcade, time varies	www.cambridge.org/venturesarcade

Unit Goals

Identify family members
Describe a family picture
Interpret a housing application

2 Listen

A Listen and repeat.

STUDENT TK 15
CLASS CD1 TK 29

1. daughter 2. father 3. grandfather
4. grandmother 5. mother 6. son

B Listen and circle.

STUDENT TK 16
CLASS CD1 TK 30

1. (a.)  b. 

2. a. 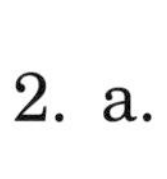  (b.) 

3. a. 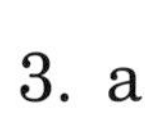  (b.)  

4. a.  (b.) 

Listen again. Check your answers.

3 After you listen

Talk with a partner. Point to a picture and ask. Your partner says the words.

Who's that?
The grandmother.

LESSON B Family members

1 Vocabulary focus

Listen and repeat.

CLASS CD1 TK 31

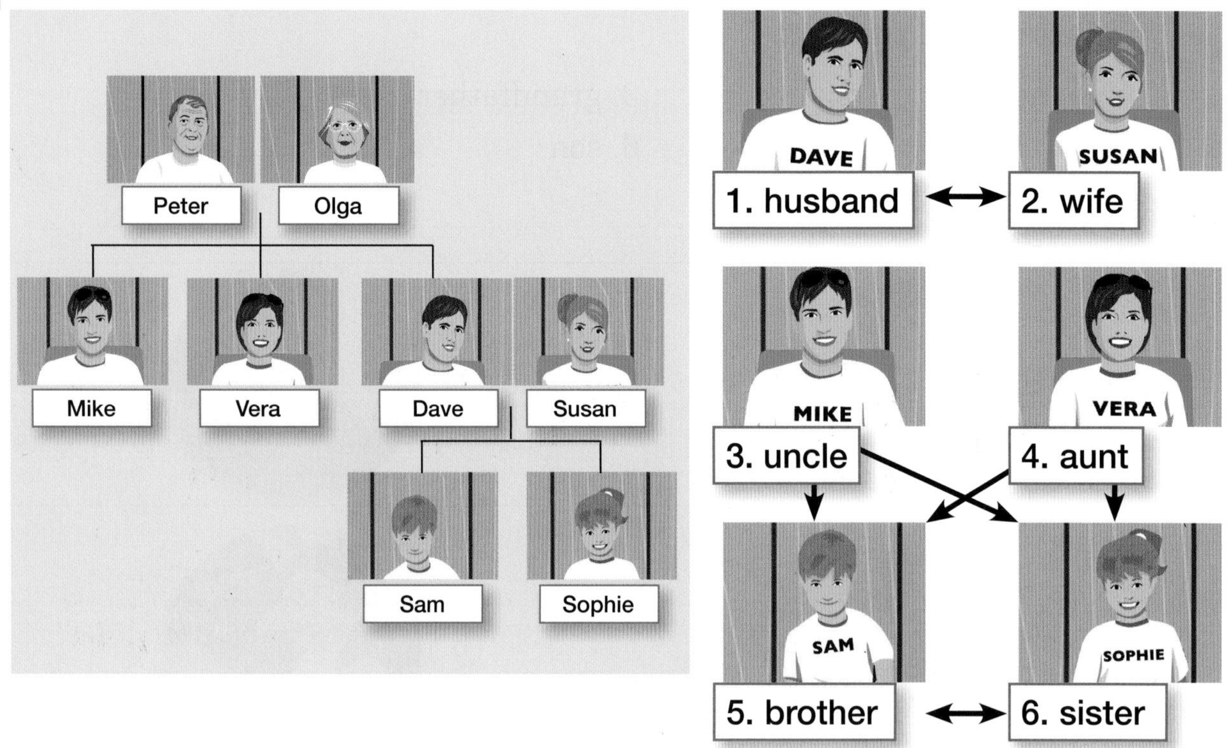

2 Practice

A Read and match.

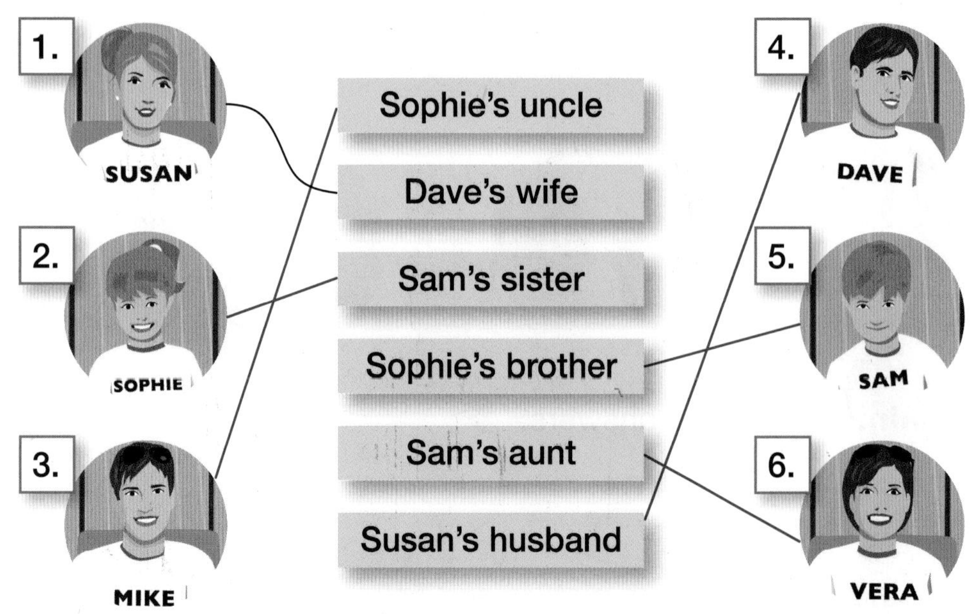

Lesson objectives

- Introduce additional vocabulary for family relationships
- Practice asking and answering questions about family relationships

Warm-up and review

- Before class. Write today's lesson focus on the board.
  Lesson B:
  Family members
  Who is Susan? Dave's wife.
- Before class. Write the key vocabulary from Lesson A on the board: *daughter*, *father*, *grandfather*, *grandmother*, *mother*, *son*.
- Begin class. Books open. Ask Ss to identify the family members in the picture on page 32. Tell Ss, for example: *Point to the grandmother.*
- Draw on the board a simple, unlabeled family tree that includes all the vocabulary words. Make sure that the people are clearly male or female. Ask for volunteers to come to the board and write, for example, the word *grandmother* next to the appropriate picture.

Presentation

- Point to the words *Family members* at the top of page 34 in the Student's Book. Say the words aloud and ask Ss to repeat after you. Tell the class: *Family members are people in a family.*
- Point to the key vocabulary written on the board and tell Ss: *These people are family members. Today, you will learn more words for family members.*
- Direct Ss' attention to the family tree in Exercise **1**. Ask: *Who are these people? Are they a family?* (Yes.)
- Go over the family members' names. Point to the man at the top of the family tree and say, for example: *His name is Peter. Peter. What's his name?* (Peter.)

Practice

- Read aloud the instructions for Exercise **1**. Point to the vocabulary words under the smaller pictures in the exercise.

Class Audio CD1 track 31 Play or read the audio program (see audio script, page T-157). Listen and repeat the vocabulary along with Ss. Repeat the audio program as needed.

- Listen carefully to Ss' pronunciation and correct as needed.

Expansion activity (student pairs)

- Before class. Create a table with two columns and four rows. In the top left cell, draw a simplified male figure. In the top right cell, draw a simplified female figure wearing a skirt. Make enough copies of this table for each pair of Ss.
- Make another copy of the table, and in the remaining cells, type or write the six vocabulary words from Exercise **1**, using large letters.
- Make a copy of this table for each pair of Ss. Cut out the cells as "vocabulary cards."
- Give each pair of Ss a copy of the original document to use as a grid along with a set of the words. Ask Ss to arrange the words in the appropriate columns, identifying them as either male or female family members.

  Option When Ss are finished, give them a new set of cards based on the key vocabulary from Lesson A, and ask them to arrange those words according to gender.

Practice

- Direct Ss' attention to Exercise **2A**. As you read aloud the instructions, hold up the Student's Book and indicate that Ss should read the words and then draw a line between the pictures and the corresponding words.
- Model the task. Hold up the Student's Book. Point to the first picture. Ask: *Who is this?* (Dave's wife.) Say: *Match the pictures with the words.*
- Ss complete the exercise individually. Help as needed.

Comprehension check

- Write the numbers *1–6* on the board. Ask a few Ss to come to the board and write the answers to Exercise **2A** on the board.
- Ask different Ss to read the answers written on the board. After each answer is read, ask: *Is this correct?* Ask another S to make corrections on the board.

Teaching tip

Since this is the first time the *'s* possessive form is used, you may want to clarify its meaning using the already familiar *my* possessive adjective. For example, you could show the class your notebook (*My notebook is on my desk.*), then a S's notebook (*Linda's notebook is on her desk.*), and write both sentences on the board for Ss to read and repeat. You could also compare your own family relationships (*My wife is Julieta.*) with the family in these exercises (*Dave's wife is Susan.*).

Literacy tip

For an alternative activity, refer literacy Ss to pages 32–33 in the *Literacy Workbook* at any time during the lesson.

LESSON **B** Family members

Presentation

- Direct Ss' attention to the picture in Exercise **2B**. Tell the class: *This is a family picnic.* Write on the board and say the word *picnic.* Ask Ss to repeat after you.
- Point to the picture and ask: *Who do you see? Who is at the picnic?* Elicit and write on the board the names of the family members in the picture.
- Direct Ss' attention to the word bank. Read the words aloud and ask Ss to repeat after you.
- Read the instructions for Exercise **2B** aloud.

Practice

- Read aloud the first part of the instructions for Exercise **2B**.
- Class Audio CD1 track 32 Model the task. Say: *Listen and repeat.* Play or read the audio program for number 1 (see audio script, page T-157) and point to Vera in the picture as you repeat. Say: *Then write.* Point to the word *aunt* written in the chart. Make sure Ss understand the task.
- Class Audio CD1 track 32 Play or read the complete audio program (see audio script, page T-157). Ss listen and repeat. Encourage Ss to point to the people in the picture as they repeat.
- Ss complete the chart individually. Repeat the audio program as needed.
- Check answers with the class. Write the numbers *1–6* on the board, and ask for volunteers to write their answers on the board. Point to each answer and ask the class: *Yes? Is this correct?* Make corrections on the board.
- Read aloud the second part of the instructions for Exercise **2B**. Point to and model the example conversation.
- Call on a pair of volunteers to read the example conversation aloud for the class.
- Point to another person in the picture on page 35. Ask a S: *Who is (name)?* Elicit the answer. Repeat with different people in the picture. Indicate that Ss should ask and answer questions about all the people.
- Ss complete the exercise in pairs. Walk around and help as needed.

Application

- Direct Ss' attention to Exercise **3** and read the instructions aloud.
- Point to and read aloud the chart headings and the information written in the chart. Read the example question and answer aloud and ask Ss to repeat after you. Point to where Habib and brother have been written in the chart as examples.
- Model the task. Duplicate the chart on the board, and talk to the class as you complete it for your own family, for example: *Name: John. Family member: father.*
- Choose a S to act as your partner. Point to the example question in his or her book and say: *Please ask me this question.* Point to your chart and say: *Ask me about my family.* When the S asks, *Who is John?*, say: *My father.*
- Ss complete the chart individually and then ask and answer questions about their charts in pairs.

Community building *(individual work)*

- Have Ss make their own family trees. Model the task by showing Ss your own family tree drawn on a large piece of poster paper. Talk about your family relationships using unit vocabulary, for example: *This is Rita. She is my aunt. She is also my mother's sister.*
- Give each S a large piece of poster paper and markers. When Ss are finished, help them tape their family trees to the classroom walls. Ask Ss to talk to the class about their families.

Teaching tip

When making your own family tree, include only living family members in order to avoid the use of the past tense. When Ss are making their trees, be aware that some Ss may have lost family members in ways they don't want to talk about in class, or they may have family situations that differ from the family shown in the unit. Encourage Ss to reveal only as much personal information as they are comfortable with. Some Ss may even prefer to draw the tree of a fictional family.

Evaluation

- Direct Ss' attention to the lesson focus written on the board and to the large picture in Exercise **1** on page 34. Ask Ss questions about the family relationships between people in the picture, for example: *Who is Olga's husband?* (Peter.) *Who is Sam's mother?* (Susan.)
- Call on Ss to ask their classmates questions similar to the ones in Exercise **2B** on page 35, for example: *Who is Olga?* (Sophie's grandmother, Peter's wife.)
- Check off each part of the lesson focus as Ss demonstrate an understanding of what they have learned in the lesson.

More Ventures, Unit 3, Lesson B	
Literacy workbook, 15–30 min.	
Basic Workbook, 15–30 min.	
Writing worksheets, 15–30 min.	www.cambridge.org/myresourceroom
Student Arcade, time varies	www.cambridge.org/venturesarcade

CLASS CD1 TK 32

B Listen and repeat. Then write.

aunt brother husband sister uncle wife

Who is . . . ?		Who is . . . ?	
1. Vera	Sam's *aunt*	4. Susan	Dave's *wife*
2. Mike	Sam's *uncle*	5. Sam	Sophie's *brother*
3. Sophie	Sam's *sister*	6. Dave	Susan's *husband*

Talk with a partner. Ask and answer.

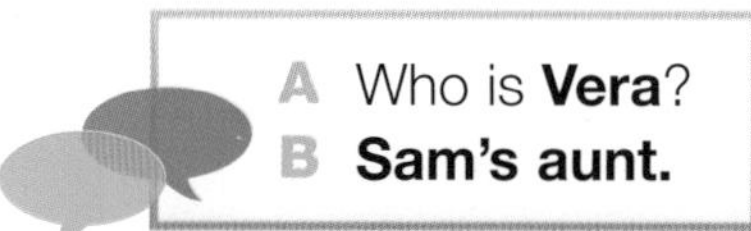

3 Communicate

Complete the chart about your family.
Then talk with a partner.

Name	Family member
Habib	*brother*
(Answers will vary.)	

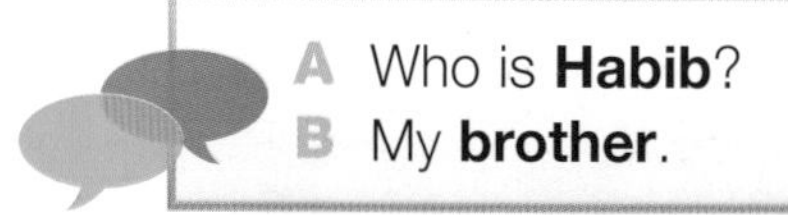

LESSON C Do you have a sister?

1 Grammar focus: *Do you have . . . ?*

Questions	Answers		
Do you **have** a sister?	Yes, I / we **do**.	No, I / we **don't**.	

don't = do not

2 Practice

A Read and circle. Then write.

1. A Do you have a brother?

   B *Yes, I do.*

   Yes, I do. No, I don't.

2. A Do you have a sister?

   B *No, we don't.*

   Yes, we do. No, we don't.

3. A Do you have a son?

   B *Yes, I do.*

   Yes, I do. No, I don't.

4. A Do you have a daughter?

   B *Yes, we do.*

   Yes, we do. No, we don't.

5. A Do you have a wife?

   B *No, I don't.*

   Yes, I do. No, I don't.

Listen and repeat. Then practice with a partner.

CLASS CD1 TK 33

Lesson objectives

- Introduce *Yes / No* questions with *have*
- Introduce short answers: *Yes, I do. / No, I don't.*
- Practice asking and answering questions about family relationships

Warm-up and review

- Before class. Write today's lesson focus on the board:
  Lesson C:
  Do you have a ____?
  Yes, I do. / No, I don't.
- Before class. Write all the vocabulary for family members on the board: *a grandmother, a grandfather, a mother, a father, an aunt, an uncle, a husband, a wife, a sister, a brother, a son, a daughter.*
- Begin class. Books closed. Point to and say each vocabulary word on the board and ask Ss to repeat.
- Books open. Direct Ss' attention to the large picture in Exercise **1** on page 34. Ask Ss questions about the family, for example: *This is a family. Does the family have a grandmother?* (Yes.) *Who is the grandmother? What's her name?* (Olga.) *Does Olga have a daughter?* (Yes.) *Who is Olga's daughter?* (Vera.) *Does Vera have a brother?* (Yes. Two brothers.)
- Continue in this manner, asking questions to help Ss recall the vocabulary.

Teaching tip

This warm-up activity gives Ss the opportunity to retrieve the meaning of previously learned vocabulary without putting pressure on them to do much speaking.

Presentation

- Direct Ss' attention to the grammar chart in Exercise **1** on page 36. Read each question and short answer aloud and ask Ss to repeat after you.
- Point to the small box beside the grammar chart. Hold up one finger and tell Ss: *One word: "don't."* Hold up two fingers and say: *Two words: "do not." They are equal. They are the same.*
- Draw three simple faces on the board and label them: *Mike, Vera, Dave.*
- Tell the class: *Let's talk to Mike.* Look toward the picture of Mike on the board and ask: *Mike, do you have a sister?* Draw a speech bubble coming from Mike's mouth and indicate that Ss should say Mike's answer. Elicit and write in the speech bubble: *Yes, I do.*
- Erase Mike's speech bubble. Tell the class: *Let's talk to Mike and Dave.* Look toward the pictures and ask the question from the grammar chart: *Mike and Dave, do you have a sister?* Draw speech bubbles coming from both men. Elicit and write in the bubbles: *Yes, we do.*
- Erase the speech bubbles and repeat the whole procedure verbally to convey to Ss that the word *you* can be singular or plural and to practice the short answers.

Expansion activity (whole group)

- Write on the board:
  Yes, I do. I have one sister / two sisters / three sisters.
  No, I don't.
- Point to and say the answer choices and have Ss repeat. Then ask several different Ss: *Do you have a sister?* When Ss answer, *Yes, I do*, ask them: *What's her name?* or *What are their names?* Write the names of your Ss' sisters on the board. Ask Ss how to spell the names.
- Repeat the procedure with the question: *Do you have a brother?*

Practice

- Direct Ss' attention to the first picture in Exercise **2A**. Read aloud the example conversation using different voices for Speaker A and Speaker B. When you read Speaker B's line, show Ss the two choices under the blank and ask: *Yes, I do, or No, I don't?* Elicit: *Yes, I do.*
- Read aloud the instructions for Exercise **2A**. Point to where *Yes, I do* has been circled and written for number 1.
- Ss complete the exercise individually. Walk around and help as needed.

Literacy tip

Literacy Ss will need to work with higher-level Ss in Exercise **2A**, pointing to or saying the answers after the higher-level S reads the question and answer choices aloud. For an alternative activity, refer literacy Ss to pages 34–35 in the *Literacy Workbook* at any time during the lesson.

Comprehension check

- Read aloud the second part of the instructions for Exercise **2A**.
- Class Audio CD1 track 33 Play or read the audio program (see audio script, page T-157). Ss listen and repeat as they check their answers.
- Write the numbers *1–5* on the board. Ask volunteers to come to the board and write the answers they circled. Make any necessary corrections on the board.
- Ss in pairs. Ask Ss to choose Role A or B and practice the questions and answers in Exercise **2A**. Then have Ss switch roles and practice again. Walk around and help as needed.
- Ask several pairs to say the questions and answers for the rest of the class.

LESSON C Do you have a sister?

Presentation

- Direct Ss' attention to the pictures in Exercise 2B. Point to and read aloud the labels with the pictures. Write the names of the woman's family members on the board and ask Ss to repeat after you.
- Make the following matching task on the board:

Ken	*grandmother*
Rose	*son*
Diana	*sister*
Danny	*husband*

- Ask Ss about each person; for example: *Who is Ken?* Ss should be able to guess from the illustration who the people are. Elicit: *The woman's husband* or *Her husband.* Draw lines on the board to show the family relationships or ask Ss to come to the board and draw the lines.

Practice

- Read aloud the first part of the instructions for Exercise 2B.
- Class Audio CD1 track 34 Model the task. Say: *Listen and repeat.* Play or read the audio program for number 1 (see audio script, page T-157) and point to the woman's sister Diana as you repeat. Say: *Then write.* Point to the word *yes* written in the chart. Make sure Ss understand the task.
- Class Audio CD1 track 34 Play or read the complete audio program (see audio script, page T-157). Ss listen and repeat. Encourage Ss to point to the people in the pictures as they repeat.
- Ss complete the chart individually. Repeat the audio program as needed.
- Check answers with the class. Write the numbers *1–6* on the board and ask for volunteers to write their answers on the board. Point to each answer and ask the class: *Yes? Is this correct?* Make any necessary corrections on the board.
- Read aloud the second part of the instructions for Exercise 2B. Point to and model the example conversation.
- Call on a pair of volunteers to read the example conversation aloud for the class. Then ask the same two Ss to model a different conversation about the family in the pictures on page 37 using, for example, *brother* or *son*.
- Indicate that Ss should ask and answer questions about all the family members in the chart. Make sure Ss understand the task.
- Ss complete the exercise in pairs. Walk around and help as needed.

Application

- Direct Ss' attention to Exercise 3 and read the instructions aloud. Point to and read aloud the questions in the first column of the chart, and ask Ss to repeat after you.
- Point to the name *Dinh* in the top of the chart and say the name aloud. Tell Ss: *"Dinh" is a first name.* Draw a stick figure on the board and label it *Dinh*.
- Say to the class: *Let's ask Dinh the questions.* Look toward "Dinh" and ask: *Do you have a son?* Point to the check marks in the first column. Draw a speech bubble coming from Dinh's mouth. Elicit and write in the bubble: *No, I don't.*
- Tell Ss: *Write two classmates' names. Ask your classmates the questions.* Make sure Ss understand the task.
- Ss stand up, walk around, and talk with two classmates. Ss could also complete the exercise in groups of four. Walk around and help as needed.

Expansion activity (individual work)

- Write on the board:
  I have a sister. / You have a sister.
  He has a sister. / She has a sister.
- Read the sentences aloud and ask Ss to repeat after you. Explain that *have* changes to *has* in sentences with *he* and *she*.
- Ask Ss to report to the rest of the class information from the charts they completed in Exercise 3.
- Model the task. Say to one S, for example: *Tell me about Rafael.* Write on the board: *Rafael has a ______.* Elicit sentences such as: *Rafael has a son. Rafael has a sister.*
- Have each S give information about a classmate.

Evaluation

- Direct Ss' attention to the lesson focus written on the board. Ask Ss questions about their own families, for example: *Do you have a brother? Do you have a wife?* Elicit short answers: *Yes, I do. / No, I don't.*
- Call on Ss to ask you questions about your family using *Do you have a ______?*
- Check off the lesson focus as Ss demonstrate an understanding of what they have learned in the lesson.

More Ventures, Unit 3, Lesson C	
Literacy workbook, 15–30 min. **Basic Workbook,** 15–30 min.	
Writing worksheets, 15–30 min.	www.cambridge.org/myresourceroom
Student Arcade, time varies	www.cambridge.org/venturesarcade

CLASS CD1 TK 34

B Listen and repeat. Then write.

Do you have a . . . ?		Do you have a . . . ?	
1. sister	*yes*	4. son	*yes*
2. brother	*no*	5. daughter	*no*
3. husband	*yes*	6. grandmother	*yes*

Talk with a partner. You are Ana. Ask and answer.

A Do you have **a sister**?
B **Yes, I do.**
A What's **her** name?
B **Diana.**
A Do you have a **brother**?
B **No, I don't.**

3 Communicate

Talk with your classmates. Complete the chart.

	Dinh		*(Answers will vary.)*			
Do you have a . . . ?	**Yes**	**No**	**Yes**	**No**	**Yes**	**No**
son		✓				
daughter	✓					
sister	✓					
brother	✓					

LESSON D Reading

1 Before you read

Talk about the picture. What do you see?

2 Read

Listen and read.

STUDENT TK 17
CLASS CD1 TK 35

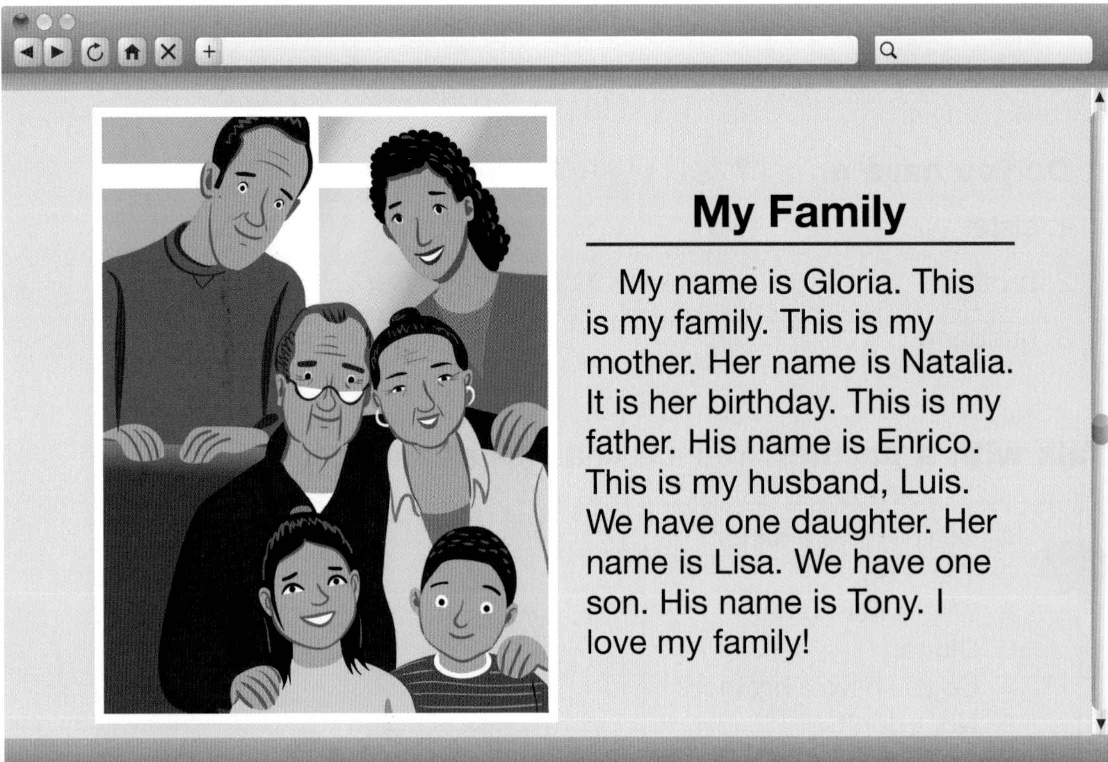

My Family

My name is Gloria. This is my family. This is my mother. Her name is Natalia. It is her birthday. This is my father. His name is Enrico. This is my husband, Luis. We have one daughter. Her name is Lisa. We have one son. His name is Tony. I love my family!

3 After you read

Read and circle. Then write.

1. Luis is Gloria's *husband*.
   father (husband)
2. Natalia is Gloria's *mother*.
   daughter (mother)
3. Tony is Gloria's *son*.
   brother (son)
4. Enrico is Gloria's *father*.
   (father) mother
5. Lisa is Gloria's *daughter*.
   sister (daughter)

Lesson objectives

- Introduce and read "My Family"
- Introduce vocabulary for talking about people
- Practice using new topic-related words

Warm-up and review

- Before class. Write today's lesson focus on the board.
  Lesson D:
  Read "My Family"
  Words for people
- Begin class. Books open. Direct Ss' attention to the family picture in Exercise **2**. Ask the class: *Who are these people?* Ss should recognize the family from the picture on page 32.
- Ask Ss to turn to page 32. Review the key vocabulary by pointing to and asking about each family member in the picture. For example, point to the grandmother and ask: *Who is she?* (The grandmother.) Point to the younger man and ask: *Who is he?* (The father.) Continue in this manner.

Expansion activity *(whole group)*

- If Ss have a good grasp of the family names they have learned so far, teach them the words *granddaughter* and *grandson*. Write the words on the board, say them aloud, and ask Ss to repeat them. Point to the picture on page 32 and ask: *Who is the granddaughter? Who is the grandson?* Ss may be able to guess that the words refer to the young girl and the young boy in the picture.

Presentation

- Direct Ss' attention to the picture in Exercise **2** on page 38 and read the instructions aloud. Ask Ss: *What do you see?* Ss should recognize the family from the picture on page 32. Elicit and write on the board any vocabulary about the picture that Ss know, such as: *family, grandmother, son, daughter.*

Practice

- Direct Ss' attention to Exercise **2**. Point to the title of the paragraph and ask: *What is the title?* (My Family) or *What is the reading about?* (Gloria's family.)

Class Audio CD1 track 35 Play or read the audio program and ask Ss to read along (see audio script, page T-157). Repeat the audio program as needed.

- Read aloud each sentence of the reading and ask Ss to repeat after you.
- Point to the family picture in Exercise **2** and ask the class: *Who is Gloria?* (Ss should indicate the mother of the children in the picture.)
- Answer any questions Ss have about the reading.

Learner persistence *(individual work)*

Self-Study Audio CD track 17 Exercise **2** is recorded on the CD at the back of the Student's Book. Ss can listen to the CD at home for reinforcement and review and also for self-directed learning when class attendance is not possible.

Expansion activity *(whole group)*

- Ask Ss to turn to page 32. Read the paragraph aloud, and ask Ss to point to each person as they hear their name.
- Walk around and check to see that Ss are pointing to the correct person. Continue until all the people in the picture have been identified by name.

Literacy tip

Literacy Ss should be able to talk about the picture and listen to and repeat the lines of the reading passage. They may also be able to assist in Exercise **3** by saying or pointing to the answers while a higher-level S writes the words.

Comprehension check

- Read aloud the instructions in Exercise **3**.
- Model the task. Point to and read aloud the first item. Then point to the answer choices and ask Ss: *Father or husband?* Elicit: *husband.* Point to where *husband* has been circled and written for number 1.
- Ss circle and write their answers individually. Walk around and help as needed.
- Go over answers with the class. Write the sentence prompts from Exercise **3** on the board with blanks after them. Call on Ss to write their answers on the board.
- Point to and read aloud each completed sentence on the board and ask the class: *Is this correct?* Ask Ss to read aloud or point to that part of the reading. Ask, for example: *Where is the answer in the reading?*

Literacy tip

For an alternative activity, refer literacy Ss to pages 36–37 in the *Literacy Workbook* at any time during the lesson.

LESSON D Reading

Presentation

- Direct Ss' attention to the picture dictionary in Exercise 4. Point to and say the word *People.* Tell Ss: *Today, we will learn more words to talk about people.*
- Read aloud the instructions for Exercise 4A.

Class Audio CD1 track 36 Play or read the audio program (see audio script, page T-157). Listen to Ss' pronunciation as they repeat the words. Correct pronunciation as needed.

Expansion activity *(student pairs)*

- Copy and cut out one set of the Unit 3 picture dictionary cards from the *Online Teacher's Resource Room* for each S.
- Have Ss play "Match the Pictures" in pairs. Ss hold their picture cards like playing cards. S1 places a card faceup on the desk or table and says the corresponding word. S2 finds the same picture card in his or her set and places it next to the matching card.
- Ss take turns putting down a card and finding the matching card.

Teaching tip

Ask Ss to write the vocabulary words on the backs of their picture cards and take them home to use as flash cards.

Learner persistence *(individual work)*

Self-Study Audio CD track 18 Exercise 4A is recorded on the Ss' self-study CD at the back of the Student's Book. Ss can listen to the CD at home for reinforcement and review and also for self-directed learning when class attendance is not possible.

Practice

- Direct Ss to Exercise 4B and read the instructions aloud. Ask two Ss to read the example conversation aloud.
- Model the task. Hold out your Student's Book and say to a S: *Show me the baby.* As the S points to the picture of the baby, he or she says: *Here's the baby.* Reverse the procedure so that the S asks you to show him or her one of the pictures.
- Ss complete the activity in pairs. Walk around and help as needed.

Expansion activity *(whole group)*

- Make four columns on the board with the headings *Girl*, *Boy*, *Man*, *Woman.*
- Have Ss turn back to the pictures of the families on pages 34 and 38 and decide which column to write each person's name in. For example, *Enrico*, the name of the grandfather from page 38, would be written under the heading *man*.

Evaluation

- Direct Ss' attention to the lesson focus written on the board. Ask Ss to turn back to the reading on page 38. Call on individual Ss to answer questions about Gloria's family; for example: *Who is Natalia?* (Gloria's mother.) *Does Gloria have a son?* (Yes, Tony.)
- Play "Name That Picture." Hold up a picture card and name it incorrectly. For example, hold up the picture card of the baby and say: *This is a man.* Ss correct the statement.
- Check off each part of the lesson focus as Ss demonstrate understanding of what they have learned in the lesson.

More Ventures, Unit 3, Lesson D	
Literacy workbook, 15–30 min. **Basic Workbook,** 15–30 min.	
Picture Dictionary activities, 30–45 min. **Writing worksheets,** 15–30 min.	www.cambridge.org/myresourceroom
Student Arcade, time varies	www.cambridge.org/venturesarcade

4 Picture dictionary People

1. baby 
2. girl 
3. boy 
4. teenager 
5. woman 
6. man

STUDENT TK 18
CLASS CD1 TK 36

A Listen and repeat. Look at the picture dictionary.

B Talk with a partner. Say a word. Your partner points to the picture.

A Show me the **man**.
B Here's the **man**.

LESSON E Writing

1 Before you write

A Talk with a partner. Complete the words.

B Talk with a partner. Look at the picture. Complete the story.

My Wonderful Family

My name is Frank. This is my family. This is my ___wife___ (1), Marie. This is our ___son___ (2). His name is Patrick. This is our ___daughter___ (3). Her name is Annie. This is our new ___baby___ (4), Jason. He is a boy. Patrick is his ___brother___ (5). Annie is his ___sister___ (6). I have a wonderful family!

Lesson objectives

- Practice writing vocabulary words from the unit
- Complete sentences about families

Warm-up and review

- Before class. Write today's lesson focus on the board.
  Lesson E:
  Write words for family members
  Complete sentences about families
- Before class. Write the following on the board:
  My mother's mother is my _____.
  My mother's father is my _____.
  My father's sister is my _____.
  My father's brother is my _____.
  My son's sister is my _____.
- Begin class. Books open. Review vocabulary for family members by asking Ss to solve the "riddles" on the board. Elicit: *grandmother*, *grandfather*, *aunt*, *uncle*, *daughter.*

Presentation

- Direct Ss' attention to the picture in Exercise **1A**. Point to the title above the picture and ask Ss: *Is this my family?* (No.) Tell Ss: *You're right. It's Frank's family.*
- Read the instructions for Exercise **1A** aloud. Tell Ss: *These are words for Frank's family members.*
- Point to the first item and say: *Number 1. Blank a-u-g-h-t-e-r . . . What's the word?* (Daughter.) *What letter do we need?* (d) Point to where the letter *d* has been written for number 1.

Practice

- Ss work in pairs to complete the words.
- When Ss are finished, call on different pairs to write their completed words on the board. Review the alphabet by asking Ss who write answers on the board to say the letters aloud. Have Ss make any necessary corrections on the board.

Literacy tip

For an alternative activity, refer literacy Ss to pages 38–39 in the *Literacy Workbook* at any time during the lesson.

- Read the instructions for Exercise **1B** aloud. Write the title of the story on the board and tell Ss that *wonderful* means "very good."
- Model the task. Begin to read the story aloud, but stop when you get to the first blank. Ask Ss: *What word do we need?* (Wife.) Point to the word *wife* in the picture and then to where *wife* has been written as an example. Make sure Ss understand that they are to fill in the blanks with the words from the picture.
- Ss work in pairs to fill in the blanks in the story.
- Check answers as a class. Write the numbers *1–6* on the board, and ask for volunteers to write their answers on the board. Point to and say each answer and ask the class: *Is this correct?* Make any necessary corrections on the board.
- Read aloud each line of the story and ask Ss to repeat after you. Answer any questions Ss have about the story.

Expansion activity (student pairs)

- Have Ss read the completed story aloud to each other in pairs.

Expansion activity (whole group)

- List on the board the names of Frank's family members: *Marie*, *Patrick*, *Annie*, *Jason.*
- Ask Ss about each family member, for example: *Who is Marie?* (Frank's wife.)
- Make four columns on the board with the headings *Man*, *Woman*, *Boy*, *Girl*, *Baby.*
- Have Ss write the names of Frank's family members in the appropriate columns.

LESSON E Writing

Presentation

- Ask Ss' to turn back to the family pictures on pages 32, 34, 35, and 38. Tell Ss: *These are pictures of families.*
- Draw on the board a simple picture of your family, either posed for a family portrait or doing some activity they like to do. Talk to Ss about your family as you draw the picture.
- Direct Ss' attention to Exercise **2A** on page 41 and read the instructions aloud. Reassure Ss that they do not need to be artists to draw a simple picture of their family.
- Give Ss time to draw their pictures. Walk around and ask friendly questions as Ss are drawing, for example: *Who is this?* or *Is this your daughter?*

Practice

- Direct Ss' attention to Exercise **2B** and read the instructions aloud. Point to the title and ask: *What is the title?* or *What will you write about?* (My Wonderful Family.) Read the words in the word bank and ask Ss to repeat. Explain that they can choose the words they need to write about their families.
- Model the task. Direct Ss' attention to the picture you drew on the board. Read aloud the first few prompts in the exercise, and write completed sentences on the board about your family. For example, write: *My name is Wendell. This is my family. This is my wife. Her name is Mira.*
- Ss complete the sentences individually. Walk around and help as needed.

> **Teaching tip**
> You may want to walk around and check to see that Ss are completing the sentences with information about their own families, rather than copying the information you wrote about your family.

Comprehension check

- Direct Ss' attention to Exercise **3** and read the instructions aloud.
- Model the task. Show your book (or paper) to a S, and say the sentences in Exercise **2B** using your own information. Ask that S to read and show you his or her sentences.
- Ss share their sentences in pairs. Walk around and spot-check Ss' writing.

Expansion activity *(individual work)*

- Ask each S to write one of their *This is my . . . His / Her name is . . .* sentence pairs on the board. You may want to have several Ss writing at the same time.
- Then have the Ss come back to the board, point to and say their sentences, and hold up the picture they drew as they "introduce" a family member to the class.

Learner persistence *(whole group)*

- Encourage Ss to attend class regularly and on time. If some Ss are frequently absent or late for class, talk to them and try to find out if there is a problem so that you can suggest a possible solution.

Evaluation

- Direct Ss' attention to the first part of the lesson focus written on the board. Conduct a spelling test. Ask Ss to close their books and take out a piece of paper. Tell Ss: *Listen. Write the words.* Dictate some or all of the vocabulary from the unit. When you are finished, collect the papers or call on individual Ss to come to the board and write one of the words.
- Direct Ss' attention to the second part of the lesson focus written on the board. Since Ss already wrote sentences on the board, simply ask: *Can you write sentences about families?* Point to the sentences Ss wrote on the board to help Ss understand the question. Elicit: *Yes!*
- Check off each part of the lesson focus as Ss demonstrate an understanding of what they have learned in the lesson.

More Ventures, Unit 3, Lesson E	
Literacy workbook, 15–30 min. **Basic Workbook,** 15–30 min.	
Writing worksheets, 15–30 min.	www.cambridge.org/myresourceroom

2 Write

A Draw a picture of your family.

(Answers will vary.)

B Write about your picture.

daughter father husband mother son wife

My Wonderful Family

My name is *(Answers will vary.)*. This is my family.

This is my ________. ________ name is ____________.
His Her

This is my ________. ________ name is ____________.
His Her

This is my ________. ________ name is ____________.
His Her

This is my ________. ________ name is ____________.
His Her

I love my family!

3 After you write

Talk with a partner. Share your writing.

LESSON F Another view

1 Life-skills reading

KB **Property Management Company**
230 Central Street, Philadelphia, PA 19019 (215) 555-1863

HOUSING APPLICATION
Directions: Complete the form. Please print.

What is your name? *Ali Azari*
Who will live with you in the house?

NAME	RELATIONSHIP
Shohreh Azari	*wife*
Azam Javadi	*mother*
Omid Azari	*son*
Navid Azari	*son*
Fatima Azari	*daughter*
Leila Azari	*daughter*
Soraya Azari	*daughter*

A Read the questions. Look at the housing application. Fill in the answer.

1. Who is Shohreh Azari?
   - Ⓐ Ali's daughter
   - ● Ali's wife
   - Ⓒ Ali's son
2. Who is Soraya Azari?
   - ● Ali's daughter
   - Ⓑ Ali's mother
   - Ⓒ Ali's wife
3. Who is Azam Javadi?
   - ● Ali's mother
   - Ⓑ Ali's wife
   - Ⓒ Ali's daughter
4. Who is Omid Azari?
   - Ⓐ Ali's brother
   - Ⓑ Ali's father
   - ● Ali's son

B Talk with a partner.

Who lives with you?

Lesson objectives

- Practice reading a housing application
- Review vocabulary and grammar from the unit
- Complete the self-assessment

Warm-up and review

- Before class. Write today's lesson focus on the board. *Lesson F:* *Read a housing application*
- Before class: Write in random places on the board the vocabulary from the unit: *an aunt, a baby, a boy, a brother, a daughter, a father, a girl, a grandfather, a grandmother, a husband, a man, a mother, a sister, a son, a teenager, an uncle, a wife, a woman.*
- Begin class. Books closed. Review the vocabulary for people and family members by calling on individual Ss to come to the board. Say: *Listen and circle the word.* Call out a word randomly for Ss to locate on the board and circle. When you are finished, practice saying the words with the class.

Teaching tip

Ss may not be familiar with the difference between *a* and *an*. It might be helpful to point out that we say "an aunt" because the first letter of *aunt* starts with a vowel.

Presentation

- Books open. Direct Ss' attention to the housing application in Exercise **1**. Tell Ss: *This is a housing application.* Point to and say the words *Housing Application*. Ask Ss to repeat after you.
- Tell Ss: *Sometimes you need to fill out a housing application when you want to rent a house or an apartment.*
- Write on the board: *rent.* Ask Ss: *What is rent?* Encourage Ss to respond to your question, and if they need help, tell them: *"Rent" means you pay money to live in a house or apartment.*

Teaching tip

You may need to spend some time explaining the difference between buying and renting a house or apartment in order to help Ss understand the purpose of a housing application.

- Point to the schedule and ask: *Who filled out this application? What's his name?* (Ali Azari.)
- Tell Ss: *Ali Azari has family members. How many family members does he have?* (Seven.)

Practice

- Read the instructions for Exercise **1A** aloud. This task helps prepare Ss for standardized-type tests they may have to take.
- Write the first item on the board along with the three answer choices labeled *a*, *b*, and *c*.
- Read the item and the answer choices aloud and then point to the housing application. Ask Ss: *Who is Shohreh Azari?* Continue to gesture toward the application to show Ss where to look for the information. Elicit: *wife.* Ask Ss: *Whose wife?* (Ali's wife.)
- Point to the three answer choices on the board. Ask Ss: *a*, *b*, or *c*? (b) Fill in the letter *b* and tell Ss: *Fill in the answer in your book.* Make sure Ss understand the task.
- Have Ss individually scan for and fill in the answers.

Comprehension check

- Go over the answers to Exercise **1A** together. Make sure that Ss followed instructions and filled in their answers. Ask Ss to point to the information in the housing application.

Application

- Read the instructions for Exercise **1B** aloud.
- Model the task. Talk about the people who live with you. If you live alone, talk about the people who live with your aunt, your brother, or another family member.
- Ss complete the task in pairs. When Ss are finished, ask them to find a new partner and have new conversations.

Expansion activity *(whole group)*

- Practice saying the address on the housing application. Write each line of the address on the board. Read the words and numbers aloud and ask Ss to repeat after you. Demonstrate the two common ways of pronouncing *0* – as "zero" and as "oh."

Literacy tip

For an alternative activity, refer literacy Ss to pages 40–41 in the *Literacy Workbook* at any time during the lesson.

LESSON F Another view

Presentation

- Make three columns on the board with the headings: *Male*, *Female*, *Male or female.* Over each heading, draw simplified male and female figures. For the third column, draw both figures with a slash between them.
- Read the column headings aloud and ask Ss to repeat the words after you.
- On a different part of the board, write the first three words from Exercise **2A**: *an aunt*, *a baby*, *a boy.*
- Ask Ss about each word; for example: *An aunt. Is an aunt male or female?* (Female.) When you get to the word baby, ask: *Is a baby male or female?* Make sure Ss understand that there are male babies and female babies, so the answer is *Male* or *female.*

Practice

- Books open. Read aloud the instructions for Exercise **2A**. Point to *an aunt* in the word box and then point to where *an aunt* has been written in the chart as an example.
- Ss complete the chart individually.
- Read aloud the second part of the instructions for Exercise **2A**. Ss compare their charts in pairs.
- Check answers with the class. Say each word from the word box, and call on a S to tell you which column he or she chose. Write the words in the columns you made on the board. If there are any errors, ask other Ss if they have a different answer.

> **Teaching tip**
> It might be helpful to give Ss an approximate age range for the terms *boy*, *girl*, *man*, and *woman*. Try to explain that there is no exact definition for these terms, but for many people, boys and girls might range from 0–17 years old whereas men and women might be over 17.

- Direct Ss' attention to Exercise **2B** and read the instructions aloud.
- Model the task. Ask a male S to come to the board and to bring his book. Ask the class, *Is (name of S) male or female?* (Male.) Point to the list of male family members in Exercise **2A** and ask the S about each term; for example: *Are you a boy? Are you a brother?* Each time the S answers *yes*, write that term on the board.
- Reproduce the sentence with blanks from Exercise **2B** on the board. Ask the same S to fill in the blanks with any of the terms for family members that you wrote on the board; for example: *I am a brother, a man, and an uncle.*
- If you think it would be helpful, repeat the modeling procedure with a female S.
- Have Ss fill in the blanks in Exercise **2B** individually.
- Read aloud the second part of the instructions for Exercise **2B**. Ss use their partner's information to complete the second sentence.
- Ask for several volunteers to tell the class about their partners.

Expansion activity *(whole group)*

- Teach the words *parent*, *parents*, *child*, *children.* Write and say the words and ask Ss to repeat.
- After the word *parents*, draw an equal sign and the words *mother and father.* Explain that a parent can be either male or female.
- After the word *children*, draw an equal sign and the words *son* and *daughter.* Explain that a child can be either male or female.
- Give Ss the singular and plural variants of the words by writing on the board: *1 parent*, *2 parents*, *1 child*, *2 children.* Give Ss simple example sentences using the singular and plural forms.

Evaluation

- Before asking Ss to turn to the self-assessment on page 138, do a quick review of the unit. Have Ss turn to Lesson A. Ask: *What words are on this page? What do you see in the picture?* Continue in this manner to review each lesson quickly.
- **Self-assessment** Read the instructions for Exercise **3**. Ask Ss to turn to the self-assessment page and complete the unit self-assessment.
- If Ss are ready, administer the unit test on pages T-171–T-173 of this Teacher's Edition (or on the Assessment Audio CD / CD-ROM).

More Ventures, Unit 3, Lesson F	
Literacy workbook, 15–30 min. **Basic Workbook,** 15–30 min.	
Real Life Document, 15–30 min. **Writing worksheets,** 15–30 min.	www.cambridge.org/myresourceroom

2 Fun with vocabulary

A Complete the chart.

an aunt	a father	a man	an uncle
a baby	a girl	a mother	a wife
a boy	a grandfather	a sister	a woman
a brother	a grandmother	a son	
a daughter	a husband	a teenager	

Male	Female	Male or female
a boy	*an aunt*	*a baby*
a brother	*a daughter*	*a teenager*
a father	*a girl*	
a grandfather	*a grandmother*	
a husband	*a mother*	
a man	*a sister*	
a son	*a wife*	
an uncle	*a woman*	

Talk with a partner. Compare your answers.

B Write about yourself. Use the words from 2A.

I am *(Answers will vary.)*, ____________,
and ____________.

Talk with a partner. Write about your partner.

My partner ____________ is ____________,
____________, and ____________.

3 Wrap up

Complete the **Self-assessment** on page 138.

UNIT
4 Health

LESSON A Listening

1 Before you listen

A Look at the picture. What do you see?

B Listen and point: doctor • doctor's office medicine • nurse • patient

CLASS CD1 TK 37

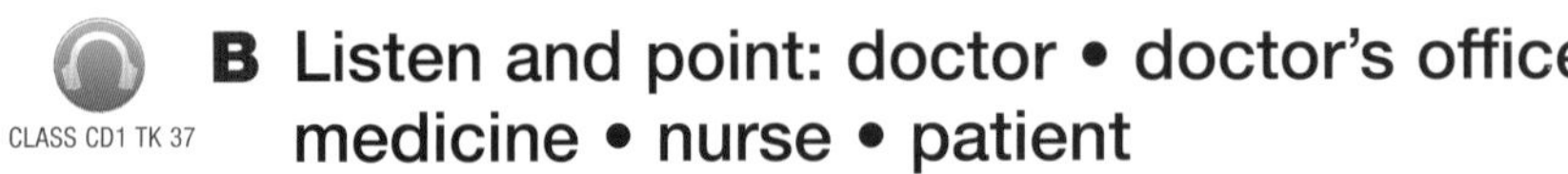

Lesson objectives

- Introduce Ss to the topic
- Find out what Ss know about the topic
- Preview the unit by talking about the picture
- Practice key vocabulary
- Practice listening skills

UNIT 4

Warm-up and review

- Before class. Write today's lesson focus on the board.

  Lesson A:
  Health problems
- Begin class. Books closed. Draw a large human stick figure on the board. Circle parts of the body and ask Ss: *What is this?* Elicit any vocabulary for body parts that Ss already know, such as: *head, arm, hand, leg, foot.*
- Point to the words *health problems* on the board. Say the words and have Ss repeat after you. Tell Ss: *This unit is about health problems. Problems with the body.*
- Point to a part of the body on the board that your Ss know the word for, for example, *head.* Pantomime a headache and ask Ss: *What's my health problem?* Elicit or provide: *headache.*

Teaching tip

Not all the Ss in your class will know vocabulary for parts of the body or health problems. This warm-up is meant to activate any prior knowledge of the subject that Ss have and to help you assess that knowledge.

Literacy tip

If you have literacy Ss in your class, it might be helpful to spend time at the beginning of any activity that contains art or photos talking about the pictures before focusing Ss' attention on the printed words in the exercise. Have Ss work in pairs. Tell them to ask each other: *What do you see?* Encourage Ss to describe the pictures to each other. Consider pairing literacy Ss with Ss who can help them read the text in the exercise. This will help preview the exercise for literacy Ss and make them more confident as the exercise continues.

Presentation

- Books open. Set the scene. Hold up the Student's Book. Show Ss the picture on page 44. Tell the class: *These people have health problems. They need a doctor.*
- Ask: What do you see? Elicit and write on the board any vocabulary that Ss know, such as: *chairs, desk, teenagers, man, woman, cap.*

Teaching tip

If possible, bring in real examples of medicine to show Ss the different forms it can take, for example, tablets, capsules, and liquids. For each example, tell Ss: *This is medicine.*

Practice

- Direct Ss' attention to the key vocabulary in Exercise **1B**. Read aloud each word or phrase while pointing to the corresponding part of the picture. Ask Ss to repeat and point.

Class Audio CD1 track 37 Play or read the audio program (see audio script, page T-157). Tell Ss: *Listen and point to the picture.* As Ss hear the key vocabulary, check to see that Ss are pointing to the correct part of the picture. Repeat the audio program as needed.

Comprehension check

- Ask Ss *Yes / No* questions about the picture. Tell Ss: *Listen. Say "yes" or "no."*

  Point to the picture. Ask: *Is this a classroom?* (No.)

  Point to the picture. Ask: *Is this a doctor's office?* (Yes.)

  Point to the nurse. Ask: *Is she a patient?* (No.)

  Point to the doctor. Ask: *Is he a doctor?* (Yes.)

  Point to the woman with the stomachache. Ask: *Is she a patient?* (Yes.)

  Point to the boy with the tissue. Ask: *Is he a doctor?* (No.)

  Point to the medicine. Ask: *Is this medicine?* (Yes.)

  Point to the nurse. Ask: *Is she a nurse?* (Yes.)

Teaching tip

Direct Ss' attention to the two teenagers in the picture, Mario and Tony, since they appear again later in the unit. Practice saying the boys' names, ask Ss how old they think the boys are (teenagers in the 13–19-year-old age range), and ask Ss about the boys' clothing (baseball uniforms).

Literacy tip

For an alternative activity, refer literacy Ss to pages 42–43 in the *Literacy Workbook* at any time during the lesson.

LESSON A Listening

Presentation

- Before class. Bring to class full-page clip art images to illustrate each of the key vocabulary terms. Save the images to use later in the lesson and in other parts of the unit.
- Direct Ss' attention to Exercise **2A** and read the instructions aloud. As you say each word or phrase, hold up the appropriate picture, and ask Ss to repeat after you.

Practice

Class Audio CD1 track 38 Play or read the audio program (see audio script, page T-157). Ss listen and repeat the vocabulary as you hold up the clip art images. Repeat the audio program as needed.

- Listen carefully to Ss' pronunciation and make corrections as needed.

Learner persistence *(individual work)*

Self-Study Audio CD track 19 Exercise **2A** is recorded on the CD at the back of the Student's Book. Ss can listen to the CD at home for reinforcement and review. They can also listen to the CD for self-directed learning when class attendance is not possible.

Literacy tip

Use the clip art images you found to make smaller picture flash cards for your literacy Ss.

- Direct Ss' attention to Exercise **2B** and read the instructions aloud.

Class Audio CD1 track 39 Model the task. Hold up the Student's Book and say: *Number one.* Play or read the audio program for number 1 (see audio script, page T-157). Point to the two answer choices in number 1 and ask Ss: *What did you hear – a or b?* Elicit: *b.* Point to the letter *b* next to the second picture and tell Ss: *Circle the letter "b."*

Class Audio CD1 track 39 Play or read the complete audio program (see audio script, page T-157). Ss listen and circle the correct answers. Repeat the audio as needed.

Class Audio CD1 track 39 Read aloud the second part of the instructions for Exercise **2B**. Play or read the audio program again so that Ss can listen and check their answers.

Learner persistence *(individual work)*

Self-Study Audio CD track 20 Exercise **2B** is recorded on the CD at the back of the Student's Book. Ss can listen to the CD at home for reinforcement and review and also for self-directed learning when class attendance is not possible.

Comprehension check

- Write the numbers *1–4* on the board. Ask a few Ss to come to the board and write the correct answers to Exercise **2B** next to each number.

Class Audio CD1 track 39 Play or read the audio program again. Pause the audio program after each conversation. Point to the answer written on the board and ask: *Is this correct?* Ask another S to make any necessary corrections.

Teaching tip

Use the same spatial arrangement as the textbook when replicating exercises on the board. This makes the process of checking answers less demanding for Ss and allows them to concentrate on the language.

Application

- Direct Ss' attention to Exercise **3** and read the instructions aloud.
- Model the task. Hold up the Student's Book and point to the pictures in Exercise **2B**. Say to one S: *Point to a picture.* Say to the first S's partner: *Say the word.*
- Ss complete the exercise in pairs. Walk around and help as needed.

Expansion activity *(student pairs)*

- Have Ss practice the conversations from Exercise **2B** in pairs. Ask Ss to turn to the self-study audio script on page 154 in the Student's Book.
- Ask Ss to choose Role A or B and read aloud the conversations. Then have Ss switch roles and read the conversations again. Walk around and help as needed.

Evaluation

- Direct Ss' attention to the lesson focus written on the board. Arrange the large clip art images that you used in Exercise **2A** on the chalk tray or on a table so that Ss can see all of them. Say the key vocabulary in random order, and call on individual Ss to select the corresponding image and hold it up for everyone to see. Have Ss replace the image each time so that every S can choose from all five.
- Check off the lesson focus as Ss demonstrate an understanding of what they have learned in the lesson.

More Ventures, Unit 4, Lesson A	
Literacy Workbook, 15–30 min. **Basic Workbook,** 15–30 min.	
Writing worksheets 15–30 min.	www.cambridge.org/myresourceroom
Student Arcade, time varies	www.cambridge.org/venturesarcade

Unit Goals
Identify health problems
Interpret a medicine label
Identify reasons for a visit to a doctor

2 Listen

A Listen and repeat.

STUDENT TK 19
CLASS CD1 TK 38

1. doctor 2. doctor's office 3. medicine 4. nurse 5. patient

B Listen and circle.

STUDENT TK 20
CLASS CD1 TK 39

1. a.  (b.) 

2. (a.)  b. 

3. (a.)  b. 

4. (a.) 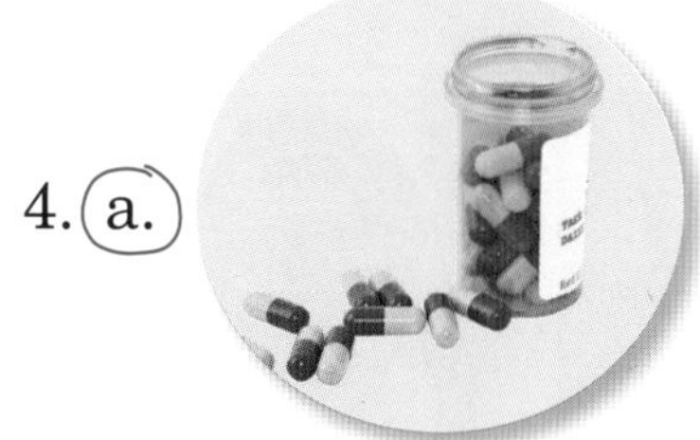 b. 

Listen again. Check your answers.

3 After you listen

Talk with a partner. Point to a picture.
Your partner says the word.

☑ Listen for and identify a patient's request

LESSON B Parts of the body

1 Vocabulary focus

Listen and repeat.

CLASS CD1 TK 40

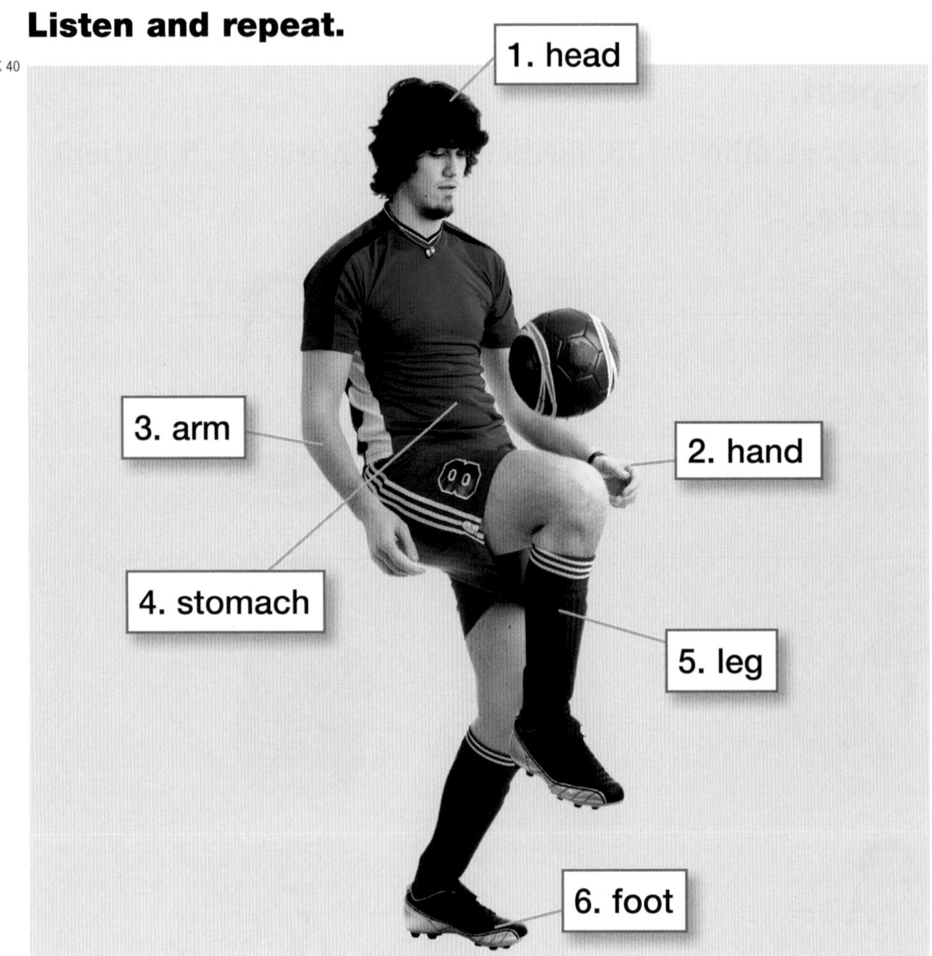

2 Practice

A Read and match.

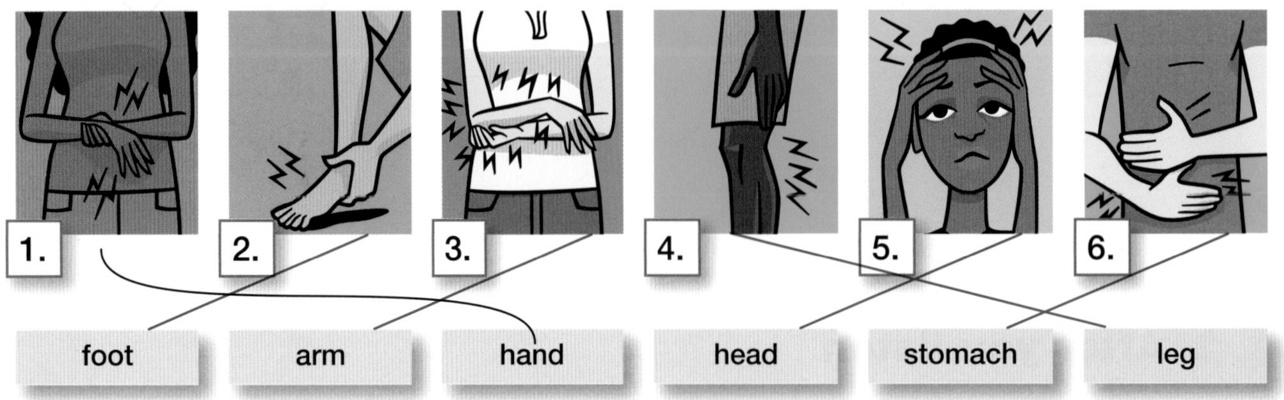

Lesson objectives

- Introduce vocabulary for parts of the body
- Practice asking and answering questions about health problems

Warm-up and review

- Before class. Write today's lesson focus on the board.
  Lesson B:
  Parts of the body
  What's the matter?
- Before class. Write the key vocabulary from Lesson A on the board: *doctor*, *doctor's office*, *medicine*, *nurse*, *patient*.
- Begin class. Books open. Point to and say each of the key vocabulary items from Lesson A, and ask Ss to repeat after you.
- Have Ss identify the vocabulary in the picture on page 44. Tell Ss, for example: *Point to the doctor.*
- If you used large clip art images in Lesson A, hold up the images in random order, and have Ss say the corresponding words.

Presentation

- Point to the words *Parts of the body* at the top of page 46. Say the words aloud and ask Ss to repeat after you. Draw a stick figure on the board and then draw a circle around the whole figure. Tell Ss: *This is the body.* Draw smaller circles around a few body parts, for example, the head, an arm, and a foot. Tell Ss: *These are parts of the body.*
- Direct Ss' attention to the picture in Exercise **1**. Tell Ss: *Today, you will learn words for parts of the body.*

Practice

- Read aloud the instructions for Exercise **1**.

Class Audio CD1 track 40 Play or read the audio program (see audio script, page T-157). Listen and repeat the vocabulary along with Ss. Repeat the audio program as needed.

- Listen carefully to Ss' pronunciation and correct as needed.
- Direct Ss' attention to Exercise **2A**. As you read aloud the instructions, hold up the Student's Book and indicate that Ss should look at the pictures of body parts and match them to the corresponding words.
- Model the activity. Hold up the Student's Book. Point to the first picture. Ask: *What body part is this?* (Hand.) Say: *Match the picture with the word.*
- Ss complete the exercise individually. Help as needed.

Comprehension check

- Write the numbers *1–6* on the board. Ask a few Ss to come to the board and write the answers to Exercise **2A** on the board.
- Ask different Ss to read the answers written on the board. Ask: *Is this correct?* After each answer is read, ask: *Is this correct?* Ask another S to make any necessary corrections on the board.

Expansion activity *(individual work)*

- Help Ss review the unit vocabulary by preparing a worksheet that lists the new words from Lesson A and Lesson B with all the vowels left out and replaced with blanks; for example:
  d _ c t _ r
  p _ t _ n t
  s t _ m _ c h

  Option 1 Allow Ss to use their Student's Book to help with spelling.

  Option 2 Bring in a prize for the S who finishes in the shortest amount of time.
- When Ss are finished, ask volunteers to write the words on the board.

Community building

- Many hospitals, clinics, and doctor's offices provide information in a number of languages. Call local health providers in your area, and ask them to send you information such as their hours, their location, and the types of services they provide in English and in your Ss' native languages. You can also ask if they are able to provide translators for patients. Give Ss information about local health providers in English and, whenever possible, in Ss' own languages.

Learner persistence

- Tell Ss what you would like them to do if they have a health problem and can't come to class. For example, give Ss your office phone number or e-mail address and ask them to contact you, or have them exchange phone numbers with a specific classmate. You can also suggest that Ss use the Self-study Audio to review the language they have already studied and to keep up with any lessons that they are missing.

Literacy tip

For an alternative activity, refer literacy Ss to pages 44–45 in the *Literacy Workbook* at any time during the lesson.

LESSON B Parts of the body

Presentation

- Direct Ss' attention to the picture in Exercise 2B. Tell the class: *These people have health problems.* Point to the second part of the lesson focus written on the board and repeat the words *health problems.*
- Direct Ss' attention to the word bank. Read each word aloud and ask Ss to repeat after you. Then point to the appropriate person in the picture and say, for example: *Her arm hurts.*

Teaching tip
Help Ss understand the meaning of the word *hurts* by acting out each health problem in the picture as you go over the vocabulary for body parts. For example, rub your arm when you say *Her arm hurts*, and make noises as if you are in pain.

Practice

- Read aloud the first part of the instructions for Exercise 2B.
- Class Audio CD1 track 41 Model the task. Say: *Listen and repeat.* Play or read the audio program for number 1 (see audio script, page T-157), and point to the first woman in line in the picture as you repeat. Say: *Then write.* Point to the word *hand* written as an example. Make sure Ss understand the task.
- Class Audio CD1 track 41 Play or read the complete audio program (see audio script, page T-157). Ss listen and repeat. Encourage Ss to point to the people in the picture as they repeat.
- Ss complete the exercise individually. Repeat the audio program as needed. Encourage them to find the words they need in the word bank.
- Check answers with the class. Write the numbers *1–6* on the board. Point to each number and ask Ss: *What hurts?* Elicit, for example: *my hand.* Write the words for parts of the body next to the numbers on the board. If Ss give an incorrect answer, ask the class if anyone has a different answer.
- Read aloud the second part of the instructions for Exercise 2B. Model the exercise by pointing to the woman in the picture with the hurt hand. Then read the conversation aloud using different voices for the two roles and acting as if your hand is hurt.
- Ask two Ss to read aloud the example conversation and act it out. Ask two different Ss to point to another person in the picture and have a new conversation as they act out his or her health problem.

Teaching tip
Write on the board: *What's the matter?* Tell Ss that they can ask this question when someone looks sad, sick, or hurt.

- Have pairs of Ss practice asking and answering questions about the people in the picture as they act out the problems. Walk around and help as needed.
- When Ss are finished, call on different pairs to perform the conversations for the rest of the class.

Application

- Direct Ss' attention to Exercise 3 and read the instructions aloud. Read the example question and answer aloud, and ask Ss to repeat after you.
- Model the task. Have a S ask you: *What's the matter?* Pantomime one of the health problems and say, for example: *My stomach hurts.*
- Ss ask and answer questions with new partners. When they are finished, have Ss switch partners and repeat the exercise.

Expansion activity *(whole group)*

- Practice using possessive pronouns and adjectives by talking about the people in the picture in Exercise 2B.
- Write on the board:
  What's the matter with (him / her)?
  (His / Her) _____ hurts.
- Point to and ask Ss about each person in the picture, for example: *What's the matter with her?* Elicit: *Her hand hurts.*

Evaluation

- Direct Ss' attention to the lesson focus written on the board. Indicate parts of your own body and have Ss say the words for the body parts.
- Ask several different Ss: *What's the matter?* Have them pantomime a sore body part as they did in Exercise 3. Then have Ss ask their classmates the question.
- Check off each part of the lesson focus as Ss demonstrate an understanding of what they have learned in the lesson.

More Ventures, Unit 4, Lesson B	
Literacy Workbook, 15–30 min. **Basic Workbook,** 15–30 min.	
Writing worksheets, 15–30 min.	www.cambridge.org/myresourceroom
Student Arcade, time varies	www.cambridge.org/venturesarcade

CLASS CD1 TK 41

B **Listen and repeat.** Then write.

arm foot hand head leg stomach

What hurts?

1. My hand.
2. My head.
3. My leg.
4. My stomach.
5. My arm.
6. My foot.

Talk with a partner. Ask and answer.

A What's the matter?
B My **hand** hurts.

3 Communicate

Talk with a partner.
Act it out. Ask and answer.

LESSON C My feet hurt.

1 Grammar focus: singular and plural

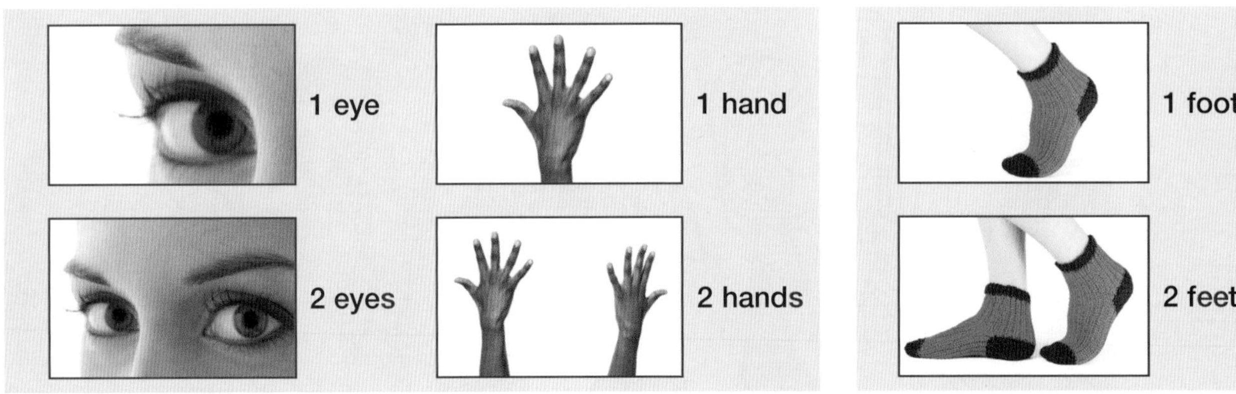

2 Practice

A Read and circle. Then write.

1. A What hurts?

   B My hands .
   hand (hands)

2. A What hurts?

   B My eyes .
   eye (eyes)

3. A What hurts?

   B My arm .
   (arm) arms

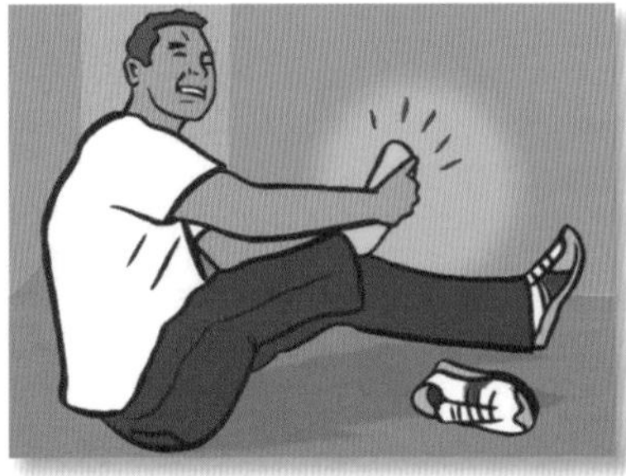

4. A What hurts?

   B My foot .
   (foot) feet

5. A What hurts?

   B My legs .
   leg (legs)

6. A What hurts?

   B My hand .
   (hand) hands

B Listen and repeat. Then practice with a partner.

CLASS CD1 TK 42

Lesson objectives

- Introduce singular and plural nouns
- Practice asking and answering questions about health problems

Warm-up and review

- Before class. Write today's lesson focus on the board.
  Lesson C:
  Singular and plural
  What hurts?
- Begin class. Books closed. Draw an outline of your hand on the board. Point to the drawing and ask Ss: *What is this?* Elicit and write on the board: *hand.*
- Draw another hand on the board and circle the two hands. Ask Ss: *What are these?* Elicit or provide the word *hands* and write it on the board. Point to and say the singular and plural forms and ask Ss to repeat after you. Circle the letter *S*.
- Repeat the procedure with *arm / arms*, *leg / legs*, and *foot / feet*. Direct Ss' attention to the first part of the lesson focus. Say and have Ss repeat: *one hand*, *two hands*; *one arm*, *two arms*; *one leg*, *two legs*; *one foot*, *two feet*.
- Point to the first part of the lesson focus on the board. Say the words aloud and ask Ss to repeat. Hold up one hand. Say: *One hand is singular.* Hold up two hands. Say: *Two hands are plural.*

Presentation

- Books open. Direct Ss' attention to the grammar chart in Exercise 1. Read each phrase aloud and ask Ss to repeat after you.

Teaching tip

Since the words *eye* and *eyes* may be new to Ss, be sure to practice pronouncing them with the class.

- Use your own body to help Ss practice the singular and plural forms. Hold up one hand and wiggle your fingers to elicit *one hand*. Close one eye to elicit that phrase; then open both eyes wide to elicit *two eyes*. Sit on your desk or table and wiggle one or both of your feet, then continue with your legs and arms, and so on.

Teaching tip

You may want to ask a S who is not easily embarrassed to stand next to you as you complete the review of vocabulary for body parts by gesturing to your two heads and your two stomachs.

Expansion activity *(student pairs)*

- Expand on the presentation of singular and plural nouns and recycle vocabulary for school supplies and classroom objects by asking Ss to count items in the classroom.
- Photocopy and give each pair of Ss a list of items you want them to count, for example: *computer(s)*, *chair(s)*, *desk(s)*, *map(s)*, *eraser(s)*, *ruler(s)*, *stapler(s).* Be sure to include some singular items.
- Increase the difficulty of the task by listing items that are likely to be numerous or that require Ss to talk to their classmates, for example, *pencils* or *notebooks.*
- Have Ss walk around the room and write the quantities on their lists. When Ss are finished, call on Ss to report their numbers to the class. Ask Ss who disagree on a number to demonstrate how they counted the items.

Practice

- Direct Ss' attention to the first picture in Exercise 2A. Ask two Ss to read the example conversation aloud.
- Read aloud the instructions for Exercise 2A. Point to where *hands* has been circled and written for number 1.
- Ss complete the exercise individually. Walk around and help as needed.

Comprehension check

- Read aloud the second part of the instructions for Exercise 2A.

Class Audio CD1 track 42 Play or read the audio program (see audio script, page T-157). Ss listen and repeat as they check their answers.

- Write the numbers *1–6* on the board. Ask volunteers to come to the board and write the words they circled. Make any necessary corrections on the board.
- Ss in pairs. Ask Ss to choose Role A or B and practice the questions and answers in Exercise 2A. Then have Ss switch roles and practice again. Walk around and help as needed.
- Ask several pairs to act out the situations and say the questions and answers for the rest of the class.

Literacy tip

For an alternative activity, refer literacy Ss to pages 46–47 in the *Literacy Workbook* at any time during the lesson.

LESSON C My feet hurt.

Presentation

- Direct Ss' attention to the pictures in Exercise 2B. Point to each picture and ask the class: *What is this?* or *What are these?* Elicit the appropriate singular or plural form of each noun. When Ss say the words, ask: *Singular or plural?*

Practice

- Read aloud the first part of the instructions for Exercise 2B.
- Class Audio CD1 track 43 Model the task. Say: *Listen and repeat.* Play or read the audio program for number 1 (see audio script, pages T-157–158), and point to the man in the first picture as you repeat. Make sure Ss understand the task.
- Class Audio CD1 track 43 Play or read the complete audio program (see audio script, pages T-157–158). Ss listen and repeat. Encourage Ss to point to the people in the pictures as they repeat.

Teaching tip

Write on the board the phrase *Oh, I'm sorry.* Tell Ss that they can use the phrase when people tell them about a health problem. Demonstrate the use of the expression by telling Ss that various parts of your body hurt; for example: *My head hurts.* Point to the board and elicit from Ss: *Oh, I'm sorry.*

- Read aloud the second part of the instructions in Exercise 2B. Call on two Ss to read aloud the example conversation. Then, point to one of the pictures in the exercise, and ask two Ss to model a new conversation using the appropriate body part.
- Indicate that Ss should ask and answer questions about all six pictures. Make sure Ss understand the task.
- Ss ask and answer questions about the pictures in pairs. When Ss are finished, ask them to switch partners and have new conversations.

Expansion activity *(student pairs)*

- Ask pairs of Ss to practice the conversations in Exercise 2A on page 48 again, but this time, have them add the sympathetic expression: *Oh, I'm sorry.*

Application

- Direct Ss' attention to Exercise 3 and read the instructions aloud. Read aloud the two column headings in the chart.
- Point to the name *Sasha* in the top line of the chart, and tell Ss that it is a first name. Point to the word *head* in the chart and ask Ss: *What hurts?* (Sasha's head.)
- Call on two Ss to read the example question and answer aloud.
- Tell the class: *Write your classmates' names. Ask them the question. Write their answers.* Make sure Ss understand the task.
- Ss complete the exercise in small groups or else walk around and talk to at least three classmates.
- Walk around and help as needed. When Ss are finished, ask for volunteers to perform one of their conversations for the class.

  Option Ask the class about several of the Ss, for example: *Tell me about Lor. What's the matter with Lor?* Elicit, for example: *His stomach hurts.*

Evaluation

- Direct Ss' attention to the lesson focus written on the board. Check Ss' understanding of singular and plural nouns by gesturing toward or wiggling parts of your own body and eliciting the words for those body parts from Ss.
- Direct Ss' attention to the picture in Exercise 2B on page 47, and ask Ss about people in the picture. For example, point to the girl with the hurt hand and ask: *What hurts?* Elicit: *Her hand.* As Ss answer, say: *Oh, I'm sorry.*
- Have Ss ask and answer questions about this picture in pairs. Walk around and monitor Ss' use of the language points.
- Check off each part of the lesson focus as Ss demonstrate an understanding of what they have learned in the lesson.

More Ventures, Unit 4, Lesson C	
Literacy Workbook, 15–30 min. **Basic Workbook,** 15–30 min.	
Writing worksheets, 15–30 min.	www.cambridge.org/myresourceroom
Student Arcade, time varies	www.cambridge.org/venturesarcade

CLASS CD1 TK 43

B Listen and repeat.

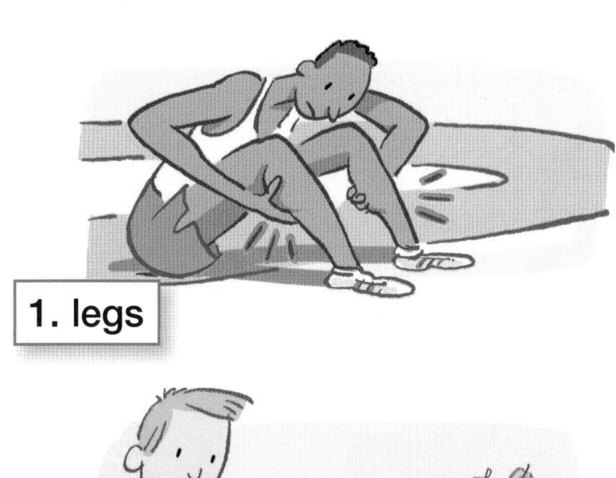
1. legs

2. hand

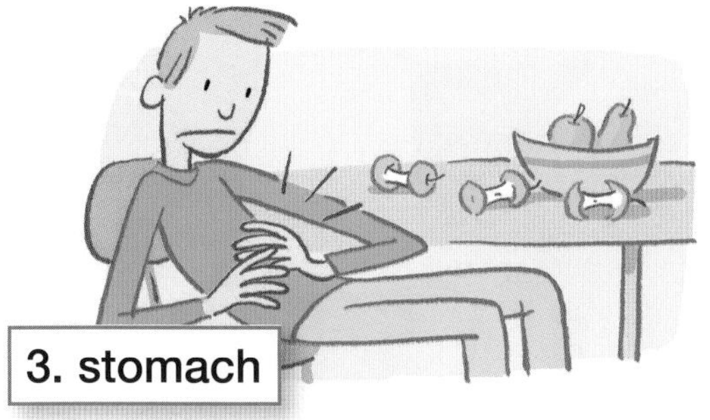
3. stomach

4. feet

5. eyes

6. head

Talk with a partner. Act it out. Ask and answer.

A What hurts?
B My **legs**.
A Oh, I'm sorry.

3 Communicate

Talk with your classmates. Complete the chart.

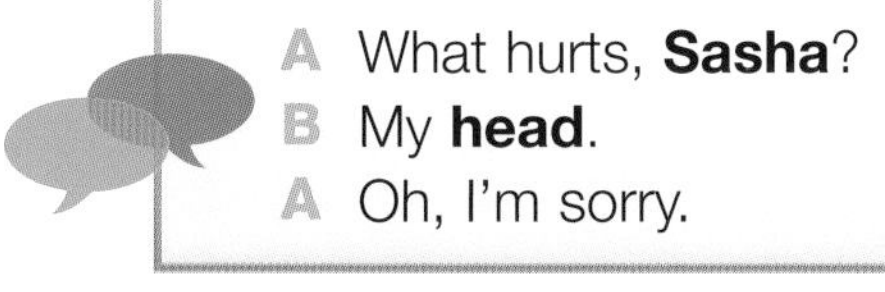

A What hurts, **Sasha**?
B My **head**.
A Oh, I'm sorry.

Name	What hurts?
Sasha	*head*
(Answers will vary.)	

LESSON D Reading

1 Before you read

Talk about the picture. What do you see?

2 Read

STUDENT TK 21
CLASS CD1 TK 44

Listen and read.

At the Doctor's Office

Tony and Mario are at the doctor's office. They are patients. Tony's leg hurts. His head hurts, too. He has a headache. Mario's arm hurts. His hands hurt, too. Tony and Mario are not happy. It is not a good day.

3 After you read

Read the sentences. Check (✓) the names.

	Tony	Mario
His arm hurts.		✓
His head hurts.	✓	
His leg hurts.	✓	
His hands hurt.		✓
He is not happy.	✓	✓

Lesson objectives

- Introduce and read "At the Doctor's Office"
- Introduce vocabulary for talking about health problems
- Practice using new topic-related words

Warm-up and review

- Before class. Write today's lesson focus on the board.
  Lesson D:
  Read "At the Doctor's Office"
  Learn words for health problems
- Begin class. Books open. Direct Ss' attention to the picture in Exercise 1. Ask the class: *Who are these boys?* Ss should recognize Mario and Tony from the picture on page 44.
- Ask Ss: *Are Mario and Tony happy?* (No.) Ask: *What's the matter?* Elicit vocabulary and grammar from the unit, for example: *His hands hurt. His leg hurts.*

Presentation

- Read aloud the instructions for Exercise 1. Ask Ss: *What do you see?* Elicit and write on the board any vocabulary about the picture that Ss know, such as: *doctor, patients, medicine.*

Practice

- Direct Ss' attention to Exercise 2. Point to the title of the paragraph and ask: *What's the title?* ("At the Doctor's Office.") Point to the first part of the lesson focus and tell Ss: *Today, you'll read about Mario and Tony at the doctor's office.*

Literacy tip

Make a list of the words for body parts that appear in the reading passage (*leg*, *head*, *arm*, *hands*) and give it to the literacy Ss in your class. Have the literacy Ss match the words on the list with the same words in the reading passage while the rest of the class reads the paragraph silently.

Class Audio CD1 track 44 Play or read the audio program and ask Ss to read along (see audio script, page T-158). Repeat the audio program as needed.

- Read aloud each sentence of the reading and ask Ss to repeat after you.
- Answer any questions Ss have about the reading.

Learner persistence (individual work)

Self-Study Audio CD track 21 Exercise 2 is recorded on the CD at the back of the Student's Book. Ss can listen to the CD at home for reinforcement and review and also for self-directed learning when class attendance is not possible.

Comprehension check

- Read aloud the instructions for Exercise 3.
- Model the task. Point to and read aloud the two column headings. Then point to and read aloud the first item in the chart: *His arm hurts.* Ask Ss: *Tony? Mario?* (Mario.) Point to the reading and ask: *Where is the answer?* Elicit the appropriate sentence from the reading.
- Ss scan the reading and fill out the chart individually. Walk around and help as needed.
- Go over answers with the class. Write the chart from Exercise 3 on the board. Call on Ss to make a check mark in the appropriate column and tell the class where they found the answer in the reading.

Expansion activity (student pairs)

- Direct Ss' attention to the woman with the stomachache in the picture on page 44. With the class, decide what the woman's name might be. Then ask Ss to rewrite the paragraph about Mario and Tony so that it is about the woman, changing the information as needed.
- Help Ss get started by writing the title on the board: *At the Doctor's Office.* Then begin the first sentence with the woman's name, and ask Ss what comes next; for example: *Beatrice is at the doctor's office.*
- Walk around and help as needed, checking to see that Ss write the correct form of *be* for the feminine subject pronoun and the feminine possessive adjective. Follow up by asking different pairs to add a sentence to the paragraph on the board. Ask for a volunteer to read the completed paragraph aloud.

Literacy tip

For an alternative activity, refer literacy Ss to pages 48–49 in the *Literacy Workbook* at any time during the lesson.

LESSON D Reading

Presentation

- Direct Ss' attention to the picture dictionary in Exercise 4. Point to and say the words *Health problems* in the book and in the second part of the lesson focus written on the board. Tell Ss: *Today, we will learn more words for health problems.*
- Read aloud the instructions for Exercise 4A.

Class Audio CD1 track 45 Play or read the audio program (see audio script, page T-158). Listen to Ss' pronunciation as they repeat the words. Correct pronunciation as needed.

Teaching tip

Give pairs of Ss additional practice with the picture dictionary. Ask one S to point to a picture, and ask that S's partner to say the health problem. Then have Ss switch roles. Walk around and help with pronunciation.

Expansion activity (student pairs)

- Write on the board the following sentences: *He has a cold. She has a cold.* Say the sentences aloud and ask Ss to repeat after you.
- Point to the first picture in the picture dictionary and to the sentences on the board. Ask Ss: *Which sentence: "He has a cold." or "She has a cold."?* Elicit: *He has a cold.*
- Write on the board: *He has a headache. She has a headache.* Say the sentences aloud and ask Ss to repeat after you.
- Point to the third picture in the picture dictionary and to the sentences on the board. Ask Ss which sentence is correct. Elicit: *She has a headache.*
- Write the following example conversation on the board:

  A: *What's the matter?*

  B: *He has a cold.*
- Have pairs of Ss practice the conversation using the pictures in the picture dictionary. Model the task by asking one S to point to a picture and ask: *What's the matter?* Ask his or her partner to respond with: *He / She has a* _____.

Learner persistence (individual work)

Self-Study Audio CD track 22 Exercise 4A is recorded on the CD at the back of the Student's Book. Ss can listen to the CD at home for reinforcement and review and also for self-directed learning when class attendance is not possible.

Practice

- Direct Ss' attention to Exercise 4B and read the instructions aloud. Read the example conversation aloud using two different voices as you act out having a cold, for example: pretend to cough and sneeze, and talk as if your nose is stuffy.
- Hold up your Student's Book and indicate all six pictures. Tell Ss: *Act out the health problem.*
- Ss complete the activity in pairs. Walk around and make sure Ss are practicing all the new vocabulary.
- When Ss are finished, ask them to change partners and have new conversations.

Evaluation

- Direct Ss' attention to the lesson focus written on the board. Point to the picture of Mario and Tony at the doctor's office on page 50 and ask Ss: *Where are Mario and Tony?* (At the doctor's office.) If Ss don't understand the question, ask: *Is this a doctor's office?* (Yes.)
- Ask Ss: *What's the matter with Mario? What's the matter with Tony?* Elicit information from the reading, for example: *His leg hurts. His hands hurt.*
- Act out the health problems from the picture dictionary in random order and ask Ss: *What's the matter?* Elicit, for example: *You have a sore throat.*
- Check off each part of the lesson focus as Ss demonstrate understanding of what they have learned in the lesson.

More Ventures, Unit 4, Lesson D	
Literacy Workbook, 15–30 min. **Basic Workbook,** 15–30 min	
Picture Dictionary activities, 30–45 min. **Writing worksheets,** 15–30 min.	www.cambridge.org/myresourceroom
Student Arcade, time varies	www.cambridge.org/venturesarcade

4 Picture dictionary Health problems

1. a cold
2. a fever 
3. a headache 
4. a sore throat 
5. a stomachache 
6. a toothache 

STUDENT TK 22
CLASS CD1 TK 45

A Listen and repeat. Look at the picture dictionary.

B Talk with a partner. Act it out. Ask and answer questions.

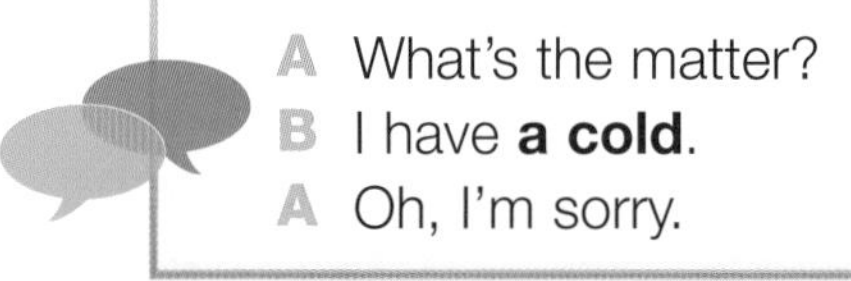

A What's the matter?
B I have **a cold**.
A Oh, I'm sorry.

☑ Read about patients at a doctor's office; use vocabulary for health problems

LESSON **E** Writing

1 Before you write

Talk with a partner. Check (✓) the reason for the visit.

1. Name: *Regina*
Reason for visit:
- ☐ cold
- ☐ fever
- ☐ headache
- ☐ sore throat
- ☐ stomachache
- ☑ toothache

2. Name: *Isaac*
Reason for visit:
- ☐ cold
- ☐ fever
- ☐ headache
- ☑ sore throat
- ☐ stomachache
- ☐ toothache

3. Name: *Joe*
Reason for visit:
- ☐ cold
- ☑ fever
- ☐ headache
- ☐ sore throat
- ☐ stomachache
- ☐ toothache

4. Name: *Esperanza*
Reason for visit:
- ☑ cold
- ☐ fever
- ☐ headache
- ☐ sore throat
- ☐ stomachache
- ☐ toothache

5. Name: *James*
Reason for visit:
- ☐ cold
- ☐ fever
- ☐ headache
- ☐ sore throat
- ☑ stomachache
- ☐ toothache

6. Name: *Sue*
Reason for visit:
- ☐ cold
- ☐ fever
- ☑ headache
- ☐ sore throat
- ☐ stomachache
- ☐ toothache

Lesson objectives

- Review vocabulary from the unit
- Complete a sign-in sheet at the doctor's office

Warm-up and review

- Before class. Write today's lesson focus on the board.
  Lesson E:
  Review words for health problems
  Complete a sign-in sheet at the doctor's office
- Before class. Write the vocabulary from Lesson D in random order on the board: *a cold*, *a fever*, *a headache*, *a sore throat*, *a stomachache*, *a toothache.*
- Begin class. Books closed. Direct Ss' attention to the first part of the lesson focus. Point to and read aloud the vocabulary for health problems written on the board. Ask Ss to repeat the words after you.
- Pantomime one of the health problems; for example, hold your fingers to your temples and look distressed. Ask the class: *What's the matter? or What's my health problem?* Elicit, for example: *A headache. Say to Ss: Right. My head hurts. I have a headache.*
- Call on a S to come to the board and circle the word headache.
- Repeat the procedure with the rest of the words for health problems.

Teaching tip

As you review the vocabulary, encourage Ss to express sympathy with your health problems by saying *Oh, I'm sorry.*

Presentation

- Books open. Direct Ss' attention to the picture in Exercise **1**. Point to each person and ask the class: *What's his / her name? What's his / her health problem?*
- Write a sentence about each person on the board, for example: *Regina has a toothache.* Then go over each sentence, reading it aloud and having Ss repeat it in order to practice the pronunciation of the names and the health problems.

Practice

- Read aloud the instructions for Exercise **1**. Explain the meaning of the word *reason.* Write on the board: *Why?* Tell Ss: *This is the question. The "reason" is the answer.* Use the situations in the picture to give examples. Ask Ss: *Why is Regina at the doctor's office?* Elicit: *Regina has a toothache.* Tell Ss: *Right. That's her reason for going to the doctor.*
- Model the task. Point to the first form and ask Ss: *What's her name?* (Regina.) *What's the reason for her visit to the doctor's office?* (A toothache.) Point to where *toothache* has been checked for number 1.
- Ss work in pairs to complete the forms. Walk around and help as needed.
- When Ss are finished, call on different pairs and say, for example: *Number 2. Isaac. What's the reason for Isaac's visit?* If Ss give any incorrect answers, direct their attention to the appropriate person in the picture, act out the person's symptoms, and say the word for his or her health problem. Make sure Ss have checked the correct boxes.

Literacy tip

Pair literacy Ss with higher-level Ss to complete Exercise **1**. Have the higher-level Ss ask their partners about the people in the picture. The literacy Ss can say the health problems while their partners check the appropriate boxes.

Expansion activity *(whole group)*

- Write in large letters on the board: *Doctor's Office.*
- Ask for six volunteers to sit at the front of the room. Give each volunteer a health problem written on a small piece of paper. Indicate that the volunteers shouldn't say or show their problem to anyone.
- Tell the volunteers: *OK, please act out your health problem.* As the volunteers pretend to have a cold, a sore throat, and so on, ask the class about each person, for example: *What's the matter with Lee? What's the reason for his visit?* Elicit the correct health problem.

Literacy tip

For an alternative activity, refer literacy Ss to pages 50–51 in the *Literacy Workbook* at any time during the lesson.

LESSON E Writing

Practice

- Direct Ss' attention to Exercise 2A and read the instructions aloud. Indicate the partial words in the exercise and tell Ss: *These words need some letters.*
- Model the task. Point to the first item and ask: *What's the health problem?* (Sore throat.) *What letter did "sore" need?* (o.) *What letter did "throat" need?* (o.) Point to the letters written in number 1.
- Tell Ss that if they need help, they can look at the words on page 52.
- Ss complete the words in pairs. Walk around and help as needed.
- When Ss are finished, ask each pair to join another pair and compare their answers.

Presentation

- Direct Ss' attention to Exercise 2B and read the instructions aloud.
- Explain the idea of a sign-in sheet. If you use a sign-in sheet to take attendance, show the sheet to Ss and tell them: *At the doctor's office, you write your name and the reason for your visit.* Otherwise, show Ss a clipboard with a piece of paper or just a page in your notebook. Act out a scene in which you arrive at the doctor's office *(Hello. I need to see the doctor)* and sign in *(Please write your name and the reason for your visit).*
- Point to and read aloud the parts of the sign-in sheet. Read aloud the example sentence or call on a S to read it aloud. Make sure Ss understand that the information they need can be found in the forms on the previous page.
- Point to the last sentence where there is a blank line. Point to students and say: *You have a health problem. Write your name and health problem here.*

Practice

- Ss complete the sign-in sheet individually or in pairs.
- When Ss are finished, call on Ss using the names on the form, for example: *Regina, what's the reason for your visit?* Elicit, for example: *I have a toothache.*

Literacy tip

For Exercise 2B, you might want to write the first letter of each health problem in the appropriate blank in your literacy Ss' books. Then encourage Ss to try to copy the words from Exercise 2A.

Comprehension check

- Direct Ss' attention to Exercise 3 and read the instructions aloud.
- Model the task. Show your sign-in sheet to a S and say one of the sentences in Exercise 2B. Ask that S to read and show you one of his or her sentences.
- Ss share their sentences in pairs. Walk around and spot-check Ss' writing.

Community building *(whole group)*

- Write the six health problems from the lesson on the board. Give Ss a chance to show their practical and cultural knowledge by conducting a class discussion about home remedies for each problem.
- Point to each health problem and ask, for example: *What is good for a fever? What can I do?* Help Ss get started by giving a few examples: *Is cold water good for a fever? Can I take a cold shower?* (Pantomime taking a cold shower.)
- You may need to help extensively with vocabulary. Allow Ss to use bilingual dictionaries or to draw pictures on the board in order to convey their ideas. Do whatever is necessary to make the discussion comprehensible for all Ss in the class.

Evaluation

- Direct Ss' attention to the first part of the lesson focus written on the board. Read the phrase aloud and ask Ss to repeat. Point to the people in the picture on page 52, and ask Ss to say the words for the health problems. Ask different Ss to write the words on the board.
- Direct Ss' attention to the second part of the lesson focus written on the board. Read it aloud and ask Ss to repeat. Draw on the board a sign-in sheet similar to the one in Exercise 2B. Call on individual Ss to write their name and the reason for their visit on the board.
- Check off each part of the lesson focus as Ss demonstrate an understanding of what they have learned in the lesson.

More Ventures, Unit 4, Lesson E	
Literacy Workbook, 15–30 min. **Basic Workbook,** 15–30 min.	
Real Life Document, 15–30 min. **Writing worksheets,** 15–30 min.	www.cambridge.org/myresourceroom

2 Write

A Talk with a partner. Complete the words.

1. s _o_ r e t h r _o_ a t
2. c _o_ l d
3. s t _o_ m a c h a c h e
4. h _e_ a d a c h e
5. f _e_ v e r
6. t _o_ o t h a c h e
7. s _o_ r e h _a_ n d

B Look at page 52. Then complete the patient sign-in sheet.

Patient Sign-In Sheet

Name of Patient	Reason for Visit
Regina	I have a _toothache_ .
Isaac	I have a _sore throat_ .
Joe	I have a _fever_ .
Esperanza	I have a _cold_ .
James	I have a _stomachache_ .
Sue	I have a _headache_ .
________ (you)	I have a _(Answers will vary.)_ .

3 After you write

Talk with a partner. Share your writing.

LESSON F Another view

1 Life-skills reading

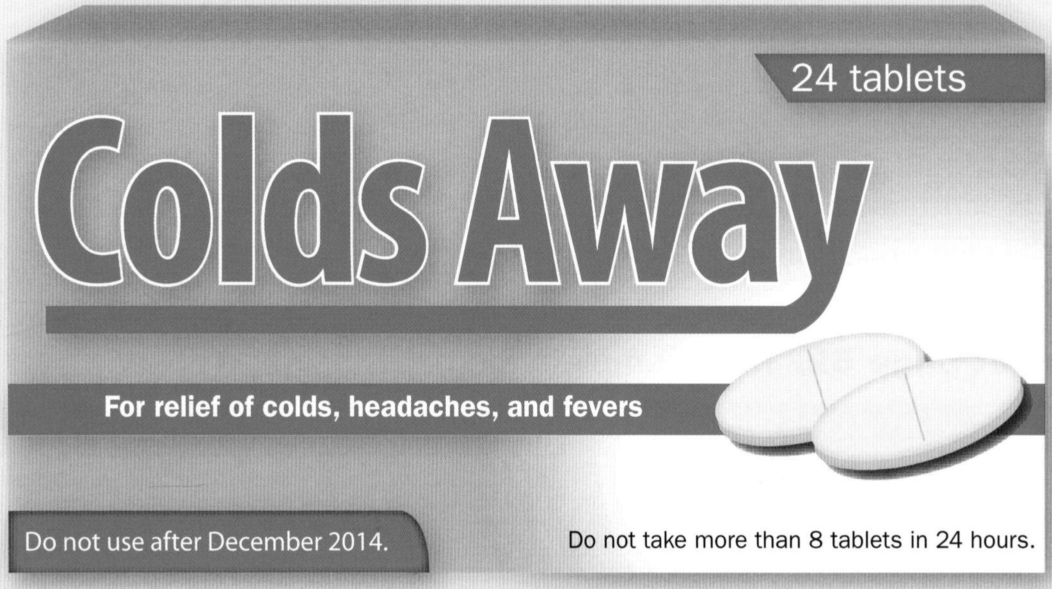

A Read the sentences. Look at the label. Fill in the answer.

1. This medicine is for ____.
   - Ⓐ a sore throat
   - Ⓑ a stomachache
   - ● a cold

2. This medicine is for ____.
   - ● a headache
   - Ⓑ a backache
   - Ⓒ a toothache

3. This medicine is for ____.
   - Ⓐ a stomachache
   - ● a fever
   - Ⓒ a sore throat

4. Do not take this medicine after ____.
   - Ⓐ 2013
   - ● 2014
   - Ⓒ 2015

B Talk with a partner.

What is this medicine not for?

Lesson objectives

- Practice reading a label on a medicine bottle
- Review vocabulary and grammar from the unit
- Complete the self-assessment

Warm-up and review

- Before class. Write today's lesson focus on the board.
  Lesson F:
  Read a medicine label
- Before class. If possible, bring to class real bottles of medicine.
- Begin class. Hold up an example of a real medicine bottle and ask the class: *What is this?* (Medicine.)
- Books closed. Write on the board: *a label.* Say the word aloud and ask Ss to repeat it after you. Ask Ss if they know what a label is. Show Ss the medicine bottles and indicate each bottle's label as you say the word.
- Tell Ss: *You need to read medicine labels. It's very important.* Pantomime reading one of the labels.
- Direct Ss' attention to the lesson focus written on the board and say: *Today, we will read a medicine label.*

Presentation

- Books open. Direct Ss' attention to the medicine label in Exercise **1**. Tell Ss: *This is a medicine label.* Point to and say the words *Colds Away.* Tell Ss that this is the name of the medicine.
- To help Ss preview the medicine label, go over each section and ask comprehension questions. For example, read aloud: *For relief of colds, headaches, and fevers. Ask Ss: What health problems is this medicine for?* (Colds, headaches, and fevers.) Continue in this manner by asking: *How many tablets do we have? When can we use this medicine?*

Teaching tip

As with many reading tasks, Ss do not need to understand every word on the medicine label in order to get the main ideas and complete the exercises. Give a brief overview of the medicine label. Then let Ss try to answer the questions. They may be surprised by how much they understand.

Practice

- Read the instructions for Exercise **1A** aloud. This task helps prepare Ss for standardized-type tests they may have to take.
- Write the first sentence on the board along with the three answer choices labeled *a*, *b*, and *c*.
- Read the item and the answer choices aloud and then point to the medicine label. Ask: *Is the medicine for a sore throat?* Show Ss where to look for the information. Elicit: *No.*
- Point to the three answer choices on the board. Ask Ss: *a*, *b*, or *c*? (c) Fill in the letter *c* and tell Ss: *Fill in the answer in your book*. Make sure Ss understand the task.
- Have Ss individually scan and fill in the correct answers.

Comprehension check

- Go over the answers to Exercise **1A** together. Make sure that Ss followed instructions and filled in their answers. Ask Ss to point to the information on the medicine label.

Application

- Read the instructions and the question in Exercise **1B** aloud. Tell Ss: *Talk with your partner. Ask and answer the question.*
- Ss complete the task in pairs. When Ss are finished, ask for a volunteer to tell the class what the medicine is not for. Accept all plausible answers.

Expansion activity (whole group)

- Go over and explain the new vocabulary from the medicine label: *away*, *relief*, *tablets*, and *Do not use after December 2014.*
- Teach *away* as part of the phrase *go away* using pantomime and gestures.
- Demonstrate *relief* by pretending to have a cold and then feeling better. Tell Ss: *My cold went away!*
- Draw a picture of a tablet as a 3-D circle with a line down the middle.
- Draw a timeline on the board with points labeled *now* and *December 2014.* Use shading and words to indicate the periods before December 2014 (between *now* and *December 2014*) and after December 2014. Explain that the medicine is good in the first period of time but bad after that, so *Do not use after December 2014* means that people should not take the medicine after that month in that year.

Literacy tip

For an alternative activity, refer literacy Ss to pages 52–53 in the *Literacy Workbook* at any time during the lesson.

LESSON F Another view

Presentation

- Books closed. Write on the board: *How many?* Point to your eyes and ask Ss: *How many eyes do I have? One eye? Two eyes?* (Two eyes.) Tell Ss: *I have two eyes.*
- Repeat the procedure with *head*, *arms*, *legs*, *hands*, and *feet*. Finish with the word *ears*. Since Ss have not seen the word ears previously in the unit, be sure to point to your ears, write the word on the board, and practice pronouncing the word with the class.

Practice

- Books open. Direct Ss' attention to the picture of the monster in Exercise 2A. Pretend to be frightened and say, for example: *Eek! It's a monster!*
- Read the instructions for Exercise 2A aloud. Write on the board and say the word *monster.* Ask Ss to repeat the word after you.

> **Teaching tip**
> Feel free to be dramatic and have fun when you talk about the monster in this exercise. Ss will enjoy the creative aspect of the exercise.

- Model the task. Point to and read aloud the two column headings in the chart. Then read aloud the question and the first body part: *How many heads?* Ask Ss: *How many heads does the monster have?* (Two.) Ask Ss: *How many heads do you have?* (One.) Point to where the numbers have been written in the chart.
- Ss complete the chart individually. Walk around and help as needed.
- Read aloud the second part of the instructions for Exercise 2A.
- Write on the board: *The monster has _____. I have _____.* Read aloud each sentence using the numbers in the example from the chart: *The monster has two heads. I have one head.* Ask Ss to repeat the sentences after you. Encourage Ss to use complete sentences as they compare charts with their partners.

Expansion activity (student pairs)

- Ask Ss to take out a piece of paper and draw a picture of a different monster.
- Have Ss share their pictures in pairs and talk about how many of each body part their monsters have.

Practice

- Direct Ss' attention to Exercise 2B. Ask the class: *What do the words need?* (Letters.) Read the instructions aloud.
- Model the task. Point to the first item and ask: *What's the word?* (Patient.) *What letter does "patient" need?* (i) Point to the letter *i* written for number 1.
- Ss complete the words individually or in pairs. When Ss have finished, ask volunteers to write the words on the board.
- Read aloud the second part of the instructions in Exercise 2B.
- Model the task. Point to the first item and ask Ss: *What letter do we need in number 1?* (i) Read aloud the numbers under the blanks in the new word and stop when you get to number 1. Tell Ss: *Write the letter "i" for number 1.* Make sure Ss understand the task.
- Ask a volunteer to write the new word on the board.

Evaluation

- Before asking Ss to turn to the self-assessment on page 139, do a quick review of the unit. Have Ss turn to Lesson A. Ask the class to talk about what they remember about this lesson. Prompt Ss, if necessary, with questions, for example: *What words are on this page? What do you see in the picture?* Continue in this manner to review each lesson quickly.
- **Self-assessment** Read the instructions for Exercise 3. Ask Ss to turn to the self-assessment page and complete the unit self-assessment.
- If Ss are ready, administer the unit test on pages T-174–T-176 of this Teacher's Edition (or on the Assessment Audio CD / CD-ROM).

More Ventures, Unit 4, Lesson F	
Literacy Workbook, 15–30 min.	
Basic Workbook, 15–30 min.	
Writing worksheets, 15–30 min.	www.cambridge.org/myresourceroom

2 Fun with vocabulary

A Complete the chart. How many?

	The monster	You
heads	2	1
eyes	6	2
ears	8	2
arms	5	2
legs	4	2
feet	4	2

Talk with a partner. Compare your answers.

B Write the missing letters.

p a t _i_ e n t (1)

f _e_ e t (2)

s t o _m_ a c h (3)

_n_ u r s e (4)

t o o t h a _c_ h e (5)

_d_ o c t o r (6)

o f f _i_ c e (7)

_e_ y e (8)

Write the letters. Make a word.

m	e	d	i	c	i	n	e
3	2	6	1	5	7	4	8

3 Wrap up

Complete the **Self-assessment** on page 139.

Review

1 Listening

Read. Then listen and circle.

CLASS CD1 TK 46

1. Who is Sonya?
   (a.) Tom's aunt
   b. Tom's brother
2. Who is David?
   a. Tom's aunt
   (b.) Tom's brother
3. Who is Tina?
   a. Ray's sister
   (b.) Ray's wife
4. Who is Jay?
   (a.) Barbara's son
   b. Barbara's brother
5. What hurts?
   a. her hand
   (b.) her head
6. What hurts?
   a. his leg
   (b.) his foot

Talk with a partner. Ask and answer.

2 Vocabulary

Write. Complete the story.

cold | doctor's office | medicine | patients | stomach

A Visit to the Doctor

Marisa and her family are at the *doctor's office* (1). They are *patients* (2). Peter is Marisa's son. His *stomach* (3) hurts. Antonia is Marisa's daughter. She has a *cold* (4). They need *medicine* (5). Marisa isn't happy. She has a headache!

Lesson objectives

- Review vocabulary and grammar from Units 3 and 4
- Introduce the pronunciation of *e* as in read, *i* as in *five*, and *u* as in *June*

UNITS 3 & 4

Warm-up and review

- Before class. Write today's lesson focus on the board.
  Review unit:
  Review vocabulary and grammar from Units 3 and 4.
  Pronounce "e" as in "read," "i" as in "five," and "u" as in "June."
- Begin class. Books open. Direct Ss' attention to the lesson focus written on the board.
- Review vocabulary from Unit 3. Direct Ss' attention to the family picture on page 34. Ask individual Ss, for example:
  What's the grandmother's name? (Olga.)
  What's the grandfather's name? (Peter.)
  Who is Vera? (Sam and Sophie's aunt; Mike and Dave's sister; Peter and Olga's daughter.)
  Who is Mike's mother? (Olga.)
  Who is Sophie's father? (Dave.)
  Do Peter and Olga have a son? (Yes, they have two sons: Mike and Dave.)
  Do Dave and Susan have a daughter? (Yes: Sophie.)

Teaching tip

Write the above questions on the board if it would help your Ss' comprehension. On the other hand, if your Ss struggle with reading, present the questions orally. The point of the questions is to help Ss retrieve previously learned vocabulary, so present them in the way that is easiest for your Ss to understand.

Practice

- Direct Ss' attention to Exercise **1** and read the instructions aloud. Read the question and answer choices in number 1 aloud.

Class Audio CD1 track 46 Model the task. Play or read only the first conversation on the audio program (see audio script, page T-158). Point to the two answer choices in number 1 and ask: *Tom's aunt or Tom's brother?* (Tom's aunt.) Point to where the letter *a* has been circled.

- Read aloud the remaining questions and answer choices. Say: *Now listen and circle the correct answers.*

Class Audio CD1 track 46 Play or read the complete audio program (see audio script, page T-158). Ss listen and circle the correct answers. Repeat the audio program as needed.

- Check answers with the class. Read each question aloud and call on different Ss to answer.

Teaching tip

After Ss read their answers to the questions, play the audio program again to check their answers.

- Read aloud the second part of the instructions for Exercise **1**. Ss practice asking and answering the questions in pairs. Walk around and help as needed.
- Ask several pairs to ask and answer the questions for the rest of the class.

Practice

- Direct Ss' attention to Exercise **2**. Point to the title of the story and ask: *What's the title?* (A Visit to the Doctor.) Help Ss by reading the title aloud if necessary.
- Read aloud the instructions for Exercise **2**. Point to the words in the word bank and tell Ss: *Write these words in the story.*
- Model the task. Read aloud the beginning of the first sentence: *Marisa and her family are at the . . .* Elicit: *doctor's office.* Point to *doctor's office* in the word bank and in the blank for number 1.
- Ss read the story and fill in the blanks individually. Walk around and help as needed.
- Write the numbers *1–5* on the board. Ask Ss to come up to the board to write the answers.
- Read the story aloud using Ss' answers. If there is an error, say: *This is not correct. Who has a different answer?* Make any necessary corrections on the board.

Comprehension check

- Ask Ss comprehension questions about the reading, for example:
  Who is Peter? (Marisa's son.) *Who is Antonia?* (Marisa's daughter.)
  What's the matter with Peter? What hurts? (His stomach hurts. / He has a stomachache.)
  What's the matter with Antonia? (She has a cold.)
  What do the children need? (Medicine.)
  What's the matter with Marisa? (She's not happy. She has a headache.)

Review

Warm-up and review

- Review singular and plural nouns from Unit 4. Direct Ss' attention to the picture of Mario and Tony on page 50. Ask Ss: *What's the matter with Tony? What hurts?* (His leg, his head.) Ask Ss: *What's the matter with Mario? What hurts?* (His arm, his hands.)
- Draw one side of a human figure on the board with one eye, one arm, one leg, and one foot. Elicit singular nouns by pointing to the body parts and saying: *He / She has one* _____. Then complete the drawing on the board and elicit plural nouns: *He / She has two* _____.

Practice

- Direct Ss to Exercise **3A**. Read the instructions aloud.
- Model the task. Read the question in number 1: *What hurts? His leg or legs?* (Leg.) Point to where *leg* has been circled and written for number 1.
- Ss circle and write their answers individually. Check answers by calling on Ss to read the sentences aloud. As Ss read the sentences, write their answers on the board.

> **Teaching tip**
> If Ss need to review short answers with *do*, go over the grammar chart on page 36. Then ask questions using *you* (singular) and *you* (plural), for example: *Do you* (a student) *have a brother? Do you* (the class) *have your books?*

- Direct Ss to Exercise **3B**. Read the instructions aloud.
- Model the task. Read the question in number 1 without the first word: *Hmm . . . you have a daughter?* Ask Ss: *Do or don't? (Do.)* Point to where *Do* has been written for number 1, and read the complete question aloud.
- Ss complete the questions individually. Check answers by calling on Ss to read the sentences aloud.

Expansion activity (whole group)

- Before class. Create a chart similar to the one on page 37 in Unit 3, but with words for school supplies in the left-hand column.
- Have Ss walk around and ask at least three classmates the questions from the chart; for example: *Do you have a pencil?* Ask Ss to answer using *Yes, I do. / No, I don't.*

Presentation

- Direct Ss' attention to the second part of the lesson focus written on the board.
- Write on the board: *read, need.* Point to and say each word and ask Ss to repeat. Underline the vowels in each of the words. Say a long e /iː/ sound before repeating each word, for example: /iː/, *read*. Ask Ss to repeat after you.
- Write on the board: *five, write.* Repeat the procedure, underlining the *i* and pronouncing a long i /aː/ sound.
- Write on the board: *June, rule.* Repeat the procedure, underlining the *u* and pronouncing a long u /uː/ sound.

Practice

Class Audio CD1 track 47 Direct Ss' attention to Exercise **4A** and read the instructions aloud. Play or read the audio program (see audio script, page T-158). Ss listen to examples of the three vowel sounds.

Class Audio CD1 track 48 Direct Ss' attention to Exercise **4B** and read the instructions aloud. Play or read the audio program (see audio script, page T-158). Ss listen and repeat what they hear.

- Read aloud the second part of the instructions for Exercise **4B**. Model the task. Point to the three charts and tell one S: *Say a word.* After that S says any word from the charts, tell his or her partner: *Point to the word.*
- Ss complete the task in pairs. Help as needed.

Class Audio CD1 track 49 Direct Ss' attention to Exercise **4C** and read the instructions aloud. Model the task. Play or read the first word on the audio program (see audio script, page T-158). Ask: *Which letter is it:* e, i, *or* o? (i) Point to where the letter has been checked.

Class Audio CD1 track 49 Play or read the complete audio program (see audio script, page T-158). Ss listen and make a checkmark under the letter they hear.

Class Audio CD1 track 49 Reproduce the chart from Exercise **4C** on the board, and play or read the audio program again. Pause after each word and ask a S to check the appropriate letter in the chart on the board.

Evaluation

- Direct Ss' attention to the lesson focus on the board.
- Draw on the board a simple family tree. Identify people by name and whether they are male or female. Ask Ss questions about the people; for example: *Who is Martina?*
- Ask as many Ss as possible: *What hurts?* Have Ss act out and say a health problem; for example: *My feet hurt.*
- Give each S a slip of paper with a number and a part of the body, for example: *2 feet, 3 heads, 1 eye, 2 ears,* and so on. Have each S ask a classmate the question: *Do you have* _____? Classmates should answer: *Yes, I do. / No, I don't.*
- Write on the board: *need, write, rule.* Call on individual Ss as you point to one of the words and ask them to say it. Listen to the vowel sounds and help as needed.
- Check off each part of the lesson focus as Ss demonstrate an understanding of what they have learned in the lesson.

3 Grammar

A Read and circle. Then write.

1. What hurts? His ___leg___.
   (leg) legs
2. What hurts? His ___arms___.
   arm (arms)
3. What hurts? Her ___hand___.
   (hand) hands
4. What hurts? Her ___foot___.
   (foot) feet

B Complete the sentences. Use *do* or *don't*.

A ___Do___(1) you have a daughter?
B Yes, we ___do___(2).

A ___Do___(3) you have a son?
B Yes, we ___do___(4).

A ___Do___(5) you have a sister?
B No, I ___don't___(6).

4 Pronunciation

CLASS CD1 TK 47

A Listen to the *e* sound, the *i* sound, and the *u* sound.

e	i	u
read	five	June

CLASS CD1 TK 48

B Listen and repeat.

e	read	need

i	five	write

u	June	rule

Talk with a partner. Say a word. Your partner points. Take turns.

CLASS CD1 TK 49

C Listen and check (✓).

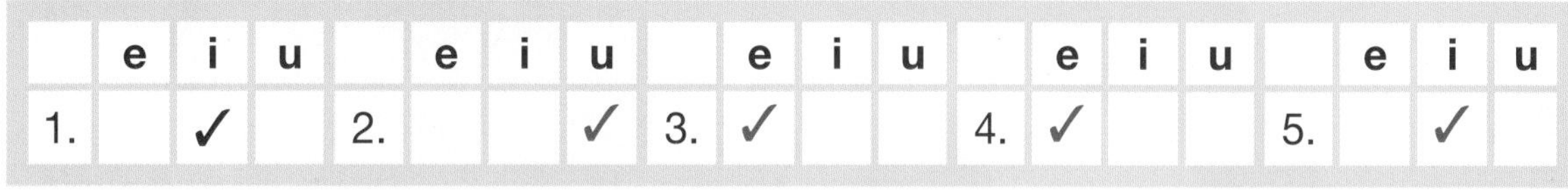

	e	i	u		e	i	u		e	i	u		e	i	u		e	i	u
1.		✓		2.			✓	3.	✓			4.	✓			5.		✓	

UNIT
5 Around town

LESSON A Listening

1 Before you listen

A Look at the picture. What do you see?

CLASS CD1 TK 50

B Listen and point: bank • library • restaurant school • street • supermarket

Lesson objectives
- Introduce Ss to the topic
- Find out what Ss know about the topic
- Preview the unit by talking about the picture
- Practice key vocabulary
- Practice listening skills

UNIT 5

Warm-up and review

- Before class. Write today's lesson focus on the board.

  Lesson A:
  Places and locations
- Before class. Place a few classroom objects in various places, such as on the table, on the desk, and on the floor.
- Begin class. Books closed. Write on the board: *Where?* Remind Ss of the meaning of this question word, and recycle vocabulary for classroom objects by asking questions, such as: *Where's my notebook? Where's my stapler?* Elicit correct responses from Ss.
- Point to the lesson focus *places and locations* written on the board. Say the words and have Ss repeat after you. Tell Ss: *"Where" tells us about places and locations.* Gesture to the room around you and ask: *Where are we?* Elicit: *in the classroom*; *at school*; etc.
- Write on the board the name of the school or other place where your class is held. Say the name and tell Ss: *This is a "place."* Ask Ss if they can think of some other places in your community.

Literacy tip

For an alternative activity, refer literacy Ss to pages 54–55 in the *Literacy Workbook* at any time during the lesson.

Literacy tip

If you have literacy Ss in your class, it might be helpful to spend time at the beginning of any activity that contains art or photos talking about the pictures before focusing Ss' attention on the printed words in the exercise. Have Ss work in pairs. Tell them to ask each other: *What do you see?* Encourage Ss to describe the pictures to each other. Consider pairing literacy Ss with Ss who can help them read the text in the exercise. This will help preview the exercise for literacy Ss and make them more confident as the exercise continues.

Presentation

- Books open. Set the scene. Hold up the Student's Book. Show Ss the picture on page 58. Tell the class: *These are places.*
- Ask: *What do you see?* Elicit and write on the board any vocabulary that Ss know, such as: *school*, *street*, *car*, *bicycle*, *buildings*, *bench.*

Practice

- Direct Ss' attention to the key vocabulary in Exercise **1B**. Read aloud each word or phrase while pointing to the corresponding part of the picture. Ask Ss to repeat and point.

Class Audio CD1 track 50 Play or read the audio program (see audio script, page T-158). Tell Ss: *Listen and point to the picture.* As Ss hear the key vocabulary, check to see that they are pointing to the correct part of the picture. Repeat the audio program as needed.

Comprehension check

- Ask Ss *Yes / No* questions about the picture. Tell Ss: *Listen. Say "yes" or "no."*

  Point to the bank. Ask: *Is this a bank?* (Yes.)
  Point to the school. Ask: *Is this a restaurant?* (No.)
  Point to the woman leaving the bakery. Ask: *Is this a woman?* (Yes.)
  Point to the woman's child. Ask: *Is this a boy?* (No.)
  Point to the school. Ask: *Is this a school?* (Yes.)
  Point to the library. Ask: *Is this a supermarket?* (No.)
  Point to the supermarket. Ask: *Is this a supermarket?* (Yes.)

Expansion activity *(whole group)*

- Recycle the *'s* possessive from Unit 3, using some of the names for places in the picture.
- Remind Ss of the *'s* possessive form by writing a few phrases for family relationships on the board, for example: *Dave's wife*, *Sophie's mother*, *Vera's brother.* Circle the *'s* in each name and ask Ss: *What is this? What does it mean?* Elicit from Ss some explanation of possession – for example, that *Dave has a wife.*
- Write on the board: *Jim's Barbershop*, *Sal's Bakery*, *Rosie's Restaurant.* Point to and say the name of each business, and ask Ss to repeat after you.
- Circle the *'s* in each name and ask Ss: *What is this? What does it mean?* Make sure Ss understand that the businesses in some way belong to the people – for example, that *Jim has a barbershop.*

LESSON A Listening

Presentation

- Direct Ss' attention to the words in Exercise 2A. Say each word aloud and ask Ss to repeat after you.
- Ask Ss questions to elicit the new vocabulary.

  Draw a dollar sign on the board. Say: *I need money. Where can I get money?* (Bank.)
  Hold up a book. Say: *I need books. Where can I get books?* (Library; or possibly school.)
  Rub your hand on your stomach. Say: *I'm hungry. Where can I get food?* (Supermarket, restaurant.)
  Pantomime hands on a steering wheel. Say: *I'm in my car. Where can I drive my car?* (Street.)
  Say: *I need to learn English. Where can I learn English?* (School.)
- Read aloud the instructions for Exercise 2A.

Practice

Class Audio CD1 track 51 Play or read the audio program (see audio script, page T-158). Ss listen and repeat the vocabulary. Repeat the audio program as needed.

- Listen carefully to Ss' pronunciation and make corrections as needed.

Learner persistence (individual work)

Self-Study Audio CD track 23 Exercise 2A is recorded on the CD at the back of the Student's Book. Ss can listen to the CD at home for reinforcement and review. They can also listen to the CD for self-directed learning when class attendance is not possible.

- Direct Ss' attention to Exercise 2B and read the instructions aloud.

Class Audio CD1 track 52 Model the task. Hold up the Student's Book and say: *Number one.* Play or read the audio program for number 1 (see audio script, page T-158). Point to the two answer choices in number 1 and ask Ss: *What did you hear – a or b?* Elicit: *a*. Point to the letter *a* next to the first picture and tell Ss: *Circle the letter "a."*

Class Audio CD1 track 52 Play or read the complete audio program (see audio script, page T-158). Ss listen and circle the correct answers. Repeat the audio as needed.

Class Audio CD1 track 52 Read aloud the second part of the instructions for Exercise 2B. Play or read the audio program again so that Ss can listen and check their answers.

Learner persistence (individual work)

Self-Study Audio CD track 24 Exercise 2B is recorded on the CD at the back of the Student's Book. Ss can listen to the CD at home for reinforcement and review and also for self-directed learning when class attendance is not possible.

Comprehension check

- Write the numbers *1–4* on the board. Ask a few Ss to come to the board and write the correct answers to Exercise 2B next to the numbers.

Class Audio CD1 track 52 Play or read the audio program again. Pause the audio program after each conversation. Point to the answer written on the board and ask: *Is this correct?* Ask another S to make any necessary corrections.

Application

- Direct Ss' attention to Exercise 3 and read the instructions aloud.
- Model the task. Hold up the Student's Book and point to the pictures in Exercise 2B. Say to one S: *Point to a picture.* Say to the first S's partner: *Say the word.*
- Ss complete the exercise in pairs. Walk around and help as needed.

Expansion activity (student pairs)

- Have Ss practice the conversations from Exercise 2B in pairs. Ask Ss to turn to the self-study audio script on page 155 in the Student's Book.
- Ask Ss to choose Role A or B and read aloud the conversations. Then have Ss switch roles and read the conversations again. Walk around and help as needed.

Evaluation

- Direct Ss' attention to the lesson focus written on the board. Write the key vocabulary words in random places around the board. Then call on Ss to come up to the board and point to the word you say.
- Ask Ss questions similar to the ones you used in the presentation of Exercise 2A; for example: *Where can I get money?* (Bank.) *Where can I learn English?* (School.)
- Check off each part of the lesson focus as Ss demonstrate an understanding of what they have learned in the lesson.

More Ventures, Unit 5, Lesson A	
Literacy Workbook, 15–30 min.	
Basic Workbook, 15–30 min.	
Writing worksheets, 15–30 min.	www.cambridge.org/myresourceroom
Student Arcade, time varies	www.cambridge.org/venturesarcade

Unit Goals

Identify places around town
Identify places on a map
Draw a map and write about it

2 Listen

STUDENT TK 23
CLASS CD1 TK 51

A Listen and repeat.

1. bank 2. library 3. restaurant
4. school 5. street 6. supermarket

STUDENT TK 24
CLASS CD1 TK 52

B Listen and circle.

1. (a.) 

b. 

2. a. 
(b.) 

3. a. 

(b.) 

4. (a.) 
b. 

Listen again. Check your answers.

3 After you listen

Talk with a partner. Point to a picture.
Your partner says the word.

LESSON **B** Places around town

1 Vocabulary focus

CLASS CD1 TK 53

Listen and repeat.

1. pharmacy

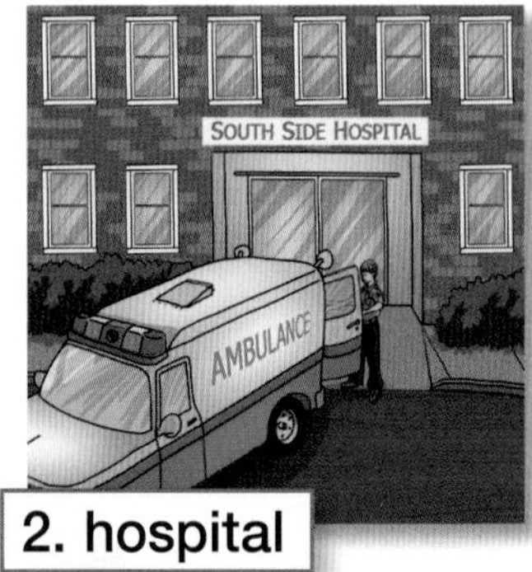

2. hospital

3. laundromat

4. post office

5. movie theater

6. gas station

2 Practice

A Read and match.

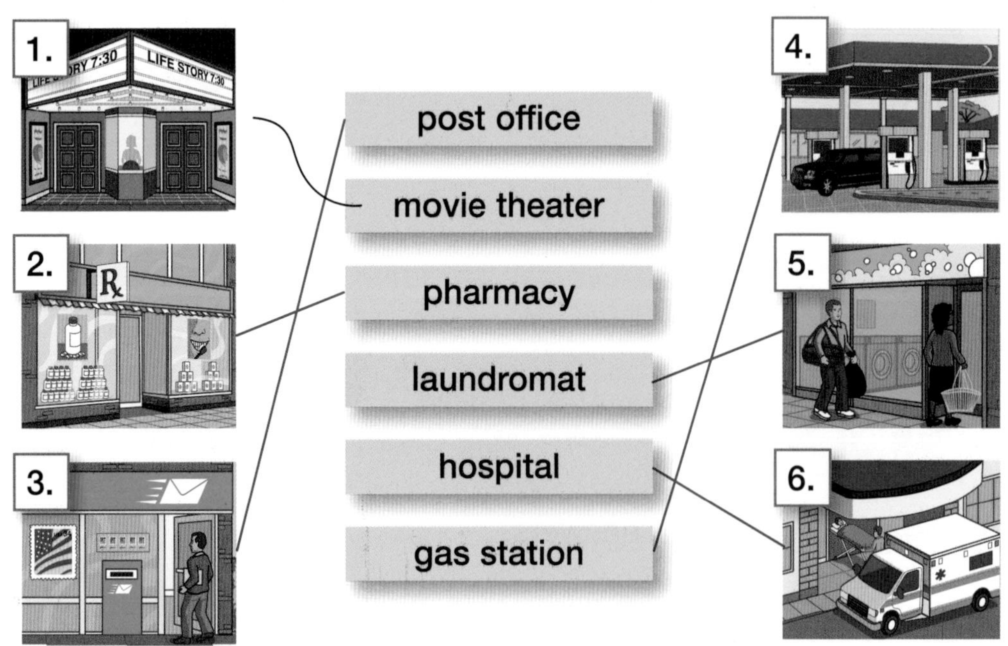

Lesson objectives

- Introduce additional vocabulary for buildings and places
- Practice identifying buildings and places
- Practice asking and answering questions about where someone is

Warm-up and review

- Before class. Write today's lesson focus on the board.
  Lesson B:
  Places around town
  Where's Minh?
- Before class. Find or draw large, simple images that correspond with the key vocabulary from Lesson A, for example: a magazine picture of a plate of spaghetti (for *restaurant*) or a bag of groceries (for *supermarket*).
- Begin class. Books open. Point to and say each of the key vocabulary items from Lesson A and ask Ss to repeat after you. Then tape the pictures under the words in random order across the board. Tell the class: *We need to match the words and the pictures. Match.*
- Ask a volunteer to come to the board. Tell the class, for example: *Felipe needs help. Help him match the words and the pictures.* Tell the volunteer: *Listen. Your classmates will help you.*
- Encourage Ss to call out advice as the volunteer draws lines between the words and the pictures. When the class is satisfied with the matches, erase any lines that are incorrect. Ask for a different volunteer to fix the errors.

Presentation

- Point to the words *Places around town* at the top of page 60 in the Student's Book. Say the words aloud and ask Ss to repeat after you. Point to the vocabulary from Lesson A written on the board and tell Ss: *These are places.*
- Explain the meaning of *around town* by writing on the board *town*, *city*, and the name of the community where you live. Hold up your Student's Book and show Ss the picture on page 58. Tell Ss: *A town or a city has places like banks, restaurants, and libraries.*
- Direct Ss' attention to the pictures in Exercise **1**. Tell Ss: *Today, you will learn more words for places.* Read aloud the instructions for Exercise **1**.

Class Audio CD1 track 53 Play or read the audio program (see audio script, page T-158). Listen and repeat the vocabulary along with Ss. Repeat the audio program as needed.

- Listen carefully to Ss' pronunciation and correct as needed.

> **Teaching tip**
> Exploit the art in this exercise by asking Ss questions similar to the ones you asked for the presentation of Exercise **2A** in Lesson A. For example, say: *I need a doctor. Where can I see a doctor?* (hospital.) *My father needs gas. Where can he go?* (gas station)

Practice

- Direct Ss' attention to Exercise **2A**. As you read aloud the instructions, hold up the Student's Book and indicate that Ss should look at the pictures of places and match them to the corresponding words.
- Model the task. Hold up the Student's Book. Point to the first picture. Ask: *What place is this?* (Movie theater.) Say: *Match the picture with the word.*
- Ss complete the exercise individually. Help as needed.

> **Literacy tip**
> Ask higher-level Ss to work with literacy Ss on Exercise **2A**. Have the higher-level Ss point to and read aloud the words while the literacy Ss draw the lines to the pictures.

Comprehension check

- Write the numbers *1–6* on the board. Ask a few Ss to come to the board and write the answers to Exercise **2A** on the board.
- Ask different Ss to read the answers written on the board. After each answer is read, ask: *Is this correct?* Ask another S to make corrections on the board.

Community building (small groups)

- Create a matching exercise with the names of local, well-known places in one column and the vocabulary from the unit in the other. Include the names of, for example, a pharmacy, a restaurant, a street, a hospital, a movie theater, and a drugstore. Give each group of 3 or 4 Ss a copy of the handout and ask them to work together to match the names and the places.
- Go over the answers with the class, and if possible, have Ss share what they know about the places. If a discussion is not possible, ask Ss to point in the direction of the places. Ask, for example: *Which way is Summit Street?* Point in various directions to illustrate the meaning of your question.

> **Literacy tip**
> For an alternative activity, refer literacy Ss to pages 56–57 in the *Literacy Workbook* at any time during the lesson.

LESSON B Places around town

Presentation

- Direct Ss' attention to the pictures in Exercise **2B** and to the word bank. Read each word aloud and ask Ss to repeat after you. Indicate the pictures and ask Ss: *Which picture shows the pharmacy?* (Number 3, the picture with Mr. Lopez.) Do the same with the other places and pictures.
- Go over the names by pointing to each picture and saying, for example: *This is Minh. Minh. Please repeat.*

Practice

- Read aloud the first set of instructions for Exercise **2B**.
- Class Audio CD1 track 54 Model the task. Say: *Listen and repeat.* Play or read the audio program for number 1 (see audio script, page T-158), and point to Minh in the picture as you repeat. Say: *Then write.* Point to the words *movie theater* written in the chart. Make sure Ss understand the task.
- Class Audio CD1 track 54 Play or read the complete audio program (see audio script, page T-158). Ss listen and repeat. Encourage Ss to point to the people in the pictures as they repeat.
- Ss complete the chart individually, using the words from the word bank. Repeat the audio program as needed.
- Check answers with the class. Write the numbers *1–6* on the board, and ask for volunteers to write their answers on the board, Make any necessary corrections.

Literacy tip

Your literacy Ss may need an alternate assignment to Exercise **2B**. You could, for example, photocopy the pictures from Exercise **1** on page 60, covering the labels. Then ask Ss to find the words from the pictures in the word box. Model this process by starting with number 5, the movie theater. Point to the words on the building and then scan the word box and circle *movie theater*.

- Read aloud the second part of the instructions for Exercise **2B**. Point to and model the example conversation.
- Call on a pair of volunteers to read the example conversation aloud for the class.
- Point to another person in the pictures on page 61. Ask: *Where's (name)?* Elicit the answer from a volunteer. Repeat with different people and places in the pictures. Indicate that Ss should ask and answer questions about all the people and places in the pictures.
- Ss complete the exercise in pairs. Walk around and help as needed.
- When Ss are finished, ask them where each person is. Make sure Ss answer using the phrase, *At the* ______.

Application

- Direct Ss' attention to Exercise **3** and read the instructions aloud.
- Read aloud the example conversation in Exercise **3** as you point to the picture.
- Write on the board the questions: *Where is he? Where is she?* Read each question aloud and ask Ss to repeat after you. Point to the people in the pictures in Exercise **2B** as you repeat the questions to reinforce the difference between *he* and *she*.
- Model the task. Ask two Ss to stand beside you. Pantomime being at a movie theater, for example, eating popcorn and staring at an imaginary screen. S1 asks: *Where is she?* S2 guesses: *At the movie theater?* You say: *Right!*
- Ask S1 to pantomime being at a different place. S2 asks: *Where is he?* You guess. S1 says *Right!* or *No!* Make sure Ss understand the task.
- Ss play the guessing game in small groups. Walk around and help as needed. Then ask each group to pantomime one place for the rest of the class.

Expansion activity *(small groups)*

- Before class. Create cards for a "Concentration" game using the six people's names and the six places from the lesson. Each group needs one set of 12 cards.
- Place all of the cards facedown in three rows of four cards on a desk or table where Ss can see the cards easily. The first S turns over two cards. If the cards match, the S must make a sentence with the matching cards, for example: *Isabel is at the gas station.* If the sentence is correct, the S keeps the cards. If the cards don't match, the S puts the cards back. Then the second S tries to find a matching pair. The game continues until all the matching pairs have been found. The winner is the person with the most cards.

Evaluation

- Direct Ss' attention to the lesson focus written on the board. Point to Exercise **2B** and ask individual Ss about the location of people in the exercise: *Where's Minh?* (At the movie theater.) Then have Ss ask their classmates the questions.
- Check off each part of the lesson focus as Ss demonstrate an understanding of what they have learned in the lesson.

More Ventures, Unit 5, Lesson B	
Literacy Workbook, 15–30 min. **Basic Workbook,** 15–30 min.	
Writing worksheets, 15–30 min.	www.cambridge.org/myresourceroom
Student Arcade, time varies	www.cambridge.org/venturesarcade

CLASS CD1 TK 54

B Listen and repeat. Then write.

gas station hospital laundromat
movie theater pharmacy post office

1. Minh

2. Alan

3. Mr. Lopez

4. Paula

5. Jackie

6. Isabel

Name	Place	Name	Place
1. Minh	*movie theater*	4. Paula	*laundromat*
2. Alan	*hospital*	5. Jackie	*post office*
3. Mr. Lopez	*pharmacy*	6. Isabel	*gas station*

Talk with a partner. Ask and answer.

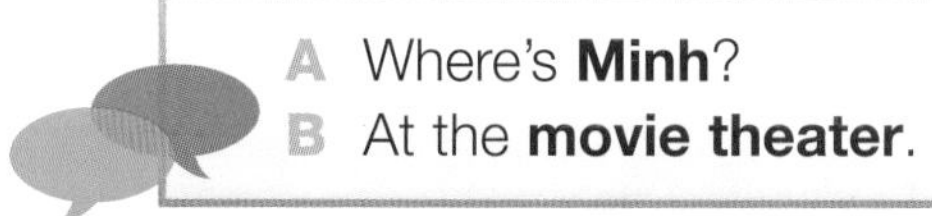

A Where's **Minh**?
B At the **movie theater**.

3 Communicate

Work in a group. Play a game. Ask and guess.

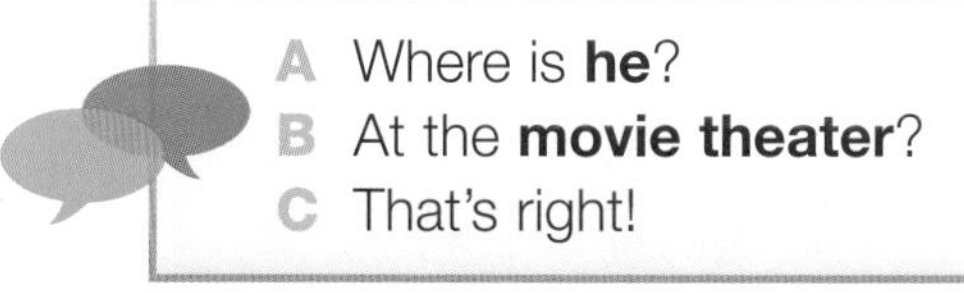

A Where is **he**?
B At the **movie theater**?
C That's right!

LESSON C The school is on Main Street.

1 Grammar focus: *on, next to, across from, between*

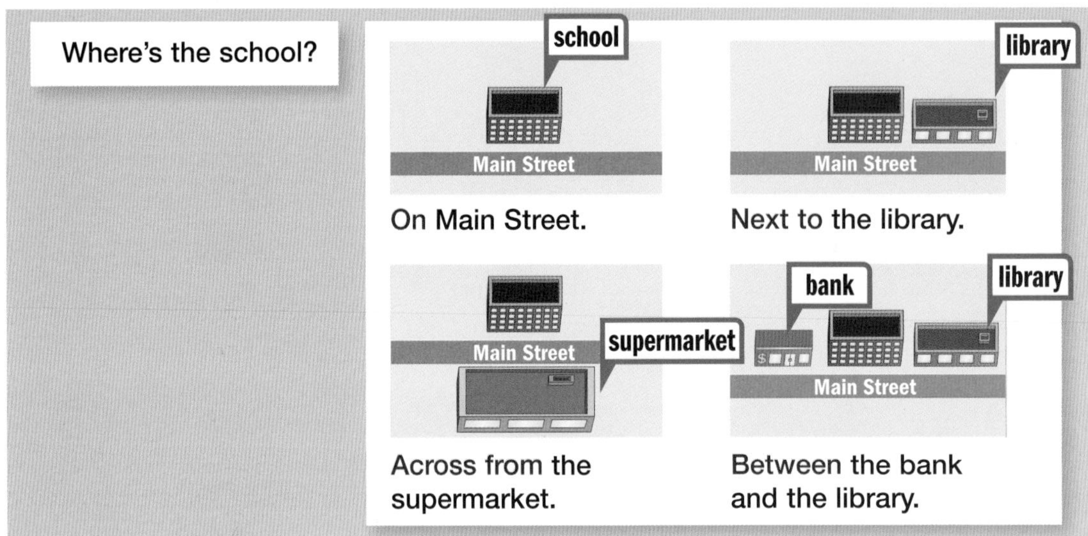

2 Practice

A Read and circle. Then write.

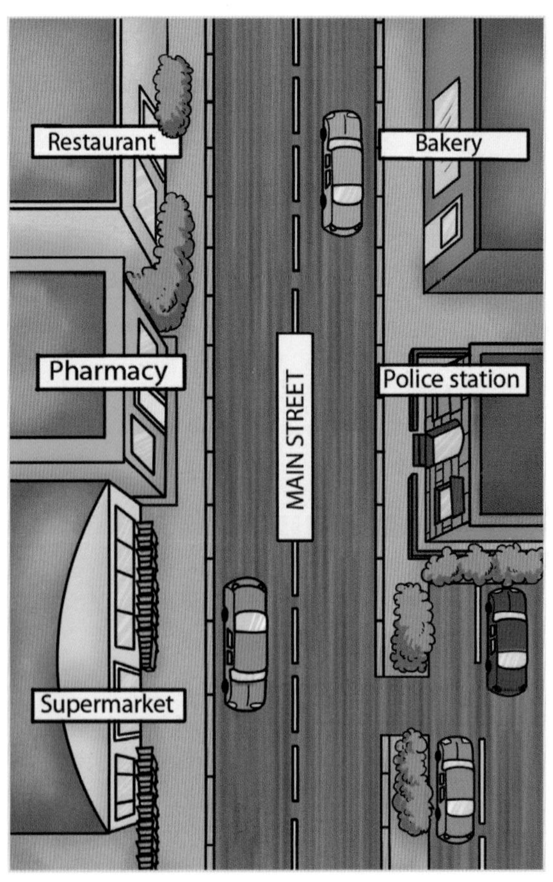

1. A Where's the pharmacy?
   B ___Between___ the restaurant
   (Between) Across from
   and the supermarket.
2. A Where's the supermarket?
   B ___On___ Main Street.
   Across from (On)
3. A Where's the restaurant?
   B ___Next to___ the pharmacy.
   Between (Next to)
4. A Where's the bakery?
   B ___Across from___ the restaurant.
   Next to (Across from)
5. A Where's the police station?
   B ___Next to___ the bakery.
   On (Next to)

CLASS CD1 TK 55

Listen and repeat. Then practice with a partner.

Lesson objectives

- Introduce the prepositions of location *on*, *next to*, *across from*, *between*
- Practice asking and answering questions about the location of buildings and places

Warm-up and review

- Before class. Write today's lesson focus on the board.
  Lesson C:
  on, next to, across from, between
  Where's the school?
- Before class. Write on the board the vocabulary from Lessons A and B: *bank*, *library*, *restaurant*, *school*, *street*, *supermarket*, *pharmacy*, *hospital*, *laundromat*, *movie theater*, *post office*, *gas station*.
- Begin class. Books open. Point to and say the vocabulary words and ask Ss to repeat after you.
- Direct Ss' attention to the picture on page 58. Say the first six vocabulary words again, and ask Ss to point to the corresponding parts of the picture. Walk around and check to see that Ss are pointing to the correct items in the picture.
- Direct Ss' attention to the six pictures on page 60. Say the next six vocabulary words and ask Ss to point to the corresponding picture. Walk around and check to see that Ss are pointing to the correct pictures.

Presentation

- Point to the first part of the lesson focus written on the board. Say each word or phrase aloud and ask Ss to repeat it after you. Tell Ss: *These words tell us where places are.*
- Direct Ss' attention to the grammar chart in Exercise **1** on page 62. Read the question aloud and ask Ss to repeat after you. Then do the same with the prepositional phrases.
- To show the question-and-answer relationship between the question and the prepositional phrases, say to a S: *Please say the question.* Elicit: *Where's the school?* Answer the question with one of the prepositional phrases.
- Repeat the procedure with at least three more Ss, each time answering with the phrases from the grammar box.
- Finally, have Ss practice asking and answering the question in pairs while pointing to the pictures and phrases in the grammar chart.

Literacy tip

Lesson C presents several challenges for literacy Ss. You may want to set up alternate activity stations around the room with, for example, flash cards that have pictures photocopied from the book on one side and the corresponding words on the other, or worksheets with the unit vocabulary words followed by the same words with one or two letters missing, for Ss to complete.

Teaching tip

Although the meanings of *next to* and *between* are easy to show using physical objects, being *on* a street and *across from* something are more idiomatic. In the first case, buildings are not literally on a street; otherwise they would block traffic. In the second case, there is an implied space between one thing and another, such as a street, a hallway, or an aisle. Since these issues are rather complex, use the pictures in the book to help Ss understand the meanings of these phrases.

Practice

- Direct Ss' attention to the map in Exercise **2A**. Read aloud the example conversation using different voices for Speaker A and Speaker B. When you read Speaker B's line, show Ss the two answer choices under the blank and ask: *"Between" or "Across from"?* Elicit: *Between.*
- Read aloud the instructions for Exercise **2A**. Point to where *Between* has been circled and written for number 1.
- Ss complete the exercise individually. Walk around and help as needed.

Comprehension check

- Read aloud the second part of the instructions for Exercise **2A**.

Class Audio CD1 track 55 Play or read the audio program (see audio script, page T-158). Ss listen and repeat as they check their answers.

- Write the numbers *1–5* on the board. Ask volunteers to come to the board and write the answers they circled. Make any necessary corrections on the board.
- Ss in pairs. Ask Ss to choose Role A or B and practice the questions and answers in Exercise **2A**. Then have Ss switch roles and practice again. Walk around and help as needed.
- Ask several pairs to say the questions and answers for the rest of the class.

Literacy tip

For an alternative activity, refer literacy Ss to pages 58–59 in the *Literacy Workbook* at any time during the lesson.

LESSON C The school is on Main Street.

Presentation

- Direct Ss' attention to the pictures in Exercise 2B. Point to each picture and ask the class: *What places do you see?* Elicit the names of the places, for example, *bank* and *supermarket*.
- Point to the prepositional phrase under each picture and say to Ss: *What's this? Please say the words.* Elicit the phrases.

Practice

- Read aloud the first part of the instructions for Exercise 2B.

Class Audio CD1 track 56 Play or read the audio program (see audio script, pages T-157–158). Ss listen and repeat the conversations.

- Write on the board: *Excuse me. Where's the _____?* Tell Ss that they can use the question to ask people on the street where places are. Model the use of the question by pretending to be a stranger who needs directions.
- Read aloud the second part of the instructions in Exercise 2B. Call on two Ss to read aloud the example conversation. Call on two different Ss to model a new conversation using Picture 2.
- Indicate that Ss should ask and answer questions about all six pictures. Make sure Ss understand the task.
- Ss ask and answer questions about the pictures in pairs. When Ss are finished, ask them to switch partners and repeat the conversations.

Expansion activity (student pairs)

- Before class. Prepare blank map grids similar to the map in Exercise 2A on page 62. Include a list of places from the unit that Ss can use to name the places shown on the map. Hand out a grid to each S.
- Have Ss work individually to fill in the grid with the names of places, or have literacy Ss work with higher-level Ss, pointing to the squares where they would like the places to be written.
- Have Ss ask and answer questions about each other's maps in pairs. The first S shows the map to his or her partner and asks questions, such as: *Where's the school? Where's the pharmacy?*
- The second S answers using prepositional phrases. In many cases, more than one phrase will be correct, so as you walk around, encourage Ss to think of all the ways they can express the location of a place, such as: *Next to the movie theater. Across from the bank.*
- When Ss are finished, ask them to switch roles and talk about the second S's map.

Application

- Direct Ss' attention to Exercise 3 and read the instructions and the example conversation aloud.
- Model the task. Say to a S: *Say the question.* Elicit: *Where are you?* Point to the pictures in Exercise 2B and say to the first S's partner: *You are at one of these places. Where?* Elicit one of the prepositional phrases. Ask the first S to guess the place. Make sure Ss understand the task.
- Ss complete the exercise in pairs. Walk around and help as needed.
- When Ss are finished, ask several different Ss: *Where are you?* As Ss answer with prepositional phrases, call on different Ss to guess the place where their classmate is.

Evaluation

- Direct Ss' attention to the lesson focus written on the board. Write on the board: *Where's the _____?*
- Direct Ss' attention to the picture on page 58. Call on Ss to ask a classmate the question written on the board about the picture. Have the S who answers ask the next question.
- Repeat the procedure with the map on page 62. Monitor Ss' accuracy in using prepositional phrases.
- Check off each part of the lesson focus as Ss demonstrate an understanding of what they have learned in the lesson.

More Ventures, Unit 5, Lesson C	
Literacy Workbook, 15–30 min. **Basic Workbook,** 15–30 min.	
Writing worksheets, 15–30 min.	www.cambridge.org/myresourceroom
Student Arcade, time varies	www.cambridge.org/venturesarcade

CLASS CD1 TK 56

B Listen and repeat.

1. next to

2. across from

3. between

4. on

5. next to

6. across from

Talk with a partner. Ask and answer.

A Excuse me. Where's the **bank**?
B **Next to the supermarket.**
A Thanks.

3 Communicate

Talk with a partner. Play a game.
Ask and guess.

A Where are you?
B **Next to the supermarket.**
A At the **bank**?
B Yes, that's right.

LESSON D Reading

1 Before you read

Talk about the picture.
What do you see?

2 Read

Listen and read.

STUDENT TK 25
CLASS CD1 TK 57

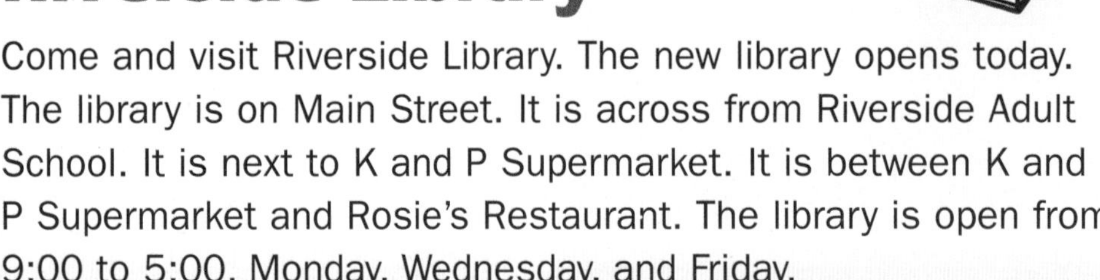

Notice from Riverside Library

Come and visit Riverside Library. The new library opens today. The library is on Main Street. It is across from Riverside Adult School. It is next to K and P Supermarket. It is between K and P Supermarket and Rosie's Restaurant. The library is open from 9:00 to 5:00, Monday, Wednesday, and Friday.

3 After you read

Complete the map. Share your map with a partner.

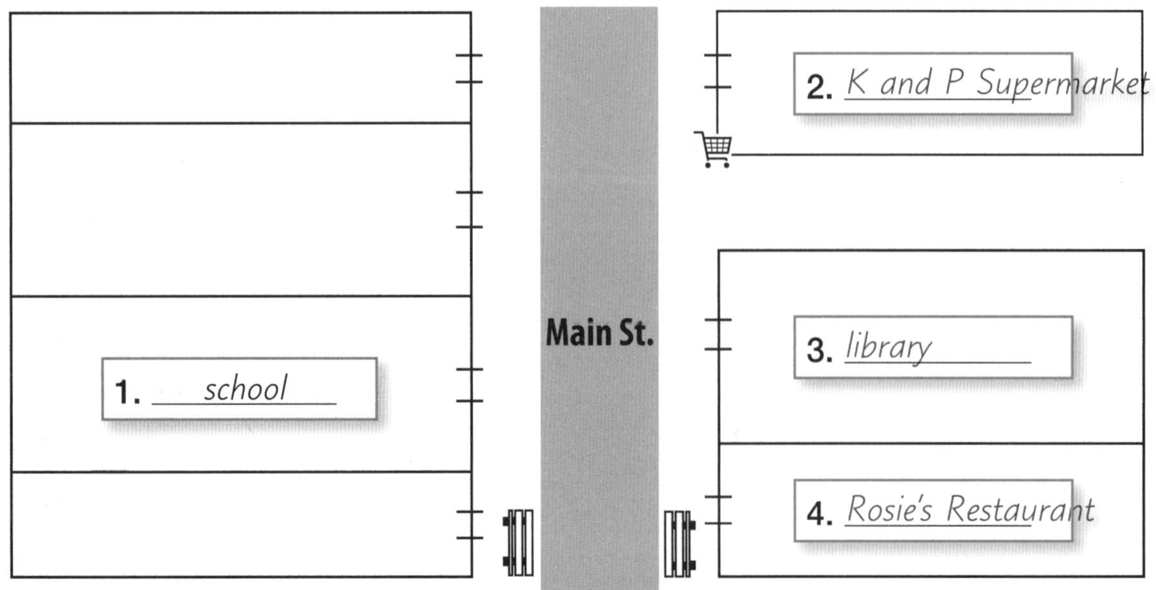

Lesson objectives

- Introduce and read "Notice from Riverside Library"
- Introduce transportation vocabulary
- Practice using new topic-related words

Warm-up and review

- Before class. Write today's lesson focus on the board.
  Lesson D:
  Read "Notice from Riverside Library"
  Learn transportation words
- Before class. Take out the six images you used in the Warm-up in Lesson B, and find six new images to represent the vocabulary from Lesson B (you will have 12 images in all). For example, you might find a clip art image of a letter to represent *post office*, a magazine picture of a gas pump to represent *gas station*, and a picture of a box of popcorn to represent *movie theater.*
- Before class: Write on the board the vocabulary from Lessons A and B: *bank*, *library*, *restaurant*, *school*, *street*, *supermarket*, *pharmacy*, *hospital*, *laundromat*, *movie theater*, *post office*, *gas station.*
- Begin class. Books closed. Point to and say the vocabulary words and ask Ss to repeat after you.
- One by one, hold up the images and ask Ss: *What's this?* or *Where can I find this?* Elicit the names of the places written on the board.

Presentation

- Read aloud the first part of the lesson focus written on the board and ask Ss to repeat after you. Write on the board and say to Ss: *The library opens today!* Ask Ss to repeat.
- Ask: *What does this mean?* Elicit any ideas Ss have. If they need help understanding the meaning, go over the difference between places being *open* and *closed.* Then explain that the library is *new.* This is the first day the library is open.
- Books open. Direct Ss' attention to the picture in Exercise **1**. Ask the class: *What is this place?* (The library.) Ask Ss to look for this library in the picture on page 58.
- Read aloud the instructions for Exercise **1**. Ask: *What do you see?* Elicit and write on the board any vocabulary about the picture that Ss know, such as: *man*, *woman*, *bicycle*, *door.*

Practice

- Direct Ss' attention to Exercise **2**. Point to the title of the paragraph and ask Ss: *What's the title?* ("Notice from Riverside Library.") Explain that a notice is similar to a note, which they saw an example of in Unit 2, but a notice is for all of the people in town, whereas a note is usually for one person.

Class Audio CD1 track 57 Play or read the audio program and ask Ss to read along (see audio script, page T-159). Repeat the audio program as needed.

- Read aloud each sentence of the reading and ask Ss to repeat after you.
- Answer any questions Ss have about the reading.

Literacy tip

Literacy Ss should be able to talk about the picture and listen to and repeat the lines of the reading passage. They may also be able to assist in the map activity by pointing to the places on the map while a higher-level S writes the names of the places.

Learner persistence *(individual work)*

Self-Study Audio CD track 25 Exercise **2** is recorded on the CD at the back of the Student's Book. Ss can listen to the CD at home for reinforcement and review and also for self-directed learning when class attendance is not possible.

Comprehension check

- Read aloud the instructions for Exercise **3**.
- Model the task. Point to where *school* has been written on the map. Ask Ss: *What's this place?* (School or Riverside Adult School.)
- Point to the reading and ask Ss: *Where's the library?* Begin reading aloud at the sentence: *The library is on Main Street. It is across from Riverside Adult School.*
- Point to the map and say: *The school! The library is across from the school.* Ask Ss: *Where do you write "library"?* (Line 3.) Point to line 3 and say: *Write "library" here.*
- Ss scan the reading and fill in the map individually. Walk around and help as needed.
- Go over answers with the class. Duplicate the map from Exercise **3** on the board. Call on Ss to write the names of the places in the appropriate places and tell the class where they found the answer in the reading.
- Have Ss compare their maps with the picture on page 58.

Literacy tip

For an alternative activity, refer literacy Ss to pages 60–61 in the *Literacy Workbook* at any time during the lesson.

LESSON D Reading

Presentation

- Direct Ss' attention to the picture dictionary in Exercise 4. Point to and say the word *Transportation* in the Student's Book and in the second part of the lesson focus written on the board. Tell Ss: *Today, we will learn transportation words.* Ask Ss to brainstorm some modes of transportation. Write their ideas on the board, such as *bus, plane, car, etc.*
- Read aloud the instructions for Exercise 4A.
- Help Ss preview the pictures by holding up the Student's Book and saying, for example: *Number one. What do you see?* Elicit any vocabulary about the pictures that Ss already know. If Ss know the word for the transportation form pictured, write it on the board; for example: *bicycle.* If Ss don't know the word, tell them the word, write it on the board, say it, and ask Ss to repeat.

Teaching tip

The phrase *on foot* is an exception to the pattern in the picture dictionary, since it uses a different preposition and there is no mechanical vehicle involved. Ss should know the word *foot*, but they may also know the word *walk* and wonder why it is not being used. If this is the case, teach Ss the phrase *by walking* in addition to *on foot*.

Class Audio CD1 track 58 Play or read the audio program (see audio script, page T-159). Listen to Ss' pronunciation as they repeat the words. Correct pronunciation as needed.

Expansion activity (student pairs)

- Before class. Photocopy and cut out enough of the picture dictionary cards for Unit 5 to give each S one card.
- Write a story to read in class about someone's busy day in which they go to at least six of the places in the unit via the six forms of transportation in the picture dictionary; for example: *Today is Wednesday. Gina goes to the library on foot.*
- Tell Ss to hold up their card when they hear the transportation words in the story.

Learner persistence (individual work)

Self-Study Audio CD track 26 Exercise 4A is recorded on the CD at the back of the Student's Book. Ss can listen to the CD at home for reinforcement and review. They can also listen to the CD for self-directed learning when class attendance is not possible.

Practice

- Direct Ss' attention to Exercise 4B and read the instructions aloud. Read the example conversation aloud or have two Ss read it.
- Point to and read aloud the two column headings in the chart. Point to where Ben's information has been written as an example.
- Ss stand up, walk around, and talk to at least four classmates about how they get to school.
- When Ss are finished, ask them follow-up questions about their classmates, such as: *How does Walter get to school? Who can tell me?*

Expansion activity (whole group)

- Draw on the board a chart with seven columns. Label the first six columns with the phrases from the picture dictionary, and label the last column *Other.*
- Ask the class: *How do you get to school?* Have Ss come to the board and check the appropriate column to indicate how they get to school. Then have a volunteer add up the checkmarks in each column.

  Option Point to each column and ask questions using *How many?* For example, point to the first column and ask: *How many people get to school by bicycle?*

Expansion activity (whole group)

- Ask Ss who work outside the home to tell the class how they get to work.

Evaluation

- Direct Ss' attention to the first part of the lesson focus written on the board. Point to the reading passage and ask: *What place did we read about?* (Riverside Library.) Ask: *Is the library opening today?* (Yes.) Ask: *Where is the library?* Elicit prepositional phrases.
- Direct Ss' attention to the second part of the lesson focus. Ask Ss to take out the picture dictionary cards you gave them in the first expansion activity. Tell Ss: *You are going to the supermarket. Use the words on the cards to tell me how you go.* Ask individual Ss: *How do you get to the supermarket?* Elicit the phrases from Ss' cards. Then have Ss ask each other the same question.
- Check off each part of the lesson focus as Ss demonstrate understanding of what they have learned in the lesson.

More Ventures, Unit 5, Lesson D	
Literacy Workbook, 15–30 min. **Basic Workbook,** 15–30 min.	
Picture Dictionary activities, 30–45 min. **Writing worksheets,** 15–30 min.	www.cambridge.org/myresourceroom
Student Arcade, time varies	www.cambridge.org/venturesarcade

4 Picture dictionary Transportation

1. by bicycle
2. by bus 
3. by car 
4. by taxi 
5. by train 
6. on foot 

A Listen and repeat. Look at the picture dictionary.

STUDENT TK 26
CLASS CD1 TK 58

B Talk with your classmates. Complete the chart.

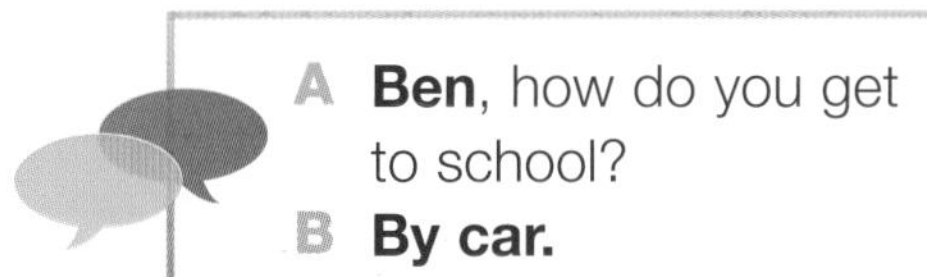

A **Ben**, how do you get to school?
B **By car.**

Name	Transportation
Ben	*by car*
(Answers will vary.)	

LESSON E Writing

1 Before you write

A Talk with a partner. Complete the words.

1. s u p e r m a r _k_ e t
2. p _h_ a r m a c y
3. p o s t o f _f_ i c e
4. r e s _t_ a u r a n t
5. l i _b_ r a r y
6. s _c_ h o o l

B Talk with a partner. Look at the map. Complete the story.

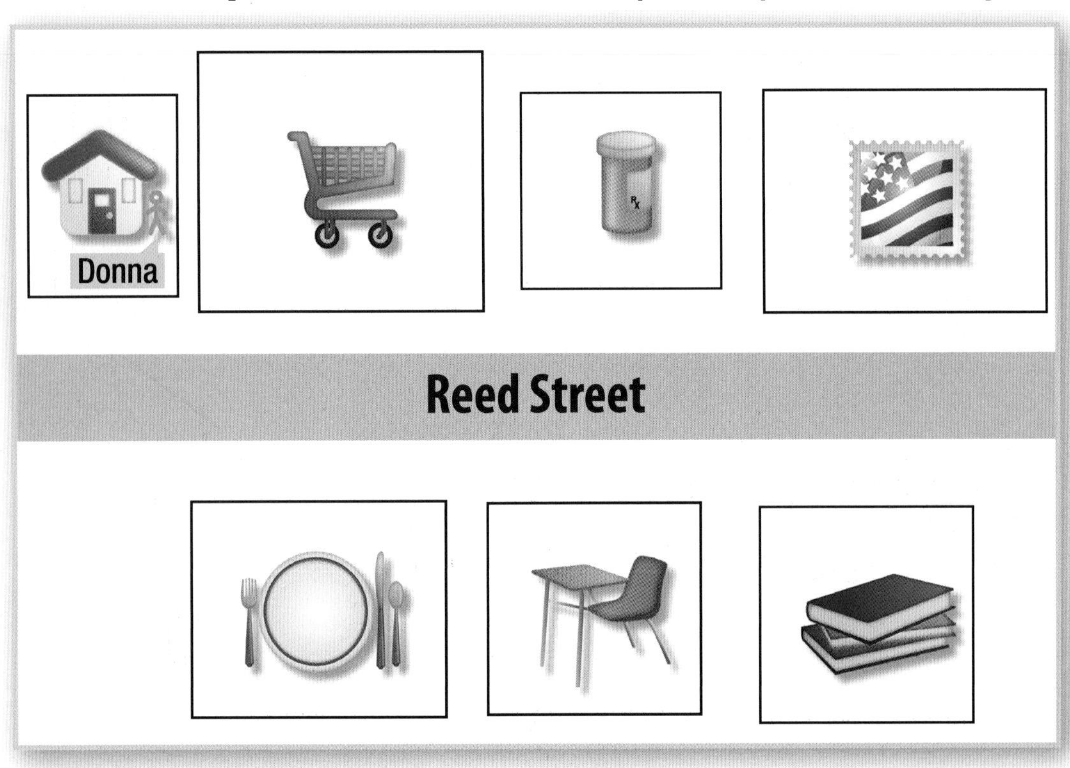

Donna lives on Reed ___Street___(1). She lives near a big supermarket. The supermarket is next to a ___pharmacy___(2). A ___restaurant___(3) is across from the supermarket. A ___post___ ___office___(4) is on Reed Street, too. It is across from the ___library___(5). A ___school___(6) is between the restaurant and the library.

Lesson objectives

- Review vocabulary and grammar from the unit
- Complete sentences about directions to your house

Warm-up and review

- Before class. Write today's lesson focus on the board.
  Lesson E:
  Review words for places
  Review *on*, *next to*, *across from*, *between*
  Complete sentences about directions to your house
- Before class. Draw on the board a map of a community similar to the map on page 64. Label the places on the map with vocabulary from the unit.
- Begin class. Books closed. Direct Ss attention to the map on the board. Ask questions, such as: *Where's the post office? Where's the laundromat?* Elicit from Ss prepositional phrases, such as: *Next to the bank* and *Between the supermarket and the library.*

Presentation

- Books open. Direct Ss' attention to Exercise **1A** and read the instructions aloud. Point to the first item and say to Ss: *Number one. What's the word?* (Supermarket.) Ask: *What letter do we need?* (k.) Pretend to write the letter *k* in the blank for number 1.

Practice

- Ss work in pairs to complete the words.
- When Ss are finished, call on different pairs to write their completed words on the board. Review the alphabet by asking Ss who write answers on the board to say the letters aloud. Have Ss make any necessary corrections on the board.

Literacy tip

Your literacy Ss should be able to handle Exercise **1A** without special help, but for the other exercises in the lesson, you may want to provide alternate work such as tracing letters or filling in blanks in the other vocabulary words from the unit. Refer Ss to Literacy Workbook. (pages 62–63).

- Read the instructions for Exercise **1B** aloud.
- Ss work in pairs to fill in the blanks in the story using the map and the words in Exercise **1A**.
- Check answers as a class. Write the numbers *1–6* on the board, and ask for volunteers to write their answers on the board.
- Read the passage aloud. When you get to each blank, point to and say the answer written on the board. Ask the class: *Is this correct?* Make any necessary corrections on the board.

Expansion activity *(student pairs)*

- Create a fill-in-the-blank exercise using "Directions to Donna's House" with blanks instead of the prepositions.
- Have one S in each pair read aloud the passage from the book while the other fills in the blanks.
- When Ss are finished, ask them to compare their passage with the original in the Student's Book.

Expansion activity *(small groups)*

- For each group, write the vocabulary for places from the unit on 12 index cards or small pieces of paper.
- Draw a simple map using at least half of the places. Don't show the map to Ss.
- Tell Ss to listen as you make statements about the map you are looking at. Have Ss arrange the "places" on a desk or table. You may need to read through your statements several times.
- When Ss are finished, walk around and see which groups have recreated your map. If a group has made a mistake, give them the relevant information they need to repair it; for example: *The bank is "across from" the restaurant, not "next to" the restaurant.*

Expansion activity *(whole group)*

- Tell Ss you are going to draw a map of the location of your school on the board. Brainstorm nearby businesses. Write their names on the board.
- Draw a rough map of the area on the board, showing streets. Draw rectangles for nearby buildings.
- Ask volunteers to come up and write the names of nearby streets and businesses on the map.
- Ask Ss to make statements about the school's location, for example: *The school is next to a gas station. The school is on _____ street.*

LESSON E Writing

Practice

- Direct Ss' attention to Exercise **2A** and read the instructions aloud. Tell Ss: *Draw the places on your street. Write the words.*
- Ss draw their maps individually. Walk around and help as needed.
- Read aloud the instructions for Exercise **2B**. Help Ss get started by modeling sentences about your street on the board. Start writing and then say, for example: *I live on . . . What do I need here?* (A street.) *Correct. I live on Milton Street.*
- Continue in this manner if your Ss need a model to refer to or direct them to the passage on page 66 for help.

Teaching tip

Exercises **2A** and **2B** are necessarily open-ended, since Ss live in different places. Be prepared to help Ss think of places in their neighborhoods to put on their maps, but ask Ss not to include places they haven't studied in the unit, for example, clothing stores, veterinarians' offices, or any other places that classmates may not know the words for. If any Ss live on a street with only houses, suggest that they draw a different street that they know well. Help them change the wording of the sentences in Exercise **2B** accordingly.

Literacy tip

Literacy Ss may have trouble writing the names of buildings and completing the sentences in Exercise **2B**. Instead, assign pages 62–63 from the *Literacy Workbook*.

Comprehension check

- Direct Ss' attention to Exercise **3** and read the instructions aloud. Hold your Student's Book close to you and tell Ss: *Don't let your partner see your map. Tell your partner about your map.*
- Ss read aloud their sentences and draw maps in pairs. When Ss are finished, have them compare their maps with their partner's original map. Then ask them to switch roles so that both partners have said their sentences and drawn a map.
- Walk around and help as needed, and check to see that Ss have written the names of places correctly.

Expansion activity *(individual work)*

- Ask Ss to write their completed sentences from Exercise **2B** on a piece of paper to hand in.

Community building *(whole group)*

- Before class. Draw a simple map of the neighborhood where your class is held. Label places on the map with vocabulary from the unit.
- Give each S a copy of the map, and ask a few questions about where places are. Then tell Ss anything you know about the places, for example, which restaurant has good food or that the nearby laundromat is very expensive. Encourage Ss to share their information about the places with the class.

Evaluation

- Direct Ss' attention to the lesson focus written on the board. Read the first two lines aloud and ask Ss to repeat. Ask the class: *Can you do this? Can you talk about where places are?* Elicit: *Yes!*
- Direct Ss' attention to the picture on page 58 and to the map on page 62, and have them ask and answer questions about where the places are.
- Direct Ss' attention to the third line of the lesson focus. Read it aloud and ask Ss to repeat. Write sentence prompts on the board similar to the ones in Exercise **2B**. Call on individual Ss to complete the sentences on the board with any appropriate vocabulary from the unit.
- Check off each part of the lesson focus as Ss demonstrate an understanding of what they have learned in the lesson.

More Ventures, Unit 5, Lesson E	
Literacy Workbook, 15–30 min.	
Basic Workbook, 15–30 min.	
Writing worksheets, 15–30 min.	www.cambridge.org/myresourceroom

2 Write

A Draw a map of your street.

(Answers will vary.)

B Write about your street.

I live on ___*(Answers will vary.)*___.
I live near a ______________.
A ______________ is across from a ______________.
A ______________ is between the ______________ and
the ______________.

3 After you write

Listen to your partner. Draw your partner's street.

(Answers will vary.)

LESSON **F** Another view

1 Life-skills reading

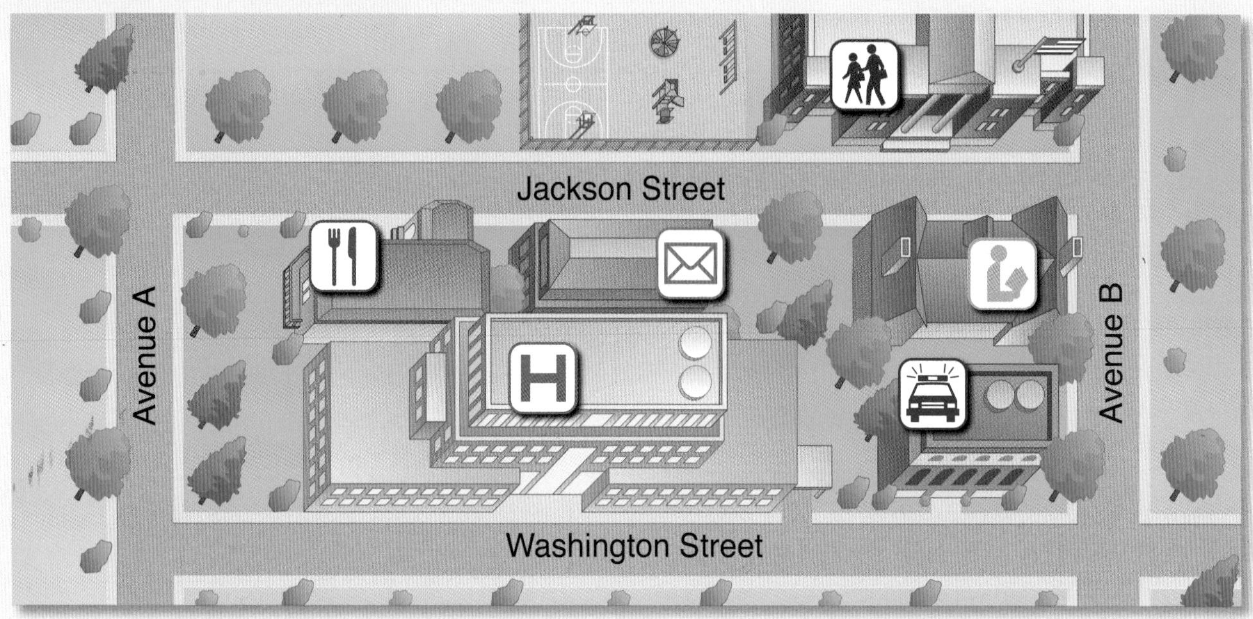

A Read the sentences. Look at the map. Fill in the answer.

1. The hospital is ____.
   - Ⓐ on Jackson Street
   - Ⓑ on Washington Street
   - Ⓒ on Avenue B

2. The post office is ____.
   - Ⓐ next to the police station
   - Ⓑ next to the school
   - Ⓒ next to the restaurant

3. The post office is ____.
   - Ⓐ between the restaurant and the library
   - Ⓑ across from the library
   - Ⓒ on Washington Street

4. The hospital is ____.
   - Ⓐ across from the school
   - Ⓑ next to the police station
   - Ⓒ between the restaurant and the school

B Talk with a partner about the places on the map.

Where is the police station?

On Washington Street.

Where is the school?

Across from the library.

Lesson objectives

- Practice reading a map
- Review vocabulary and grammar from the unit
- Complete the self-assessment

Warm-up and review

- Before class. Write today's lesson focus on the board.
  Lesson F:
  Read a map
- Before class. Draw a simple map on the board. Draw six buildings and label them with the symbols used in the Student's Book: dollar sign for bank, book for library, letter for post office, etc.
- Begin class. Books closed. Review vocabulary and grammar from the unit by pointing to each building on the map and asking Ss: *What's this?* Ask Ss to come to the board and label the buildings on the map.
- When the map is completed, ask Ss questions with *Where*, for example: *Where's the pharmacy?* Elicit prepositional phrases such as: *Next to the library.*

Presentation

- Books open. Direct Ss' attention to the map in Exercise **1**. Ask Ss: *What places do you see?* As Ss say the names of the places represented with icons on the map, list the words on the board. Repeat and spell words as you list them.

Practice

- Read the instructions in Exercise **1A** aloud. This task helps prepare Ss for standardized-type tests they may have to take.
- Write the first item on the board along with the three answer choices labeled *a*, *b*, and *c*.
- Read the item and answer choices aloud and then point to the map. Ask Ss: *Is the hospital on Jackson Street, Washington Street, or Avenue B?* Show Ss where to look on the map for the information. Elicit: *On Washington Street.*
- Point to the three answer choices on the board. Ask Ss: *a*, *b*, or *c*? (b) Fill in the letter *b* and tell Ss: *Fill in the answer.* Make sure Ss understand the task.
- Have Ss individually scan for and fill in the answers.

Literacy tip

Literacy Ss will likely have trouble with Lesson F, so you may want to provide alternative activities to work on at their desks or at self-access centers in the classroom.

Comprehension check

- Go over the answers to Exercise **1A** together. Make sure that Ss followed instructions and filled in their answers. Ask Ss to point to the places on the map.

Application

- Read the instructions for Exercise **1B** aloud. Call on two Ss to read the speech bubbles aloud. Have a volunteer point to the library on the map.
- Ss ask and answer questions in pairs. When Ss are finished, ask them to find a new partner and talk to him or her about where places are on the map.

Expansion activity *(student pairs)*

- Write on the board: *How do you get to ______?* Say the sentence using the name of a place and ask Ss to repeat after you.
- Have a volunteer ask you the question about any place on the map. Hold up your Student's Book, point to page 65, and answer the question using a phrase from the picture dictionary.
- Ss ask and answer questions in pairs.

  Option Before class. Photocopy and cut out a set of the picture dictionary cards for each pair of Ss, and have them place the cards in a pile facedown. When the first S asks the question, the second S picks up the top card and answers using the form of transportation pictured on the card.

Literacy tip

For an alternative activity, refer literacy Ss to pages 64–65 in the *Literacy Workbook* at any time during the lesson.

LESSON F Another view

Practice

- Direct Ss' attention to Exercise **2A** and read the instructions aloud.
- Model the task. Point to the first picture and ask: *Where is this?* Elicit: *Post office.* Point to the words and the line connecting the picture to the words *post office.*
- Tell Ss: *Match the pictures and the words.*
- Ss complete the exercise individually. Then Ss compare their answers with a partner's.

Expansion activity *(whole group)*

- Teach vocabulary for items in the pictures in Exercise **2A**.
- Point to each picture in turn and ask Ss: *What do you see?* List on the board any vocabulary Ss know, and provide additional words, such as: *stamp*, *envelope*, *dollar bills*, *coins or change*, *clothes*, *towels*, *laundry basket*, *medicine*, *tooth brushes*, *tickets*, *popcorn*, *pastries*, *rolls.*
- Talk about items according to Ss' interest, and whenever possible, show Ss real examples of the items.

Practice

- Direct Ss' attention to the word puzzle in Exercise **2B**. Ask the class: *What is this? What do you see?* Ss may say that they see letters.
- Read the instructions for Exercise **2B** aloud. Point to the word *puzzle* and tell Ss: *This is a puzzle.* Say the word aloud and ask Ss to repeat after you.
- Model the task. Point to and say the word *foot* in the word box. Point to the puzzle and ask Ss: *Do you see "foot" here?* Ss should point to the circled example.
- Ss find the words individually or in pairs. When most of the Ss have finished, ask Ss if there are words they can't find in the puzzle. Have other Ss in the class show them where the words are.

Evaluation

- Before asking Ss to turn to the self-assessment on page 140, do a quick review of the unit. Have Ss turn to Lesson A. Ask the class to talk about what they remember about this lesson. Prompt Ss, if necessary, with questions, such as: *What words are on this page? What do you see in the picture?* Continue in this manner to review each lesson quickly.
- **Self-assessment** Read the instructions for Exercise **3**. Ask Ss to turn to the self-assessment page and complete the unit self-assessment.
- If Ss are ready, administer the unit test on pages T-177–T-179 of this Teacher's Edition (or on the Assessment Audio CD / CD-ROM).
- If Ss are ready, administer the midterm test on pages T-180–T-183 of this Teacher's Edition (or on the Assessment Audio CD / CD-ROM).

More Ventures, Unit 5, Lesson F	
Literacy Workbook, 15–30 min.	
Basic Workbook, 15–30 min.	
Writing worksheets, 15–30 min.	www.cambridge.org/myresourceroom

2 Fun with vocabulary

A Read and match.

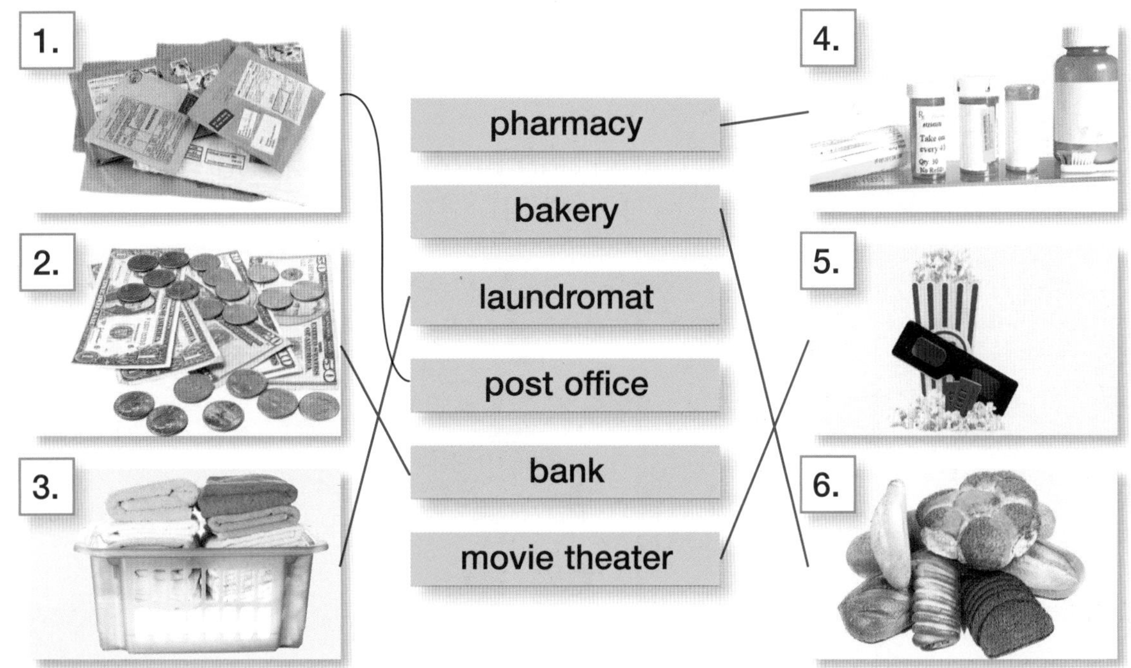

Talk with a partner. Check your answers.

B Circle the words in the puzzle.

bicycle bus car foot taxi train

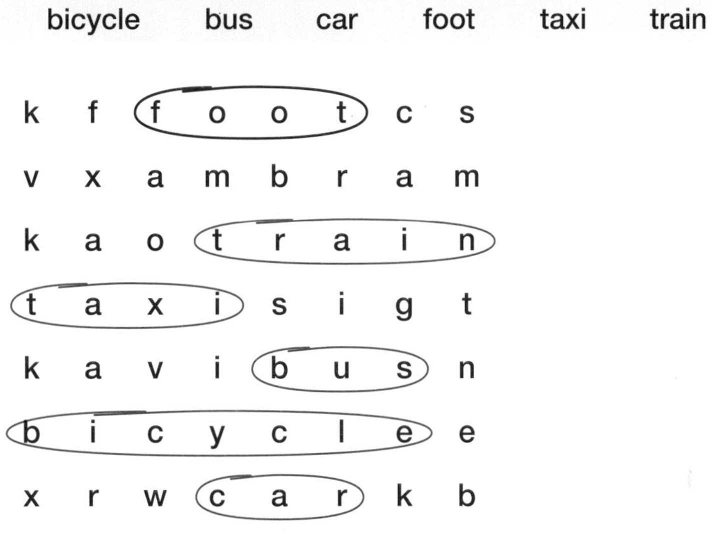

3 Wrap up

Complete the **Self-assessment** on page 140.

UNIT
6 Time

LESSON A Listening

1 Before you listen

A Look at the picture. What do you see?

CLASS CD2 TK 2

B Listen and point: 7:00 • 9:00 • 10:00
10:30 • 2:30 • 6:30

Lesson objectives

- Introduce Ss to the topic
- Find out what Ss know about the topic
- Preview the unit by talking about the picture
- Practice key vocabulary
- Practice listening skills

UNIT **6**

Warm-up and review

- Before class. Write today's lesson focus on the board.
  Lesson A:
  Time vocabulary
- Begin class. Books closed. Write the phrase *shopping mall* on the board. Point to the words. Read them aloud and ask Ss to repeat. Ask: *What's this?* Elicit appropriate responses. Ask: *What stores are in the mall?*

Teaching tip

Ask Ss to say the names of local malls in your area. If you don't have a mall, ask Ss to brainstorm the names of local stores.

- Draw three rectangles on the board, with three more rectangles across from them to represent stores facing each other in the mall. Ask: *What are the names of some stores?* Elicit: *clothes store*, *shoe store*, etc., or use actual names. Write the names of the stores in the rectangles.
- Point to two adjacent stores. Ask: *Where is (name of store)?* (It's next to ______.)
- Continue by asking more questions about the stores. Encourage Ss to use the prepositions *on*, *next to*, *across from*, and *between*.

Literacy tip

If you have literacy Ss in your class, it might be helpful to spend time at the beginning of any activity that contains art or photos talking about the pictures before focusing Ss' attention on the printed words in the exercise. Have Ss work in pairs. Tell them to ask each other: *What do you see?* Encourage Ss to describe the pictures to each other. Consider pairing literacy Ss with Ss who can help them read the text in the exercise. This will help preview the exercise for literacy Ss and make them more confident as the exercise continues.

Presentation

- Books open. Set the scene. Hold up the Student's Book. Show Ss the picture on page 70. Tell Ss: *This is a shopping mall.*
- Ask: *What do you see?* Elicit and write on the board any vocabulary that Ss know, such as: *shopping mall*, *movie theater*, *restaurants*, *woman*.

Practice

- Direct Ss' attention to the key vocabulary in Exercise **1B**. Read each time phrase aloud while pointing to the times in the picture. Ask Ss to repeat and point.

Class Audio CD2 track 2 Play or read the audio program (see audio script, page T-159). Tell Ss: *Listen and point to the picture.* As Ss hear the key vocabulary, check to see that they are pointing to the correct part of the picture. Repeat the audio program as needed.

Comprehension check

- Ask Ss *Yes / No* questions about the picture. Tell Ss: *Listen. Say "yes" or "no."*
  Point to the picture. Ask: *Is this a shopping mall?* (Yes.)
  Point to the gym. Ask: *Is this a movie theater?* (No.)
  Point to the soup restaurant. Ask: *Is this restaurant next to Brown's Deli?* (Yes.)
  Point to the woman in front of the movie theater. Ask: *Is Teresa next to Brown's Deli?* (No.)
  Point to the woman sitting in front of Brown's Deli. Ask: *Is Joan next to the movie theater?* (No.)
  Point to the sign at the movie theater. Ask: *Is the next movie at 2:30?* (Yes.)
  Point to the sign at Brown's Deli. Ask: *Is the breakfast special from 8:00 a.m. to 10 a.m.?* (No.)
  Point to the clock on the movie theater. Ask: *Is it 10:30?* (Yes.)
  Point to the circled time in the daily planner. Ask: *Is this 10:00?* (Yes.)

Teaching tip

It might be helpful to explain the difference between *a.m.* and *p.m.* to the class, or ask Ss to explain it for the rest of the class.

Expansion activity *(whole group and student pairs)*

- Write different times on the board, such as: *10:00 a.m.*, *9:30 p.m.*, *10:00 p.m.*, *6:30 a.m.*, and *7:30 p.m.* Use only times on the hour or half hour, since Ss will not be familiar with other time phrases. Ask a S to come to the board. Say: *Please circle "10:00 p.m."* Ask the rest of the class: *Is that correct?* If a S is not correct, ask another S to help find the correct answer.

LESSON A Listening

Presentation

- Direct Ss' attention to Exercise **2A**. Tell Ss: *We are going to practice saying the different times.*
- Read aloud the instructions for Exercise **2A**.

Practice

Class Audio CD2 track 3 Play or read the audio program (see audio script, page T-159). Ss listen and repeat the vocabulary. Repeat the audio program as needed.

- Listen carefully to Ss' pronunciation and make corrections as needed.

Learner persistence *(individual work)*

Self-Study Audio CD track 27 Exercise **2A** is recorded on the CD at the back of the Student's Book. Ss can listen to the CD at home for reinforcement and review. They can also listen to the CD for self-directed learning when class attendance is not possible.

- Direct Ss' attention to Exercise **2B** and read the instructions aloud.

Class Audio CD2 track 4 Model the task. Hold up the Student's Book and say: *Number one.* Play or read the audio program for number 1 (see audio script, page T-159). Point to the two answer choices in number 1 and ask Ss: *What did you hear – a or b?* Elicit: *b.* Point to the letter *b* next to the second picture and tell Ss: *Circle the letter "b."*

Class Audio CD2 track 4 Play or read the complete audio program (see audio script, page T-159). Ss listen and circle the correct answers. Repeat the audio as needed.

Class Audio CD2 track 4 Read aloud the second part of the instructions for Exercise **2B**. Play or read the audio program again so that Ss can listen and check their answers.

Learner persistence *(individual work)*

Self-Study Audio CD track 28 Exercise **2B** is recorded on the CD at the back of the Student's Book. Ss can listen to the CD at home for reinforcement and review and also for self-directed learning when class attendance is not possible.

Comprehension check

- Write the numbers *1–4* on the board. Ask a few Ss to come to the board and write the correct answers to Exercise **2B** next to each number.

Class Audio CD2 track 4 Play or read the audio program again. Pause the audio program after each conversation. Point to the answer written on the board and ask: *Is this correct?* Ask another S to make any necessary corrections.

Literacy tip

For an alternative activity, refer literacy Ss to pages 66–67 in the *Literacy Workbook* at any time during the lesson.

Useful language

Read the tip box aloud and ask Ss to repeat the times after you. Write several times (on the hour and half hour) on the board, and practice saying them with the class.

Application

- Direct Ss' attention to Exercise **3** and read the instructions aloud.
- Model the task. Hold up the Student's Book and point to the answer choices in Exercise **2B**. Say to one S: *Point to a picture.* Say to the first S's partner: *Say the word.*
- Ss complete the exercise in pairs. Walk around and help as needed.

Expansion activity *(student pairs)*

- Peer dictation. Ask Ss to write five time phrases on a piece of paper. Ask them to write only times that are on the hour or half hour.
- Ss in pairs. Say: *Don't show your paper to your partner. Tell your partner the time phrases in your notebook. Your partner will write them in his or her notebook.*
- When Ss are finished, ask them to switch roles.
- Help as needed. When Ss are finished, ask them to check their work by looking at their partners' notebooks. On the half hour or hour in your class, ask: *What time is it?* Elicit the correct response.

Evaluation

- Direct Ss' attention to the lesson focus written on the board. Check Ss' understanding of time vocabulary by asking them to point to the times that are written on signs in the picture on page 70 in the Student's Book: *7:00*, *9:00*, *10:00*, *10:30*, *2:30*, and *6:30.* Walk around and check that Ss are pointing to the correct items.
- Check off the lesson focus as Ss demonstrate an understanding of what they have learned in the lesson.

More Ventures, Unit 6, Lesson A	
Literacy Workbook, 15–30 min.	
Basic Workbook, 15–30 min.	
Writing worksheets 15–30 min.	www.cambridge.org/myresourceroom
Student Arcade, time varies	www.cambridge.org/venturesarcade

Unit Goals

Read clock time
Make a schedule
Identify parts of an invitation

2 Listen

STUDENT TK 27
CLASS CD2 TK 3

A Listen and repeat.

1. 7:00 2. 9:00 3. 10:00
4. 10:30 5. 2:30 6. 6:30

STUDENT TK 28
CLASS CD2 TK 4

B Listen and circle.

1. a. 

(b.) 

2. a. 

(b.) 

3. (a.) 

b. 

4. a. 

(b.) 

Listen again. Check your answers.

3 After you listen

Talk with a partner. Point to a picture and ask. Your partner says the time.

USEFUL LANGUAGE

Say times like this.
3:00 = *three o'clock*
6:30 = *six-thirty*

LESSON B Events

1 Vocabulary focus

CLASS CD2 TK 5

Listen and repeat.

SEPTEMBER

Sunday	Monday	Tuesday	Wednesday	Thursday	Friday	Saturday
		1. appointment	1	2	3	4
5	6	7 1:30	8	9 2. meeting	10 3:30	11
12	13	14 3. class	15 page 6 8:30	16	17 4. movie	18 7:30
19	20	21	22	23	24	25
26 5:00	27 5. party	28	29 6. TV show	30 4:30		

2 Practice

A Read and match.

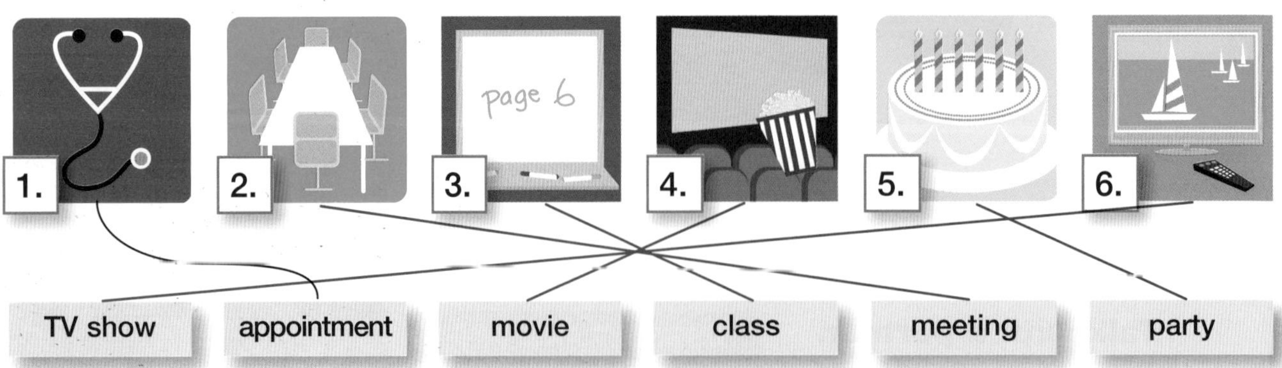

Lesson objective

- Introduce and practice vocabulary for events

Warm-up and review

- Before class. Write today's lesson focus on the board.
  Lesson B:
  Events
  What time is the appointment?
- Begin class. Books open. Direct Ss' attention to the picture on page 70. Review key vocabulary from the unit by asking Ss to point to the following times in their books: *7:00, 9:00, 10:00, 10:30, 2:30, 6:30.*
- Walk around and check to see that Ss are pointing to the correct items in the picture.
- Write the word *planner* on the board. Ask Ss: *What is a planner?* If Ss don't respond, hold up the Student's Book on page 70. Point to Teresa's planner. Say: *This is a planner. Teresa has a meeting with Joan on Wednesday at 10:00.*
- Ask Ss what other types of planners they use. Many Ss may use an iCalendar or other calendar apps on their phones.

Presentation

- Set the scene. Write on the board: *appointment, meeting, class, movie, party, TV show.* Say the words aloud. Ask Ss to repeat after you.
- Point to the word *Events* at the top of page 72 in the Student's Book. Have Ss repeat it after you. Point to the vocabulary on the board and say: *These are events. We often write them on a calendar to remember them.*
- Explain the difference between *appointment* and *meeting.* Say: *A meeting is when people get together. You can have a meeting at work or at your child's school. An appointment is a plan to be at a place at a certain time, like the doctor's office.*
- Direct Ss' attention to the calendar in Exercise **1**. Ask questions about the events on the calendar, pointing to them as you ask: *What time is the appointment?* (1:30) *What time is the meeting?* (3:30) *What time is the class?* (8:30.) *What time is the movie?* (7:30.) *What time is the party?* (5:00.) *What time is the TV show?* (4:30.)
- Read aloud the instructions for Exercise **1**.

Class Audio CD2 track 5 Play or read the audio program (see audio script, page T-159). Listen and repeat the vocabulary along with Ss. Repeat the audio program as needed.

- Listen carefully to Ss' pronunciation and correct as needed.

Expansion activity (student pairs)

- Direct Ss' attention to the calendar in Exercise **1**. Say: *Ask your partner questions.* For example: *When is the meeting?* (September 10.) *When is the class?* (September 15.) *When is the movie?* (September 18.)
- When Ss are finished, ask them to switch roles. Help as needed.

Community building (whole class)

- Show Ss a calendar that you have in the classroom (if there isn't one in the classroom, bring one in). Ask: *What events are happening in our community this month?* Write key words for the events on the board. Keep a class calendar at school. Ask Ss to write important events on the calendar as they come up during the school year.

Practice

- Direct Ss' attention to Exercise **2A**. As you read aloud the instructions, hold up the Student's Book and indicate that Ss should look at the pictures for various events and match them to the corresponding words.
- Model the task. Hold up the Student's Book. Point to the first picture. Ask: *What event is this?* (appointment) Say: *Match the picture with the word.*
- Ss complete the exercise individually. Help as needed.

Literacy tip

For an alternative activity, refer literacy Ss to pages 68–69 in the *Literacy Workbook* at any time during the lesson.

Comprehension check

- Write the numbers *1–6* on the board. Ask a few Ss to come to the board and write the answers to Exercise **2A** on the board.
- Ask different Ss to read the answers written on the board. After each answer is read, ask: *Is this correct?* Ask another S to make any necessary corrections on the board.

Learner persistence (individual work)

- Encourage Ss to use daily planners to keep track of their assignments, quizzes, and tests. Show Ss an example of how to use a daily planner for the class.

LESSON B Events

Presentation

- Direct Ss' attention to the pictures in Exercise 2B. Say: *These are notices about events. What events do you see?* Point to each event in turn. Elicit: *appointment, class, TV show, meeting, movie, party.*
- Ask Ss questions about the events in the pictures. Ask: *What time is the English class?* (8:30.) *What day is the appointment?* (Friday.) *Where is the meeting?* (At Riverside School.)

Practice

- Read aloud the first part of the instructions in Exercise 2B.
- Class Audio CD2 track 6 Model the task. Say: *Listen and repeat.* Play or read the audio program for number 1 (see audio script, page T-159) and point to the appointment card in the first picture as you repeat. Say: *Then write.* Point to *1:30* and *Friday* written in the chart. Make sure Ss understand the task.
- Class Audio CD2 track 6 Play or read the complete audio program (see audio script, page T-159). Ss listen and repeat. Encourage Ss to point to the information in the pictures as they repeat.
- Ss complete the charts individually. Repeat the audio program as needed.
- Check answers with the class. Write the numbers *1–6* on the board, and ask for volunteers to write their answers on the board. Point to each answer and ask the class: *Yes? Is this correct?* Make corrections on the board.
- Read aloud the second part of the instructions for Exercise 2B. Point to and model the example conversation.
- Call on a pair of volunteers to read the example conversation aloud for the class.
- Point to another event on page 73. Ask: *What time is the TV show?* (At 4:30 on Friday.) Repeat with different events in the pictures. Indicate that Ss should ask and answer questions about all the events in the pictures.
- Ss complete the exercise in pairs. Walk around and help as needed.

Expansion activity (student pairs)

- Draw a rectangle on the board. This represents a page in a daily planner. Write today's date at the top of the "page." Write different times on the hour and half hour on the left-hand side of the daily planner page. Write events such as *doctor's appointment, movie, birthday party,* and *meeting* in the time slots.
- Point to one of the events on the page. Ask: *What time is the (name of event)?* Elicit: *It's at (time of event).*
- Encourage Ss to continue asking each other about the events on the board in pairs.
- Ask Ss to draw a daily planner page in their notebooks and write events on it. Tell them that the events can be real or imaginary. They can use the events in Exercise 2B as a guide. Encourage them to ask and answer questions about the events with a different partner.

Application

- Direct Ss' attention to Exercise 3, and read the instructions aloud. Have Ss write the times and days of a TV show and a party in the chart. They can be real or imaginary.
- Model the task. Ask two Ss to read the question and answer aloud. Hold up the Student's Book and point to the words *movie, 7:30,* and *Saturday* as the Ss are saying the conversation. Make sure Ss understand the task.
- Ss then circulate and ask other classmates about the events in their charts. Walk around and help as needed.
- Ask several Ss to ask and answer the questions for the rest of the class.

Learner persistence (whole group)

- If you have some Ss who regularly miss class, recycle the words in this lesson to remind them of the days and times your class meets. Ask the class: *What days does this class meet?* Ask: *What times does this class meet?* Elicit appropriate responses.

Evaluation

- Direct Ss' attention to the lesson focus written on the board. Check Ss' understanding of the key vocabulary by naming an event and asking them to point to the events in the pictures in Exercise 2B on page 73: *appointment, TV show, movie, class, party, meeting.* Walk around and check that Ss are pointing to the correct items.
- Check off the lesson focus as Ss demonstrate an understanding of what they have learned in the lesson.

More Ventures, Unit 6, Lesson B	
Literacy Workbook, 15–30 min.	
Basic Workbook, 15–30 min.	
Writing worksheets, 15–30 min.	www.cambridge.org/myresourceroom
Student Arcade, time varies	www.cambridge.org/venturesarcade

CLASS CD2 TK 6

B Listen and repeat. Then write.

1. 

2. 

3. 

4. 

5. 

6. 

Event	Time	Day
appointment	*1:30*	*Friday*
TV show	*4:30*	*Friday*
movie	*9:00*	*Saturday*

Event	Time	Day
class	*8:30*	*Friday*
party	*5:00*	*Saturday*
meeting	*3:00*	*Saturday*

Talk with a partner. Ask and answer.

A What time is the **appointment**?
B At **1:30** on **Friday**.

3 Communicate

Complete the chart. Write a time and day for each event. Then talk with your classmates.

Event	Time	Day
movie	*7:30*	*Saturday*
TV show	*(Answers will vary.)*	
party		
meeting		

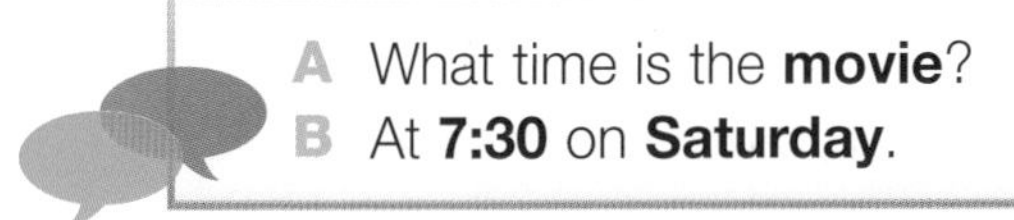

A What time is the **movie**?
B At **7:30** on **Saturday**.

LESSON C Is your class at 11:00?

1 Grammar focus: *Yes / No* questions with *be*

Questions			Answers	
Is	your class	at 11:00?	Yes, No,	it is. it isn't.

isn't = is not

2 Practice

A Read and circle. Then write.

Class	Time
English	11:00

1. A Is your class at 11:00?

B *Yes, it is.*

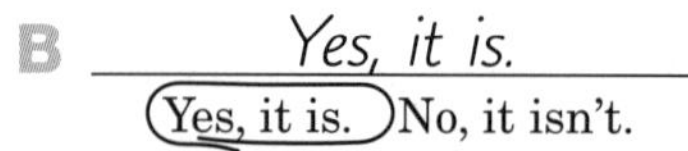

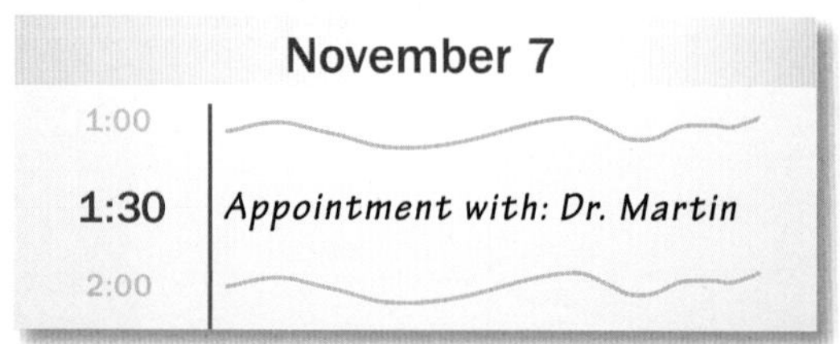

2. A Is your appointment at 12:30?

B *No, it isn't.*

Yes, it is. No, it isn't.

3. A Is your concert at 8:00?

B *No, it isn't.*

Yes, it is. No, it isn't.

4. A Is your movie at 6:00?

B *Yes, it is.*

Yes, it is. No, it isn't.

5. A Is your party at 4:00?

B *Yes, it is.*

Yes, it is. No, it isn't.

Ch. 3 Singing Stars
7:00 Who wins? Final three singers.

6. A Is your TV show at 7:30?

B *No, it isn't.*

Yes, it is. No, it isn't.

Listen and repeat. Then practice with a partner.

Lesson objective

- Introduce and practice *Yes / No* questions with *be*

Warm-up and review

- Before class. Write today's lesson focus on the board:
  Lesson C:
  Yes / No questions with be
- Begin class. Books closed. Write several hour and half hour times on the board. Point to the first one. Ask: *Is this class at (time)?* Elicit: *Yes, it is.* or *No, it isn't.*
- Continue the exercise. Write names of events under the times on the board. Point to each time and event. Ask: *Is the movie at (time)? Is the meeting at (time)?* Elicit appropriate responses.
- If your school has several scheduled weekly classes, ask Ss to brainstorm them by asking: *What classes do we have at this school?* Write the names of the classes on the board. Point to the names of the classes on the board in turn. Ask: *What time is this class?*

Presentation

- Books open. Direct Ss' attention to the grammar chart in Exercise **1**. Read the question and the corresponding answers aloud. Ask Ss to repeat after you.
- Point to the small box beside the grammar chart. Hold up one finger and tell Ss: *One word: isn't.* Hold up two fingers and say: *Two words: is not. They are equal. They are the same.*
- Ask Ss the question in the grammar chart about the time of their own English class. Ss should answer appropriately.

Practice

- Direct Ss' attention to the first picture in Exercise **2A**. Ask two Ss to read the example aloud.
- Read aloud the instructions for Exercise **2A**. Point to where *Yes, it is* has been circled and written for number 1. Say: *Circle the correct answer. Then write it in the blank.*
- Ss complete the exercise individually. Walk around and help as needed.

Comprehension check

- Read aloud the second part of the instructions in Exercise **2A**.

Class Audio CD2 track 7 Play or read the audio program (see audio script, page T-159). Ss listen and repeat as they check their answers.

- Write the numbers *1–6* on the board. Ask volunteers to come to the board and write the answers they circled. Make any necessary corrections on the board.
- Ss in pairs. Ask Ss to choose Role A or B and practice the questions and answers in Exercise **2A**. Then have Ss switch roles and practice again. Walk around and help as needed.
- Ask several pairs to say the questions and answers for the rest of the class.

Literacy tip

Ask literacy Ss to copy the times from Exercise **2A** in their notebooks. Say: *Work with a partner. Say one of the times in your notebook. Your partner will point to it. Then change roles.*

Expansion activity *(student pairs)*

- Focus Ss' attention on the pictures in Exercise **2A**. Write on the board: *1. What kind of class is it?* Continue writing questions on the board as Ss ask and answer in pairs.
  2. What kind of appointment is it? (A doctor's appointment.)
  3. What concert is it? (Toni Tucker.)
  4. What movie is it? (The Lost Clues.)
  5. What kind of party is it? (A birthday party.)
  6. What TV show is it? (Singing Stars.)

Teaching tip

Do not expect Ss to answer the questions in complete sentences. The purpose of this exercise is to understand the meaning of the question and answer with the correct information.

Literacy tip

For an alternative activity, refer literacy Ss to pages 70–71 in the *Literacy Workbook* at any time during the lesson.

LESSON C Is your class at 11:00?

Presentation

- Write on the board: *planner.* Say the word. Ask Ss to repeat. Ask: *Do you remember what this is?* If Ss don't remember, say: *A planner tells you the events for different days in a week.*

> **Teaching tip**
> If you have a planner, it might be helpful to show it to the Ss. Ss learn new vocabulary quickly by visualizing it. Ask Ss if any of them use a planner. If they do, ask them to hold it up for the class to see.

- Direct Ss' attention to the planner page in Exercise 2B. Say: *This is an example of a page from a planner.* Ask: *What's the month?* (April.) *What are the days in the planner?* (Monday, Tuesday, Wednesday, Thursday, Friday, Saturday, Sunday.)
- Ask: *What time is the doctor's appointment in this planner?* (3:30.) *What time is the concert?* (9:00.)

Practice

- Read aloud the first part of the instructions for Exercise 2B. Focus Ss' attention on the words below the planner page. Hold up the Student's Book. Point to the doctor's appointment on Monday in the planner. Ask: *What time is the appointment?* (3:30.) Point to the line connecting *appointment* to *three-thirty.*
- Ss complete the exercise individually. Walk around and help as needed.

> **Teaching tip**
> If Ss need help with writing numbers in words, refer them to page 5 in the Welcome Unit. It might be helpful to write the word *thirty* on the board. Tell Ss that this is how *30* is spelled in English.

- Write the numbers *1–6* on the board. Ask a few Ss to come to the board and write the time for each number on the board. Ask: *Are these times correct?* Ask other Ss to make corrections if needed.
- Read aloud the second part of the instructions for Exercise 2B. Model the task. Ask two Ss to read the example conversation. Call on two different Ss to model a new conversation using another event in the planner.
- Indicate that Ss should ask and answer questions about all the events in the planner. Make sure Ss understand the task.
- Ss ask and answer questions about the items in the planner in pairs. When Ss are finished, ask them to switch partners and repeat the conversations.
- Ask several pairs to say their conversations to the rest of the class.

Application

- Direct Ss' attention to Exercise 3 and read the instructions aloud.
- Focus Ss' attention on the word bank. Say: *Use these words for the calendar.* Ss complete the task individually. Walk around and help as needed.

> **Teaching tip**
> It might be helpful to teach Ss the verb *fill in.* Hold up the calendar in Exercise 3. Point to the empty boxes. Tell the Ss that when they write the words, they are filling in the calendar. This is a useful phrase that Ss may encounter when they fill in information on forms.

- Direct Ss' attention to the example conversation below the calendar. Model the task. Ask two Ss to read the example conversation. Point to the information in the calendar as they read.
- Ss complete the exercise in pairs, asking and answering questions about their own calendars. Walk around and help as needed.

Expansion activity (student pairs)

- Ask Ss to draw a larger calendar of the current month in their notebooks. Say: *Write events from your life in your calendar.* Walk around and help as needed.
- Say: *Now show your calendar to your partner. Your partner will ask questions about your calendar. For example: Is your English class on Tuesday? Is your son's birthday on (date)?*
- Encourage partners to respond appropriately.
- Ask several pairs to ask and answer questions about Ss' real-life calendars for the rest of the class.

Evaluation

- Direct Ss' attention to the lesson focus written on the board. Write different times and events on the board such as *movie* and *2:00.* Ask Ss to form *Yes / No* questions and answers with these words. Say: *Is the movie at 2:00?* Elicit: *Yes, it is.* or *No, it isn't.*
- Check off the lesson focus as Ss demonstrate an understanding of what they have learned in the lesson.

More Ventures, Unit 6, Lesson C	
Literacy Workbook, 15–30 min.	
Basic Workbook, 15–30 min.	
Writing worksheets, 15–30 min.	www.cambridge.org/myresourceroom
Student Arcade, time varies	www.cambridge.org/venturesarcade

B Read and match.

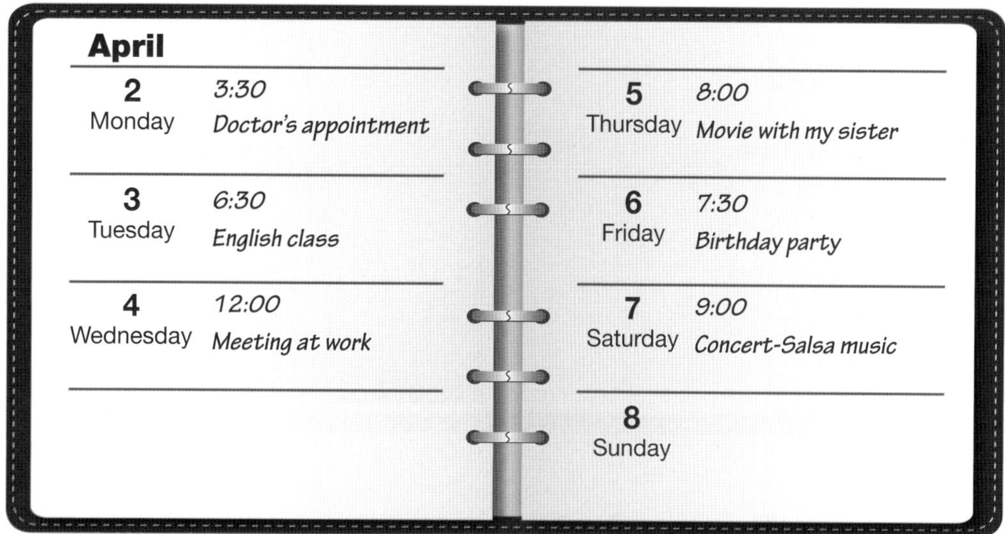

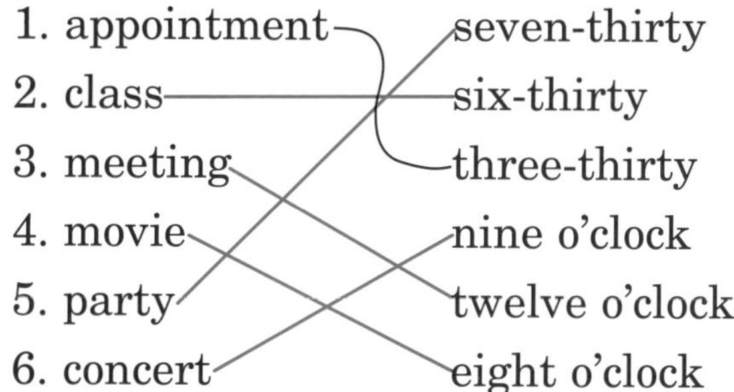

Talk with a partner. Ask and answer.

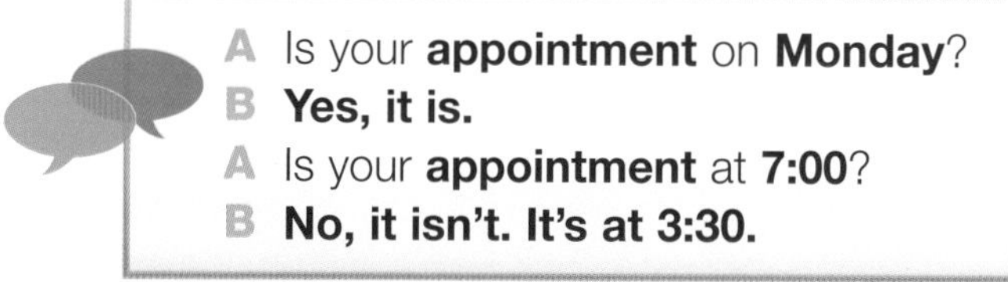

3 Communicate

Complete the chart. Write an event and time for each day. Then talk with a partner.

appointment   class   concert   meeting   party

Monday	Tuesday	Wednesday	Thursday	Friday
class – 5:00	*(Answers will vary.)*			

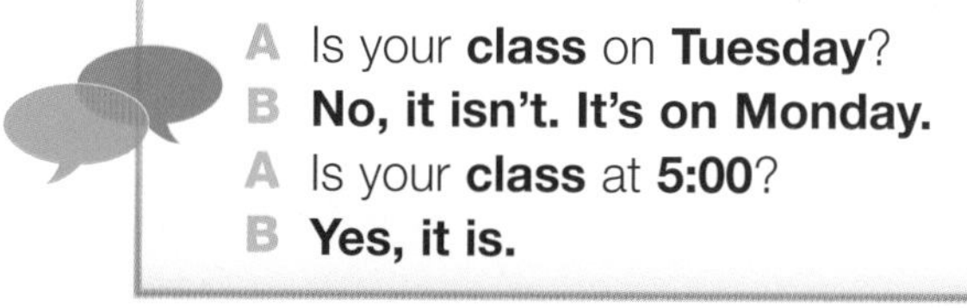

LESSON D Reading

1 Before you read

Talk about the picture.
What do you see?

2 Read

Listen and read.

STUDENT TK 29
CLASS CD2 TK 8

Teresa's Day

Teresa is busy today. Her meeting with her friend Joan is at 10:00 in the morning. Her doctor's appointment is at 1:00 in the afternoon. Her favorite TV show is at 4:30. Her class is at 6:30 in the evening. Her uncle's birthday party is also at 6:30. Oh, no! What will she do?

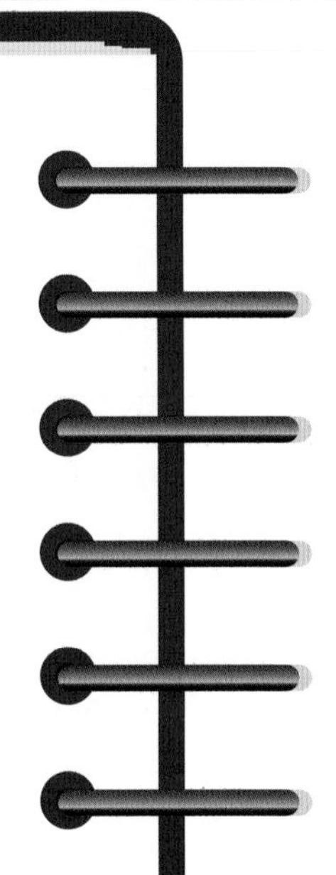

3 After you read

Write the answers.

1. What time is Teresa's meeting? At 10:00.
2. What time is Teresa's TV show? At 4:30.
3. What time is Teresa's class? At 6:30.
4. Is Teresa's appointment at 4:00? No, it isn't.
5. Is her uncle's party at 6:30? Yes, it is.

Lesson objectives

- Introduce and read "Teresa's Day"
- Practice using words about events and time
- Learn the phrases for times of the day

Warm-up and review

- Before class. Write today's lesson focus on the board.
  Lesson D:
  Read "Teresa's Day"
  Discuss the events in Teresa's day
  Learn phrases for times of the day
- Begin class. Books closed. Ask: *What are some words for events?* Elicit: *TV show*, *appointment*, *party*, *movie*, *meeting*, *concert.* Write the words on the board as Ss say them.
- Point to some of the words on the board. Ask: *Do you have an appointment today? Do you have a meeting today? What time is the appointment or meeting?* Elicit appropriate responses.
- Books open. Direct Ss' attention to the picture on page 70. Hold up the Student's Book. Point to the picture of Teresa. Ask: *What's her name?* (Teresa.) *Where is she?* (At the mall.) *What day is it?* (Wednesday.) *What time is her meeting with Joan?* (At 10:00.)

Teaching tip

It might be helpful to point to each part of the picture that corresponds to the answers to the questions you are asking. Doing this gives Ss visual cues that will help them answer the questions correctly.

Presentation

- Direct Ss' attention to the picture in Exercise **1** on page 76.
- Read aloud the instructions for Exercise **1**. Ask: *What do you see?* Elicit and write on the board any vocabulary that Ss know, such as: *Teresa*, *her planner*, *Wednesday*, *10:00.*
- Say: *Now we will read about Teresa's day.*

Teaching tip

Do not expect Ss to answer the question in complete sentences. The purpose of this exercise is to prepare Ss for the reading about Teresa's day that follows.

Practice

- Direct Ss' attention to Exercise **2**. Read the instructions aloud.

Class Audio CD2 track 8 Play or read the audio program and ask Ss to read along (see audio script, page T-159). Repeat the audio program as needed.

- Read aloud each sentence of the reading and ask Ss to repeat after you.
- Write *in the morning*, *in the afternoon*, and *in the evening* on the board. Point to each phrase in turn and say it aloud. Ask Ss to repeat after you. Ask Ss: *What time is the morning? What time is the afternoon? What time is the evening?* (Elicit appropriate responses – correct Ss if necessary).

Learner persistence *(individual work)*

Self-Study Audio CD track 29 Exercise **2** is recorded on the CD at the back of the Student's Book. Ss can listen to the CD at home for reinforcement and review, and also for self-directed learning when class attendance is not possible.

Comprehension check

- Read aloud the instructions for Exercise **3**.
- Model the task. Ask two Ss to read aloud the first question and answer. Ask a S to point to the part of the reading that gives the answer.
- Point out to Ss that questions 2 and 3 will have the same kind of answer as number 1. Direct Ss' attention to numbers 4 and 5. Ask: *What kind of answers will these questions have?* Elicit *Yes, it is.* and *No, it isn't.* Write these answers on the board as a reference.
- Ss complete the exercise individually. Walk around and help as needed.
- Go over answers with the class. Write the numbers *1–5* on the board. Call on volunteers to write their answers on the board.
- Read aloud each answer on the board and ask: *Is this correct?*
- Ask several pairs to ask and answer the questions for the class.

Literacy tip

For an alternative activity, refer literacy Ss to pages 72–73 in the *Literacy Workbook* at any time during the lesson.

Learner persistence *(individual work)*

- Encourage Ss to tell you if they have to miss class for any reason. Practice using the vocabulary from this unit to help Ss explain their absences. Write on the board: *I'm sorry. I can't come to class tomorrow. I have a doctor's appointment at 9:00 a.m.*
- Tell Ss to practice writing excuses using the model on the board.

LESSON D Reading

Presentation

- Direct Ss' attention to the picture dictionary in Exercise 4. Point to and say the words *Times of the day* and ask Ss to repeat them after you.
- Write on the board: *morning, afternoon, evening, night.* Ask Ss: *What time of day is it right now?* If Ss are unsure, point to the appropriate picture in the picture dictionary. Say: *It is (time phrase) right now.* Ask Ss to repeat the sentence after you.
- Direct Ss' attention back to the picture dictionary. Read the instructions for Exercise 4A aloud.

Class Audio CD2 track 9 Play or read the audio program (see audio script, page T-159). Listen to Ss' pronunciation as they repeat the times of the day. Correct pronunciation as needed.

Teaching tip

It might be helpful to tell Ss that it is common to refer to 12:00 p.m. as *twelve noon* and 12:00 a.m. as *twelve midnight.* Tell Ss that to avoid confusion, Americans often say *at midnight* or *at noon* as opposed to *at 12:00 a.m.* or *at 12:00 p.m.*

Learner persistence (individual work)

Self-Study Audio CD track 30 Exercise 4A is recorded on the CD at the back of the Student's Book. Ss can listen to the CD at home for reinforcement and review and also for self-directed learning when class attendance is not possible.

Expansion activity (whole group)

- Name That Picture. Before class. Cut out the picture dictionary cards that correspond to this unit. Hold up a picture card and name it incorrectly. For example, hold up the picture card of *in the evening.* Say: *Is this in the morning?* Listen as Ss say *No*, and correct the statement. Continue until you have gone through all the cards. Expand questioning to different types of questions besides *Yes / No.* For example, *Is this morning or afternoon? What time of day is this?*

Useful language

Read the tip box aloud. Ask Ss to repeat the examples after you. Ask: *Is it a.m. or p.m. right now?* Elicit an appropriate answer.

Practice

- Direct Ss' attention to Exercise 4B and read the instructions aloud. Read the example conversation aloud using two different voices.
- Point to and read aloud the column headings in the chart. Point to the check mark under the "At noon" heading. Say: *Make conversations about the other times. Check the correct boxes.* Make sure Ss understand the task.
- Ss complete the activity in pairs. Walk around and help as needed.
- Ask several pairs to say the conversations for the class.

Learner persistence

- If any of your Ss are having problems learning the new vocabulary from this chapter, make them a set of the picture dictionary cards from the *Online Teacher's Resource Room.* Tell Ss to use them as flash cards to learn the new words. Say: *Look at the pictures. Say the times of the day. Then look at the backs of the cards to see if you are right.*

Evaluation

- Direct Ss' attention to the first part of the lesson focus written on the board. Ask: *What were the events in Teresa's day?* Elicit: *doctor's appointment, TV show, class, birthday party.*
- Direct Ss' attention to the third part of the lesson focus. Point to the pictures in Exercise 4A on page 77 in the Student's Book. Ask: *What time do you think it is?* for each picture. Elicit answers, such as: *Maybe it's (time).*
- Check off each part of the lesson focus as Ss demonstrate understanding of what they have learned in the lesson.

More Ventures, Unit 6, Lesson D	
Literacy Workbook, 15–30 min. **Basic Workbook,** 15–30 min.	
Picture Dictionary activities, 30–45 min. **Writing worksheets,** 15–30 min.	www.cambridge.org/myresourceroom
Student Arcade, time varies	www.cambridge.org/venturesarcade

4 Picture dictionary Times of the day

1. in the morning

2. in the afternoon

3. in the evening

4. at noon

5. at night

6. at midnight

STUDENT TK 30
CLASS CD2 TK 9

A Listen and repeat. Look at the picture dictionary.

B Talk with a partner. Complete the chart.
Check (✓) the time of the day.

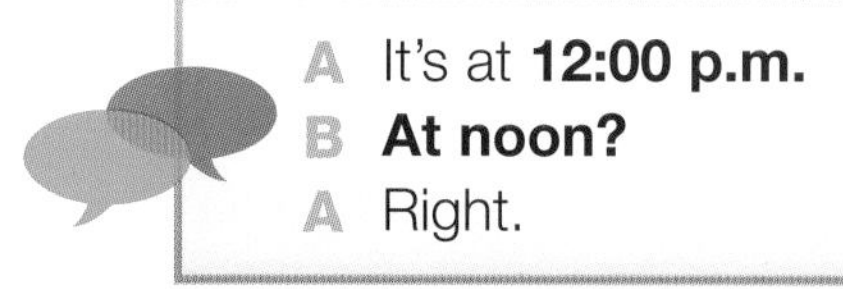

USEFUL LANGUAGE

a.m. = from midnight to noon
p.m. = from noon to midnight

	In the morning	In the afternoon	In the evening	At noon	At midnight
12:00 p.m.				✓	
3:00 p.m.		✓			
6:00 a.m.	✓				
12:00 a.m.					✓
6:00 p.m.			✓		

LESSON **E** Writing

1 Before you write

A Talk with a partner. Complete the words.

1. m o v __i__ __e__
2. c l a __s__ __s__
3. a p p __o__ __i__ n t m e n t
4. p __a__ __r__ t y
5. TV __s__ __h__ o w
6. m __e__ __e__ t i n g

B Talk with a partner. Look at the memo. Complete the story.

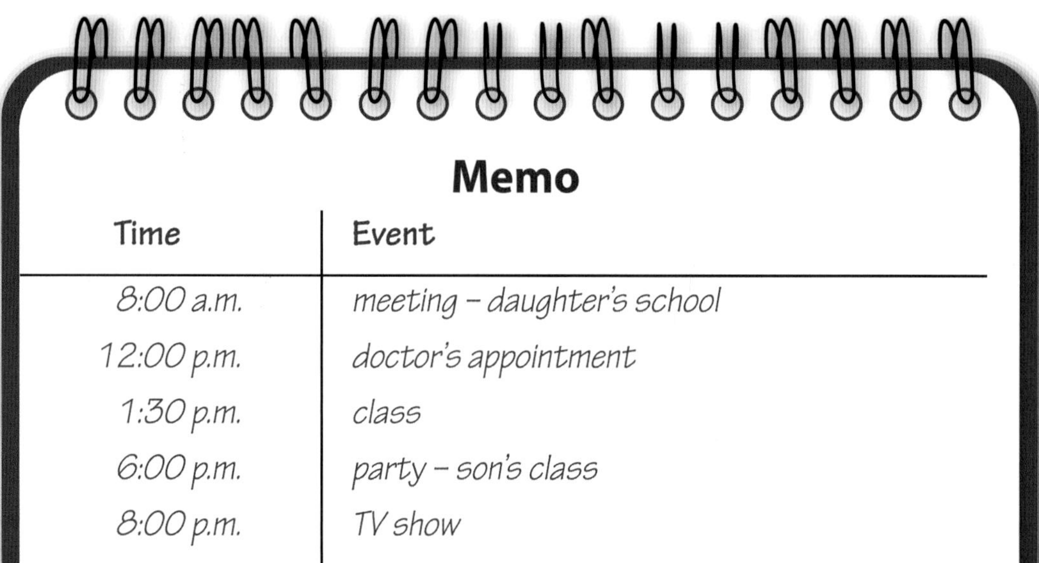

Memo

Time	Event
8:00 a.m.	meeting – daughter's school
12:00 p.m.	doctor's appointment
1:30 p.m.	class
6:00 p.m.	party – son's class
8:00 p.m.	TV show

My Busy Day

Today is a busy day. My ___meeting___ (1) at my daughter's school is at 8:00 in the morning. Then my doctor's ___appointment___ (2) is at noon. My English ___class___ (3) is at 1:30. What time is my son's class ___party___ (4)? Oh, yes. At 6:00 in the evening. Dinner with my family is at 7:00. And my favorite TV ___show___ (5) is at 8:00 at night. It's a very busy day.

Lesson objective

- Discuss and write about a busy day

Warm-up and review

- Before class. Write today's lesson focus on the board.
  Lesson E:
  Write about a busy day
- Begin class. Books closed. Write *busy* on the board. Point to the word. Say it aloud. Ask Ss to repeat after you. Ask: *What does this word mean?* Elicit an appropriate response, such as: *having a lot of things to do.*
- Ask: *Do you have a busy day today?* Elicit *Yes* / *No* responses. If a S responds with yes, ask: *Why?* Elicit an appropriate response, such as a list of things to do that day.

Presentation

- Direct Ss' attention to Exercise **1A** and read the instructions aloud.
- Point to the first item and say: *Number 1. What's the word?* (movie) Ask: *What letters do we need?* (i *and* e) Point to where the letters are written in the blanks. Say: *Now you complete the rest of the words.*

Practice

- Ss work in pairs to complete the words.
- When Ss are finished, call on different pairs to write their completed words on the board. Review the alphabet by asking Ss who write answers on the board to say the letters aloud.
- Go over the answers with the class. Ask: *Are these words spelled correctly?* Make corrections as needed.

Presentation

- Books open. Direct Ss' attention to Exercise **1B** and read the instructions aloud.
- Write the word *memo* on the board. Point to the word. Say it aloud, and ask Ss to repeat after you. Ask: *What does this word mean?* Elicit an appropriate response, such as: *A short note to help you remember something.*
- Ask five Ss to read each part of the memo aloud.
- Model the exercise. Hold up the Student's Book. Read the first two sentences of the story aloud. Point to *meeting* and *8:00* in the memo. Say: *Complete the story.*
- Ss work in pairs to fill in the blanks in the story using the information in the memo. Walk around and help as needed.
- Check answers as a class. Ask several Ss to read sentences from the story aloud. After each sentence ask: *Is that word correct?* Correct any errors if needed.

  Option Ask Ss to read the story to each other in pairs.
- Write the numbers *2–5* on the board, and ask volunteers to write their answers on the board. Make any corrections on the board.

Community building *(whole class)*

- Ask: *Do you often have busy days? What do you do on busy days?*

Expansion activity *(whole class)*

- Hangman game. Draw on the board an outline for the game Hangman as follows:

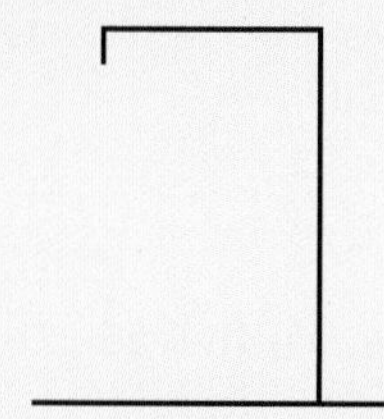

- Think of one of the words from Exercise **1A**. Write blanks to represent each letter of the word under the above diagram.
- Ask Ss to guess the word by guessing different letters. If they guess a letter that is in the word, write it in the corresponding blank. If the letter is not in the word, write it on the right side of the diagram. Then draw a part of a body hanging from the vertical line on the left of the diagram.
- If the Ss guess the word, they win. If an entire figure is drawn in the hangman diagram, the teacher wins.
- Continue the game by asking Ss to think of different words. Draw blanks under the diagram to represent each letter in the new words. Encourage Ss to use any word that they have learned in English class up to this point.

Teaching tip

This is a good way for Ss to practice saying the names of letters of the alphabet in English. It also reinforces vocabulary learned in the unit.

LESSON E Writing

Presentation

- Say: *Remember the memo on page 78? Now you are going to write your own memo about events in your life. They can be real events or imaginary events.*
- Direct Ss' attention to Exercise **2A** and read the instructions aloud. Ask: *What are your plans for today?*
- Draw a vertical line on the board to make two columns. Write *Time* and *Event* as headings.
- Model the task. Ask a S to come to the board and write a time and an event in the columns. Repeat with one or two other Ss.

> **Teaching tip**
> Remind Ss that they don't have to use real-life events. Give them some examples of imaginary events if they don't know what to write in the memo.

Practice

- Ss complete the exercise individually. Walk around and help as needed.
- Direct Ss' attention to Exercise **2B** and read the instructions aloud.
- Model the activity. Point to the time and event examples on the board. Say: *Make a sentence about the time and event.* Write: *My (event) is at (time).* beside each example. Have Ss fill in the blanks on the board.
- Direct Ss' attention to the paragraph in Exercise **2B**. Say: *Now make sentences about the events in your memo.*
- Ss complete the exercise individually. Walk around and help as needed.

> **Literacy tip**
> For an alternative activity, refer literacy Ss to pages 74–75 in the *Literacy Workbook* at any time during the lesson.

- Direct Ss' attention to Exercise **3**. Read the instructions aloud. Say: *Tell your partner about your busy day.* Encourage Ss to read their paragraphs to their partners. Walk around and help as needed.

> **Teaching tip**
> This exercise asks Ss to work together to share their writing. Encourage Ss to peer-correct each other's writing if necessary. Say: *Help your partner with any mistakes. Then your partner will help you.*

- Ask several Ss to read their paragraphs aloud for the rest of the class.

  Option Ask several Ss to write their memos from Exercise **2A** on the board. Then ask them to explain their schedules to the rest of the class.

Community building *(whole group)*

- If appropriate for your class, ask Ss to write their daily schedules in their notebooks. Define and discuss carpooling. If there are any Ss in your class who need rides to English class, ask them to compare their schedules to see if carpooling might be a possibility.

Expansion activity *(whole group)*

- Dictation. Ask Ss to take out a piece of paper and write the numbers *1–5* on it. Dictate the following sentences:
  1. *My meeting is at 10:00 a.m.*
  2. *My TV show is at 11:00 a.m.*
  3. *My appointment is at 12:30 p.m.*
  4. *My English class is at 5:00 p.m.*
  5. *The concert is at 8:00 p.m.*
- Ask Ss to write their sentences on the board. Ask other Ss: *Are the sentences correct?* Ask different Ss to correct any errors if needed.

Evaluation

- Direct Ss' attention to the lesson focus written on the board.
- Ask different Ss to come to the board and write sentences about events in their day. They should include the name of the event and the time.
- Check off the lesson focus as Ss demonstrate understanding of what they have learned in the lesson.

More Ventures, Unit 6, Lesson E	
Literacy Workbook, 15–30 min. **Basic Workbook,** 15–30 min.	
Real Life Document, 15–30 min. **Writing worksheets,** 15–30 min.	www.cambridge.org/myresourceroom

2 Write

A Complete the memo. Write four times and four events for you.

Memo

Time	Event
(Answers will vary.)	

B Write about your day.

My Busy Day

Today is a busy day.

My *(Answers will vary.)* ________ is at ________.

My ________ is at ________.

My ________ is at ________.

And my ________ is at ________.

It's a very busy day.

3 After you write

Talk with a partner. Share your writing.

LESSON F Another view

1 Life-skills reading

It's a party!

Lily is 50! It's her surprise party!
When: *Saturday, October 2*
What time: *8:00 p.m.*
Where: *Katya and Alex's house*
874 Lake Road
RSVP: *555-6188*

A Read the sentences. Look at the invitation. Fill in the answer.

1. It's a party for ____.
   - Ⓐ Lily
   - Ⓑ Katya and Alex
   - Ⓒ Katya

2. The party is ____.
   - Ⓐ in the morning
   - Ⓑ in the afternoon
   - Ⓒ at night

3. The party is at ____.
   - Ⓐ 2:00 p.m.
   - Ⓑ 4:00 p.m.
   - Ⓒ 8:00 p.m.

4. The party is on ____.
   - Ⓐ Friday
   - Ⓑ Saturday
   - Ⓒ Sunday

B Talk with a partner about the party.

Tell the day, the time, and the place.

Lesson objectives
- Practice reading a party invitation
- Review vocabulary and grammar from the unit
- Complete the self-assessment

Warm-up and review

- Before class. Write today's lesson focus on the board.
  Lesson F:
  Read and answer questions about a party invitation
  Practice writing times on clocks
  Complete the self-assessment
- Begin class. Books closed. Write the word *invitation* on the board. Point to the word. Say it aloud and ask Ss to repeat. Ask: *What kinds of invitations are there?* Elicit appropriate responses, such as: *birthday*, *graduation*, *wedding*.

Teaching tip
It might be helpful to bring in an example of a blank invitation card to show Ss what an invitation is. Alternatively, draw a card on the board that says *You're invited to a party!* You could also discuss e-mail invitations, such as e-vites. Ask Ss if they have ever written or received an e-vite.

Presentation

- Books open. Direct Ss' attention to the invitation in Exercise **1A**.
- Hold up the Student's Book. Point to the invitation. Ask: *What kind of party is this invitation for?* Elicit: *It's a party for Lily. It's her birthday.*

Teaching tip
Make sure Ss know the meaning of the word *surprise.* Say: *A surprise is when you don't know the party is for you.* Ask Ss if they have ever attended a surprise party or had one themselves.

Practice

- Read the instructions for Exercise **1A** aloud. This task helps prepare Ss for standardized-type tests they may have to take.
- Write the first item on the board along with the three answer choices labeled *a*, *b*, and *c*.
- Read the item and the answer choices aloud and then point to the invitation. Ask Ss: *Who is the party for?* Show Ss where to look for the information. Elicit: *Lily.*
- Point to the three answer choices on the board. Ask Ss: *a*, *b*, or *c?* (a) Fill in the letter *a* and tell Ss: *Fill in the answer.* Make sure Ss understand the task.
- Have Ss individually scan for and fill in the answers.

Comprehension check

- Go over the answers to Exercise **1A** with the class. Make sure that Ss followed instructions and filled in their answers. Ask Ss to point to the information in the invitation.

Application

- Read the instructions for Exercise **1B** aloud.
- Model the task. Ask: *What day is the party?* (Saturday.) *What time is the party?* (8:00 p.m.) *Where is the party?* (Katya and Alex's house.)
- Say: *Now tell your partner this information about the party.*
- Ss complete the exercise in pairs. Walk around and help as needed.

Literacy tip
For an alternative activity, refer literacy Ss to pages 76–77 in the *Literacy Workbook* at any time during the lesson.

Expansion activity *(individual work, student pairs)*
- Ask Ss to write an invitation to an imaginary party in their notebooks. Tell them to model their invitation after the one in Exercise **1A**. Encourage them to change the information in their invitation to make the party different.
- Ss in pairs. Say: *Look at your partner's invitation. Ask questions about the party. Use these question words: What day*, *What time*, *and Where.*
- Walk around and help as needed.

Community building *(whole group)*
- If you plan to have a real party in your class in the future (for example, the last day of the course), talk about the party and make an invitation for the party on the board. Ask different Ss to write different parts of the invitation on the board in turn. This might be a good time to teach Ss words like *potluck* and *casual dress.*

LESSON F Another view

Presentation

- Books closed. Draw five rectangles on the board to represent five digital clocks.
- Ask a few Ss to come to the board and write different times in the clocks, such as *10:00* or *11:30*.
- Point to each clock in turn. Ask different Ss: *What time is it?* Elicit appropriate responses.

Practice

- Books open. Direct Ss' attention to Exercise **2A** and read the instructions aloud. Hold up the Student's Book. Point to the first row of clocks. Say: *Write times on this row of clocks only.*
- Ss complete the task individually. Walk around and help as needed.
- Direct Ss' attention to the second part of the instructions for Exercise **2A**. Model the task. Ask two Ss to read the example conversation. Hold up the Student's Book. Point to the second row of clocks. Say: *Write the time your partner says on these clocks.*
- Ss complete the exercise in pairs. Walk around and help as needed.
- Erase the times on the clocks on the board. Then ask several pairs to say their conversations for the rest of the class. The S who asks the question should write the answer in a clock on the board.

Expansion activity (whole class)

- Competition. Draw a vertical line on the board, dividing the board in half. Draw a large rectangle on each side of the line, to represent digital clocks. Divide the class into two teams. Say: *I am going to tell you a time. One person from each team will go to the board and write the time in the clock.*
- Model the activity. Ask a S to stand up. Say: *10:00 a.m.* The S goes to the board and writes the time in the rectangle on his or her side of the board.
- Begin the game. Ask Ss to write the following times, or make up other times to match the ability of your class:
  9:30 a.m. 11:00 p.m. 6:30 a.m. 8:00 a.m. 4:30 p.m.
- The S who writes the time correctly first earns a point. The team with the most points at the end of the game wins.

Practice

- Direct Ss' attention to Exercise **2B**. Read the instructions aloud.
- Model the task. Point to the first item and ask: *What's the word?* (day) *What letter does it need?* (d) Point to the letter *d* written in the blank.
- Ss complete the words individually or in pairs. Walk around and help as needed.
- Ask individual Ss to write the words on the board. Point to each word. Ask other Ss: *Is this word correct?* Ask Ss to correct the spelling if necessary.
- Read aloud the second part of the instructions in Exercise **2B**.
- Model the task. Point to the first item and ask: *What letter do we need in number 1?* (d) Read aloud the numbers under the blanks in the puzzle and stop when you get to number 1. Tell Ss: *Write the letter "d" for number 1.* Make sure Ss understand the task.
- Ss complete the task individually.
- Ask a S to write the answer to the puzzle on the board.

Evaluation

- Before asking Ss to turn to the self-assessment on page 141, do a quick review of the unit. Have Ss turn to Lesson A. Ask the class to talk about what they remember about this lesson. Prompt Ss, if necessary, with questions, such as: *What words are on this page? What do you see in the picture?* Continue in this manner to review each lesson quickly.
- **Self-assessment** Read the instructions for Exercise **3**. Ask Ss to turn to the self-assessment page and complete the unit self-assessment.
- If Ss are ready, administer the unit test on pages T-184–T-186 of this Teacher's Edition (or on the Assessment Audio CD / CD-ROM).

More Ventures, Unit 6, Lesson F	
Literacy Workbook, 15–30 min. **Basic Workbook,** 15–30 min.	
Writing worksheets, 15–30 min. **Real Life Document,** 15–30 min.	www.cambridge.org/myresourceroom

2 Fun with vocabulary

A Write times on the clocks.

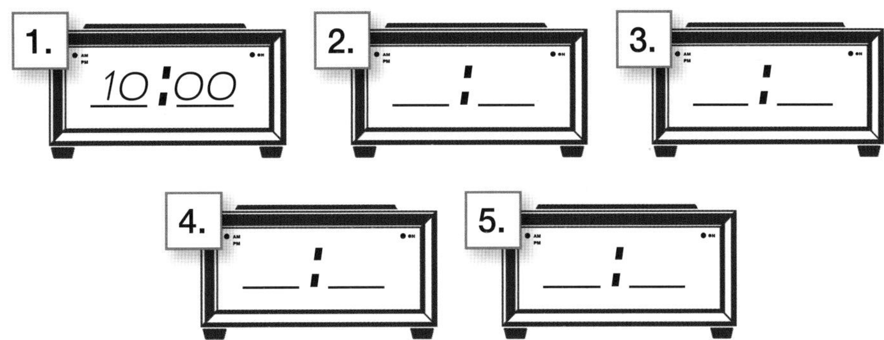

Talk with a partner. Listen and write your partner's times.

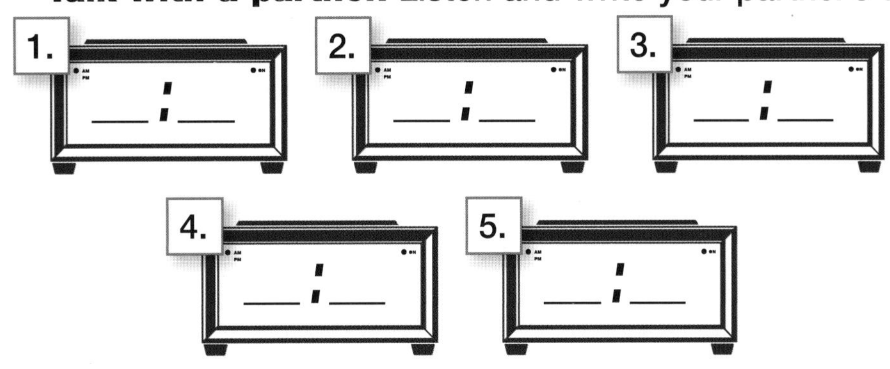

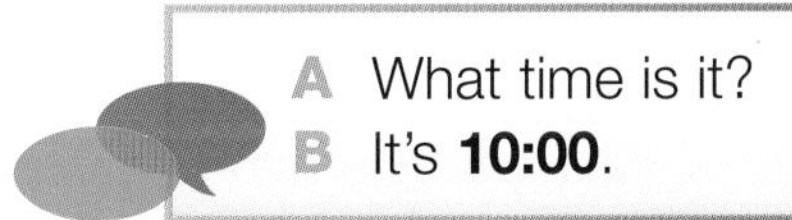

A What time is it?
B It's **10:00**.

B Write the missing letters.

d (1) ay — m (2) ovie — at noo n (3) — at nig h (4) t

in the even i (5) ng — in the af t (6) ernoon

in the mornin g (7) — appo i (8) ntment

What time is it? Write the letters below.

m (2) i (8) d (1) n (3) i (5) g (7) h (4) t (6)

3 Wrap up

Complete the **Self-assessment** on page 141.

Review

1 Listening

CLASS CD2 TK 10

Read. Then listen and circle.

1. Is the meeting on Friday?
   - (a.) Yes, it is.
   - b. No, it isn't.
2. What time is the meeting?
   - a. at 2:30
   - (b.) at 10:30
3. What time is the appointment?
   - (a.) at 2:00
   - b. at 4:00
4. Where's the school?
   - a. next to the bank
   - (b.) across from the bank
5. Where's the movie theater?
   - a. between the supermarket and the pharmacy
   - (b.) next to the supermarket
6. Is the movie at 7:30?
   - (a.) Yes, it is.
   - b. No, it isn't.

Talk with a partner. Ask and answer.

2 Vocabulary

Write. Complete the story.

afternoon class 8:30 hospital meeting

Tan's Day

Tan's English _class_ (1) is at _8:30_ (2) in the morning. His _meeting_ (3) is at 1:00 in the _afternoon_ (4). The meeting is at the _hospital_ (5), next to the school. It's a busy day.

Lesson objectives

- Review vocabulary and grammar from Units 5 and 6
- Introduce the pronunciation of *a* as in *at* and *o* as in *on*

Warm-up and review

- Before class. Write today's lesson focus on the board.
  Review unit:
  Review vocabulary and grammar from Units 5 and 6.
  Pronounce a as in at and o as in on.
- Begin class. Books closed. Ask the following questions and elicit appropriate responses:
  Where is our English class?
  What time is our English class?
  What time is our English class over?
  What building is next to our school?

Practice

- Books open. Say: *Listen to conversations about events and places.*
- Direct Ss' attention to Exercise **1** and read the instructions aloud. Ask a S to read the question and answer choices in number 1 aloud.
- Class Audio CD2 track 10 Model the task. Play or read only the first conversation on the audio program (see audio script, page T-159). Point to the two answer choices in number 1 and ask: *Yes, it is or No, it isn't?* (Yes, it is.) Point to where letter *a* has been circled. Say: *Yes, the meeting is on Friday.*
- Read aloud the remaining questions and answer choices. Say: *Now listen and circle the correct answers.*
- Class Audio CD2 track 10 Play or read the complete audio program (see audio script, page T-159). Ss listen and circle the answers. Repeat the audio program as needed.
- Check answers with the class. Read each question aloud and call on different Ss to answer.
- Read aloud the second part of the instructions for Exercise **1**. Ss practice asking and answering the questions in pairs. Walk around and help as needed.
- Ask several pairs to ask and answer the questions for the rest of the class.

Learner persistence (student pairs)

- If you have any Ss who are struggling in class, try to pair them with stronger Ss who like to help others in the class. From time to time, ask Ss to pick new partners so that everyone gets a chance to practice with Ss of different ability levels.

Practice

- Direct Ss' attention to Exercise **2**. Point to the title of the story and ask: *What's the title?* (Tan's Day) Ask: *What do you think this story is about?* Elicit any words that Ss might think will be in the story, such as *English class, meeting, morning.*
- Read aloud the instructions for Exercise **2**. Point to the words in the word bank and tell the Ss: *Write these words in the story.*
- Model the task. Read aloud the first sentence: *Tan's English . . .* Elicit *class.* Point to *class* in the word bank and in the blank for number 1.
- Ss read the story and fill in the blanks individually. Walk around and help as needed.
- Write the numbers *1–5* on the board. Ask Ss to come up and write the answers on the board.
- Ask individual Ss to read sentences from the story aloud. After each sentence, ask: *Is the answer correct?* Ask different Ss to correct any errors.

Expansion activity (small groups)

- Before class. Prepare copies of the picture dictionary cards from Units 5 and 6. Divide the class into small groups. Give each group copies of the picture cards. Say: *Make sentences with the two sets of cards.*
- Model the activity. Write on the board: *I go* _____. Ask Ss to complete the sentence with a place they go every day. Elicit endings, such as: *to school, home, to work.*
- Hold up a picture dictionary card from Unit 6, for example: *in the morning.* Put it next to a sentence. Say the sentence aloud, for example: *I go to school in the morning.*
- Hold up a picture dictionary card from Unit 5, for example: *by bus.* Put it next to the card from Unit 6. Form a longer sentence using the two picture dictionary cards. Say the sentence aloud, for example: *I go to school in the morning by bus.*
- Tell Ss to use this order when forming sentences: *I go to school + (picture card from Unit 6) + (picture card from Unit 5).*

> **Teaching tip**
> If appropriate, tell Ss that the order of the phrases in the sentences can be changed, for example: *In the morning I go to school by bus.*

- Ss complete the activity in small groups. Encourage them to make as many sentences as possible. They can write the sentences in their notebooks for further writing practice.
- Ask each group to write a sentence on the board.

Review

Warm-up and review

- Books closed. Draw some buildings on the board. Label them with names of places learned in Unit 5. Make sure they are located across from, between, and next to each other.
- Point to a building. Ask: *What's this?* (Elicit the name of the building.) Ask: *Where is it?* (Elicit an appropriate response.) Continue by asking about all the buildings.

Practice

- Direct Ss' attention to Exercise **3A**. Read the instructions aloud.
- Model the task. Ask a S to read the first example. Ask: *Is it correct to say "The library is on the bank?"* (No.) Say: *No, the library is across from the bank.* Point to where *across from* has been circled and written.
- Ss circle and write their answers individually. Walk around and help as needed.
- Write the numbers *1–4* on the board. Ask individual Ss to write the answers from Exercise **3** on the board. Ask other Ss to read the words aloud. Ask: *Are these words correct?* Ask different Ss to correct any errors.
- Direct Ss' attention to the planner page in Exercise **3B** and ask: *What do you see?* Elicit any vocabulary that Ss know. Read the instructions aloud.
- Model the task. Ask two Ss to read the example question and answer aloud. Hold up the Student's Book. Point to where it says *movie* in the memo. Ask: *Is the movie at 6:00?* Elicit: *No, it isn't. It's at 6:30.*
- Ss complete the exercise individually. Walk around and help as needed.
- Ss check their answers in pairs. Say: *Ask and answer the questions with your partner. Check to see if your answers are the same or different.*
- Ask several pairs to ask and answer the questions for the rest of the class.

Presentation

- Direct Ss' attention to the second part of the lesson focus written on the board.
- Write on the board: *at, class, map.* Point to and say each word and ask Ss to repeat. Underline the *a* in the words. Say a short a (/æ/) sound before repeating each word, for example: /æ/, *at.* Ask Ss to repeat after you.
- Write on the board: *on, clock, not.* Repeat the procedure, underlining the *o* in the words and pronouncing a short *o* (/ɒ/) sound, for example: /ɒ/, *on.*

Practice

Class Audio CD2 track 11 Direct Ss' attention to Exercise **4A** and read aloud the instructions. Play or read the audio program (see audio script, page T-159). Ss listen to examples of the two vowel sounds.

Expansion activity *(whole group)*

- Draw a vertical line on the board. Write *at* in one column and *on* in the other. Say: *Let's think of other words that have these sounds.* As Ss say words with these sounds, write them in the correct column. Point to each word and ask Ss to repeat.

Class Audio CD2 track 12 Direct Ss' attention to Exercise **4B** and read the instructions aloud. Play or read the audio program (see audio script, page T-159). Ss listen and repeat what they hear.

- Read aloud the second part of the instructions for Exercise **4B**. Model the task. Point to the two charts and tell one S: *Say a word.* Tell his or her partner: *Point to the word.*
- Ss complete the task in pairs. Walk around and help as needed.

Class Audio CD2 track 13 Direct Ss' attention to Exercise **4C** and read the instructions aloud. Model the task. Play or read the first word on the audio program (see audio script, page T-159). Ask: *Which letter is it:* a *or* o*?* (o) Point to where the letter has been checked in the chart.

Class Audio CD2 track 13 Play or read the complete audio program (see audio script, page T-159). Ss listen and make a checkmark under the letter they hear.

Class Audio CD2 track 13 Reproduce the chart from Exercise **4C** on the board, and play or read the audio program again. Pause after each word and ask a S to check the appropriate letter in the chart.

Evaluation

- Direct Ss' attention to the lesson focus.
- Go around the room. Ask each S to say a sentence about Tan from Exercise **2** on page 82 in the Student's Book.
- Write on the board: *class, clock.* Call on individual Ss as you point to one of the words, and ask them to say it. Listen carefully to the vowel sounds and provide help and correction as needed.
- Check off the items in the lesson focus as Ss demonstrate understanding of what they have learned in the lesson.

3 Grammar

A **Read and circle.** Then write.

1. The library is ___*across from*___ the bank.
   on (across from)
2. The post office is ___*between*___ the bank and the library.
   next to (between)
3. The restaurant is ___*on*___ Main Street.
   (on) between
4. The hospital is ___*across from*___ the gas station.
   (across from) between

B **Read the memo and answer.** Write *Yes, it is* or *No, it isn't.*

1. Is the movie at 6:00?
   ___*No, it isn't*___.
2. Is the class at 9:00?
   ___*Yes, it is*___.
3. Is the meeting in the morning?
   ___*No, it isn't*___.
4. Is the appointment in the afternoon?
   ___*Yes, it is*___.

Morning
9:00 class

Afternoon
2:00 – meeting with Ms. Morales
4:30 – appointment with Dr. Morgan

Evening
6:30 – movie

4 Pronunciation

A **Listen to the *a* sound and the *o* sound.**

CLASS CD2 TK 11

a	o
at	on

B **Listen and repeat.**

CLASS CD2 TK 12

a	at	class	map

o	on	clock	not

Talk with a partner. Say a word. Your partner points. Take turns.

C **Listen and check (✓).**

CLASS CD2 TK 13

	a	o		a	o		a	o		a	o		a	o
1.		✓	2.		✓	3.	✓		4.	✓		5.		✓

UNIT
7 Shopping

LESSON A Listening

1 Before you listen

A Look at the picture. What do you see?

CLASS CD2 TK 14

B Listen and point: a dress • pants • a shirt
shoes • socks • a T-shirt

Lesson objectives

- Introduce Ss to the topic
- Find out what Ss know about the topic
- Preview the unit by talking about the picture
- Practice key vocabulary
- Practice listening skills

UNIT 7

Warm-up and review

- Before class. Write today's lesson focus on the board.
  Lesson A:
  Shopping
  Vocabulary for clothes shopping
- Begin class. Write the word *clothes* on the board. Point to the word. Say it aloud and ask Ss to repeat after you. Ask: *What are some examples of clothes?* Encourage Ss to say any names of clothes that they know or to point to different types of clothes on Ss in the classroom. Write the different types that Ss say on the board. Explain the new words by pointing to examples in the class.
- Say: *Today's class is about shopping for clothes. Where do you go shopping for clothes?* Elicit appropriate responses. Ask: *What clothes stores do you like?* Elicit appropriate responses.

Literacy tip

If you have literacy Ss in your class, it might be helpful to spend time at the beginning of any activity that contains art or photos talking about the pictures before focusing Ss' attention on the printed words in the exercise. Have Ss work in pairs. Tell them to ask each other: *What do you see?* Encourage Ss to describe the pictures to each other. Consider pairing literacy Ss with Ss who can help them read the text in the exercise. This will help preview the exercise for literacy Ss and make them more confident as the exercise continues.

Presentation

- Books open. Set the scene. Hold up the Student's Book. Show Ss the picture on page 84. Ask: *What do you see?* Elicit and write on the board any vocabulary that Ss know, such as: *clothes store, sale, dress, pants, T-shirt.*

Teaching tip

If Ss don't know the meaning of the word *sale*, say: *"Sale" means a time of lower prices.* If possible, bring in a circular from a newspaper that has the word *sale* in it. Show it to the class. Point to the sale items. Say: *These items are on sale.*

Practice

- Direct Ss' attention to the key vocabulary in Exercise **1B**. Read each word or phrase aloud while pointing to the corresponding items in the picture. Ask Ss to repeat and point.

Class Audio CD2 track 14 Play or read the audio program (see audio script, page T-160). Tell Ss: *Listen and point to the picture.* As Ss hear the key vocabulary, check to see that they are pointing to the correct part of the picture. Repeat the audio program as needed.

Comprehension check

- Ask Ss *Yes / No* questions about the picture. Ask about new vocabulary and recycle words learned in previous units. Say: *Listen to the questions. Answer "Yes, it is." or "No, it isn't."*

  Point to the picture. Ask: *Is this a shopping mall?* (No, it isn't.)
  Point to the store. Ask: *Is this a shoe store?* (No, it isn't.)
  Point to the sundress in the store window. Ask: *Is this a dress?* (Yes, it is.)
  Point to a T-shirt. Ask: *Is this a pair of pants?* (No, it isn't.)
  Point to a pair of pants. Ask: *Is this a pair of pants?* (Yes, it is.)

Teaching tip

Review, if necessary, the grammar point learned in Lesson C of Unit 6. This grammar point asks questions with the pattern *Is your class at 11:00?* and has the same answers *Yes, it is* and *No, it isn't* as in this exercise.

Expansion activity (whole group)

- Draw a large stick figure on the board. Say: *We are going to put clothes on this person.* Ask a S to come to the board. Say: *Please draw pants on this person.* Continue by asking different Ss to draw other clothes on the figure.

  Option Ask a S to tell the other Ss what to draw. Write: *Draw a _____ on the person.* to help the S with the directions.

Literacy tip

For an alternative activity, refer literacy Ss to pages 78–79 in the *Literacy Workbook* at any time during the lesson.

LESSON A Listening

Presentation

- Direct Ss' attention to Exercise **2A**. Tell Ss: *These are different types of clothes.*
- Hold up or point to real examples of the clothing as you read each word aloud. Ask Ss to repeat the words after you. If there is an item that no one is wearing (for example, a dress), draw a quick sketch and label it on the board.
- Read aloud the instructions for Exercise **2A**.

Practice

Class Audio CD2 track 15 Play or read the audio program (see audio script, page T-160). Ss listen and repeat the vocabulary. Repeat the audio program as needed.

- Listen carefully to Ss' pronunciation and make corrections as needed.

Learner persistence *(individual work)*

Self-Study Audio CD track 31 Exercise **2A** is recorded on the CD at the back of the Student's Book. Ss can listen to the CD at home for reinforcement and review. They can also listen to the CD for self-directed learning when class attendance is not possible.

- Direct Ss' attention to Exercise **2B** and read the instructions aloud.

Class Audio CD2 track 16 Model the task. Hold up the Student's Book and say: *Number one.* Play or read the audio program for number 1 (see audio script, page T-160). Point to the two answer choices in number 1 and ask Ss: *What did you hear – a or b?* Elicit: *a.* Point to the letter *a* next to the first picture and tell Ss: *Circle the letter "a."*

Class Audio CD2 track 16 Play or read the complete audio program (see audio script, page T-160). Ss listen and circle the correct answers. Repeat the audio as needed.

Class Audio CD2 track 16 Read aloud the second part of the instructions for Exercise **2B**. Play or read the audio program again so that Ss can listen and check their answers.

Learner persistence *(individual work)*

Self-Study Audio CD track 32 Exercise **2B** is recorded on the CD at the back of the Student's Book. Ss can listen to the CD at home for reinforcement and review and also for self-directed learning when class attendance is not possible.

Comprehension check

- Write the numbers *1–4* on the board. Ask a few Ss to come to the board and write the correct answers to Exercise **2B** next to each number.

Class Audio CD2 track 16 Play or read the audio program again. Pause the audio program after each conversation. Point to the answer written on the board and ask: *Is this correct?* Ask another S to make any necessary corrections.

Application

- Direct Ss' attention to Exercise **3** and read the instructions aloud.
- Model the task. Hold up the Student's Book and point to the answer choices in Exercise **2B**. Say to one S: *Point to a picture.* Say to the first S's partner: *Say the word.*
- Ss complete the exercise in pairs. Walk around and help as needed.

Evaluation

- Direct Ss' attention to the lesson focus written on the board. Check Ss' understanding of clothing vocabulary by asking them to point to the following clothing items in the picture on page 84 in the Student's Book: *dress*, *pants*, *shirt*, *shoes*, *socks*, *T-shirt.* Walk around and check that Ss are pointing to the correct items.
- Check off the lesson focus as Ss demonstrate an understanding of what they have learned in the lesson.

More Ventures, Unit 7, Lesson A	
Literacy Workbook, 15–30 min.	
Basic Workbook, 15–30 min.	
Writing worksheets, 15–30 min.	www.cambridge.org/myresourceroom
Student Arcade, time varies	www.cambridge.org/venturesarcade

Unit Goals
Identify prices
Complete a shopping list
Interpret a receipt

2 Listen

A Listen and repeat.

STUDENT TK 31
CLASS CD2 TK 15

1. a dress 2. pants 3. a shirt
4. shoes 5. socks 6. a T-shirt

B Listen and circle.

STUDENT TK 32
CLASS CD2 TK 16

1. 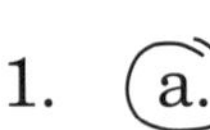 a.  b. 

2. a.   b. 

3. a.   b. 

4. a.  b. 

Listen again. Check your answers.

3 After you listen

Talk with a partner. Point to a picture. Your partner says the word.

LESSON **B** Clothing

1 Vocabulary focus

Listen and repeat.

CLASS CD2 TK 17

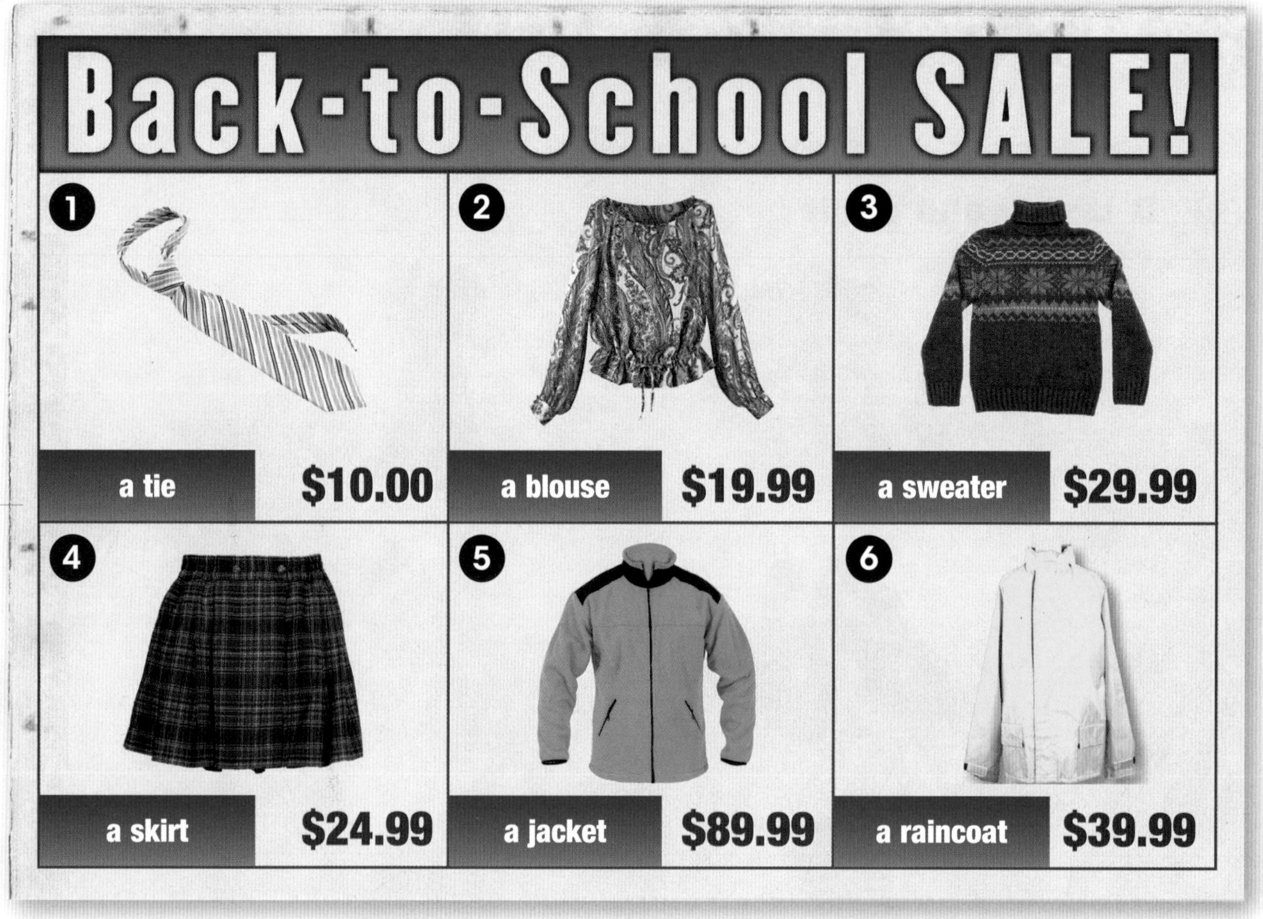

Back-to-School SALE!
1
a tie
$10.00
2
a blouse
$19.99
3
a sweater
$29.99
4
a skirt
$24.99
5
a jacket
$89.99
6
a raincoat
$39.99

2 Practice

A Read and match.

1.
2.
3.
4.
5.
6.

a tie | a blouse | a jacket | a skirt | a raincoat | a sweater

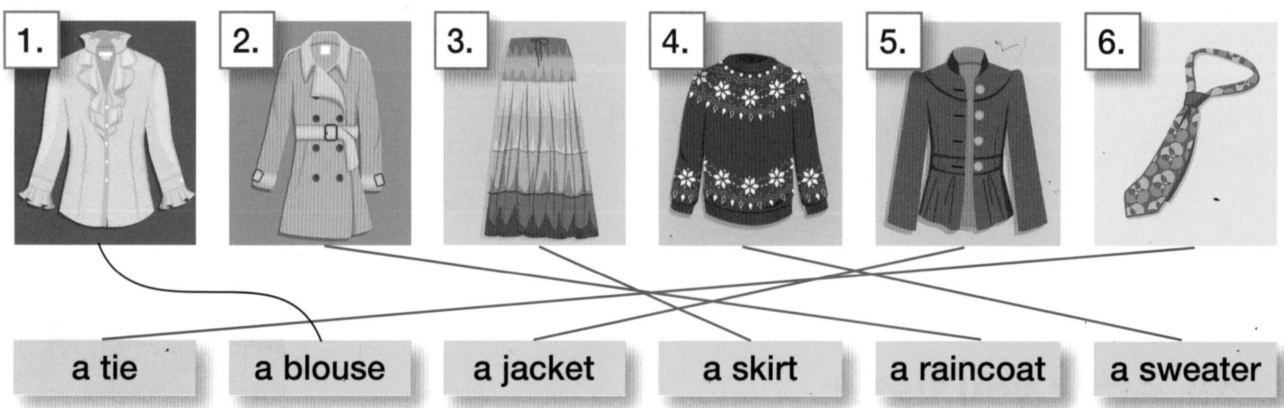

Lesson objectives

- Introduce and practice more clothing vocabulary
- Practice questions and answers about prices with *How much?*

Warm-up and review

- Before class. Write today's lesson focus on the board.
  Lesson B:
  Clothing vocabulary
  How much?
  Prices
- Begin class. Books open. Direct Ss' attention to the picture on page 84. Review key vocabulary from the unit by asking: *What are some names of clothes in this picture?* Elicit: *dress, pants, shirt, shoes, socks, T-shirt.* Ask Ss to point to these items.
- Walk around and check to see that Ss are pointing to the correct items in the picture.
- Point out to students that *clothes* and *clothing* mean the same thing.
- Write the words *Back-to-School Sale!* on the board. Point to the words. Say them aloud. Ask Ss to repeat them after you. Ask: *What is this?* If necessary, remind Ss of the sale sign in the picture on page 84. If Ss don't know what a back-to-school sale is, say: *It's a sale just before school starts. It's for buying clothes for school.*

Community building (whole class)

- If you have Ss with school-age children, ask if they go to back-to-school sales at the beginning of the school year. Ask: *What store has good back-to-school sales?* Elicit appropriate answers. Ask other Ss if they shop at back-to-school sales for themselves.

Presentation

- Set the scene. Write on the board: *advertisement.* Point to the word. Say it aloud. Ask: *What's this?* Elicit an appropriate response.

> **Teaching tip**
> It might be helpful to bring some advertisements to class. Show them to the class. Say: *These are advertisements, or "ads" for short.* Erase the letters to show how *advertisement* becomes *ad.*

- Read aloud the instructions for Exercise **1**.
- Class Audio CD2 track 17 Play or read the audio program (see audio script, page T-160). Listen and repeat the vocabulary along with Ss. Repeat the audio program as needed.
- Listen carefully to Ss' pronunciation and correct as needed.

Expansion activity (student pairs)

- Write on the board: *Is this a (name of clothing item)? Yes, it is. / No, it isn't.*
- Model the activity. Point to the picture of a blouse in Exercise **1**. Ask a S: *Is this a blouse?* The S answers: *Yes, it is.* Point to the picture of a raincoat. Ask another S: *Is this a jacket?* The S answers: *No, it isn't.*
- Ss continue pointing and asking about the pictures with their partners.
- Walk around and help as needed.

Practice

- Direct Ss' attention to Exercise **2A**. As you read aloud the instructions, hold up the Student's Book and indicate that Ss should look at the pictures of clothing items and match them to the corresponding words.
- Model the task. Hold up the Student's Book. Point to the first picture. Ask: *What clothing item is this?* (a blouse) Say: *Match the picture with the word.*
- Ss complete the exercise individually. Help as needed.

> **Teaching tip**
> Sometimes Ss have difficulty distinguishing between a blouse and a shirt. Draw a frilly blouse on the board, or ask a S wearing one to stand up. Draw a plainer shirt on the board, or ask a S wearing one to stand up. Point to the blouse and shirt one at a time and say: *This is a blouse. This is a shirt.*

> **Literacy tip**
> Literacy Ss may be able to complete this activity with help. Pair stronger Ss with literacy Ss. Tell literacy Ss to refer to Exercise **1** when completing Exercise **2A**.

Comprehension check

- Write the numbers *1–6* on the board. Ask a few Ss to come to the board and write the answers to Exercise **2A** on the board.
- Ask different Ss to read the answers written on the board. After each answer is read, ask: *Is this correct?* Ask another S to make any necessary corrections on the board.

LESSON B Clothing

Presentation

- Direct Ss' attention to the word bank in Exercise **2B**. Say: *Repeat these words after me.* Say each word aloud. Listen to Ss' pronunciation as they repeat the words after you.
- Read the instructions for Exercise **2B** aloud.
- Say: *You are going to listen to conversations about prices.* Write on the board: *How much?* Point to the words. Say: *When we ask about prices, we say, "How much?"*

Practice

Class Audio CD2 track 18 Model the task. Say: *Listen and repeat.* Play or read the audio program for number 1 (see audio script, page T-160), and point to the tie as you repeat. Say: *Then write.* Point to the word *tie* written in the blank. Make sure Ss understand the task.

Class Audio CD2 track 18 Play or read the complete audio program (see audio script, page T-160). Ss listen and repeat. Encourage Ss to point to the clothing pictures as they repeat.

- Ss complete the sentences individually using words from the word bank. Repeat the audio program as needed.
- Check answers with the class. Write the numbers *1–6* on the board, and ask for volunteers to write their answers on the board. Point to each answer and ask the class: *Yes? Is this correct?* Make any necessary corrections on the board.
- Read aloud the second part of the instructions for Exercise **2B**. Point to and model the example conversation.
- Call on a pair of volunteers to read the example conversation aloud for the class.
- Point to another clothing picture on page 87. Ask: *How much is the jacket?* ($48.99.) Repeat with different clothing items. Indicate that Ss should ask and answer questions about all the clothing in the pictures.
- Ss complete the exercise in pairs. Walk around and help as needed.

Teaching tip

It might be helpful to go over the different ways prices can be said in English. Write *$9.99* on the board. Say: *In English, we can say this price in two ways. One way is "nine ninety-nine." The second way is "nine dollars and ninety-nine cents."* Continue by asking Ss to read the prices in Exercise **2B** two ways.

Literacy tip

For an alternative activity, refer literacy Ss to pages 80–81 in the *Literacy Workbook* at any time during the lesson.

Expansion activity *(student pairs)*

- Bring clothing ads from department and other stores to class. Ask Ss to find examples of the clothing items in Lessons A and B in the ads.
- Write: *How much is the ______?* Say: *Point to a clothing item. Ask your partner, "How much is it?"* Walk around and help as needed.
- Ask several pairs to ask and answer questions about the clothing in the ads for the rest of the class.

Application

- Direct Ss' attention to Exercise **3** and read the instructions aloud. Have the Ss write their own prices for each of the items.
- Model the task. Ask two Ss to read the question and answer aloud. Hold up the Student's Book and point to where $24.99 is written under the skirt as the Ss are saying the conversation. Make sure the Ss understand the task.
- Ss complete the exercise in pairs. Walk around and help as needed.
- Ask several pairs to ask and answer the questions for the rest of the class.

Evaluation

- Direct Ss' attention to the lesson focus written on the board. Check Ss' understanding of the key vocabulary by asking them to point to the clothing in the pictures in Exercise **2B** on page 87: *tie*, *blouse*, *jacket*, *raincoat*, *skirt*, *sweater.* Walk around and check that Ss are pointing to the correct items.
- Focus Ss' attention on *How much?* in the lesson focus. Ask Ss to ask questions about the prices of the items in Exercise **2B** with *How much?* Ask other Ss to answer the questions.
- Check off each part of the lesson focus as Ss demonstrate an understanding of what they have learned in the lesson.

More Ventures, Unit 7, Lesson B	
Literacy Workbook, 15–30 min.	
Basic Workbook, 15–30 min.	
Writing worksheets, 15–30 min.	www.cambridge.org/myresourceroom
Student Arcade, time varies	www.cambridge.org/venturesarcade

CLASS CD2 TK 18

B Listen and repeat. Then write.

blouse jacket raincoat skirt sweater tie

1. 
The *tie* is $9.99.

2. 
The *raincoat* is $26.95.

3. 
The *skirt* is $35.95.

4. 
The *sweater* is $39.99.

5. 
The *jacket* is $48.99.

6. 
The *blouse* is $25.95.

Talk with a partner. Ask and answer.

A How much is the **tie**?
B **$9.99.**

USEFUL LANGUAGE

$9.99 = *nine ninety-nine*
or
nine dollars and ninety-nine cents

3 Communicate

Write prices. Your partner asks the price. You answer.

$ *24.99* $ *(Answers will vary.)* $ ______ $ ______ $ ______

A How much is the **skirt**?
B **$24.99.**

LESSON C How much are the shoes?

1 Grammar focus: *How much is? / How much are?*

Questions			Answers
How much	**is**	the shirt?	$15.99.
	are	the shoes?	$68.95.

2 Practice

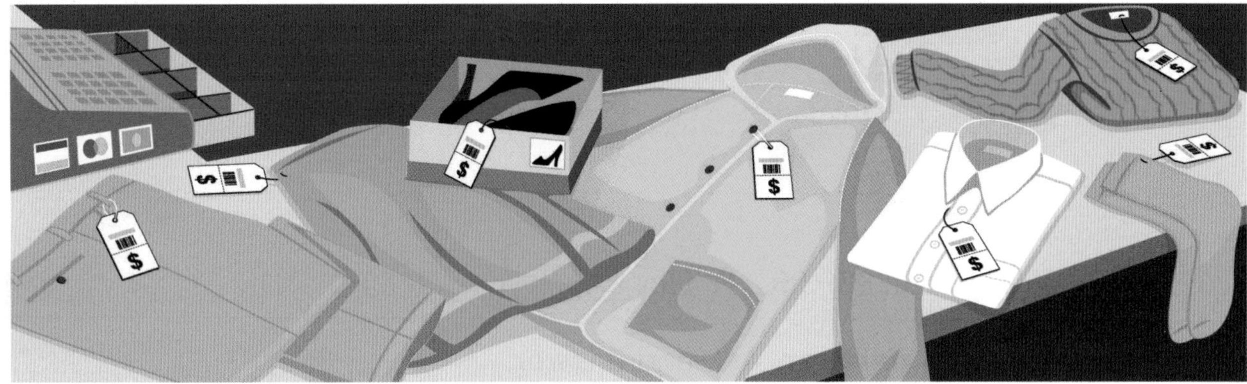

A Read and circle. Then write.

1. A How much *are* (is / **are**) the pants?
   B $24.99.
2. A How much *is* (**is** / are) the skirt?
   B $18.99.
3. A How much *is* (**is** / are) the raincoat?
   B $16.95.
4. A How much *are* (is / **are**) the shoes?
   B $58.99.
5. A How much *is* (**is** / are) the sweater?
   B $31.99.
6. A How much *are* (is / **are**) the socks?
   B $5.95.

CLASS CD2 TK 19

Listen and repeat. Then practice with a partner.

Lesson objective

- Review *How much is?* and introduce *How much are?*

Warm-up and review

- Before class. Write today's lesson focus on the board.
  Lesson C:
  How much is?
  How much are?
- Begin class. Books closed. Write the names of clothing learned in Lesson B on the board: *blouse*, *jacket*, *raincoat*, *skirt*, *sweater*, *tie*. Write a price under each item: *$10.00*, *$24.99*, *$32.50*, *$12.99*, *$6.99*.
- Point to the word *blouse*. Ask: *What's this?* (A blouse.) Ask: *How much is it?* ($10.00.)
- Continue the exercise. Point to each clothing item on the board. Ask Ss the prices.

Presentation

- Books open. Direct Ss' attention to the grammar chart in Exercise **1**. Read the questions and the corresponding answers aloud. Ask Ss to repeat after you.
- Ask: *Why do we sometimes say "How much is" and sometimes say "How much are"?* If Ss don't know the answer, say: *Use "is" for a singular item (one item) and "are" for a plural item (more than one).*
- Write *singular* and *plural* on the board. Point to each word. Say it aloud. Ask Ss to repeat it after you. Pick up a pen and show it to the class. Ask: *Is this singular or plural?* (Singular.) Pick up two books. Ask: *Are these singular or plural?* (Plural.)

> **Teaching tip**
> Remind Ss that plurals in English usually have an *s* on the end of the singular form. Give Ss examples to remind them of the singular and plural forms in English.

Comprehension check

- Write the words *pants*, *socks*, and *shoes* on the board. Include a price for each item: *$24.99*, *$4.99*, *$62.50*. Point to the word *pants*. Write on the board: *How much is?* and *How much are?* Ask: *Which question do I use with "pants"?* Elicit: *How much are the pants?* If Ss need more explanation, circle the *s* in pants. Say: *Remember that plural words use "are" in this question.*
- Point to the singular words written on the board at the beginning of the lesson (*blouse*, *jacket*, etc.). Ask: *Which question do I use with "blouse"?* Elicit: *How much is the blouse?*
- Point to all the words in turn, switching from plural words to singular ones. Check to make sure Ss understand the difference between the two question forms.

Practice

- Direct Ss' attention to the picture in Exercise **2A**. Ask: *Where is this picture?* (In a store.) *What do you see?* Elicit: *pants*, *a skirt*, *a raincoat*, *shoes*, *a sweater*, *a shirt*, *socks*.

> **Teaching tip**
> Do not expect Ss to answer the questions in complete sentences. The purpose of this exercise is to understand the meaning of the question and answer with the correct information.

- Read aloud the example conversation in number 1. When you read Speaker B's line, show Ss the two answer choices under the blank and ask: *is* or *are*? Elicit *are*.
- Read aloud the instructions for Exercise **2A**. Point to where *are* has been circled and written for number 1.
- Ss complete the exercise individually. Walk around and help as needed.

Comprehension check

- Read aloud the second part of the instructions in Exercise **2A**.

Class Audio CD2 track 19 Play or read the audio program (see audio script, page T-160). Ss listen and repeat as they check their answers.

- Write the numbers *1–6* on the board. Ask volunteers to come to the board and write the answers they circled. Make any necessary corrections on the board.
- Ss in pairs. Ask Ss to choose Role A or B and practice the questions and answers in Exercise **2A**. Then have Ss switch roles and practice again. Walk around and help as needed.
- Ask several pairs to read the conversations to the rest of the class.

> **Literacy tip**
> For an alternative activity, refer literacy Ss to pages 82–83 in the *Literacy Workbook* at any time during the lesson.

LESSON C How much are the shoes?

Presentation

- Books closed. Write on the board: *yard sale.* Say the words. Ask Ss to repeat. Ask: *What is a yard sale?* If Ss don't know these words, say: *A yard sale is when people sell their used items outside their houses.* If Ss still do not understand, ask them to open their books and look at the picture in Exercise 2B for further clarification.

> **Teaching tip**
> It might be interesting to ask Ss if they ever go to yard sales. Ask if they have ever had a yard sale themselves.

> **Culture tip**
> If Ss are new to the United States, they may not be familiar with yard sales. It might be interesting to ask them their opinions about yard sales. Ask if any Ss have these types of sales in their countries. Explain that many Americans like to go to yard sales to find bargains or unique items.

Practice

- Books open. Direct Ss' attention to the picture in Exercise 2B. Say: *This is a picture of a yard sale. What do you see?* Elicit as many vocabulary words as possible.
- Read aloud the first part of the instructions for Exercise 2B. Focus Ss' attention on the shopping list beside the picture.

Class Audio CD2 track 20 Model the task. Say: *Listen and repeat.* Play or read the audio program for number 1 (see audio script, page T-160) and point to the T-shirt in the picture as you repeat. Say: *Then write.* Point to where *$2.00* has been written beside *T-shirt* in the shopping list. Make sure Ss understand the task.

Class Audio CD2 track 20 Play or read the complete audio program (see audio script, page T-160). Ss listen and repeat. Encourage Ss to point to the clothing in the picture as they repeat.

- Ss work individually as they write the prices in the shopping list. Repeat the audio program as needed.
- Write the numbers *1–8* on the board. Ask a few Ss to come to the board and write the word and the price for each clothing item on the board. Ask Ss to read each price aloud. Ask: *Are these prices correct?* Ask other Ss to make corrections.
- Read aloud the second part of the instructions for Exercise 2B. Model the task. Ask two Ss to read the first example conversation. Then ask two different Ss to read the second example conversation.
- Indicate that Ss should ask and answer questions about all the clothing. Make sure Ss understand the task.
- Ss ask and answer questions about the clothing in the picture in pairs. When Ss are finished, ask them to switch partners and repeat the conversations.
- Ask several pairs to say their conversations to the rest of the class.

Application

- Direct Ss' attention to Exercise 3 and read the instructions aloud. Have the Ss write their own prices for the items.
- Model the task. Ask two Ss to read the example conversation aloud. Hold up the Student's Book and point to where *$5.00* is written under the socks as the Ss are saying the conversation. Make sure Ss understand the task.
- Ss complete the exercise in pairs. Walk around and help as needed.

Community building *(whole group)*

- If Ss are interested in visiting a yard sale, tell them how to find out where yard sales are taking place. Tell Ss that they can look for yard sale signs in their neighborhoods or look for listings in the classified ads section of their local newspaper.

Evaluation

- Direct Ss' attention to the lesson focus written on the board. Ask Ss to look at the picture on page 84. Ask them to make questions about the clothing items in the picture using *How much is?* and *How much are?* Ask different Ss to answer the questions.
- Check off each part of the lesson focus as Ss demonstrate an understanding of what they have learned in the lesson.

More Ventures, Unit 7, Lesson C	
Literacy Workbook, 15–30 min. **Basic Workbook,** 15–30 min.	
Writing worksheets, 15–30 min.	www.cambridge.org/myresourceroom
Student Arcade, time varies	www.cambridge.org/venturesarcade

CLASS CD2 TK 20

B Listen and repeat. Then write.

1. T-shirt $2.00
2. shoes $3.00
3. jacket $8.00
4. sweater $4.00
5. raincoat $5.00
6. pants $6.00
7. socks $1.00
8. blouse $7.00

Talk with a partner. Ask and answer.

A How much **is the T-shirt**?
B **$2.00.**
A **$2.00?** Thanks.

A How much **are the shoes**?
B **$3.00.**
A **$3.00?** Thanks.

3 Communicate

Write prices. Your partner asks the price. You answer.

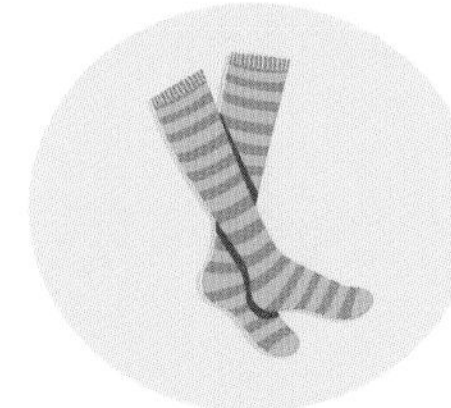

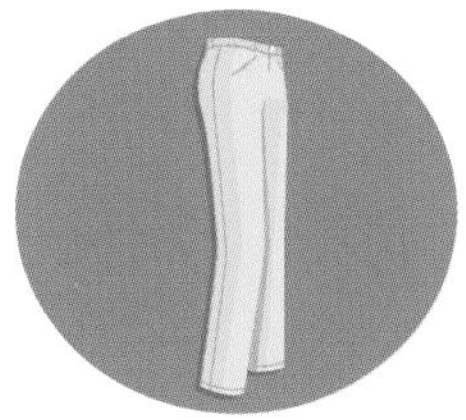

$ 5.00 $ (Answers will vary.) $ ______ $ ______ $ ______

A How much **are the socks**?
B **$5.00.**

LESSON D Reading

1 Before you read

Talk about the picture.
What do you see?

2 Read

Listen and read.

STUDENT TK 33
CLASS CD2 TK 21

New Message

From: Rose
To: Patty
Subject: Shopping

Hi Patty,

This morning, Samuel and I are going to The Clothes Place. Samuel needs blue pants. He needs a tie, too. I need a red dress and black shoes. Dresses are on sale. They're $49.99. Shoes are on sale, too. They're $34.99. That's good.

Call you later,

Rosc

3 After you read

Read and match.

Lesson objectives

- Introduce and read an e-mail message
- Practice using topic-related words

Warm-up and review

- Before class. Write today's lesson focus on the board.
Lesson D:
Read an e-mail message about shopping
Learn new vocabulary about clothes shopping
- Begin class. Books closed. Write *clothes* on the board. Point to the word. Ask: *What are the names of some clothes?* Elicit appropriate responses and write them on the board. Point to each of the words on the board in turn. Ask: *What is a good price for this item?* Elicit appropriate responses. Write the prices on the board next to the items.
- Write *Sale* on the board. Ask: *Do you remember this word on a sign in the first picture of this unit? What does the sign mean?* Elicit appropriate responses.

Community building (whole group)

- Ask Ss if there are any good sales going on in stores in the vicinity of the school. Encourage Ss to tell each other when good sales are happening.

Presentation

- Books open. Direct Ss' attention to the picture in Exercise **1**.
- Read the instructions aloud. Ask: *What do you see?* Elicit and write on the board any vocabulary that Ss know, such as: *sale*, *pants*, *dress*, *shoes*.
- Write *e-mail* on the board. Point to the word. Say it aloud and ask Ss to repeat after you. Ask: *What's this?* Elicit an appropriate answer such as: *It's a message on the computer.* Ask: *Do you write e-mails?*
- Say: *Now we will read an e-mail about shopping.*

Practice

- Direct Ss' attention to Exercise **2**. Read the instructions aloud.

Class Audio CD2 track 21 Play or read the audio program and ask Ss to read along (see audio script, page T-160). Repeat the audio program as needed.

- Read aloud each sentence of the e-mail and ask Ss to repeat after you.
- Answer any questions Ss have about the reading.

Community building

- If any Ss in your class have e-mail addresses, ask them if they would like to share them with others in the class. Explain that Ss can practice their writing and get to know their classmates better through e-mail. They can also find out about missed assignments if they are absent from English class.

Learner persistence (individual work)

Self-Study Audio CD track 33 Exercise **2** is recorded on the CD at the back of the Student's Book. Ss can listen to the CD at home for reinforcement and review and also for self-directed learning when class attendance is not possible.

Comprehension check

- Direct Ss' attention to Exercise **3** and read the instructions aloud.
- Hold up the Student's Book. Point to the first picture. Point to the line matching Picture 1 to the correct sentence. Ask a S to read the example sentence aloud. Say: *Draw a line to match each picture with the correct sentence.*
- Ss complete the exercise individually. Walk around and help as needed.
- Ask individual Ss to read each sentence aloud and say which picture the sentence matches.

Expansion activity (individual)

- Question-and-answer activity. Say: *Walk around the room. Write down the names of five Ss in the class. Then write their clothing next to their names.*
- Model the activity. Ask a S: *What's your name?* Write the S's name on the board. Ask the class: *What clothes is he / she wearing?* After the class responds, write the S's clothing next to his / her name. For example: *jeans, T-shirt, shoes.*

Teaching tip

Tell Ss that they don't have to ask the S what he or she is wearing. They can simply look and write down the other S's clothing.

LESSON D Reading

Presentation

- Books closed. Write the word *colors* on the board. Point to the word and say it aloud. Ask Ss to repeat it after you.
- Ask: *What colors can you say in English?* Write Ss' responses on the board.

Teaching tip
It might be helpful to point out examples of the colors in the room as you write the names of the color words on the board.

- Books open. Direct Ss' attention to the picture dictionary in Exercise 4. Hold up the Student's Book. Point to the pictures of baseball caps. Say: *These are baseball caps. They are all different colors.* Write *baseball caps* on the board. Say the words aloud and ask Ss to repeat.
- Point to the names of colors under each picture. Read the words aloud and ask Ss to repeat them after you.
- Read the instructions for Exercise 4A aloud.

Class Audio CD2 track 22 Play or read the audio program (see audio script, page T-160). Listen to Ss' pronunciation as they repeat the colors. Correct pronunciation as needed.

Learner persistence (individual work)

Self-Study Audio CD track 34 Exercise 4A is recorded on the CD at the back of the Student's Book. Ss can listen to the CD at home for reinforcement and review and also for self-directed learning when class attendance is not possible.

Practice

- Direct Ss' attention to Exercise 4B and read the instructions aloud. Ask two Ss to read the example conversations aloud. Then have them ask about a third S's clothing. Encourage Ss to try to use all the colors in the picture dictionary in their conversations.
- Ss complete the exercise in pairs. Walk around and help as needed.
- Ask several pairs to ask and answer the questions for the rest of the class, indicating who they are talking about. Check that they are using *his* and *her* correctly.

Teaching tip
It might be helpful to review possessive adjectives for this exercise. Point to a male and female S in the class. Ask: *What's his name? What's her name?* Write *his* and *her* on the board. Remind Ss to use the correct one when practicing the conversations in Exercise 4B.

Literacy tip
For an alternative activity, refer literacy Ss to pages 84–85 in the *Literacy Workbook* at any time during the lesson.

- Direct Ss' attention to Exercise 4C and read the instructions aloud.
- Focus Ss' attention on the example in Exercise 4C. Point to the words written in the chart. Say: *This student's name is Eliza. Her sweater is red. Her socks are yellow. Her blouse is white.* Hold up the Student's Book and point to each item in the chart.
- Model the task. Write *Name* and the colors horizontally across the board in the same order as in the Student's Book. Ask a volunteer to come to the front of the class Write the S's name on the board under *Name.* Point to the first color on the board. Say: *Look at Stefan's clothes. What is red? Anything? No.* Leave the chart cell blank. Point to the next color on the board. Ask: *What is yellow? His T-shirt. Yes!* Write *T-shirt* under *yellow* on the board. Continue with the rest of the colors: *Is Stefan wearing red?* If the answer is yes, ask: *What clothing item is red?* Elicit an appropriate response. Hold up the Student's Book again. Point to the corresponding cell in the chart. Say: *Write the name of the clothing item in this square.*
- Ss complete the chart in pairs, writing about the clothing of four classmates. Walk around and help as needed. Ss may ask for help with other clothing or color vocabulary.

Evaluation

- Direct Ss' attention to the first part of the lesson focus written on the board. Ask: *Where is Rose going shopping?* Elicit: *The Clothes Place.* Ask: *What is Rose going to buy?* Elicit: *Blue pants, a tie, a red dress, black shoes.*
- Direct Ss' attention to the baseball caps in the picture dictionary. Say: *Please name the color and the item. For example, number one. A black baseball cap.* Continue by asking different Ss to say the colors and names of the items.
- Check off each part of the lesson focus as Ss demonstrate understanding of what they have learned in the lesson.

More Ventures, Unit 7, Lesson D	
Literacy Workbook, 15–30 min. **Basic Workbook,** 15–30 min.	
Picture Dictionary activities, 30–45 min. **Writing worksheets,** 15–30 min.	www.cambridge.org/myresourceroom
Student Arcade, time varies	www.cambridge.org/venturesarcade

4 Picture dictionary Colors

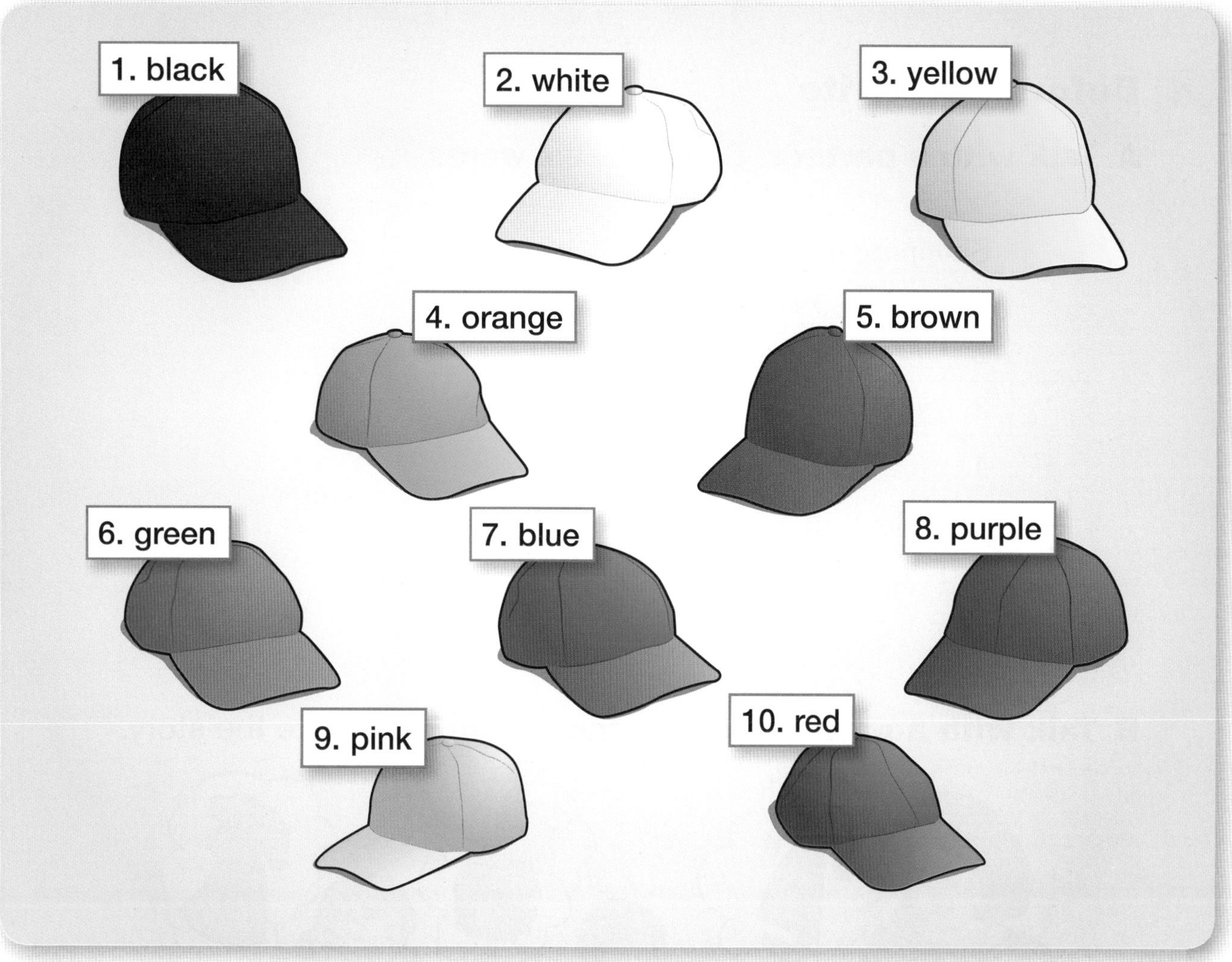

1. black
2. white
3. yellow
4. orange
5. brown
6. green
7. blue
8. purple
9. pink
10. red

STUDENT TK 34
CLASS CD2 TK 22

A Listen and repeat. Look at the picture dictionary.

B Talk with a partner. Look around your classroom. Ask and answer.

A What color is **her sweater**?
B **Blue.**

A What color are **his shoes**?
B **Brown.**

C Talk with a partner. Choose four classmates. Complete the chart.

Name	red	yellow	green	black	white	brown	blue
Eliza	*sweater*	*socks*			*blouse*		
(Answers will vary.)							

LESSON E Writing

1 Before you write

A Talk with a partner. Complete the words.

Shopping list
1. _s_ _k_ i r t
2. _d_ _r_ e s s
3. _s_ _h_ o e s
4. _b_ _l_ o u s e
5. _s_ _w_ e a t e r
6. T- _s_ _h_ i r t

B Talk with a partner. Look at the picture. Complete the story.

Sun Mi and her children are shopping today. They need clothes for school. Sun Mi needs a _dress_ (1) and _shoes_ (2). Her son Roger needs a _T-shirt_ (3) and a _sweater_ (4). Her daughter Emily needs a _blouse_ (5) and a _skirt_ (6).

Lesson objectives

- Discuss and write about shopping
- Write a shopping list

Warm-up and review

- Before class. Write today's lesson focus on the board.
  Lesson E:
  Write about shopping
  Write a shopping list
- Begin class. Books closed. Write *shopping list* on the board. Point to the words. Say them aloud. Ask Ss to repeat after you. Ask: *What does this mean?* Elicit an appropriate response, such as: *A list of things to buy.*
- Ask: *Do you write shopping lists?* Elicit *Yes* / *No* responses. Ask Ss who respond with *yes*: *When do you write shopping lists?* Elicit an appropriate response, such as: *For food shopping, clothes shopping.*
- Ask: *Are you going shopping after English class?* Elicit *Yes* / *No* responses. If a S responds with *yes*, ask: *Do you have a shopping list?* Elicit a *Yes* / *No* response.

Presentation

- Direct Ss' attention to Exercise **1A**.
- Say: *This is an example of a shopping list. What kind of shopping list is it?* Elicit an appropriate response, such as: *A shopping list for clothes.* or *A back-to-school shopping list.*
- Read the instructions aloud.
- Point to the first item and say: *Number 1. What's the word?* (skirt) Ask: *What letters do we need?* (s *and* k) Point to where the letters are written in the blanks. Say: *Now you complete the rest of the words.*

Practice

- Ss work in pairs to complete the words.
- When Ss are finished, call on different pairs to write their completed words on the board. Review the alphabet by asking Ss who write answers on the board to say the letters aloud.
- Go over the answers with the class. Ask: *Are these words spelled correctly?* Ask different Ss to make corrections as needed.
- Write the numbers *1–6* on the board. Ask individual Ss to come to the board and write their answers to Exercise **1A**. Ask different Ss to read the answers aloud. Ask: *Is the word spelled correctly?* Ask different Ss to correct the spellings if necessary.
- Direct Ss' attention to the picture in Exercise **1B**. Ask: *What do you see?* Elicit as much vocabulary about the picture as possible, and write the words on the board: *mother, daughter, son, shoes, dress, skirt, blouse, T-shirt, sweater.*

Teaching tip

Encourage Ss to use language learned in previous lessons. This exercise recycles and reinforces vocabulary learned earlier in the book.

- Read the instructions aloud. Model the exercise. Ask two Ss to read the first two sentences aloud. Ask: *What does Sun Mi need?* Point to Sun Mi's thought bubble in the art and the word *dress* written in the story. (A dress and shoes.) Say: *Now complete the story.* Point out that the words they need are in the list in Exercise **1A**.
- Ss work in pairs to fill in the blanks in the story using the information in the art and the words in Exercise **1A**. Walk around and help as needed.
- Check answers as a class. Ask several Ss to read sentences from the story aloud. After each sentence ask: *Is that word correct?* Correct any errors if needed.

  Option Ask Ss to read the story to each other in pairs.

Literacy tip

For an alternative activity, refer literacy Ss to pages 86–87 in the *Literacy Workbook* at any time during the lesson.

Expansion activity *(whole class)*

- Peer dictation. Before class. Prepare copies of the following lists for your class. Make enough copies so that each S in a pair has one of the lists:

Student A	*Student B*
1. a black dress	*1. a pink blouse*
2. brown shoes	*2. orange socks*
3. a green T-shirt	*3. red pants*
4. yellow socks	*4. a purple skirt*
5. a white sweater	*5. blue shoes*

- Explain to Ss that one S will dictate words to another S. Then they will switch roles.
- Walk around and help as needed. Encourage Ss to check their writing after they finish by comparing their words to their partner's list.

LESSON E Writing

Presentation

- Say: *Sun Mi was making a shopping list. Now you are going to help complete her shopping list.*
- Direct Ss' attention to Exercise 2A and read the instructions aloud.
- Model the task. Ask: *What clothing does Sun Mi need?* Elicit: *A dress.* Point to *dress* written on the shopping list. Ask: *What else does she need?* Elicit: *Shoes.* Say: *Write "shoes" in the shopping list.*

Practice

- Ss complete the exercise individually using the information from Exercise 1B. Walk around and help as needed.
- Copy the unfinished list from Exercise 2A on the board. Ask several Ss to complete the list.
- Ask different Ss to read the words on the board. Ask: *Are these items correct?* Ask Ss to correct the list if needed.
- Direct Ss' attention to Exercise 2B. Say: *Now you are going to make your own shopping list.* Read the instructions aloud.
- Model the task. Hold up the Student's Book. Say: *Think about what you need. Then circle the clothing. For example, I need pants, socks, and a raincoat. I'm going to circle those words in this exercise.* Hold up the book and pretend to circle the items. Say: *My son needs a sweater.* Pretend to circle *sweater.*
- Ss complete the exercise individually. Walk around and help as needed.

Literacy tip

While Ss are working on Exercise 2B, help the literacy Ss by reading the words in this exercise to them. Tell them to circle the items they need.

- Direct Ss' attention to Exercise 2C. Read the instructions aloud. Say: *Write the items you circled on your list.*
- Model the task. Say: *My son needs a sweater. His name is John.* Write on the board: *John: a sweater.*
- Ss write their shopping lists individually using the list in Exercise 2A as a guide. Walk around and help as needed.
- Focus Ss' attention on Exercise 3. Read the instructions aloud.
- Ss complete the task in pairs. Walk around and help as needed.

Teaching tip

This exercise asks Ss to work together to share their writing. Encourage Ss to peer-correct each other's writing if necessary. Say: *Help your partner with any mistakes. Then your partner will help you.*

- Ask several Ss to read their lists aloud for the whole class.

  Option Ask several Ss to write their lists from Exercise 2C on the board. Then ask them to explain their lists to the rest of the class.

Expansion activity *(student pairs)*

- Focus Ss' attention on the picture on page 84. Say: *Look at the items for sale in this picture. Imagine that you are shopping at this store. Make a shopping list. What will you buy?*
- Encourage Ss to use the shopping list in Exercise 2C on page 93 as a guide. They can write the names of people on the list and the items they want to buy for them in the column under *Clothing.*
- Ask several Ss to write their shopping lists on the board.
- Expand this activity more by recycling the grammar points *How much is?* and *How much are?* from Lesson C. Ask Ss to write the prices of the items on their lists. When Ss are finished, ask them *How much is the dress?* and *How much are the shoes?*

Evaluation

- Direct Ss' attention to the lesson focus written on the board.
- Write *Shopping List* on the board. Ask different Ss to come to the board and write clothing items on the list. Ask them to include the color of the clothing.
- Check off each part of the lesson focus as Ss demonstrate understanding of what they have learned in the lesson.

More Ventures, Unit 7, Lesson E	
Literacy Workbook, 15–30 min.	
Basic Workbook, 15–30 min.	
Writing worksheets, 15–30 min.	www.cambridge.org/myresourceroom

UNIT 7

2 Write

A Complete the shopping list for Sun Mi's family.

Name	Clothing
Sun Mi:	a dress, shoes
Emily:	a blouse, a skirt
Roger:	T-shirt, a sweater

B Circle the clothes you and your family need.

a blouse	socks	a tie	a dress
a sweater	a jacket	a skirt	a raincoat
a T-shirt	a shirt	shoes	pants

C Write a shopping list for your family.

Name	Clothing
(Answers will vary.)	

3 After you write

Talk with a partner. Share your writing.

LESSON **F** Another view

1 Life-skills reading

271 Center Street
Tampa, Florida 33601
(813) 555-7200

Shoes	$29.99
T-shirt	$7.99
Subtotal:	$37.98
7% Tax:	$2.66
Total:	**$40.64**

Thank you for shopping at
The Clothes Place.
Have a nice day!

A Read the sentences. Look at the receipt. Fill in the answer.

1. The Clothes Place is a ____.
   - Ⓐ clothing store
   - Ⓑ supermarket
   - Ⓒ laundromat
2. The phone number is ____.
   - Ⓐ 555-0072
   - Ⓑ 555-7200
   - Ⓒ 813
3. The shoes are ____.
   - Ⓐ $29.99
   - Ⓑ $19.99
   - Ⓒ $40.64
4. The tax is ____.
   - Ⓐ $40.64
   - Ⓑ $37.98
   - Ⓒ $2.66

B Talk with a partner.

1. Where do you buy clothes?
2. What clothes do you need?

Lesson objectives

- Practice reading a store receipt
- Review unit vocabulary
- Complete the self-assessment

Warm-up and review

- Before class. Write today's lesson focus on the board.
  Lesson F:
  Read and answer questions about a store receipt
  Practice vocabulary in receipts
  Complete the self-assessment
- Begin class. Books closed. Say: *We are going to make a new shopping list on the board.* Ask Ss to brainstorm clothing items. List them on the board.
- Ask: *How much are these items?* Point to each item in turn and ask Ss to give you a price for it. Write the price to the right of each item in a column. Draw a line under the list of prices.
- Ask: *How much are these items together?* Ask a S to add the prices together on paper or with a calculator. When the S is finished, write the total under all the prices.
- Say: *This is the total amount of money that we will spend on these clothes.* Write the word *Total* beside the total price amount on the board. Say the word aloud. Ask Ss to repeat it after you.

Presentation

- Books open. Write on the board: *receipt.* Point to the word. Say it aloud and ask Ss to repeat. Ask: *What is this?* If Ss don't know, show them an example of a receipt from a store. Ask Ss if they have any examples of receipts with them that they can show to the class.
- Direct Ss' attention to the picture of a receipt in Exercise **1A**.
- Hold up the Student's Book. Point to the receipt. Ask: *What store is this receipt from?* (The Clothes Place.) Ask: *Where is the store?* (Tampa, Florida.) Ask: *What clothes are on the receipt?* (shoes and a T-shirt.) Ask: *What other words do you see on the receipt?* Elicit any other words Ss read on the receipt.
- Write the words *subtotal* and *tax* on the board. Say the words aloud. Ask Ss to repeat them after you. Point to the word *subtotal.* Ask: *What does this word mean?* If Ss don't know, or can't explain the definition in English, say: *It's the total amount before tax.* Point to the word *tax.* Ask: *What does this word mean?* If Ss don't know, or can't explain the definition in English, say: *It's extra money you pay when you buy something. It helps pay for government services.*

Practice

- Read the instructions for Exercise **1A** aloud. This task helps prepare Ss for standardized-type tests they may have to take.
- Write the first item on the board along with the two answer choices labeled *a*, *b*, and *c*.
- Read the item and the answer choices aloud and then point to the receipt. Ask: *Is the Clothes Place a clothing store, a supermarket, or a laundromat?* Show Ss where to look for the information. Elicit: *Clothing store.*
- Point to the three answer choices on the board. Ask Ss: *a*, *b*, or *c?* (a) Fill in the letter *a* and tell Ss: *Fill in the answer.* Make sure Ss understand the task.
- Have Ss individually scan for and fill in the answers.

Comprehension check

- Go over the answers to Exercise **1A** with the class. Make sure that Ss followed directions and filled in their answers. Ask Ss to point to the information in the receipt.

Application

- Read the instructions for Exercise **1B** aloud.
- Model the task. Ask a S: *Where do you buy clothes?* Elicit an appropriate answer.
- Say: *Now ask your partner both questions.*
- Ss complete the exercise in pairs.
- Ask several pairs to ask and answer the question for the rest of the class.

Expansion activity *(individual work, student pairs)*

- Ask Ss to make a receipt for clothing items that they "bought" in a store. It can be a real store or an imaginary store. The receipt should include the name and address of the store, the names and prices of items bought, the subtotal, the tax, and the total for the purchase.
- When Ss are finished, ask them to work with a partner. Say: *Show your partner your receipt. Then look at your partner's receipt. Ask questions. For example: How much is the _____? How much are the _____?*
- Walk around and help as needed.

LESSON F Another view

Practice

- Books closed. Write *crossword puzzle* on the board. Point to the words. Say them aloud. Ask Ss to repeat the words after you.
- Books open. Focus Ss' attention on Exercise 2. Write the words *across* and *down* on the board. Draw arrows to indicate the directions, as shown in the Student's Book. Hold up the Student's Book. Point to the clues on the left side of the page. Say: *These words go across.* Move your finger across the page to show the direction. Point to the clues on the right side of the page. Say: *These words go down.* Move your finger down the page to show the direction.
- Ask Ss: *Do you do crossword puzzles?* Elicit a *yes* or *no* response.
- Read the instructions aloud. Model the task. Hold up the Student's Book. Point to number 1 (*pants*) in the crossword puzzle. Say: *Write the words in the spaces.*
- Ss complete the exercise individually. Walk around and help as needed.
- Write the numbers *1–10* on the board. Ask individual Ss to write their answers on the board.
- Ask different Ss to read the answers aloud. Ask: *Are these answers correct?* Ask different Ss to correct the answers if needed.

Literacy tip

For an alternative activity, refer literacy Ss to pages 88–89 in the *Literacy Workbook* at any time during the lesson.

Expansion activity (small groups)

- Scrambled questions and answers. Before class, make enough copies of the following questions for small groups of four Ss in your class:
  1. *How much is the blue shirt?*
  2. *How much are the yellow shoes?*
  3. *How much is the brown sweater?*
  4. *How much are the green socks?*
  5. *How much is the purple blouse?*
- Cut up each sentence so that the words are separate. Mix up the words in each question. Put them in envelopes with the corresponding number on the envelope.
- Give each small group of Ss a set of five envelopes. Ask them to unscramble the questions. When they are finished, they should write the questions in their notebooks.
- The first group to finish unscrambling the questions wins the game.
- Write the numbers *1–5* on the board. Ask Ss to write the questions on the board.
- For further practice, ask Ss to ask a partner the questions on the board. Encourage Ss to invent prices for each item in the questions.

Evaluation

- Before asking Ss to turn to the self-assessment on page 142, do a quick review of the unit. Have Ss turn to Lesson A. Ask the class to talk about what they remember about this lesson. Prompt Ss, if necessary, with questions, such as: *What words are on this page? What do you see in the picture?* Continue in this manner to review each lesson quickly.
- **Self-assessment** Read the instructions for Exercise 3. Ask Ss to turn to the self-assessment page and complete the unit self-assessment.
- If Ss are ready, administer the unit test on pages T-187–T-189 of this Teacher's Edition (or on the Assessment Audio CD / CD-ROM).

More Ventures, Unit 7, Lesson F	
Literacy Workbook, 15–30 min.	
Basic Workbook, 15–30 min.	
Writing worksheets, 15–30 min.	www.cambridge.org/myresourceroom

2 Fun with vocabulary

Write the words in the puzzle. Some words are across (→). Some words are down (↓).

3 Wrap up

Complete the **Self-assessment** on page 142.

UNIT
8 Work

LESSON A Listening

1 Before you listen

A Look at the picture. What do you see?

CLASS CD2 TK 23

B Listen and point: cashier • custodian • mechanic receptionist • salesperson • server

Lesson objectives

- Introduce Ss to the topic
- Find out what Ss know about the topic
- Preview the unit by talking about the picture
- Practice key vocabulary
- Practice listening skills

UNIT

8

Warm-up and review

- Before class. Write today's lesson focus on the board.
  Lesson A:
  Work vocabulary
  Names of jobs
- Begin class. Write the words *jobs* on the board. Point to the word. Say it aloud and ask Ss to repeat after you. Say: *Today's class is about jobs. What are some examples of jobs?* As Ss respond, write their examples on the board.
- Ask: *Who has a job?* Ask Ss who say *yes*: *What's your job?* Write their responses on the board.

Teaching tip

If Ss ask, you can explain the difference between *jobs* and *occupations.* Tell Ss that a job is a type of work and an occupation is a profession, or a job you do for a long time.

Literacy tip

If you have literacy Ss in your class, it might be helpful to spend time at the beginning of any activity that contains art or photos talking about the pictures before focusing Ss' attention on the printed words in the exercise. Have Ss work in pairs. Tell them to ask each other: *What do you see?* Encourage Ss to describe the pictures to each other. Consider pairing literacy Ss with Ss who can help them read the text in the exercise. This will help preview the exercise for literacy Ss and make them more confident as the exercise continues.

Presentation

- Books open. Set the scene. Direct Ss' attention to the picture on page 96. Ask: *Where is this?* (a big store with a restaurant, an office, a car garage, etc.)
- Hold up the Student's Book. Show Ss the picture. Ask: *What do you see?* Elicit and write on the board any vocabulary that Ss know, such as: *people*, *a salesperson*, *a customer*, *a computer*, *a server*, *a mechanic.*

Teaching tip

Do not expect Ss to know all the new vocabulary words. These questions are intended to find out what Ss already know about work vocabulary.

Practice

- Direct Ss' attention to the key vocabulary in Exercise **1B**. Read each word aloud while pointing to the corresponding person in the picture. Ask Ss to repeat and point.

Class Audio CD2 track 23 Play or read the audio program (see audio script, page T-160). Tell Ss: *Listen and point to the picture.* As Ss hear the key vocabulary, check to see that they are pointing to the correct part of the picture. Repeat the audio program as needed.

Comprehension check

- Ask Ss *Yes* / *No* questions about the picture. Ask about new vocabulary and recycle words learned in previous units. Say: *Listen to the questions. Answer "Yes" or "No."*
  Point to the picture. Ask: *Is this a school?* (No, it isn't.)
  Point to the store sign. Ask: *Is this a store?* (Yes, it is.)
  Point to the cashier. Ask: *Is she a cashier?* (Yes, she is.)
  Point to the woman sitting at a desk. Ask: *Is she a mechanic?* (No, she isn't.)
  Point to the mechanic. Ask: *Is he a server?* (No, he isn't.)
  Point to Sara. Ask: *Is she a salesperson?* (Yes, she is.)
  Point to the server. Ask: *Is he a server?* (Yes, he is.)

Expansion activity *(student pairs)*

- If your Ss would benefit from answering more questions about the picture using a different form for the question and answer, write the following on the board: *What's his job? What's her job? He's a _____. She's a _____.*
- Ss in pairs. Say: *Look at the questions on the board. Point to different people in the picture. Ask your partner the questions.* Point to the answers on the board. Say: *Answer the questions like this.*
- Model the activity. Point to Sara. Ask: *What's her job?* Elicit: *She's a salesperson.*
- Ss complete the activity in pairs. Walk around and help as needed.
- Ask several pairs to ask and answer the questions for the rest of the class.

Literacy tip

For an alternative activity, refer literacy Ss to pages 90–91 in the *Literacy Workbook* at any time during the lesson.

LESSON A Listening

Presentation

- Direct Ss' attention to the jobs in Exercise 2A. Read them aloud. Ask Ss to repeat them after you.
- Ask Ss questions about the jobs. Focus their attention on the picture on page 96. Ask Ss to point when you ask: *Where is the cashier?* Continue with all the words in Exercise 2A.
- Focus Ss' attention on Exercise 2A again. Read the instructions aloud.

Practice

- Class Audio CD2 track 24 Play or read the audio program (see audio script, page T-160). Ss listen and repeat the vocabulary. Repeat the audio program as needed.
- Listen carefully to Ss' pronunciation and make corrections as needed.

Learner persistence (individual work)

- Self-Study Audio CD track 35 Exercise 2A is recorded on the CD at the back of the Student's Book. Ss can listen to the CD at home for reinforcement and review. They can also listen to the CD for self-directed learning when class attendance is not possible.
- Direct Ss' attention to Exercise 2B and read the instructions aloud.
- Class Audio CD2 track 25 Model the task. Hold up the Student's Book and say: *Number one.* Play or read the audio program for number 1 (see audio script, page T-160). Point to the two answer choices in number 1 and ask Ss: *What did you hear – a or b?* Elicit: *b.* Point to the letter *b* next to the second picture and tell Ss: *Circle the letter "b."*
- Class Audio CD2 track 25 Play or read the complete audio program (see audio script, page T-160). Ss listen and circle the correct answers. Repeat the audio as needed.
- Class Audio CD2 track 25 Read aloud the second part of the instructions for Exercise 2B. Play or read the audio program again so that Ss can listen and check their answers.

Learner persistence (individual work)

- Self-Study Audio CD track 36 Exercise 2B is recorded on the CD at the back of the Student's Book. Ss can listen to the CD at home for reinforcement and review and also for self-directed learning when class attendance is not possible.

Comprehension check

- Write the numbers *1–4* on the board. Ask a few Ss to come to the board and write the correct answers to Exercise 2B next to each number.
- Class Audio CD2 track 25 Play or read the audio program again. Pause the audio program after each conversation. Point to the answers written on the board and ask: *Is this correct?* Ask another S to make any necessary corrections.

Application

- Direct Ss' attention to Exercise 3 and read the instructions aloud.
- Model the task. Hold up the Student's Book and point to the answer choices in Exercise 2B. Say to one S: *Point to a picture.* Say to the first S's partner: *Say the word.*
- Ss complete the exercise in pairs. Walk around and help as needed.

Expansion activity (whole group)

- Before class. Make copies of a two-row chart, one row for Ss' names and one row for their jobs, or draw one on the board.
- Hold up the chart, or point to the one on the board. Say: *You are going to ask two questions. What are the questions?* Point to *Name.* Elicit: *What's your name?* Point to *Job.* Elicit: *What's your job?* or Write the questions on the board.
- Say: *Stand up. Walk around and ask five students for their names. Then ask about their jobs. Write their names and jobs in the chart.* You may have to assist Ss with additional job vocabulary.

> **Teaching tip**
> Encourage non-working Ss to say, as applicable: *I'm a student. I'm a homemaker. I'm a stay-at-home parent.* Define these words for Ss if necessary.

- When everyone is finished, ask several Ss to make sentences with the information in their charts, such as: *Rosa is a student. Arif is a mechanic.*

Evaluation

- Direct Ss' attention to the lesson focus written on the board. Hold up the Student's Book and point to jobs in the picture on page 96. Ask Ss to tell you the jobs as you point to them (*cashier, custodian, mechanic, receptionist, salesperson, server*). Walk around and check that Ss are pointing to the correct jobs.
- Check off the lesson focus as Ss demonstrate an understanding of what they have learned in the lesson.

More Ventures, Unit 8, Lesson A	
Literacy Workbook, 15–30 min.	
Basic Workbook, 15–30 min.	
Writing worksheets 15–30 min.	www.cambridge.org/myresourceroom
Student Arcade, time varies	www.cambridge.org/venturesarcade

Unit Goals
Identify jobs
Identify job duties
Interpret help wanted ads

2 Listen

A Listen and repeat.

STUDENT TK 35
CLASS CD2 TK 24

1. cashier 2. custodian 3. mechanic
4. receptionist 5. salesperson 6. server

B Listen and circle.

STUDENT TK 36
CLASS CD2 TK 25

1. a.  (b.) 

2. (a.)  b. 

3. a.  (b.) 

4. (a.)  b. 

Listen again. Check your answers.

3 After you listen

Talk with a partner. Point to a picture.
Your partner says the word.

LESSON **B** Job duties

1 Vocabulary focus

CLASS CD2 TK 26

Listen and repeat.

1. She answers the phone.

2. She counts money.

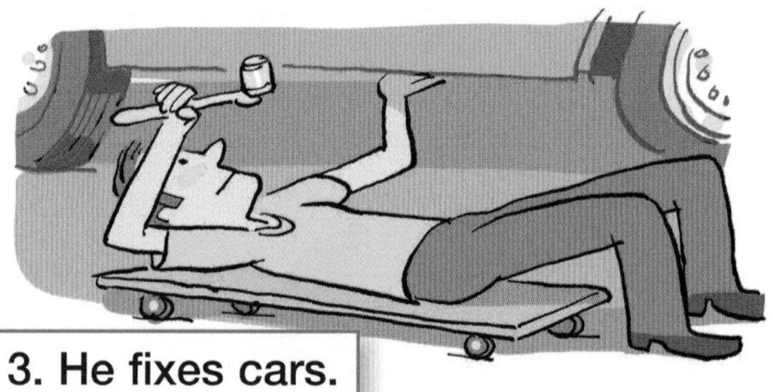

3. He fixes cars.

4. He cleans buildings.

5. She sells clothes.

6. He serves food.

2 Practice

A Read and match.

1. A receptionist	sells clothes.
2. A salesperson	cleans buildings.
3. A cashier	answers the phone.
4. A server	fixes cars.
5. A custodian	serves food.
6. A mechanic	counts money.

Lesson objectives

- Introduce and practice more vocabulary about work
- Introduce and practice sentences in the simple present about job duties

Warm-up and review

- Before class. Write today's lesson focus on the board.
  Lesson B:
  Work vocabulary
  Job duties
- Begin class. Books open. Direct Ss' attention to the picture on page 96. Review key vocabulary from the unit by asking: *What are the different jobs in this picture?* Elicit: *salesperson, cashier, receptionist, server, custodian, mechanic.* Ask Ss to point to the people with these jobs.
- Walk around and check to see that Ss are pointing to the correct people in the picture.

Presentation

- Set the scene. Write on the board: *job duties.* Point to the words. Say them aloud. Ask Ss to repeat the words after you. Say: *Job duties tell about what people in different jobs do at work.*
- Focus Ss' attention on the sentences below the pictures in Exercise **1**. Say: *These are some examples of job duties. They describe the jobs in the pictures.*
- Read aloud the instructions for Exercise **1**.

Class Audio CD2 track 26 Play or read the audio program (see audio script, page T-160). Listen and repeat the sentences along with Ss. Repeat the audio program as needed.

- Listen carefully to Ss' pronunciation and correct as needed.

Literacy tip

It might be helpful to hold up the Student's Book and point to each picture as Ss listen to the audio program. This will help literacy Ss if they are unable to read the text as they listen to the audio program.

Expansion activity *(student pairs)*

- Put Ss in pairs. Try to pair more advanced Ss with less advanced Ss, or advanced Ss with literacy Ss. Tell Ss to practice reading the job duties. They will read one of the sentences, and their partner will point to the picture that matches the description. After that, encourage Ss to switch roles.

Multilevel tip

To make this activity more challenging for advanced Ss in your class, ask them to put a piece of paper over the job descriptions. Say: *Describe the pictures. What do these people do every day at work?* Literacy Ss who have good oral skills may like the challenge of this activity as well.

Practice

- Direct Ss' attention to Exercise **2A**. As you read aloud the instructions, hold up the Student's Book and indicate that Ss should match the words for jobs with their corresponding duties.
- Model the task. Hold up the Student's Book. Point to the word *receptionist* in the example. Ask: *What does a receptionist do?* (answers the phone) Say: *Match the job with the job duty.*
- Ss complete the exercise individually. Help as needed.

Literacy tip

For an alternative activity, refer literacy Ss to pages 92–93 in the *Literacy Workbook* at any time during the lesson.

Comprehension check

- Write the numbers *1–6* on the board. Ask a few Ss to come to the board and write the answers to Exercise **2A** on the board.
- Ask different Ss to read the answers written on the board. After each answer is read, ask: *Is this correct?* Ask another S to make any necessary corrections on the board.

LESSON **B** Job duties

Presentation

- Direct Ss' attention to the word bank in Exercise **2B**. Say: *Repeat these words after me.* Say each phrase aloud. Listen to Ss' pronunciation as they repeat the phrases.
- Direct Ss' attention to the pictures below the word bank. Read aloud the names and ask Ss to repeat after you.
- Hold up the Student's Book. Point to different people and ask: *What is his or her job?* Elicit: *cashier, server, receptionist, salesperson, custodian, mechanic.*
- Read the instructions for Exercise **2B** aloud.

Practice

Class Audio CD2 track 27 Model the task. Say: *Listen and repeat.* Play or read the audio program for number 1 (see audio script, pages T-160–T-161) and point to Sandra in the first picture as you repeat. Say: *Then write.* Point to the phrase *counts money* in the Duty column beside Sandra in the chart. Make sure Ss understand the task.

Class Audio CD2 track 27 Play or read the complete audio program (see audio script, pages T-160–T-161). Ss listen and repeat. Encourage Ss to point to the people in the pictures as they repeat.

- Ss complete the charts individually using words from the word bank. Repeat the audio program as needed.
- Check answers with the class. Write the numbers *1–6* on the board, and ask for volunteers to write their answers on the board. Point to each answer and ask the class: *Yes? Is this correct?* Make any necessary corrections.
- Read aloud the second part of the instructions for Exercise **2B**. Point to and model the example conversation.
- Call on a pair of volunteers to read the example conversation aloud for the class. Then ask the same Ss to make up a new conversation about another person in the pictures on page 99. Indicate that Ss should ask and answer questions about all the people in the pictures.
- Ss complete the exercise in pairs. Walk around and help as needed.

Multilevel tip

Some Ss may wish to expand on the job duties of the jobs in this lesson. If you feel it is appropriate for your class, encourage Ss to say more job duties for these jobs if they already know them.

Application

- Direct Ss' attention to Exercise **3** and read the instructions aloud.
- Model the task. Ask two Ss to read the conversation aloud.

Useful language

Read the tip box aloud. Ask Ss to repeat the two questions after you. Tell Ss that the two questions have the same meaning.

- Ss walk around and practice the conversation with as many classmates as possible in the time allotted. Encourage them to use both of the questions in the Useful language tip box.
- Ask several pairs to ask and answer the questions for the rest of the class.

Expansion activity *(whole group)*

- Password. Prepare a list of jobs that Ss have learned in this unit. Write them in a list form on a piece of paper.
- Divide the class into two teams. Explain to Ss that the game is called Password. One person from each team will come to the front of the class. You will show them a job written on a piece of paper. The Ss will give one- or two-word clues to their team. Their team will guess the job.
- Model the game. Write *student* on the board. Ask: *What words describe this job?* Elicit: *school, study, English, books*, etc.
- Start the game. Encourage Ss to only use one or two words as clues. If Ss get stuck, help them think of words.
- Teams take turns giving clues. Whenever someone on the team guesses the job, the team gets a point. The team with the most points wins.

Evaluation

- Direct Ss' attention to the lesson focus written on the board. Check Ss' understanding of the key vocabulary by asking them to say the job duties for the jobs in the pictures in Exercise **2B** on page 99.
- Check off the lesson focus as Ss demonstrate an understanding of what they have learned in the lesson.

More Ventures, Unit 8, Lesson B	
Literacy Workbook, 15–30 min.	
Basic Workbook, 15–30 min.	
Writing worksheets, 15–30 min.	www.cambridge.org/myresourceroom
Student Arcade, time varies	www.cambridge.org/venturesarcade

CLASS CD2 TK 27

B Listen and repeat. Then write.

answers the phone	cleans buildings	counts money
fixes cars	sells clothes	serves food

Name	Duty	Name	Duty
1. Sandra	She *counts money*.	4. Oscar	He *sells clothes*.
2. Stephanie	She *serves food*.	5. Tim	He *cleans building*.
3. Alba	She *answers the phone*.	6. Ahmad	He *fixes cars*.

Talk with a partner. Ask and answer.

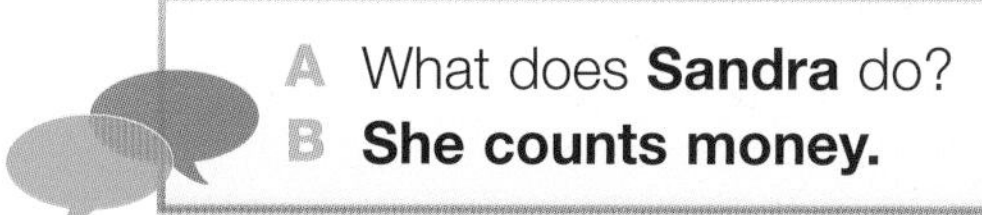

A What does **Sandra** do?
B **She counts money.**

3 Communicate

Talk with your classmates. Ask and answer.

A What do you do?
B I'm a **cashier**. **I count money.**

USEFUL LANGUAGE

What do you do? = What's your job?

LESSON C Does he sell clothes?

1 Grammar focus: *does* and *doesn't*

Questions			Answers					
Does	he / she	**sell** clothes?	Yes,	he / she	**does**.	No,	he / she	**doesn't**.

doesn't = does not

2 Practice

A Read and circle. Then write.

1. A Does he serve food?

   B No, he doesn't.
   does (doesn't)

2. A Does he clean buildings?

   B Yes, he does.
   (does) doesn't

3. A Does she answer the phone?

   B Yes, she does.
   (does) doesn't

4. A Does he sell clothes?

   B Yes, he does.
   (does) doesn't

5. A Does she fix cars?

   B No, she doesn't.
   does (doesn't)

Listen and repeat. Then practice with a partner.

CLASS CD2 TK 28

Lesson objective

- Introduce and practice *does* and *doesn't*

Warm-up and review

- Before class. Write today's lesson focus on the board.
  Lesson C:
  does
  doesn't
- Begin class. Books closed. Write a question mark on the board. Tell Ss you are going to practice making questions about jobs. Ask Ss to say the names of some jobs they have studied in this unit. Elicit any jobs Ss remember from the unit. Write them on the board (*receptionist*, *mechanic*, *server*, etc.).
- Write on the board: *What does a* ______ *do?* Point to one of the jobs on the board. Say: *Make a question.* Point to the question mark on the board. Elicit: *What does a receptionist do?* Continue until Ss make questions about each of the jobs on the board.
- Point to the word *does* on the board. Say it aloud. Ask Ss to repeat it after you.

Presentation

- Books open. Say: *Here are some Yes / No questions with "does."* Direct Ss' attention to the grammar chart in Exercise **1**. Read the questions and the corresponding answers aloud. Ask Ss to repeat after you.
- Say: *When the answer is negative, we say "doesn't."* Hold up the Student's Book. Point to the word *doesn't.* Say it aloud. Ask Ss to repeat it after you.
- Point to the small box beside the grammar chart. Hold up one finger and tell Ss: *One word: doesn't.* Hold up two fingers and say: *Two words: does not. They are equal. They are the same.*

Practice

- Direct Ss' attention to the pictures in Exercise **2A**. Hold up the Student's Book. Point to the first picture. Ask: *What's his job?* (He's a salesperson.) Ask: *What does he do?* (He sells TVs.) Ask: *Does he serve food?* (No, he doesn't.) Review the jobs in the other pictures.
- Read aloud the instructions for Exercise **2A**. Model the task. Read aloud the example conversation in number 1. When you read Speaker B's line, show Ss the two answer choices under the blank and ask: *does or doesn't?* Elicit *doesn't.*
- Point to where *doesn't* has been circled and written for number 1. Say: *Circle the correct answer. Then write it in the blank.*
- Ss complete the exercise individually. Walk around and help as needed.

Comprehension check

- Read aloud the second part of the instructions in Exercise **2A**.
- Class Audio CD2 track 28 Play or read the audio program (see audio script, page T-161). Ss listen and repeat as they check their answers.
- Write the numbers *2–5* on the board. Ask volunteers to come to the board and write the answers they circled. Make any necessary corrections on the board.
- Ss in pairs. Ask Ss to choose Role A or B and practice the questions and answers in Exercise **2A**. Then have Ss switch roles and practice again. Walk around and help as needed.
- Ask several pairs to read the conversations to the rest of the class.

Expansion activity *(student pairs)*

- Direct Ss' attention to page 98 in the Student's Book. Say: *Look at the pictures. Ask Yes / No questions about them. Use the questions and answers in Exercise* **2A** *on page 100 as a guide.*

Teaching tip

It might be helpful to remind Ss of the question form in the simple present tense. Point to the questions in the grammar chart on page 100. Remind Ss that the base verb form doesn't change in a question. Tell Ss that they can ask questions with *yes* or *no* answers as they look at the pictures on page 98.

- Model the activity. Hold up the Student's Book. Point to Picture 1. Ask: *Does she answer the phone?* (Yes, she does.) Ask: *Does she count money?* (No, she doesn't.)
- Ss complete the activity in pairs. Walk around and help as needed.
- Ask several pairs to ask and answer questions about the pictures for the rest of the class.
- If Ss need more practice, they can continue this expansion activity by asking *Yes / No* questions about the pictures on page 96, 97, and 99 in the Student's Book.

LESSON C Does he sell clothes?

Presentation

- Books open. Direct Ss' attention to the picture in Exercise 2B. Ask: *What do you see?* Elicit as many vocabulary words as possible, such as: *man, job, pants, shirt, tie, coffee.*

> **Teaching tip**
> Do not expect Ss to answer in complete sentences. The purpose of this question is to recycle any vocabulary Ss already know and to find out any new words Ss may know about the topic.

Practice

- Read aloud the first part of instructions for Exercise 2B.
- Class Audio CD2 track 29 Model the task. Say: *Listen and repeat.* Play or read the audio program for number 1 (see audio script, page T-161) and point to the man in the picture as you repeat. Say: *Then write.* Point to where the words have been written in the blanks in number 1. Make sure Ss understand the task.
- Class Audio CD2 track 29 Play or read the complete audio program (see audio script, page T-161). Ss listen and repeat. Encourage Ss to focus on the man in the picture as they repeat.
- Ss work individually as they fill in the blanks in the exercise. Repeat the audio program as needed.

> **Literacy tip**
> For an alternative activity, refer literacy Ss to pages 94–95 in the *Literacy Workbook* at any time during the lesson.

- Write the numbers *1–6* on the board. Ask a few Ss to come to the board and write the words missing from the blanks for each number on the board. Ask: *Are these words correct?* Ask other Ss to make corrections if needed.
- Read aloud the second part of the instructions for Exercise 2B.
- Model the activity. Ask: *What's his job?* Tell Ss to guess the man's job. Tell them to choose one of the jobs in the word bank.
- Ss complete the exercise in pairs. Walk around and help as needed.
- Ask for a show of hands to see how many Ss agree about the man's job.

Application

- Direct Ss' attention to Exercise 3 and read the instructions aloud.
- Focus Ss' attention on the picture in Exercise 3. Say: *They are playing a game.*
- Model the task. Ask a S to read part A of the example conversation with you. Pantomime fixing a car engine as you read the conversation. Make sure Ss understand the task.
- In small groups, Ss take turns acting out and guessing different jobs. Walk around and help as needed.

Expansion activity (student pairs)

- Before class. Find pictures of different jobs in magazines. Bring the pictures to class – you should have one for each pair of Ss. Give each pair a picture. Say: *Ask questions about the jobs in the pictures. Use "Yes, he / she does." or "No, he / she doesn't." in your answers.*
- Ss complete the activity in pairs. Walk around and help as needed.
- Ask several pairs to hold up their pictures and ask and answer questions for the class.

Evaluation

- Direct Ss' attention to the lesson focus written on the board. Ask Ss to look at the picture on page 96. Ask them to make questions and answers about the jobs in the picture using *does* and *doesn't.*
- Check off the lesson focus as Ss demonstrate an understanding of what they have learned in the lesson.

More Ventures, Unit 8, Lesson C	
Literacy Workbook, 15–30 min. **Basic Workbook,** 15–30 min.	
Writing worksheets, 15–30 min.	www.cambridge.org/myresourceroom
Student Arcade, time varies	www.cambridge.org/venturesarcade

CLASS CD2 TK 29

B Listen and repeat. Then write.

1. A ___Does___ he ___sell___ clothes?
   B ___No___, he ___doesn't___.
2. A ___Does___ he ___fix___ cars?
   B ___No___, he ___doesn't___.
3. A ___Does___ he ___clean___ buildings?
   B ___No___, he ___doesn't___.
4. A ___Does___ he ___serve___ food?
   B ___No___, he ___doesn't___.
5. A ___Does___ he ___count___ money?
   B ___No___, he ___doesn't___.
6. A ___Does___ he ___answer___ the phone?
   B ___Yes___, he ___does___.

Talk with a partner. Ask and guess his job.

cashier	custodian
mechanic	receptionist
salesperson	server

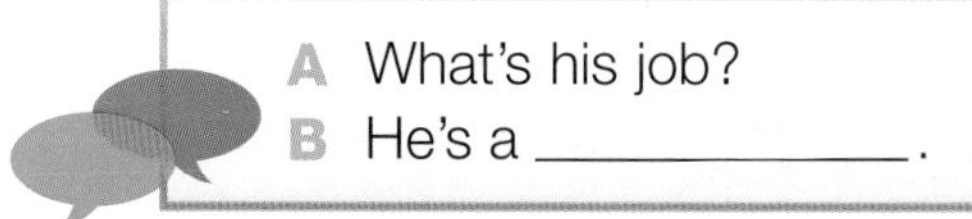
A What's his job?
B He's a ___________.

3 Communicate

Talk with your classmates. Play a game. Ask and guess.

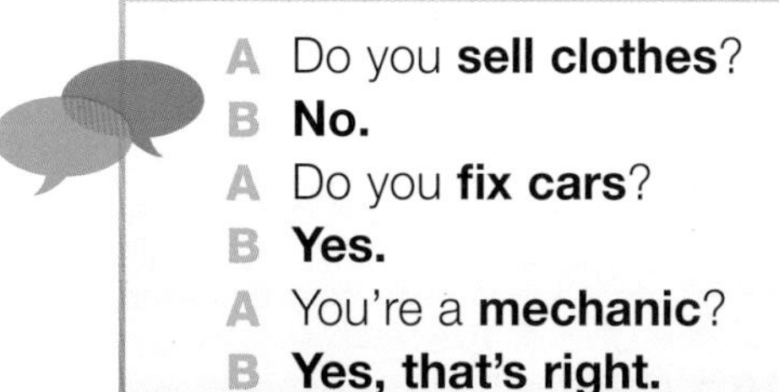
A Do you **sell clothes**?
B **No.**
A Do you **fix cars**?
B **Yes.**
A You're a **mechanic**?
B **Yes, that's right.**

LESSON D Reading

1 Before you read

Talk about the picture.
What do you see?

2 Read

STUDENT TK 37
CLASS CD2 TK 30

Listen and read.

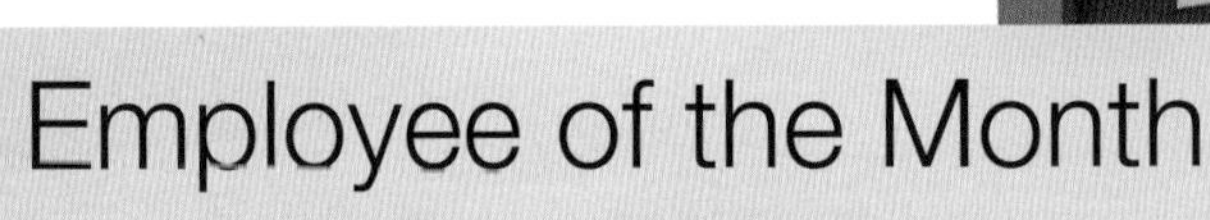

Employee of the Month:
Sara Lopez

Congratulations, Sara Lopez – Employee of the Month! Sara is a salesperson. She sells clothes. Sara's whole family works here at Shop Smart. Her father is a custodian, and her mother is a receptionist. Her Uncle Eduardo is a server. He serves food. Her sister Lucy is a cashier. She counts money. Her brother Leo fixes cars. He's a mechanic. Everybody in the store knows the Lopez family!

3 After you read

Write the job and the job duty.

1. **Name** *Leo Lopez* **Job** *mechanic*
   Job duty *He fixes cars.* $hop $mart

2. **Name** *Lucy Lopez* **Job** *cashier*
   Job duty *He counts money.* $hop $mart

3. **Name** *Eduardo Lopez* **Job** *server*
   Job duty *He serves food.* $hop $mart

4. **Name** *Sara Lopez* **Job** *salesperson*
   Job duty *She sells clothes.* $hop $mart

Lesson objectives

- Introduce and read "Employee of the Month: Sara Lopez"
- Practice using new topic-related words

Warm-up and review

- Before class. Write today's lesson focus on the board.
  Lesson D:
  Read "Employee of the Month: Sara Lopez"
  Learn new vocabulary about work
- Begin class. Books closed. Write *jobs* on the board. Point to the word. Ask: *Do any of you work right now? Do you have jobs?* If any S says *yes*, ask: *What do you do at your job every day?* Elicit short answers, such as: *I cook. I fix cars. I serve food.*

Teaching tip

Do not expect Ss to know many words to describe their jobs. If appropriate, teach them a few words to describe their work. The purpose of this exercise is to prepare Ss for the reading about work that follows.

Presentation

- Books open. Direct Ss' attention to the picture in Exercise **1**.
- Read the instructions aloud. Ask: *What do you see?* Elicit and write on the board any vocabulary that Ss know, such as: *salesperson, Sara Lopez, notice, coffee.*
- Write on the board: *Employee of the Month.* Say the words aloud. Ask Ss to repeat them after you. Ask: *What's an employee?* If Ss don't know, say: *It's a person who works at a company or business.*
- Point to the words on the board. Ask: *What's an employee of the month?* If Ss don't know, say: *It's a person who is a good worker. This person gets an award.* If Ss don't know the meaning of the word *award*, point to the plaque in the picture. Say: *This is her award.*

Community building *(whole group)*

- If appropriate for your class, ask working Ss if they have an "Employee of the Month" award at their jobs. Ask Ss with school-age children if their children's schools have a "Student of the Month" or "Student of the Week" award.

Practice

- Direct Ss' attention to Exercise **2**. Ask a S to read the title of the reading aloud. Read the instructions aloud.

Class Audio CD2 track 30 Play or read the audio program and ask Ss to read along (see audio script, page T-161). Repeat the audio program as needed.

- Read aloud each sentence of the reading, and ask Ss to repeat after you.
- Ask: *Are there any words you don't understand?* Write the words on the board. Give definitions or ask Ss if they can define the words for the rest of the class.

Expansion activity *(student pairs)*

- Bring in pictures of famous celebrities from magazines or printed from the Internet. If you don't have pictures, write the celebrities' names on index cards.
- Ss in pairs. Give each pair of Ss a few pictures or index cards with celebrities on them. Say: *Ask your partner questions about the celebrities.* Model the activity. Show a picture of a famous actor. Ask: *Who is he? What does he do?* (Elicit appropriate responses).

Learner persistence *(individual work)*

Self-Study Audio CD track 37 Exercise **2** is recorded on the CD at the back of the Student's Book. Ss can listen to the CD at home for reinforcement and review and also for self-directed learning when class attendance is not possible.

Comprehension check

- Direct Ss' attention to Exercise **3** and read the instructions aloud.
- Hold up the Student's Book. Draw Ss' attention to the first job card. Point to the word *name.* Ask: *What's his name?* (Leo Lopez.) Ask: *What's his job?* (He's a mechanic.) Ask: *What does he do?* (He fixes cars.) Point to the words written under *Name*, *Job*, and *Job duty.*
- Ss complete the exercise individually. Walk around and help as needed.
- Write the numbers *1–4* on the board. Ask three Ss to write their answers to Exercise **3** on the board. Ask different Ss to ask the questions: *What's his / her name? What's his / her job? What does he / she do?* for all three employees. The S who wrote the answers must answer the questions for his or her example.

Literacy tip

For an alternative activity, refer literacy Ss to pages 96–97 in the *Literacy Workbook* at any time during the lesson.

LESSON D Reading

Presentation

- Books closed. Write the word *jobs* on the board. Point to the word. Say: *We have learned the names of some jobs in this unit. What other job names do you know?* Write Ss' responses on the board.
- Books open. Direct Ss' attention to the picture dictionary in Exercise 4. Hold up the Student's Book. Point to the names of jobs under each picture. Read the words aloud and ask Ss to repeat them after you.

> **Teaching tip**
> It might be helpful to point out that *aide* means helper. Tell Ss that a teacher's aide helps the teacher.

- Read the instructions for Exercise 4A aloud.

Class Audio CD2 track 31 Play or read the audio program (see audio script, page T-161). Listen to Ss' pronunciation as they repeat the jobs. Correct pronunciation as needed.

Learner persistence *(individual work)*

Self-Study Audio CD track 38 Exercise 4A is recorded on the CD at the back of the Student's Book. Ss can listen to the CD at home for reinforcement and review and also for self-directed learning when class attendance is not possible.

Expansion activity *(whole group)*

- Memory game. Say: *Think of the name of a job. Write it in your notebook.* Write on the board: *I'm a _____.* Tell Ss: *Use your imagination. Maybe this isn't your real job.*
- Model the game. Say: *I'm a painter.* Ask a S to continue. Say: *Say your job. Then say my job.* The S says: *I'm a (name of job). She's a painter.* Point to yourself as the S says your job.
- Continue by asking the S next to the first S to continue saying the jobs. Ss must remember all the other jobs that have been said. If a S doesn't remember, help him or her so that the game can continue.

> **Multilevel tip**
> If this game seems too challenging, put Ss in small groups of six. This way the Ss will only have to remember six jobs for the game.

Practice

- Direct Ss' attention to Exercise 4B. Read the instructions aloud. Ask two Ss to read the conversation aloud and point to the picture in number 5 as they read. Then ask them to change the conversation to ask about another picture. Make sure Ss understand the task.
- Ss complete the exercise in pairs. Walk around and help as needed.
- Ask several pairs to ask and answer the questions for the rest of the class.

Expansion activity *(small groups)*

- Concentration. Before class. Copy and cut out the picture dictionary cards for this unit. Make two sets of cards for each small group of four Ss in your class.
- Ss in groups of four. Give each group two sets of picture cards. Tell Ss to mix up the cards and spread them out facedown on a desk.
- Tell Ss to divide each group into teams of two Ss each. One person from the first team will pick up two cards and put them faceup on the desk. If the cards match, the S must ask his or her teammate the name of the job on the card. If the teammate answers correctly, he or she keeps the cards. If the teammate doesn't answer correctly, the cards must be put back in their original places, and the other team can have a chance at saying the name of the job.
- The game continues until all matches have been found and names of jobs identified correctly. The teams count their cards. The Ss with the most cards win the game.

> **Teaching tip**
> It might be helpful to write on the board as a guideline:
> *What's his / her job? He's / She's a _____.*

Evaluation

- Direct Ss' attention to the first part of the lesson focus written on the board. Turn Ss' attention to the story on page 102. Call on several Ss to answer comprehension questions about the reading.
- Direct Ss' attention to the jobs in the picture dictionary. Ask different Ss the names of the different jobs.
- Check off each part of the lesson focus as Ss demonstrate understanding of what they have learned in the lesson.

More Ventures, Unit 8, Lesson D	
Literacy Workbook, 15–30 min. **Basic Workbook,** 15–30 min.	
Picture Dictionary activities, 30–45 min. **Writing worksheets,** 15–30 min.	www.cambridge.org/myresourceroom
Student Arcade, time varies	www.cambridge.org/venturesarcade

4 Picture dictionary Jobs

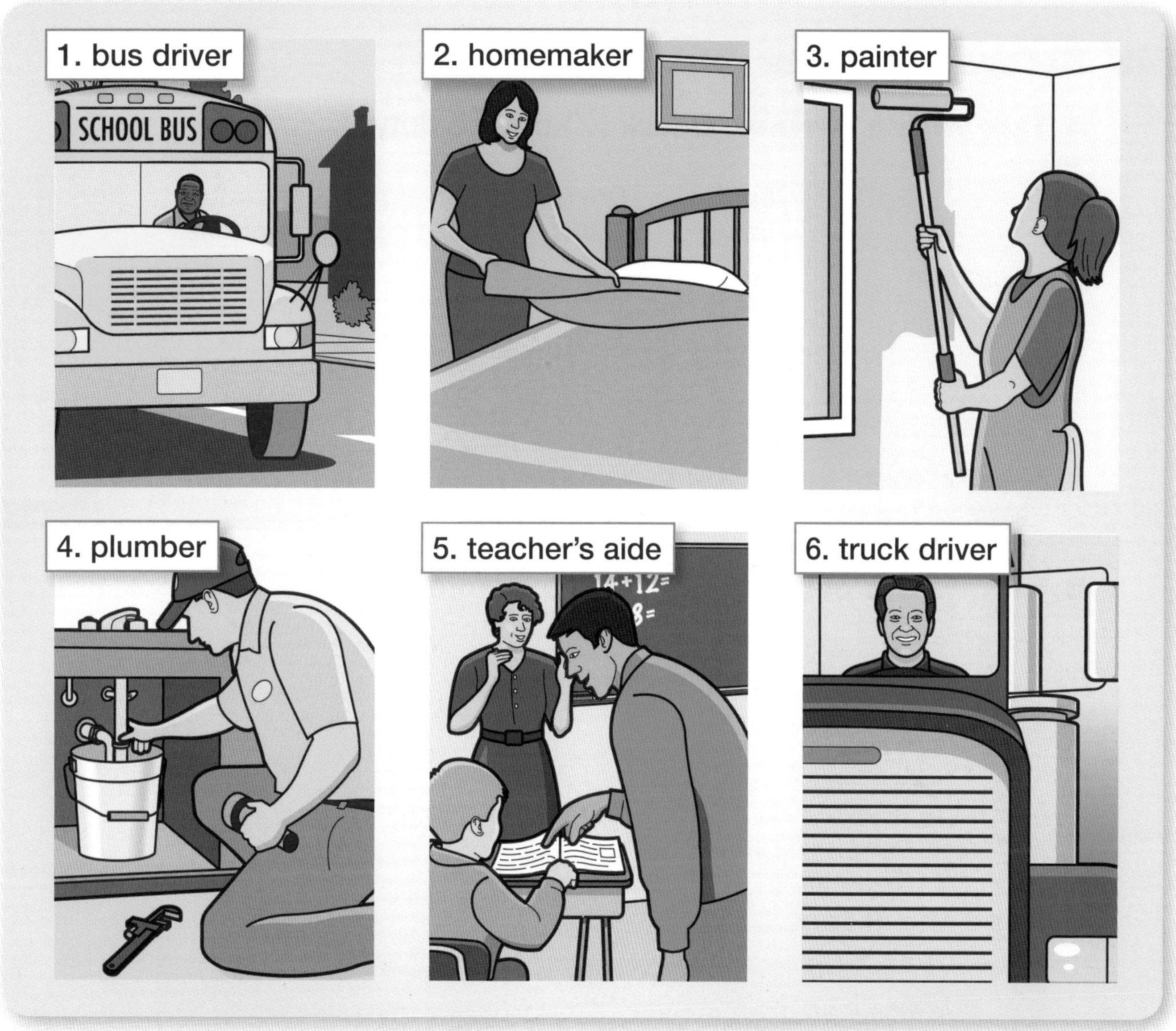

1. bus driver
2. homemaker
3. painter
4. plumber
5. teacher's aide
6. truck driver

STUDENT TK 38
CLASS CD2 TK 31

A **Listen and repeat.** Look at the picture dictionary.

B **Talk with a partner.** Point and ask. Your partner answers.

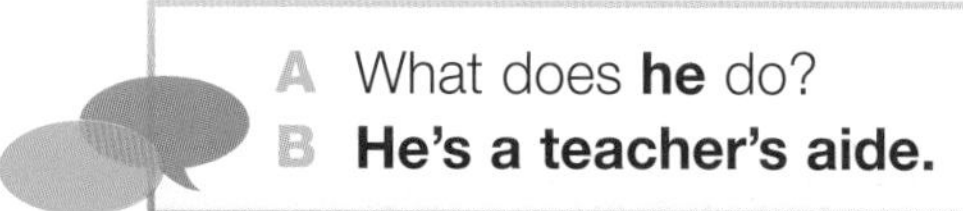

A What does **he** do?
B **He's a teacher's aide.**

LESSON E Writing

1 Before you write

A Talk with a partner. Check (✓) the job duty.

	Counts money	Drives a bus	Cleans buildings	Answers the phone	Serves food
cashier	✓				
custodian			✓		
server					✓
bus driver		✓			
receptionist				✓	

B Talk with a partner. Complete the words.

1. salesp_e_ _r_son
2. sells _c_ _l_othes
3. me_c_ _h_anic
4. fix_e_ _s_ cars
5. an_s_ _w_ers the phone
6. c_o_ _u_nts money

C Read the letter.

Dear Grandpa,

How are you? We are all well here. Luis and Maria have new jobs! Luis is a server. He serves food. Maria is a receptionist. She answers the phone. I'm a homemaker. I work at home. Write soon.

Love,
Rosa

Lesson objectives

- Discuss and complete a letter about jobs
- Write about family and friends

Warm-up and review

- Before class. Write today's lesson focus on the board. *Lesson E:* *Write about family, friends, and jobs*
- Begin class. Books closed. Write *job duties* on the board. Point to the word. Ask: *What are some examples of job duties?* Elicit appropriate responses, such as: *serve food, count money, make appointments.*

Teaching tip

If Ss can't think of any job duties, ask: *What are some things that people do at work?* Give Ss an example if needed.

Presentation

- Direct Ss' attention to Exercise **1A** and read the instructions aloud.
- Model the activity. Ask a S: *What does a cashier do?* (He / She counts money.) Ask: *Does a cashier drive a bus?* (No.) Hold up the Student's Book. Point to the check mark under *Counts money.* Continue with questions for the other columns. Make sure Ss understand the task.

Practice

- Ss complete the chart in pairs. Walk around and help as needed.
- Check Ss' answers by calling on individual Ss. Ask about each job in turn: *What does a custodian do?* (Cleans buildings.) Have Ss check each other's charts.
- Direct Ss' attention to Exercise **1B** and read the instructions aloud.
- Point to the first item and say: *Number 1. What's the word?* (salesperson) Ask: *What letters do we need?* (*e* and *r*) Point to where the letters are written in the blanks. Say: *Now you complete the rest of the words.*
- Ss work in pairs to complete the words.
- When Ss are finished, call on different pairs to write their completed words on the board. Review the alphabet by asking Ss who write answers on the board to say the letters aloud.
- Go over the answers with the class. Ask: *Are these words spelled correctly?* Make corrections as needed.

Literacy tip

Pair literacy Ss with other Ss for Exercise **1B**. Encourage the Ss to work together to fill in the blanks. The literacy S can help with oral clues while the other S can help the literacy S write the letters correctly. This kind of teamwork will make literacy Ss feel more comfortable asking other Ss questions in class.

- Write the word *letter* on the board. Point to the word. Say it aloud. Ask Ss to repeat it after you. Ask: *Do you write letters?* If Ss don't know what a letter is, say: *It's a note that you write someone.* Show Ss the letter in Exercise **1C** as an example. If any Ss answer *yes* to your question, ask: *Who do you write letters to? Where does this person live?*
- Direct Ss' attention to the letter in Exercise **1C**. Ask: *Who is the letter to?* (Grandpa.) *Who is the letter from?* (Rosa.) *How do you begin a letter in English?* (Dear [name].) *How do you finish a letter in English?* (Elicit an appropriate answer, such as *Love* or *Sincerely.*)
- Read the instructions aloud. Ask Ss to read the letter silently. Then ask a S to read the letter aloud.

Literacy tip

It might be helpful to explain the differences between different ways to sign a letter. Tell Ss that *Love* is used for people you are close to and *Sincerely* is a more formal way to sign a letter.

Expansion activity *(student pairs)*

- Say: *Ask and answer questions about the letter.* Write on the board: *What is Luis's job? What does he do? What is Maria's job? What does she do?*
- Ss in pairs. Say: *Ask your partner the questions. Then your partner will ask you the questions.*
- Walk around and help as needed.
- Ask several pairs to ask and answer the questions for the rest of the class.

LESSON E Writing

Presentation

- Direct Ss' attention to Exercise 2A and read the instructions aloud.
- Model the task. Ask a S to read the first part of the letter aloud. Ask the S to stop after the example word *salesperson*.
- Remind Ss to look at Exercise 1B on the previous page for the words to write in the blanks.

Practice

- Ss complete the exercise in pairs, using the words from Exercise 1B. Walk around and help as needed.

> **Teaching tip**
> It might be helpful to give Ss examples of how to talk with their partner about completing the exercise. Tell Ss to read the sentences aloud. Then they can ask their partner: *What is this word? What do you think?* Write the questions on the board so that Ss can refer to them as they work with their partners.

- Write the numbers *1–6* on the board. Ask different Ss to write their answers on the board.
- Ask different Ss to read the answers aloud. Ask: *Are these words correct?* Ss can correct the list if needed. Then ask a S to read the letter aloud.
- Direct Ss' attention to Exercise 2B and read the instructions aloud.
- Model the task. Hold up the Student's Book. Say: *I'm going to write about my friend. My friend's name is ______.* Use a real or imaginary friend's name for the example. Continue by telling the class about your friend's job and job duties. For example: *My friend's name is Mary. She is a receptionist. She answers the phone.*
- Ss complete the exercise individually. Walk around and help as needed.

> **Teaching tip**
> Tell Ss that they can write about real or imaginary friends and family. If Ss choose to write about real people, they may need help with names of other jobs and job duties in English. Encourage Ss to use bilingual dictionaries to find the words they are trying to use in this exercise.

> **Literacy tip**
> For an alternative activity, refer literacy Ss to pages 98–99 in the *Literacy Workbook* at any time during the lesson.

Application

- Focus Ss' attention on Exercise 3. Read the instructions aloud. Encourage Ss to read what they wrote in Exercise 2B to their partners.
- Ss complete the task in pairs. Walk around and help as needed.
- Ask several volunteers to read their sentences aloud to the class.

> **Teaching tip**
> This exercise asks Ss to work together to share their writing. Encourage Ss to peer-correct each other's writing if necessary. Say: *Help your partner with any mistakes. Then your partner will help you.*

Expansion activity *(student pairs)*

- Give each S in your class two index cards. Tell them to write the name of a job learned in this unit on one side of the card and the job duty on the back of the card. For example: *cashier* on one side and *counts money* on the other side.
- When Ss are finished, collect the cards. Mix them up, and hand out four cards to each pair of Ss.
- Ss in pairs. Say: *Show your partner the job on one of your cards. Your partner will tell you the job duty.*
- Walk around and help as needed. When Ss are finished with their four cards, encourage them to exchange cards with other Ss.

Evaluation

- Direct Ss' attention to the lesson focus written on the board.
- Ask Ss to write the names of the jobs they reviewed in this lesson on the board (*cashier*, *custodian*, *server*, *bus driver*, *receptionist*, *salesperson*, *mechanic*). Point to each job in turn. Ask individual Ss to tell you the job duty for each job.
- Check off each part of the lesson focus as Ss demonstrate understanding of what they have learned in the lesson.

More Ventures, Unit 8, Lesson E	
Literacy Workbook, 15–30 min. **Basic Workbook,** 15–30 min.	
Writing worksheets, 15–30 min.	www.cambridge.org/myresourceroom

2 Write

A Talk with a partner. Complete the letter. Use the words from 1B.

Dear Grandma,

How are you? We are all well here. Janie and Walter have new jobs!

Janie is a ___salesperson___(1). She ___sells___(2) clothes. She also ___answers___(3) the phone at work, and she ___counts___(4) money. Walter is a ___mechanic___(5). He ___fixes___(6) cars.

Write soon.

Love,

Meg

B Write about your family and friends. Write about their jobs.

My ___friend's___ name is ___Sandra___.
She is a ___receptionist___. She ___answers the phone___.

1. My ___(Answers will vary.)___'s name is ______________.
He is a ______________. He ______________.

2. My ______________'s name is ______________.
She is a ______________. She ______________.

3. My ______________'s name is ______________.
__________ is a ______________.
______________________________.

3 After you write

Talk with a partner. Share your writing.

LESSON F Another view

1 Life-skills reading

A Read the sentences. Look at the ads. Fill in the answer.

1. Job A is for a ____.
   - Ⓐ cashier
   - Ⓑ receptionist
   - ● salesperson
2. Job B is for a ____.
   - Ⓐ driver
   - ● painter
   - Ⓒ plumber
3. For Job C, ____.
   - ● write to Shop Smart
   - Ⓑ go to Shop Smart
   - Ⓒ call Shop Smart
4. Call City Bus Company ____.
   - Ⓐ in the morning
   - Ⓑ in the afternoon
   - ● in the evening

B Talk with a partner.

What job do you want?

Lesson objectives

- Read and understand job ads
- Review unit vocabulary
- Complete the self-assessment

Warm-up and review

- Before class. Write today's lesson focus on the board.
Lesson F:
Read and answer questions about job ads
Practice vocabulary about jobs
Complete the self-assessment
- Begin class. Books closed. Write on the board: *Job advertisements.* Point to the words. Say them aloud and ask Ss to repeat. Cross out *-vertisements.* Say: *These are commonly called ads. "Ads" is the short form for "advertisements."*
- Ask: *Where can you find job ads?* If Ss don't know, say: *You can find them in the newspaper and on the Internet.*

Teaching tip
It might be helpful to bring in some examples of job ads from the local newspaper.

Presentation

- Books open. Direct Ss' attention to the job ads in Exercise **1A**.
- Hold up the Student's Book. Point to the words *Help Wanted.* Say the words aloud. Ask Ss to repeat them after you. Ask Ss what they think this means. Say: *This means that some workplaces need help. If you see this sign in a workplace, it means they are looking for workers.*

Practice

- Read aloud the instructions in Exercise **1A**. This task helps prepare Ss for standardized-type tests they may have to take.
- Write the first item on the board along with three answer choices labeled *a*, *b*, and *c*.
- Read the item and the answer choices aloud and then point to the help-wanted ads. Ask Ss: *What job is Job A?* Show Ss where to look for the information. Elicit: *Salesperson.*
- Point to the three answer choices on the board. Ask Ss: *a*, *b*, or *c*? (c) Fill in the letter *c* and tell Ss: *Fill in the answer.* Make sure Ss understand the task.
- Have Ss individually scan for and fill in the answers.

Comprehension check

- Go over the answers to Exercise **1A** with the class. Make sure that Ss followed directions and filled in their answers. Ask Ss to point to the information in the job ads.

Literacy tip
For an alternative activity, refer literacy Ss to pages 100–101 in the *Literacy Workbook* at any time during the lesson.

Application

- Read the instructions for Exercise **1B** aloud.
- Model the task. Ask a S: *What job do you want?* Indicate that the S should choose from the job ads above. Elicit an appropriate answer. Say: *Now ask your partner the same question.*
- Ss complete the task in pairs.
- Ask several pairs to ask and answer the question for the rest of the class.

Teaching tip
If you do not want to limit your Ss to one of the jobs in the help-wanted ads on this page, explain that they can choose a different job that they would like to have in the future. List any new jobs that Ss come up with on the board, and ask the Ss who chose them to define them for the class.

Expansion activity *(individual work, student pairs)*

- Ask Ss to write ads for different jobs. Encourage them to use the ads in Exercise **1** as a guide.
- When Ss are finished, ask them to work with a partner. Say: *Show your partner your ad. Then look at your partner's ad. Ask questions. For example: How much is the salary? What's the phone number? Is it part-time or full-time?*
- Ask Ss: *Do you want any of the jobs in the ads? Why or why not?*

Community building *(whole group)*

- Do the expansion activity using real job ads from a local newspaper. Discuss which ads are the most interesting to Ss in your class and why they feel that way. Help Ss define any unfamiliar words in the ads.

LESSON F Another view

Practice

- Direct Ss' attention to Exercise 2A. Read the instructions aloud.
- Focus Ss' attention on the pictures. Say: *These are things that people need for their jobs.*
- Ask a S to read the names of the jobs aloud.
- Model the task. Hold up the Student's Book. Point to the first picture (a truck). Ask: *Who needs this?* (A truck driver.) Point to the line drawn from Picture number 1 to *a truck driver.* Say: *A truck driver needs this.*
- Ss complete the exercise individually. Walk around and help as needed.

> **Teaching tip**
> Some Ss may want to know how to say the names of the items in the pictures in Exercise 2A. If your Ss express interest in this, write the names of the items on the board: *1. a truck, 2. a car, 3. a cash register, 4. paints and a roller, 5. books, 6. a phone.*

- Direct Ss' attention to the second set of instructions in Exercise 2A. Read the instructions aloud.
- Ss complete the exercise in pairs. Ask: *Are your answers the same as your partner's?*
- Go over the answers with the class. Ask individual Ss to read their answers to the class. Ask: *Are the answers correct?* Ask different Ss to make corrections if needed.

Expansion activity *(individual work)*

- Dictation. Books closed. Ask Ss to take out a piece of paper and write the numbers *1–5* on it. Tell them they will listen to five sentences and write them on their papers. Dictate the following sentences:

  1. A truck driver needs a truck.

  2. A mechanic fixes cars.

  3. A receptionist answers the phone.

  4. A custodian cleans buildings.

  5. A cashier counts money.
- Write the numbers *1–5* on the board. Ask five Ss to come to the board and write one sentence each. Ask different Ss to read the sentences aloud. Ask: *Are the sentences correct?* Ask different Ss to make corrections if needed.

Practice

- Direct Ss' attention to Exercise 2B. Read the instructions aloud.
- Hold up the Student's Book. Point to where the word *fix* has been circled in the puzzle. Focus Ss' attention on the words in the word bank. Say: *Find the rest of the words in the puzzle.*
- Ss complete the exercise individually or in pairs. Walk around and help as needed.

Expansion activity *(individual work)*

- Ask Ss to write sentences using the words in the word search.

  Option Ask Ss to erase the words from the word bank in their sentences and leave a line in each word's place. Ask them to trade papers with a partner. Their partners fill in the blanks with the words from the word bank. When they are finished, they can give their papers back to their partners. The partners will check to see if the correct words were chosen or not.

Evaluation

- Before asking Ss to turn to the self-assessment on page 143, do a quick review of the unit. Have Ss turn to Lesson A. Ask the class to talk about what they remember about this lesson. Prompt Ss, if necessary, with questions such as: *What words are on this page? What do you see in the picture?* Continue in this manner to review each lesson quickly.
- **Self-assessment** Read the instructions for Exercise 3. Ask Ss to turn to the self-assessment page and complete the unit self-assessment.
- If Ss are ready, administer the unit test on pages T-190–T-192 of this Teacher's Edition (or on the Assessment Audio CD / CD-ROM).

More Ventures, Unit 8, Lesson F	
Literacy Workbook, 15–30 min.	
Basic Workbook, 15–30 min.	
Writing worksheets, 15–30 min.	www.cambridge.org/myresourceroom

2 Fun with vocabulary

A Read and match.

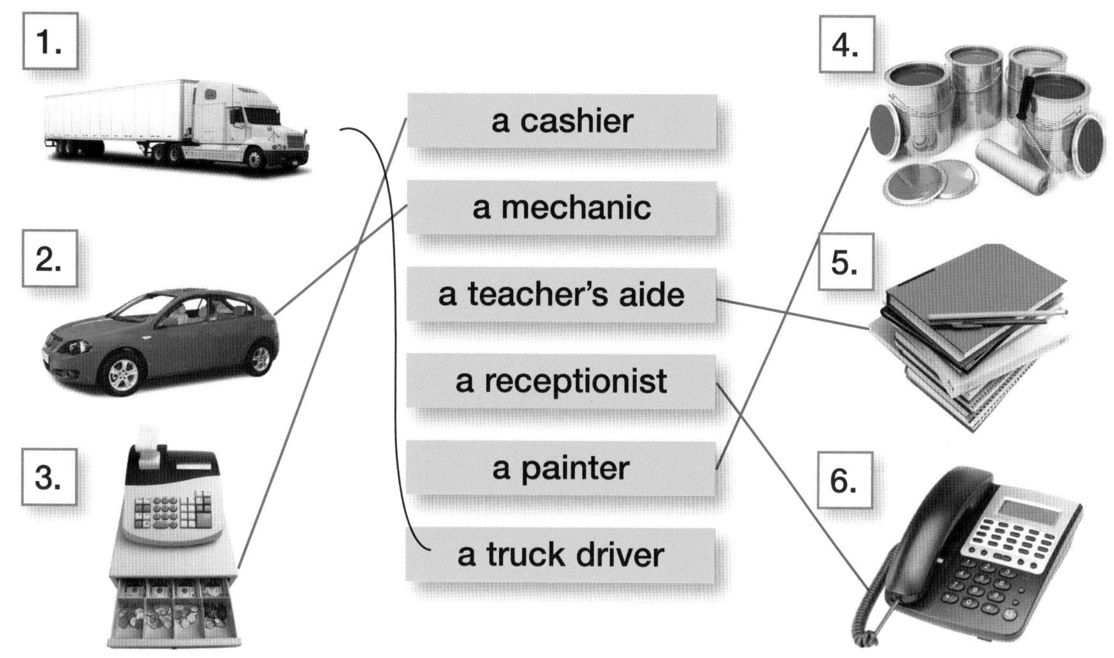

Talk with a partner. Check your answers.

B Circle the words in the puzzle.

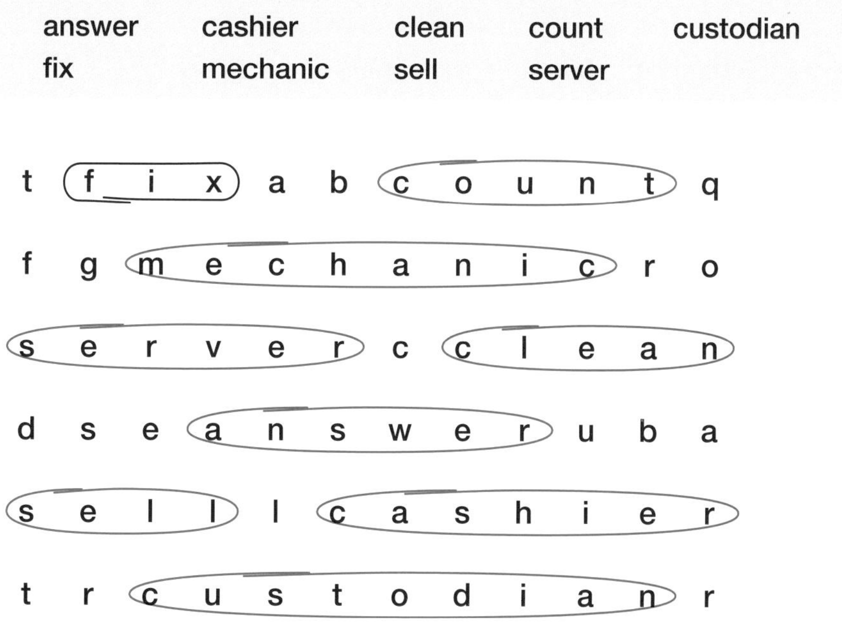

3 Wrap up

Complete the **Self-assessment** on page 143.

Review

1 Listening

CLASS CD2 TK 32

Read. Then listen and circle.

1. What does Chul do?
   (a.) He's a cashier.
   b. He's a custodian.
2. Does he serve food?
   a. Yes, he does.
   (b.) No, he doesn't.
3. What does Luz do?
   a. She's a salesperson.
   (b.) She's a receptionist.
4. Does she answer the phone?
   (a.) Yes, she does.
   b. No, she doesn't.
5. What color are the pants?
   (a.) blue
   b. green
6. How much are the pants?
   a. $9.99
   (b.) $19.99

Talk with a partner. Ask and answer.

2 Vocabulary

Write. Complete the story.

cars clothes mechanic $9.99 salesperson shirt

A New Shirt

Sam is a _mechanic_ (1). He fixes _cars_ (2). Today he is at Shop Smart. He needs a blue _shirt_ (3). Shirts are on sale. Brenda is a _salesperson_ (4). She sells _clothes_ (5) at Shop Smart. How much is the shirt? It's _$9.99_ (6).

Lesson objectives

- Review vocabulary and grammar from Units 7 and 8
- Introduce pronunciation of *e* as in *red*, *i* as in *six*, and *u* as in *bus*

UNITS **7&8**

Warm-up and review

- Before class. Write today's lesson focus on the board.
  Review unit:
  Review vocabulary and grammar from Units 7 and 8.
  Pronounce e as in red, i as in six, and u as in bus.
- Begin class. Books closed. Ask a volunteer to come to the front of the class. Ask another S: *What color is her (clothing item)?* Elicit an appropriate response.
- Point to another item of clothing on the volunteer. Ask: *What's this?* Elicit an appropriate response.
- Write the words *mechanic*, *teacher's aide*, and *receptionist* on the board. Point to each word in turn. Ask Ss: *What does a mechanic do?* (He / She fixes cars.) *What does a teacher's aide do?* (He / She helps students.) *What does a receptionist do?* (He / She answers the phone.)
- Draw a simple drawing of a T-shirt and shoes on the board. Write a price next to each clothing item, such as: *$10.99* and *$29.99*, respectively. Point to each item in turn. Ask: *How much is the T-shirt?* ($10.99) *How much are the shoes?* ($29.99)

Practice

- Books open. Direct Ss' attention to Exercise **1** and read the instructions aloud.
- Ask a S to read the question and answer choices in number 1 aloud.
- Class Audio CD2 track 32 Model the task. Play or read only the first conversation on the audio program (see audio script, page T-161). Point to the two answer choices in number 1 and ask: *Is Chul a cashier or a custodian?* (He's a cashier.) Point to where the answer *a* is circled.
- Class Audio CD2 track 32 Play or read the complete audio program (see audio script, page T-161). Ss listen and circle the correct answers. Repeat the audio program as needed.
- Check answers with the class. Read each question aloud and call on different Ss to answer.

Teaching tip

You may need to play the audio program several times in order to give Ss a chance to extract the information they need. Then, to check comprehension and to help Ss who may be struggling, play the audio program again and ask Ss to repeat the parts of the conversation that contain the answers to the questions.

- Read aloud the second part of the instructions for Exercise **1**. Ss practice asking and answering the questions in pairs. Walk around and help as needed.
- Ask several pairs to ask and answer the questions for the rest of the class.

Expansion activity *(small groups)*

- Tell Ss to write questions about their group members. Then they will ask the rest of the class the questions. They should use Exercise **1** as a guide.
- Model the activity. Point to a small group. Say: *I will give you some examples of questions about this group.* Point to one S. Ask: *What does Maria do?* Elicit an appropriate response, such as *Maria is a student.* Ask: *Does she fix cars?* Elicit a *Yes / No* response. Point to a different S in the group. Ask: *What color is her (name of clothing item S is wearing)?*
- Ss write questions in their groups. Ask them to ask the questions to other Ss in the class.

Teaching tip

You may need to remind Ss to look at the questions in Exercise **1** to use as a guide while they are writing questions about their group members.

Practice

- Direct Ss' attention to Exercise **2**. Point to the title of the story and ask Ss: *What's the title?* (A New Shirt) Help Ss by reading the title aloud if necessary.
- Direct Ss' attention to the words in the word bank. Say each word aloud. Ask Ss to repeat them after you.
- Read aloud the instructions for Exercise **2**. Point to the words in the word bank and tell Ss: *Write these words in the story.*
- Model the task. Read aloud the first two sentences of the story. Point to *mechanic* in the word bank and in the blank for number 1.
- Ss read the story and fill in the blanks individually. Walk around and help as needed.
- Write the numbers *1-6* on the board. Ask Ss to come up to the board to write the answers.
- Ask several Ss to read different sentences of the story aloud using the words on the board. Ask: *Are these words correct?* Ask different Ss to correct any errors.

Review

Warm-up and review

- Books closed. Write an example of a store receipt on the board. Use the following or make up your own:

The Clothes Shop

pants	*$16.95*	*Subtotal*	*$38.90*
socks	*$9.95*	*Tax*	*$3.15*
T-shirt	*$12.00*	*Total*	*$42.05*

- Ask Ss: *How much is the T-shirt?* ($12.) *How much are the socks?* ($9.95.) *How much are the pants?* ($16.95.) *How much is the tax?* ($3.15.) *How much is the total price?* ($42.05.).

Practice

- Direct Ss' attention to the picture in Exercise **3A**. Ask: *What do you see?*
- Read the instructions aloud. Model the task. Read number 1: *How much is or are the T-shirt?* (is) Point to where *is* has been written for number 1 and read the complete sentence aloud. Ask: *Why "is" and not "are"?* (T-shirt is singular.) Ask: *When do we use "are"?* (With plurals.)
- Ss write their answers individually. Check answers by calling on Ss to read the sentences aloud. After each question, ask: *Is this question correct?* Ask different Ss to make corrections.
- Direct Ss' attention to Exercise **3B** and read the instructions aloud.
- Model the task. Ask two Ss to read the example question and answer aloud. Ask: *Is it "Yes, she does" or "Yes, she doesn't"?* (Yes, she does.) Point to where *does* has been written for number 1. Ask: *Why is it "does"?* (It's a *Yes* answer.) Ask: *When do we use "doesn't"?* (With *No* answers.)
- Ss complete the exercise individually. Check answers by calling on Ss to read the questions and answers aloud.

Expansion activity *(whole group)*

- Expand on Exercise **3B** by asking questions about Ss' lives. Point to a S. Ask another S: *Does (student's name) come from Mexico?* Elicit an appropriate response. Continue by asking more questions about other Ss.

Presentation

- Direct Ss' attention to the second part of the lesson focus written on the board.
- Draw two vertical lines on the board, making three columns. Write *e*, *i*, and *u* as headings in each column.
- Write in the *e* column: *red, when.* Point to and say each word and ask Ss to repeat. Underline the *e* in the words. Say a short *e* (/e/) sound before repeating each word, for example: /e/, *red.* Ask Ss to repeat.
- Write in the *i* column: *six, his.* Repeat the procedure, underlining the *i* in the words and pronouncing a short *i* sound, for example: /i/, *six.*
- Write in the *u* column: *bus, much.* Repeat the procedure, underlining the *u* in the words and pronouncing a short *u* sound, for example: /u/, *bus.*

Practice

Class Audio CD2 track 33 Direct Ss' attention to Exercise **4A** and read the instructions aloud. Play or read the audio program (see audio script, page T-161). Ss listen to examples of the three vowel sounds.

Class Audio CD2 track 34 Direct Ss' attention to Exercise **4B** and read the instructions aloud. Play or read the audio program (see audio script, page T-161). Ss listen and repeat what they hear.

- Read aloud the second part of the instructions for Exercise **4B**. Model the task. Point to the three charts and tell one S: *Say a word.* After that S says any word from the charts, tell his or her partner: *Point to the word.*
- Ss complete the task in pairs. Help as needed.

Class Audio CD2 track 35 Direct Ss' attention to Exercise **4C** and read the instructions aloud. Model the task. Play or read the first word in the audio program (see audio script, page T-161). Ask: *Which letter is it: e, i, or u?* Point to where the letter has been checked in the chart.

Class Audio CD2 track 35 Play or read the complete audio program (see audio script, page T-161). Ss listen and make a check mark under the letter they hear.

Class Audio CD2 track 35 Reproduce the chart from Exercise **4C** on the board, and play or read the audio program again. Pause after each word and ask a S to check the appropriate letter in the chart.

Evaluation

- Direct Ss' attention to the lesson focus written on the board.
- Ask individual Ss questions similar to the ones in Exercise **1**. Ask real questions about Ss in the class.
- Write on the board: *red, six, bus.* Call on individual Ss as you point to one of the words and ask them to say the word. Listen carefully to the vowel sounds and provide help and correction as needed.
- Check off each part of the lesson focus as Ss demonstrate an understanding of what they have learned in the lesson.

3 Grammar

A Complete the sentences. Use *is* or *are*.

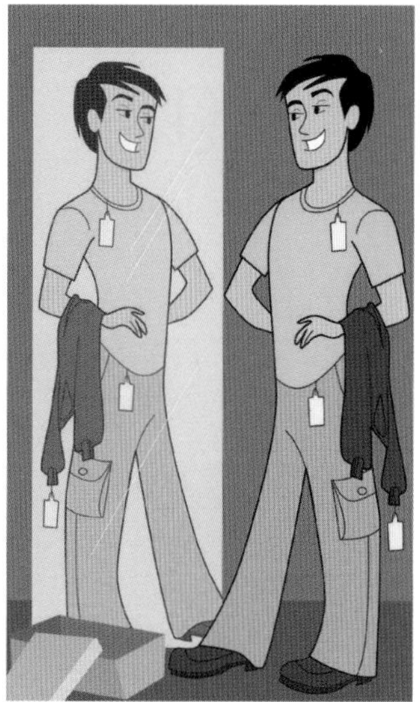

1. A How much ___is___ the T-shirt?
   B $10.99.
2. A How much ___are___ the pants?
   B $28.99.
3. A How much ___are___ the shoes?
   B $39.95.
4. A How much ___is___ the sweater?
   B $22.95.

B Read and circle. Then write.

1. A Does Kayla count money?
   B Yes, she ___does___.
   (does) doesn't
2. A Does she clean buildings?
   B No, she ___doesn't___.
   does (doesn't)
3. A Does Allen fix cars?
   B No, he ___doesn't___.
   does (doesn't)
4. A Does he serve food?
   B Yes, he ___does___.
   (does) doesn't

4 Pronunciation

CLASS CD2 TK 33

A Listen to the *e* sound, the *i* sound, and the *u* sound.

e	i	u
red	six	bus

CLASS CD2 TK 34

B Listen and repeat.

e	red	when

i	six	his

u	bus	much

Talk with a partner. Say a word. Your partner points. Take turns.

CLASS CD2 TK 35

C Listen and check (✓).

	e	i	u		e	i	u		e	i	u		e	i	u		e	i	u
1.	✓			2.			✓	3.		✓		4.		✓		5.	✓		

UNIT
9 Daily living

LESSON A Listening

1 Before you listen

A Look at the picture. What do you see?

CLASS CD2 TK 36

B Listen and point: doing homework • doing the laundry • drying the dishes • making lunch • making the bed • washing the dishes

Ping

Tao

Quan

Mei

Li

Huan

Lesson objectives

- Introduce Ss to the topic
- Find out what Ss know about the topic
- Preview the unit by talking about the picture
- Practice key vocabulary
- Practice listening skills

Warm-up and review

- Before class. Write today's lesson focus on the board.
  Lesson A:
  Daily living
  Vocabulary for daily activities
- Begin class. Books closed. Point to the words *daily activities* written in the lesson focus. Say each word aloud. Ask Ss to repeat them after you. Tell Ss some daily activities that you do in your house, such as: *washing the dishes, making the bed.*
- Ask: *What are some activities you do every day in your house?* Write Ss' responses on the board. Elicit any appropriate responses, such as: *cooking, doing the laundry.* Say: *These types of activities are called household chores.* Write *chores* on the board. Say the word and ask Ss to repeat it after you.

Teaching tip

Do not expect Ss to know the vocabulary for all daily activities. This warm-up will help you to find out what Ss know before you present the vocabulary for daily activities in this lesson.

Literacy tip

If you have literacy Ss in your class, it might be helpful to spend time at the beginning of any activity that contains art or photos talking about the pictures before focusing Ss' attention on the printed words in the exercise. Have Ss work in pairs. Tell them to ask each other: *What do you see?* Encourage Ss to describe the pictures to each other. Consider pairing literacy Ss with Ss who can help them read the text in the exercise. This will help preview the exercise for literacy Ss and make them more confident as the exercise continues.

Presentation

- Books open. Set the scene. Hold up the Student's Book. Show Ss the picture on page 110. Ask: *What do you see?* Elicit and write on the board any vocabulary that Ss know, such as: *a kitchen, a family, food, father, mother, daughter, son.*
- Ask: *What are the people's names?* (Huan, Quan, Li, Tao, Mei, Ping)

Practice

- Direct Ss' attention to the key vocabulary in Exercise **1B**. Say: *These are some daily activities or chores.* Read each phrase aloud while pointing to the corresponding chore in the picture. Ask Ss to repeat and point.
- Read the instructions for Exercise **1B** aloud.

Class Audio CD2 track 36 Play or read the audio program (see audio script, page T-161). Tell Ss: *Listen and point to the picture.* As Ss hear the key vocabulary, check to see that they are pointing to the correct part of the picture. Repeat the audio program as needed.

Comprehension check

- Ask Ss *Yes / No* questions about the picture. Tell Ss: *Listen. Say "yes" or "no."*

  Point to the mother. Ask: *Is she making lunch?* (Yes.)

  Point to the father. Ask: *Is he drying the dishes?* (No.)

  Point to the boy drying dishes. Ask: *Is he washing the dishes?* (No.)

  Point to the boy doing the laundry. Ask: *Is he doing the laundry?* (Yes.)

  Point to the girl making her bed. Ask: *Is she doing her homework?* (No.)

  Point to the girl doing her homework. Ask: *Is she making the bed?* (No.)

Expansion activity (student pairs)

- Write on the board: *Do you do this chore at home?* Hold up the Student's Book. Point to one of the activities. Ask a S: *Do you do this chore at home?* Elicit *Yes, I do.* or *No, I don't.* Write these responses on the board as a guide.
- Ss in pairs. Say: *Point to different activities in the picture. Ask your partner the question on the board.*
- Walk around and help as needed.

  Option Write on the board: *Who does this activity at your house?* Model the task. Point to an activity in the picture. Tell Ss who does the activity at your house, for example: *My husband washes the dishes.* Ask Ss to point to activities in the picture. Elicit short responses to the question on the board, such as: *My brother / sister / roommate / daughter.*

LESSON A Listening

Presentation

- Direct Ss' attention to the phrases in Exercise 2A. Tell Ss: *We are going to practice pronouncing these daily activities.* Read them aloud. Ask Ss to repeat them after you.
- Read aloud the instructions for Exercise 2A.

Practice

Class Audio CD2 track 37 Play or read the audio program (see audio script, page T-161). Ss listen and repeat the vocabulary. Repeat the audio program as needed.

- Listen carefully to Ss' pronunciation and make corrections as needed.

Learner persistence *(individual work)*

Self-Study Audio CD track 39 Exercise 2A is recorded on the CD at the back of the Student's Book. Ss can listen to the CD at home for reinforcement and review. They can also listen to the CD for self-directed learning when class attendance is not possible.

> **Literacy tip**
> For an alternative activity, refer literacy Ss to pages 102–103 in the *Literacy Workbook* at any time during the lesson.

- Direct Ss' attention to Exercise 2B and read the instructions aloud.

Class Audio CD2 track 38 Model the task. Hold up the Student's Book and say: *Number one.* Play or read the audio program for number 1 (see audio script, page T-161). Point to the two answer choices in number 1 and ask Ss: *What did you hear – a or b?* Elicit: *a.* Point to the letter *a* next to the first picture and tell Ss: *Circle the letter "a."*

Class Audio CD2 track 38 Play or read the complete audio program (see audio script, page T-161). Ss listen and circle the correct answers. Repeat the audio program as needed.

Class Audio CD2 track 38 Read aloud the second part of the instructions in Exercise 2B. Play or read the audio program again so that Ss can listen and check their answers.

Learner persistence *(individual work)*

Self-Study Audio CD track 40 Exercise 2B is recorded on the CD at the back of the Student's Book. Ss can listen to the CD at home for reinforcement and review and also for self-directed learning when class attendance is not possible.

Comprehension check

- Write the numbers *1–4* on the board. Ask a few Ss to come to the board and write the correct answers to Exercise 2B next to each number.

Class Audio CD2 track 38 Play or read the audio program again. Pause the audio program after each conversation. Point to the answer written on the board and ask: *Is this correct?* Ask another S to make any necessary corrections.

Application

- Direct Ss' attention to Exercise 3 and read the instructions aloud.
- Model the task. Hold up the Student's Book and point to the pictures in Exercise 2B. Say to one S: *Point to a picture.* Say to the S's partner: *Say the word.*
- Ss complete the exercise in pairs. Walk around and help as needed.

Expansion activity *(student pairs)*

- Write on the board: *Do you like _____?* Point to the question. Say it aloud. Ask Ss to repeat it after you. Tell Ss to ask each other the question on the board using the household chores in Exercises 2A and 2B.
- Model the activity. Hold up the Student's Book. Point to the first picture in number 1 in Exercise 2B. Ask a S: *Do you like doing homework?* Elicit a *yes* or *no* response.
- Ss in pairs. Say: *Point to the pictures in Exercise 2B. Ask your partner the question on the board.* Tell Ss to switch roles when they are finished.
- Walk around and help as needed.

Evaluation

- Direct Ss' attention to the lesson focus written on the board. Check Ss' understanding of daily activities vocabulary by asking them to point to the following activities in the picture on page 110: *doing homework, doing the laundry, drying the dishes, making lunch, making the bed,* and *washing the dishes.*
- Walk around and check that Ss are pointing to the correct parts of the picture.
- Check off the lesson focus as Ss demonstrate an understanding of what they have learned in the lesson.

More Ventures, Unit 9, Lesson A	
Literacy Workbook, 15–30 min.	
Basic Workbook, 15–30 min.	
Writing worksheets 15–30 min. **Real Life Document,** 15–30 min.	www.cambridge.org/myresourceroom
Student Arcade, time varies	www.cambridge.org/venturesarcade

Unit Goals

Identify family chores
Complete a chart about family chores
Interpret a work order

2 Listen

A Listen and repeat.

STUDENT TK 39
CLASS CD2 TK 37

1. doing homework
2. doing the laundry
3. drying the dishes
4. making lunch
5. making the bed
6. washing the dishes

B Listen and circle.

STUDENT TK 40
CLASS CD2 TK 38

1. (a.)  b. 

2. a.  (b.) 

3. (a.)  b. 

4. (a.)  b. 

Listen again. Check your answers.

3 After you listen

Talk with a partner. Point to a picture. Your partner says the words.

☑ Listen for and identify family chores

LESSON B Outside chores

1 Vocabulary focus

CLASS CD2 TK 39

Listen and repeat.

2 Practice

A Read and match.

Lesson objectives
- Introduce and practice vocabulary about outside chores
- Practice questions and answers about outside chores

Warm-up and review

- Before class. Write today's lesson focus on the board.
Lesson B:
Vocabulary about outside chores
Ask and answer questions about outside chores
- Begin class. Books open. Direct Ss' attention to the picture on page 110. Ask Ss to cover up the words in Exercise **1B**. Review key vocabulary from the unit by asking: *What are the names of daily activities in this picture?* Elicit: *doing homework*, *doing the laundry*, *drying the dishes*, *making lunch*, *making the bed*, and *washing the dishes.* Ask Ss to point to these activities.

Teaching tip
If you feel that it is too challenging for your Ss to cover up the words in Exercise **1B** for this warm-up exercise, allow Ss to look at the words while pointing to the activities in the picture.

- Walk around and check to see that Ss are pointing to the correct items in the picture.
- Point to the words *outside chores* on the board. Say them aloud. Ask Ss to repeat them after you. Ask Ss: *What are these?* Tell Ss that chores are work you do at home. If Ss don't know what *outside* means, point out the window and say: *That's outside.* If your classroom doesn't have a window, explain that *outside* is the opposite of *inside.* Use hand gestures to indicate the meanings of the two words.

Presentation

- Set the scene. Point to the words *outside chores* on the board again. Ask: *What are some examples of outside chores?* Elicit appropriate examples, such as cleaning the yard or cutting the grass. If Ss don't know any examples, direct Ss' attention to the pictures in Exercise **1**. Say: *Here are some examples of outside chores.*
- Read aloud the instructions for Exercise **1**.

Class Audio CD2 track 39 Play or read the audio program (see audio script, page T-161). Listen and repeat the vocabulary along with Ss. Repeat the audio program as needed.

- Listen carefully to Ss' pronunciation and correct as needed.

Expansion activity (student pairs)

- Write on the board: *What are your chores at home?* Point to the words. Say them aloud. Ask Ss to repeat them after you. Ss in pairs. Say: Ask your partner the question on the board. Model the activity. Ask a S the question. Elicit an appropriate response, for example: *taking out the trash*, *walking the dog*, *washing the dishes.*
- Ss continue asking the questions in pairs. Walk around and help as needed.
- Have several pairs ask and answer the question for the rest of the class.

Teaching tip
Encourage Ss to use the chores in Lesson A as well as the chores in Lesson B for this expansion activity.

Practice

- Direct Ss' attention to Exercise **2A**. As you read aloud the instructions, hold up the Student's Book and indicate that Ss should look at the pictures of outside chores and match them with the corresponding phrases.
- Model the task. Hold up the Student's Book. Point to the daughter in the first picture. Ask: *What is she doing?* Elicit: *Cutting the grass.* Point to the mother. Ask: *What is she doing?* Elicit: *Getting the mail.* Hold up the Student's Book. Point to the lines connecting the first picture to the phrases *cutting the grass* and *getting the mail.* Say: *Match the pictures and the words.*
- Ss complete the exercise individually. Help as needed.

Literacy tip
Literacy Ss may be able to complete this activity with help. Pair stronger Ss with literacy Ss. Tell literacy Ss to refer to Exercise **1** when completing Exercise **2A**.

Comprehension check

- Ask different Ss to point to each picture in Exercise **2A** and read the phrases that match the picture. After each phrase is read, ask: *Is this correct?* Ask another S to make any corrections if needed.

Community building (whole group)

- If your school has a custodian, ask: *What are the custodian's chores?* Brainstorm his or her chores. Write them on the board. Elicit appropriate responses, such as: *taking out the trash*, *cleaning the boards*, *cleaning the classroom.*

LESSON B Outside chores

Presentation

- Direct Ss' attention to the picture in Exercise 2B. Ask: *What do you see?* Elicit any words that Ss know, such as: *family chores, cutting the grass, getting the mail, walking the dog, watering the grass.*
- Tell Ss that this picture shows the Navarro family. Ask Ss to tell you the names of the people in the family (*Mr. and Mrs. Navarro, Roberto, Diego, Norma, and Rita*). Say: *Mr. and Mrs. Navarro are the father and mother. Who are Roberto and Diego?* (brothers or sons) *Who are Norma and Rita?* (sisters or daughters)
- Read the instructions for Exercise 2B aloud.

Class Audio CD2 track 40 Model the task. Say: *Listen and repeat.* Play or read the audio program for number 1 (see audio script, page T-161) and point to Mrs. Navarro in the picture as you repeat. Say: *Then write.* Point to where *watering* has been written in the chart. Make sure Ss understand the task.

Class Audio CD2 track 40 Play or read the complete audio program (see audio script, page T-161). Ss listen and repeat. Encourage Ss to point to the people in the picture as they repeat.

- Ss complete the charts individually using words from Exercises 1 and 2A. Repeat the audio program as needed.
- Check answers with the class. Write the numbers *2–6* on the board, and ask volunteers to write their answers on the board. Point to each answer and ask the class: *Is this correct?* Make any necessary corrections.
- Read aloud the second part of the instructions for Exercise 2B. Point to and model the example conversation.
- Call on a pair of volunteers to read the example conversation aloud for the class. Then ask the same Ss to make up a new conversation about another person in the Navarro family. Indicate that Ss should ask and answer questions about all the people in the family.
- Ss complete the exercise in pairs. Walk around and help as needed.

Literacy tip

For an alternative activity, refer literacy Ss to pages 104–105 in the *Literacy Workbook* at any time during the lesson.

Application

- Direct Ss' attention to Exercise 3 and read the instructions aloud.
- Model the task. Pantomime taking out the trash. Ask: *What am I doing?* Elicit: *Taking out the trash.*
- Direct Ss' attention to the picture in Exercise 3. Say: *He's acting "watering the grass." She's guessing the chore.*
- Ss complete the exercise in pairs. Have Ss act out as many chores as they can in the time allotted.
- Ask several pairs to act out the chores for the rest of the class. Encourage Ss to act out the chores learned in both Lessons A and B of this unit.

Expansion activity *(whole group)*

- Competition. Divide the class into two teams. Ask one S from each team to come to the board. Say: *I will start saying a chore. You have to finish it by writing on the board.* Model the activity. Ask a S to come to the board. Say: *Watering* _____. The S has to write *the grass* on the board. If the S doesn't understand the prompt, model the game by writing *the grass* on the board for the S. Say: *The chore is watering the grass.*
- Start the game. Use all the chores in Lessons A, B, and C. Use the following as prompts:
  cutting _____ (the grass)
  walking _____ (the dog)
  washing _____ (the dishes or the car)
  doing _____ (homework or the laundry)
  making _____ (lunch or the bed)
  taking out _____ (the trash)
  watering _____ (the grass)
  drying _____ (the dishes)
  getting _____ (the mail)
- The first S who completes the phrase correctly earns a point. The team with the most points wins.

Evaluation

- Direct Ss' attention to the lesson focus written on the board. Check Ss' understanding of the key vocabulary by asking them to point to the outdoor chores in the pictures in Exercise 2B on page 113: *cutting the grass, getting the mail, taking out the trash, walking the dog, washing the car*, and *watering the grass.* Walk around and check that Ss are pointing to the correct items.
- Check off the lesson focus as Ss demonstrate an understanding of what they have learned in the lesson.

More Ventures, Unit 9, Lesson B	
Literacy Workbook, 15–30 min.	
Basic Workbook, 15–30 min.	
Writing worksheets, 15–30 min.	www.cambridge.org/myresourceroom
Student Arcade, time varies	www.cambridge.org/venturesarcade

CLASS CD2 TK 40

B Listen and repeat. Then write.

Name	Chore
1. Mrs. Navarro	watering the grass
2. Mr. Navarro	cutting the grass
3. Roberto	washing the car
4. Diego	taking out the trash
5. Norma	getting the mail
6. Rita	walking the dog

Talk with a partner. Ask and answer.

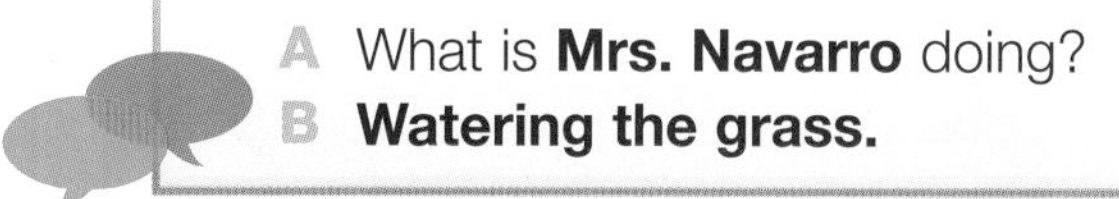

A What is **Mrs. Navarro** doing?
B **Watering the grass.**

3 Communicate

Talk with a partner. Act and guess.

LESSON C What are they doing?

1 Grammar focus: questions with *What*

Questions

What	**is**	he	**doing**?
	is	she	
	are	they	

Answers

Cutting the grass.
Walking the dog.
Washing the dishes.

2 Practice

A Read and circle. Then write.

1. A What ___*are*___ they doing?
is (are)
B Making dinner.
A What ___*is*___ he doing?
(is) are
B Washing the dishes.

2. A What ___*are*___ they doing?
is (are)
B Making the bed.
A What ___*is*___ he doing?
(is) are
B Taking out the trash.

3. A What ___*is*___ he doing?
(is) are
B Washing the car.
A What ___*is*___ she doing?
(is) are
B Watering the grass.

CLASS CD2 TK 41

Listen and repeat. Then practice with a partner.

Lesson objective

- Introduce questions with *What*

Warm-up and review

- Before class. Write today's lesson focus on the board.
  Lesson C:
  What is he doing?
  What is she doing?
  What are they doing?
- Begin class. Direct Ss' attention to the picture on page 110. Ask Ss to review the names of the activities in the picture. Model the task. Hold up the Student's Book. Point to the mother. Say: *She is making lunch.*
- Ss continue the exercise in pairs. One S should point and the other names the activity. Walk around and help as needed.
- Continue by reviewing the activities in the pictures in Exercises **1** and **2A** on page 112. This time the second S will point and the first S will name the activity.

Presentation

- Books open. Direct Ss' attention to the grammar chart in Exercise **1**. Read the questions and the corresponding answers aloud. Ask Ss to repeat after you.

Teaching tip

It might be helpful to review the verb *to be*. Write *I*, *you*, *he*, *she*, *it*, *we*, *you*, and *they* on the board in list form. Ask Ss for the correct forms of the verb *to be* (*I am*, *you are*, *he is*, *she is*, *it is*, *we are*, *you are*, *they are*).

Expansion activity (student pairs)

- Focus Ss' attention on the picture in Exercise **2B** on page 113. Point to the questions in the lesson focus. Say: *Ask your partner the questions on the board. Point to people in the picture.*
- Ss complete the exercise in pairs. Walk around and help as needed.
- Ask several pairs to ask and answer the questions for the rest of the class.

Practice

- Read aloud the instructions for Exercise **2A**. Model the task. Read aloud the example conversation in number 1. When you read Speaker A's first line, show Ss the two answer choices under the blank and ask: *is* or *are*? Elicit *are*.
- Point to where *are* has been circled and written for number 1. Say: *Circle the correct answer. Then write it in the blank.*
- Ss complete the exercise individually. Walk around and help as needed.

Comprehension check

- Read aloud the second part of the instructions for Exercise **2A**.

Class Audio CD2 track 41 Play or read the audio program (see audio script, page T-162). Ss listen and repeat as they check their answers.

- Write the numbers *1–3* on the board. Ask volunteers to come to the board and write the answers they circled. Tell Ss to write two answers for each number. Remind Ss to write only the words they circled, not the complete sentences. Make any necessary corrections on the board.
- Ss in pairs. Ask Ss to choose Role A or B and practice the questions and answers in Exercise **2A**. Then have Ss switch roles and practice again. Walk around and help as needed.
- Ask several pairs to read the conversations to the rest of the class.

Expansion activity (student pairs)

- Focus Ss' attention on Exercise **2B** on page 111. Say: *Look at the pictures. Ask your partner questions.*
- Point to the lesson focus questions written on the board. Tell Ss to use these questions as a guide to talking about the pictures.

LESSON C What are they doing?

Presentation

- Books open. Direct Ss' attention to the word bank in Exercise 2B. Say the words aloud. Ask Ss to repeat them after you.
- Focus Ss' attention on the pictures in Exercise 2B. Ask: *What do you see?* Elicit: *People doing chores.*
- Read the instructions aloud.

Practice

Class Audio CD2 track 42 Model the task. Say: *Listen and repeat.* Play or read the audio program for number 1 (see audio script, page T-162), and point to the people in picture number 1 as you repeat. Say: *Then write.* Point to where the word *getting* has been written in number 1. Make sure Ss understand the task.

Class Audio CD2 track 42 Play or read the complete audio program (see audio script, page T-162). Ss listen and repeat. Encourage Ss to point to the people in the pictures as they repeat.

- Ss work individually as they fill in the blanks in the phrases. Repeat the audio program as needed.
- Write the numbers *2–6* on the board. Ask a few Ss to come to the board and write the answers for each number on the board. Ask: *Are these words correct?* Ask other Ss to make corrections if needed.
- Read aloud the second part of the instructions for Exercise 2B. Model the task. Ask two pairs of Ss to read the example conversations aloud. Point to numbers 1 and 2 as they are reading.
- Indicate that Ss should ask and answer questions about all the pictures. Make sure Ss understand the task.
- Ss ask and answer questions about the pictures in pairs. Walk around and help as needed.
- When Ss are finished, ask them to switch partners and repeat the conversations.
- Ask several pairs to say their conversations to the rest of the class.

Application

- Direct Ss' attention to Exercise 3 and read the instructions aloud.
- Focus Ss' attention on the picture in Exercise 3. Ask two Ss to read the example conversation aloud.
- Model the task. Draw a picture of lunch items with a stick figure next to them. Point to the stick figure. Ask: *What is he doing?* (making lunch) Make sure Ss understand the task.
- Ss complete the exercise in pairs. Walk around and help as needed.
- Ask several volunteers to come to the board and draw one of the chores from Lessons A, B, or C. Encourage the other Ss to guess what the artist is drawing.

Literacy tip

For an alternative activity, refer literacy Ss to pages 106–107 in the *Literacy Workbook* at any time during the lesson.

Expansion activity *(student pairs)*

- **Materials needed:** Old magazines. Ss in pairs. Bring enough magazines to class for each pair of Ss to share. Tell Ss to look through the magazines for pictures of people doing something. Point to the lesson focus on the board: *What is he doing? What is she doing? What are they doing?*
- Tell Ss to ask their partners the questions on the board about the magazine pictures. Their partners will answer the questions. Then encourage them to switch roles.
- Walk around and listen to Ss' questions and answers. Help as needed.
- Ask several pairs to hold up their magazine pictures and ask and answer questions about them for the class.

Community building *(whole class)*

- Before class. Ask Ss to bring in a photo of themselves doing something. There can be other people in the picture, such as friends or family members. Ask Ss to show the pictures to the rest of the class and name everyone in the picture. The other Ss will ask: *What are you doing in the picture? What is (name) doing?* This exercise helps Ss practice their English and also talk about their friends and family members.

Evaluation

- Direct Ss' attention to the lesson focus written on the board. Ask Ss to look at the pictures on pages 110 and 114. Ask them to make questions about the chores in the pictures using the questions in the lesson focus on the board. Ask different Ss to answer the questions.
- Check off the lesson focus as Ss demonstrate an understanding of what they have learned in the lesson.

More Ventures, Unit 9, Lesson C	
Literacy Workbook, 15–30 min. **Basic Workbook,** 15–30 min.	
Writing worksheets, 15–30 min.	www.cambridge.org/myresourceroom
Student Arcade, time varies	www.cambridge.org/venturesarcade

B Listen and repeat. Then write.

CLASS CD2 TK 42

cutting doing drying getting making taking

1. getting the mail

2. making lunch.

3. cutting the grass.

4. doing the laundry.

5. drying the dishes.

6. taking out the trash.

Talk with a partner. Ask and answer.

A What **are they** doing?
B **Getting the mail.**

A What **is he** doing?
B **Making lunch.**

3 Communicate

Talk with a partner. Make a picture. Ask and guess.

What are they doing?

Drying the dishes.

LESSON D Reading

1 Before you read

Talk about the picture.
What do you see?

2 Read

Listen and read.

STUDENT TK 41
CLASS CD2 TK 43

New Message

From: Huan
To: Susie
Subject: Help

Dear Susie,

It's after dinner. My family is working in the kitchen. My daughter Li is washing the dishes. My daughter Mei is drying the dishes. My husband and Tao are taking out the trash. Where is my oldest son? He isn't in the kitchen. He is sleeping in the living room! I am not happy.

I need help. What can I do?

Huan

3 After you read

Read and match.

1. 

2. 

They are taking out the trash.

She is drying the dishes.

She is washing the dishes.

She is not happy.

3. 

4. 

Lesson objectives

- Read an e-mail about chores
- Practice using new topic-related words

Warm-up and review

- Before class. Write today's lesson focus on the board.
  Lesson D:
  Read an e-mail about chores
  Learn vocabulary about rooms in the house
- Begin class. Books open. Hold up the Student's Book to the picture on page 110. Ask: *Remember this family? What are they doing in this picture?* Elicit: *Chores*, or the specific names of the chores the family is doing. Say: *Now we will see another picture of this family.*

Presentation

- Direct Ss' attention to the picture in Exercise **1**. Read the instructions aloud. Ask: *What do you see?* Elicit: *teenage son, mother, house.*
- Ask: *Is the mother happy?* If Ss don't know what this word means, draw a happy face on the board to illustrate the meaning. Elicit: *No, she's not.*

Teaching tip

If appropriate for your class, teach Ss the word *angry.* Point to the picture of Huan in Exercise **1**. Say: *She is angry.* Make your face angry, or draw an angry face on the board to illustrate the meaning of the word. Write the word on the board. Ask Ss to repeat it after you.

Practice

- Direct Ss' attention to the e-mail under the picture. Ask: *What's this?* (An e-mail.) Ask: *Who is the e-mail to?* (Susie.)

Culture tip

Explain to Ss that Susie is an advice columnist and that people in the United States often write letters or e-mails to advice columnists asking for help with their problems. Ask Ss if they know about these columnists. If possible, bring an example of an advice column in the local newspaper to class. Show Ss the letters. Ask Ss if they have advice columns in newspapers in their countries.

- Say: *Now we will read an e-mail to Susie from Huan. It's about family chores.* Direct Ss' attention to Exercise **2**. Read the instructions aloud.

Class Audio CD2 track 43 Play or read the audio program and ask Ss to read along (see audio script, page T-162). Repeat the audio program as needed.

- Read aloud each sentence of the e-mail and ask Ss to repeat after you. Answer any questions Ss have about new words in the reading.

Learner persistence *(individual work)*

Self-Study Audio CD track 41 Exercise **2** is recorded on the CD at the back of the Student's Book. Ss can listen to the CD at home for reinforcement and review and also for self-directed learning when class attendance is not possible.

Expansion Activity *(individual work)*

- Tell Ss that they are going to write an e-mail to a friend, similar to the one to Susie in Exercise **2** but without a problem. Say: *Write an e-mail to a friend. Tell your friend what you and your classmates and your teacher are doing in English class.*
- Walk around the room, and make sure that Ss are using the salutation "Dear ______," and using correct paragraph formation.
- When Ss are finished, ask a few of them to read their e-mails to the rest of the class.

Comprehension check

- Direct Ss' attention to Exercise **3** and read the instructions aloud.
- Hold up the Student's Book. Direct Ss' attention to the first picture. Ask: *Is Huan happy?* (No.) Point to the line matching the first picture to the last sentence. Say: *She is not happy. Draw a line to match the picture with the correct sentence.*
- Ss complete the exercise individually. Walk around and help as needed.
- Ask individual Ss to read each sentence aloud and say which picture matches it.
- After each sentence, ask: *Is that correct?* Ask different Ss to make corrections if needed.

LESSON D Reading

Presentation

- Books closed. Write the phrase *rooms of a house* on the board. Point to the words. Say them aloud. Ask Ss to repeat them after you.
- Draw a simple picture of a floor plan of a house on the board. Tell Ss that it is a house with rooms in it. Ask Ss: *Do you know the names of the rooms of a house?* If Ss know the names, write their responses in the spaces that represent rooms in the house on the board.
- Books open. Direct Ss' attention to the picture dictionary in Exercise 4. Hold up the Student's Book. Point to the pictures of individual rooms. Say: *These are different rooms in a house.* Say the words aloud. Ask Ss to repeat them after you.
- Read the instructions for Exercise 4A aloud.

Class Audio CD2 track 44 Play or read the audio program (see audio script, page T-162). Listen to Ss' pronunciation as they repeat the names of rooms in a house. Correct pronunciation as needed.

Learner persistence (individual work)

Self-Study Audio CD track 42 Exercise 4A is recorded on the CD at the back of the Student's Book. Ss can listen to the CD at home for reinforcement and review and also for self-directed learning when class attendance is not possible.

Expansion activity (small groups)

- Copy and cut out the picture dictionary cards that correspond to this unit. You will need one set for each small group of four or five Ss in your class. Make the sets with pictures on one side of the cards and the names of the rooms on the other side.
- Ss in small groups. Have Ss show each other the pictures on the flash cards and say the names of the rooms in the pictures.
- Ss complete the exercise in small groups. Walk around and help as needed.

Practice

- Direct Ss' attention to Exercise 4B. Read the instructions aloud. Model the conversation. Ask two Ss to read the conversation aloud and point to the kitchen in the picture as they read. Then ask them to change the conversation to ask about a different room. Make sure Ss understand the task.
- Ss complete the exercise in pairs, asking and answering questions about the rooms in the house. Walk around and help as needed.
- Ask several pairs to ask and answer the questions for the rest of the class.

Literacy tip

For an alternative activity, refer literacy Ss to pages 108–109 in the *Literacy Workbook* at any time during the lesson.

Expansion activity (individual work)

- Ask Ss to draw a floor plan of their house or apartment. Model the activity. Draw a simple outline of your house or apartment on the board. Label each room with the appropriate name.
- Give each S a large blank piece of paper. Say: *You can draw your real house or an imaginary house. The house can be big or small.*
- When Ss are finished, ask several volunteers to show their floor plans to the rest of the class. Encourage them to point to each room and say: *This is the living room. This is the bedroom.*

  Option Put Ss in pairs. Ask them to describe their house floor plans to each other.

Evaluation

- Direct Ss' attention to the first part of the lesson focus written on the board. Turn Ss' attention to the e-mail on page 116. Call on several Ss to answer comprehension questions about the reading.
- Direct Ss' attention to the rooms in the picture dictionary. Say: *Please name the rooms in the house.* Ask different Ss to say the names of the rooms as you point to them.

  Option Show Ss the picture dictionary cards. Ask them to identify the different rooms in the house as you show them each card in turn.
- Check off each part of the lesson focus as Ss demonstrate understanding of what they have learned in the lesson.

More Ventures, Unit 9, Lesson D	
Literacy Workbook, 15–30 min. **Basic Workbook,** 15–30 min.	
Picture Dictionary activities, 30–45 min. **Writing worksheets,** 15–30 min.	www.cambridge.org/myresourceroom
Student Arcade, time varies	www.cambridge.org/venturesarcade

4 Picture dictionary Rooms of a house

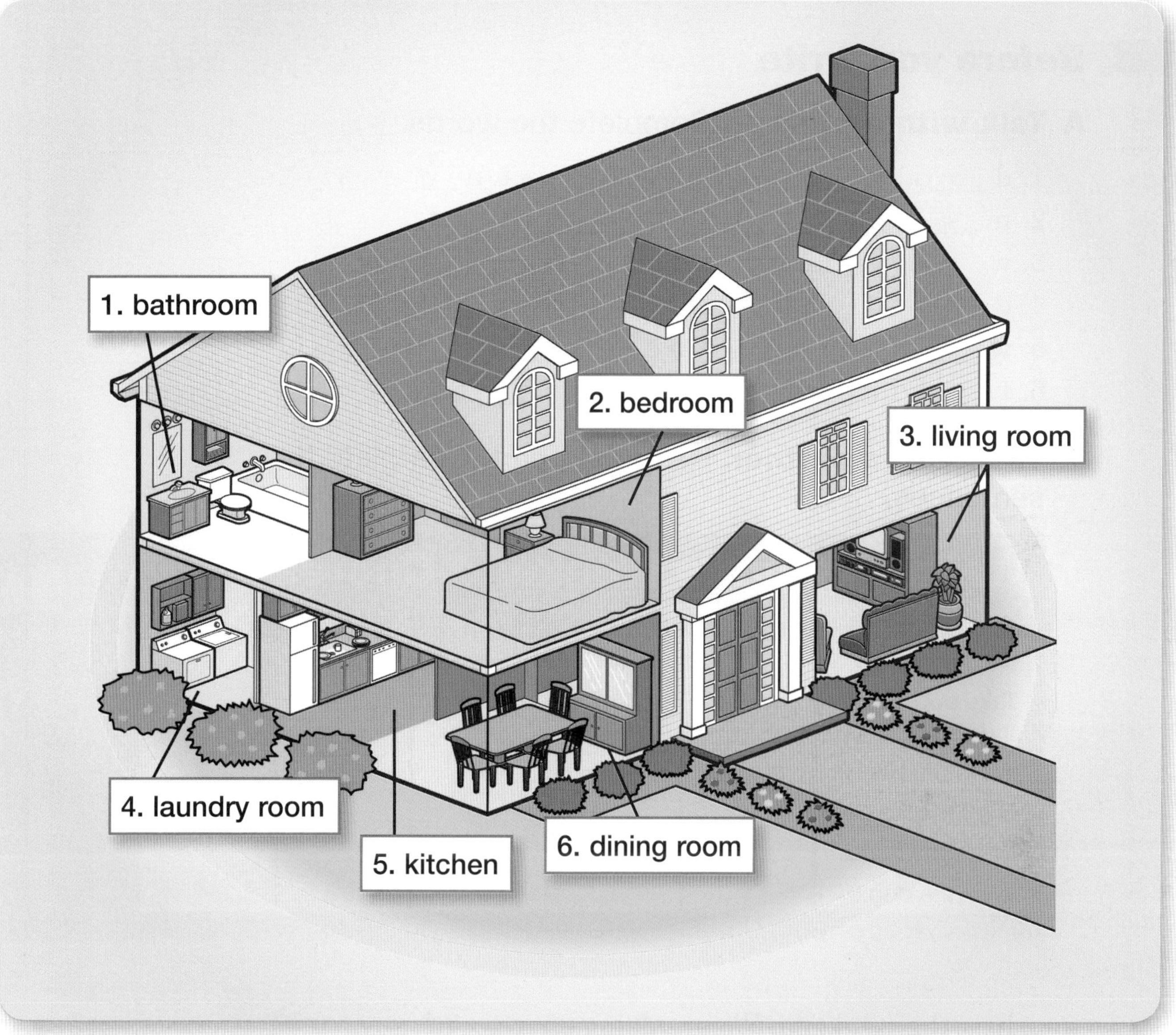

1. bathroom
2. bedroom
3. living room
4. laundry room
5. kitchen
6. dining room

A Listen and repeat. Look at the picture dictionary.

B Talk with a partner. Point to a room and ask. Your partner answers.

LESSON E Writing

1 Before you write

A Talk with a partner. Complete the words.

1. d _o_ i _n_ _g_ the _l_ aun _d_ r _y_
2. m _a_ k _i_ ng the _b_ e _d_ s
3. w _a_ l _k_ ing the _d_ o _g_
4. c _u_ tt _i_ ng the _g_ ra _s_ s
5. w _a_ s _h_ ing the _d_ is _h_ es
6. t _a_ king out the _t_ ras _h_

B Talk with a partner. Read the chart. Complete the sentences.

Walker Family's Weekend Chores

Chore	Dad	Mom	Max	Iris	Charlie
Do the laundry.		✔		✔	
Take out the trash.					✔
Wash the dishes.			✔		
Cut the grass.	✔				
Make the beds.		✔			
Walk the dog.			✔		✔

It is the weekend. We are doing chores.

1. Charlie is _taking_ _out_ _the_ _trash_.
2. Mom and Iris are _doing_ _the_ _laundry_.
3. Dad is _cutting_ _the_ _grass_.
4. Max is _washing_ _the_ _dishes_.
5. Mom is _making_ _the_ _beds_.
6. Charlie and Max are _walking_ _the_ _dog_.

Lesson objectives

- Discuss and write about chores
- Write a chore chart

Warm-up and review

- Before class. Write today's lesson focus on the board.
  Lesson E:
  Write about chores
  Write a chore chart
- Begin class. Books closed. Write *chores* on the board. Ask: *What are some chores that we have learned in this unit?* Elicit any chores from previous lessons in this unit.
- Ask: *What chores do you like?* Elicit an appropriate response, such as: *walking the dog.*
- Ask: *What chores don't you like?* Elicit an appropriate response, such as: *doing the laundry.*

Presentation

- Read the instructions aloud. Model the activity.
- Point to the first item and say: *Number 1. What's the chore?* (doing the laundry) Ask: *What letters do we need?* (o, n, g, l, d, and y) Point to where the letters are written in the blanks. Say: *Now you complete the rest of the words.*

Teaching tip

It might be helpful to write questions and answers on the board that will help Ss as they work with a partner, such as: *What chore is this? Do you think this is right?*

- Ss work in pairs to complete the words. Encourage Ss to figure out the chores together.
- When Ss are finished, call on different pairs to write their completed words on the board. Review the alphabet by asking Ss who write answers on the board to say the letters aloud.
- Go over the answers with the class. Ask: *Are these words spelled correctly?* Ask different Ss to make corrections as needed.

Teaching tip

This is a good opportunity to review the names of the letters in English. Ask the Ss who write the answers on the board to spell out the missing letters for the class. Make corrections if needed.

- Focus Ss' attention on the chart in Exercise **1B**. Ask: *What do you see?* Elicit as much vocabulary about the chart as possible, and write the words on the board: *Weekend chores*, *Walker family*, *Dad*, *Mom*, etc.
- Read the instructions aloud. Hold up the Student's Book. Point to the chart. Say: *This is a chart. It tells who needs to do the chores on the weekend.* Ask: *What days are the weekend?* (Saturday and Sunday.)

Culture tip

Explain that American families sometimes use charts to show different responsibilities in a family. Ask Ss if they use charts like this in their homes.

- Ask questions about the chart. Hold up the Student's Book, and point to the corresponding areas in the chart as you ask: *Who is in the Walker family?* (Dad, Mom, Max, Iris, and Charlie.) Say: *It's the weekend. Who is doing the laundry?* (Mom.) *Who is taking out the trash?* (Charlie.)
- Model the exercise. Focus Ss' attention on the sentences below the chart. Ask a S to read the first two sentences aloud. Ask: *What is Charlie doing?* (taking out the trash.) Point to the words written in the blanks.
- Say: *Now you complete the sentences. Use the information in the chart and the phrases in Exercise* **1A**.
- Ss complete the exercise in pairs. Walk around and help as needed.

Comprehension check

- Write the numbers *1–6* on the board. Ask individual Ss to write their answers on the board. Ask: *Is this answer correct?* Different Ss can correct the answers if needed.

Expansion activity *(student pairs)*

- Direct Ss' attention to the sentences in Exercise **1B**. Say: *Now read your sentences to your partner. Then your partner will read his / her sentences to you.*
- Walk around and listen to Ss' pronunciation. Write down any errors that you hear. When Ss are finished reading, write any words that Ss are having difficulties with on the board. Read the words aloud. Ask Ss to repeat. Correct their pronunciation if needed.

LESSON E Writing

Presentation

- Ask: *What are your chores at home?* Elicit appropriate responses.
- Direct Ss' attention to Exercise 2A and read the instructions aloud. Say: *You can write different people's names if you don't want to use your family's real names.*
- Model the task. Hold up the Student's Book. Point to the *name* category. Say: *Write the names here.* Point to the *chore* category. Say: *Write the chores here.*

Practice

- Ss complete the exercise individually. Walk around and help as needed.
- Ask several S volunteers to draw their chore charts on the board. Ask questions to preview Exercise 2B. Ask: *Who is (name of family member)? What is (name of person) doing?*
- Direct Ss' attention to Exercise 2B. Say: *Now you are going to write about your family's chores.*
- Model the task. Point to one of the chore charts on the board. Make sentences about it, such as: *(Name of person) is (chore).*
- Ss complete the exercise individually. Walk around and help as needed.

Literacy tip
For an alternative activity, refer literacy Ss to pages 110–111 in the *Literacy Workbook* at any time during the lesson.

Application

- Direct Ss' attention to Exercise 3. Read the instructions aloud. Encourage Ss to read what they wrote in Exercise 2B to their partners.
- Ss complete the task in pairs. Walk around and help as needed.
- Ask several Ss to read their sentences aloud for the whole class.

Teaching tip
This exercise asks Ss to work together to share their writing. Encourage Ss to peer-correct each other's writing if necessary. Say: *Help your partner with any mistakes. Then your partner will help you.*

Expansion activity (student pairs)

- Student dictation. Ask Ss to write the numbers *1–5* in list form in their notebooks. Ask five Ss to volunteer to read the sentences to the class. Explain that the other Ss will listen and write the sentences in their notebooks.
- Ask the five Ss to come up one at a time and read the following sentences to the class:
  1. *Mom is doing the laundry.*
  2. *Dad is taking out the trash.*
  3. *Max is walking the dog.*
  4. *Sarah is cutting the grass.*
  5. *John is making the beds.*

Teaching tip
Each S should read the sentence more than once so that Ss who are slower writers have the opportunity to complete the exercise.

- Write the numbers *1–5* on the board. Ask different Ss to write the dictated sentences on the board. Read each sentence aloud. Ask: *Is it correct?* Different Ss can make any corrections if needed.

Evaluation

- Direct Ss' attention to the lesson focus written on the board.
- Draw a chore chart on the board. Include names on the chart. Ask different Ss to come to the board and write chores on it. Check off chores for each name on your chart.
- Ask Ss questions about the chart, for example: *What is (name) doing?* Make sure Ss answer correctly.
- Check off each part of the lesson focus as Ss demonstrate understanding of what they have learned in the lesson.

More Ventures, Unit 9, Lesson E	
Literacy Workbook, 15–30 min.	
Basic Workbook, 15–30 min.	
Writing worksheets, 15–30 min.	www.cambridge.org/myresourceroom

2 Write

A **Complete the chart.** Write the weekend chores at your house. Write your family's names. Check (✓) the names.

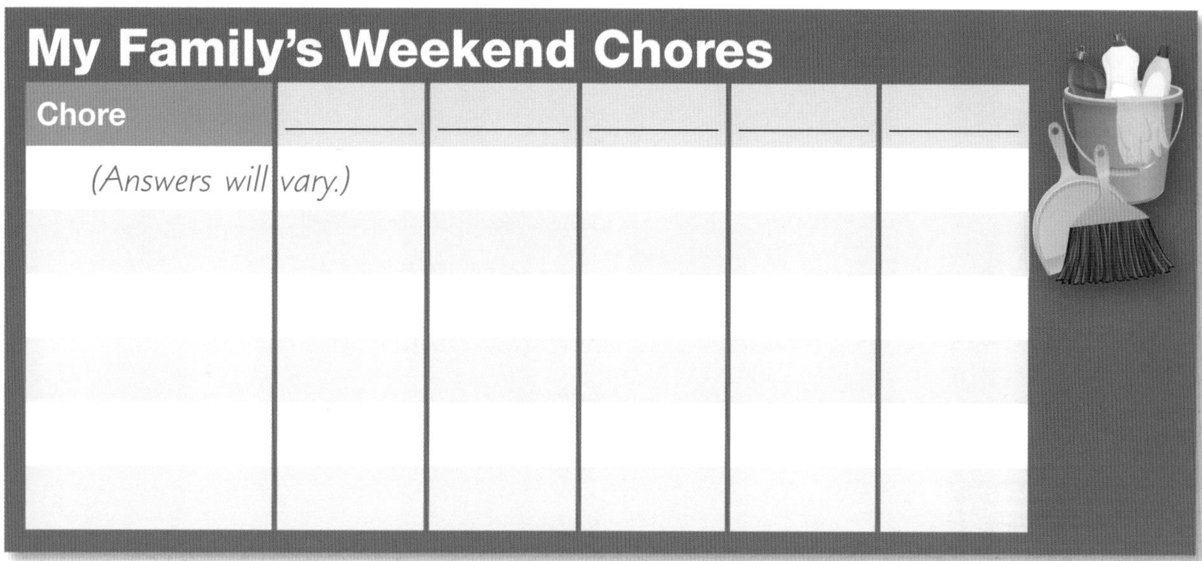

My Family's Weekend Chores

Chore	______	______	______	______	______
(Answers will vary.)					

B **Write.** It is the weekend. Tell about your family's chores. Look at 1B for help.

It is the weekend. We are doing chores.

1. I am (Answers will vary.) ______.
2. ______ is ______.
3. ______ is ______.
4. ______ is ______.
5. ______ and ______ are ______.

3 After you write

Talk with a partner. Share your writing.

LESSON F Another view

1 Life-skills reading

Friendly Cleaning Service, Inc.
Madison, WI 53714

We do your chores with a smile!

Work Order for: *1812 Franklin Street* *Madison, WI 53714*

Date: *Monday, August 27*

Name	Chore
Alma	*dishes*
Kay	*beds*
Ramiro	*grass*
Cyrus	*laundry*
Binh	*trash*

A Read the sentences. Look at the work order. Fill in the answer.

1. Alma's chore is ____.
   - Ⓐ cutting the grass
   - ● washing the dishes
   - Ⓒ making the beds

2. Kay's chore is ____.
   - ● making the beds
   - Ⓑ doing the laundry
   - Ⓒ washing the dishes

3. Ramiro's chore is ____.
   - Ⓐ doing the laundry
   - Ⓑ taking out the trash
   - ● cutting the grass

4. Binh's chore is ____.
   - Ⓐ doing the laundry
   - Ⓑ cutting the grass
   - ● taking out the trash

B Talk with a partner.

What are your chores?

Lesson objectives

- Read and discuss a work order
- Review unit vocabulary
- Complete the self-assessment

Warm-up and review

- Before class. Write today's lesson focus on the board.
  Lesson F:
  Read and answer questions about a work order
  Review vocabulary about chores
  Complete the self-assessment
- Begin class. Books closed. Write *cleaning service* on the board. Point to the words. Say them aloud. Ask Ss to repeat them after you. Say: *This is a company that cleans for people who can't or don't want to clean the house or the office themselves.*
- Ask: *What are some chores that cleaning companies do?* Elicit: *cleaning the house or office, taking out the trash, making the beds, doing the laundry, doing the dishes.*

Presentation

- Books open. Write on the board: *work order.* Point to the words. Say them aloud and ask Ss to repeat. Ask: *What is this?* If Ss don't know, direct their attention to the example of a work order in Exercise **1**. Say: *This is a work order for Friendly Cleaning Service, Inc. This shows the work the cleaning company will do on Monday, August 27.*
- Hold up the Student's Book. Point to the work order. Ask: *Where is the Friendly Cleaning Service?* (Madison, Wisconsin.) Ask: *What address is the work order for?* (1812 Franklin Street, Madison, WI 53714.) Ask: *How many people are working at this house?* (Five.) *Who are the workers on the work order?* (Alma, Kay, Ramiro, Cyrus, and Binh.)

Practice

- Read aloud the instructions in Exercise **1A**. This task helps prepare Ss for standardized-type tests they may have to take.
- Write the first item on the board along with the three answer choices labeled *a*, *b*, and *c*.
- Read the item and the answer choices aloud and then point to the work order. Ask Ss: *What is Alma's chore?* Show Ss where to look for the information. Elicit: *washing the dishes.*
- Point to the three answer choices on the board. Ask Ss: *a, b, or c?* (b) Fill in the letter *b* and tell Ss: *Fill in "b."* Make sure Ss understand the task.
- Have Ss individually scan for and fill in the answers.

Comprehension check

- Go over the answers to Exercise **1A** with the class. Make sure that Ss followed directions and filled in their answers. Ask Ss to point to the information in the work order.

Application

- Read the instructions for Exercise **1B** aloud.
- Model the task. Ask a S: *What are your chores?* Elicit an appropriate answer.
- Say: *Now ask your partner the same question.*
- Ss complete the task in pairs.
- Ask several pairs to ask and answer the question for the rest of the class.

Expansion activity *(small groups)*

- Ask Ss to form small groups of four or five Ss. Say: *Imagine that you are a cleaning service. Each of you has a job. Make a work order for your company for today.*
- Remind Ss to use the work order in Exercise **1** as a guide. Encourage Ss to think of an interesting name for their company and to change the date and address on their work orders. They should have a chore listed for each member of the group.
- Ask several small groups to come to the front of the class and write their work orders on the board. Ask one of the group members to describe the work order to the rest of the class. For example: *We are the (name of cleaning service). This is a work order for today (date). This work order is for (address). Our group is doing these chores: (names of people doing each chore).*

LESSON F Another view

Practice

- Direct Ss' attention to Exercise **2A**. Read the instructions aloud.
- Focus Ss' attention on the word bank. Say: *Use these words to complete the chores in the chart.*
- Model the exercise. Hold up the Student's Book. Point to the column with *make* as the heading. Ask: *What chores begin with "make"?* (make the bed, make lunch) Point out that there are two extra blanks, one under *wash* and one under *do.* See if Ss can come up with two more chores. (do the dishes, wash the dog.)
- Ss complete the exercise individually. Walk around and help as needed.
- Write the words *cut*, *wash*, *do*, *make*, and *dry* in list form on the board. Ask individual Ss to write their answers on the board in the correct column.
- Ask different Ss to read the answers aloud. Ask: *Are these answers correct?* Different Ss can correct the answers if needed.

Expansion activity (individual work)

- Make copies of the following grid for each S in the class.

  Option Draw the grid on the board and ask Ss to copy it into their notebooks.

Name				
What chores do you do every day?				

- Tell Ss they need to talk to four Ss in the class. They will write the names of the Ss in the first row of their grid and the answers to the question in the second row of the grid.
- Model the activity. Draw the chart on the board. Ask a S: *What chores do you do every day?* Elicit chores such as: *I wash the dishes. I make lunch.* Write the S's name in the first row and his or her answers in the second row.
- Ss complete the exercise individually. Walk around and help as needed.
- Direct Ss' attention to the puzzle in Exercise **2B**. Read the instructions aloud. Ask Ss: *What are some "-ing" words?* Write Ss' examples on the board, such as: *writing*, *doing*, *making.*
- Model the exercise. Hold up the Student's Book. Show Ss where *walking* has been circled in the puzzle. Tell Ss that all the words can be found written horizontally. Draw a line on the board to show what *horizontally* means.
- Ss complete the activity individually. Walk around and help as needed.
- Ask seven Ss to write the words they found on the board. Ask different Ss to read the words aloud. Make sure the words on the board are spelled correctly. Make corrections if needed.

  Option Ask Ss to make sentences with the words they found in the word search.

Literacy tip

For an alternative activity, refer literacy Ss to pages 112–113 in the *Literacy Workbook* at any time during the lesson.

Evaluation

- Before asking Ss to turn to the self-assessment on page 144, do a quick review of the unit. Have Ss turn to Lesson A. Ask the class to talk about what they remember about this lesson. If necessary, prompt Ss with questions, for example: *What words are on this page? What do you see in the picture?* Continue in this manner to review each lesson quickly.
- **Self-assessment** Read the instructions for Exercise **3**. Ask Ss to turn to the self-assessment page and complete the unit self-assessment.
- If Ss are ready, administer the unit test on pages T-193–T-195 of this Teacher's Edition (or on the Assessment Audio CD / CD-ROM).

More Ventures, Unit 9, Lesson F	
Literacy Workbook, 15–30 min. **Basic Workbook,** 15–30 min.	
Writing worksheets, 15–30 min. **Real Life Document,** 15–30 min.	www.cambridge.org/myresourceroom

2 Fun with vocabulary

A Talk with a partner. Complete the chart.

the bed	the car	the dishes	the dog
the grass	homework	the laundry	lunch

cut	wash	do	make	dry
the grass	the car	homework	the bed	the dishes
	the dishes	the dishes	lunch	
	the dog	the laundry		

B Circle eight ***-ing*** words in the puzzle.

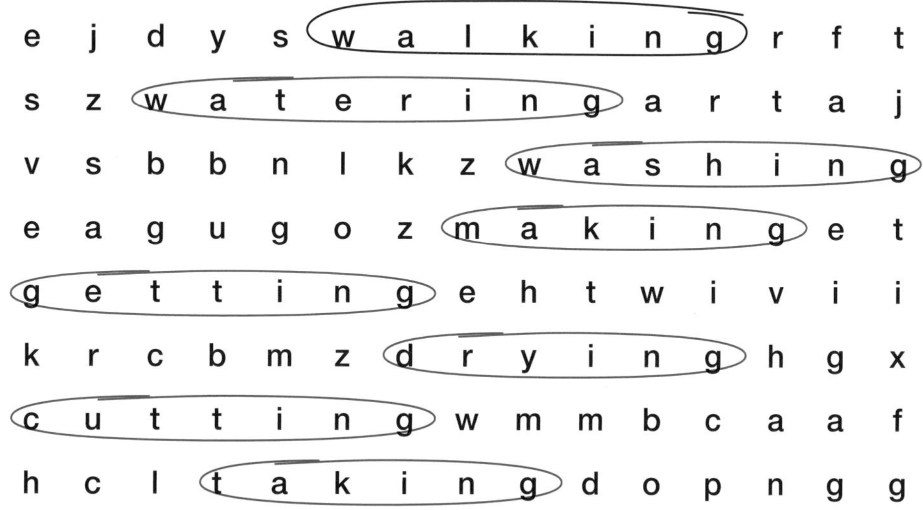

e	j	d	y	s	w	a	l	k	i	n	g	r	f	t
s	z	w	a	t	e	r	i	n	g	a	r	t	a	j
v	s	b	b	n	l	k	z	w	a	s	h	i	n	g
e	a	g	u	g	o	z	m	a	k	i	n	g	e	t
g	e	t	t	i	n	g	e	h	t	w	i	v	i	i
k	r	c	b	m	z	d	r	y	i	n	g	h	g	x
c	u	t	t	i	n	g	w	m	m	b	c	a	a	f
h	c	l	t	a	k	i	n	g	d	o	p	n	g	g

3 Wrap up

Complete the **Self-assessment** on page 144.

UNIT
10 Free time

LESSON A Listening

1 Before you listen

A Look at the picture. What do you see?

CLASS CD2 TK 45

B Listen and point: dance • exercise • fish
play basketball • play cards • swim

Lesson objectives

- Introduce Ss to the topic
- Find out what Ss know about the topic
- Preview the unit by talking about the picture
- Practice key vocabulary
- Practice listening skills

UNIT 10

Warm-up and review

- Before class. Write today's lesson focus on the board.
  Lesson A:
  Vocabulary for free-time activities
- Begin class. Books closed. Point to the words *free-time activities* on the board. Read them aloud and ask Ss to repeat after you. Explain that free-time activities are what you do in your extra time. Say: *Free time is when you don't work or go to school.* Ask: *When do you have free time?* Elicit appropriate responses, such as: *Saturday, Sunday, the weekend.* Ask: *What do you do in your free time?* Elicit appropriate responses.

Teaching tip

If Ss still don't understand the words *free time*, show them a calendar. Point to the days you work. Say: *I work on these days.* Point to your days off. Say: *I don't work on these days. I have free time.*

Literacy tip

If you have literacy Ss in your class, it might be helpful to spend time at the beginning of any activity that contains art or photos talking about the pictures before focusing Ss' attention on the printed words in the exercise. Have Ss work in pairs. Tell them to ask each other: *What do you see?* Encourage Ss to describe the pictures to each other. Consider pairing literacy Ss with Ss who can help them read the text in the exercise. This will help preview the exercise for literacy Ss and make them more confident as the exercise continues.

Presentation

- Books open. Set the scene. Show Ss' the picture on page 122. Ask: *What do you see?* Elicit and write on the board any vocabulary that Ss know, such as: *park, people, boys, basketball, music.*
- Hold up the student book. Point to each labeled person in turn. Ask: *What is his / her name?* Elicit the appropriate responses.

Practice

- Direct Ss' attention to the key vocabulary in Exercise **1B**. Hold up the Student's Book. Read each word aloud while pointing to the corresponding activity in the picture. Ask Ss to repeat and point.

Class Audio CD2 track 45 Play or read the audio program (see audio script, page T-162). Tell Ss: *Listen and point to the picture.* As Ss hear the key vocabulary, check to see that they are pointing to the correct pictures. Repeat the audio program as needed.

Comprehension check

- Ask Ss *Yes / No* questions about the picture. Tell Ss: *Listen. Say "yes" or "no."*

  Point to the picture. Ask: *Is this a park?* (Yes.)

  Point to the two teenage boys. Ask: *Are they playing baseball?* (No.)

  Point to the people dancing. Ask: *Are they dancing?* (Yes.)

  Point to the man fishing. Ask: *Is he fishing?* (Yes.)

  Point to the people swimming. Ask: *Are they fishing?* (No.)

  Point to the people playing cards. Ask: *Are they playing cards?* (Yes.)

  Point to the woman running. Ask: *Is she walking?* (No.)

Expansion activity (student pairs)

- Write on the board:

  What is he doing? He is _____.

  What is she doing? She is _____.

  What are they doing? They are _____.
- Point to the questions and incomplete answers on the board. Say: *Ask your partner questions about the people in the picture.*
- Model the activity. Hold up the Student's Book. Point to the people playing cards. Ask a S: *What are they doing?* Elicit: *They are playing cards.*
- Ss complete the activity in pairs. Encourage Ss to ask about all the people in the picture. Then tell them to switch roles.
- Ask several pairs to ask and answer questions about different people in the picture for the rest of the class.

Community building (whole group)

- Ask Ss to make a list of free-time activities that are possible to do in your local community. Write the activities on the board. Ss new to your city or town will appreciate learning about different activities to do in their free time.

LESSON A Listening

Presentation

- Direct Ss' attention to Exercise 2A. Tell Ss: *We are going to practice saying these free-time activities.* Read the words aloud. Ask Ss to repeat them after you.
- Read aloud the instructions for Exercise 2A.

Practice

- Class Audio CD2 track 46 Play or read the audio program (see audio script, page T-162). Ss' listen and repeat the vocabulary. Repeat the audio program as needed.
- Listen carefully to Ss' pronunciation and make corrections as needed.

Learner persistence *(individual work)*

- Self-Study Audio CD track 43 Exercise 2A is recorded on the CD at the back of the Student's Book. Ss can listen to the CD at home for reinforcement and review and also for self-directed learning when class attendance is not possible.

Practice

- Direct Ss' attention to Exercise 2B and read the instructions aloud.
- Class Audio CD2 track 47 Model the task. Hold up the Student's Book and say: *Number one.* Play or read the audio program for number 1 (see audio script, page T-162). Point to the two answer choices in number 1 and ask Ss: *What did you hear – a or b?* Elicit: *a*. Point to the letter *a* next to the first picture and tell Ss: *Circle the letter "a."*
- Class Audio CD2 track 47 Play or read the complete audio program (see audio script, page T-162). Ss listen and circle the correct answers. Repeat the audio program as needed.
- Class Audio CD2 track 47 Read aloud the second part of the instructions for Exercise 2B. Play or read the audio program again so that Ss can listen and check their answers.

Learner persistence *(individual work)*

- Self-Study Audio CD track 44 Exercise 2B is recorded on the CD at the back of the Student's Book. Ss can listen to the CD at home for reinforcement and review. They can also listen to the CD for self-directed learning when class attendance is not possible.

Comprehension check

- Write the numbers *1–4* on the board. Ask a few Ss to come to the board and write the correct answers to Exercise 2B next to each number.
- Class Audio CD2 track 47 Play or read the audio program again. Pause the audio program after each conversation. Point to the answer written on the board and ask: *Is this correct?* Ask another S to make any necessary corrections.

Application

- Direct Ss' attention to Exercise 3 and read the instructions aloud.
- Model the task. Hold up the Student's Book and point to the pictures in Exercise 2B. Say to one S: *Point to a picture.* Say to the first S's partner: *Say the word.*
- Ss complete the exercise in pairs. Walk around and help as needed.

Literacy tip

For an alternative activity, refer literacy Ss to pages 114–115 in the *Literacy Workbook* at any time during the lesson.

Community building *(whole class)*

- Draw a vertical line on the board, making two columns. Above the first column, write *free-time activity.* Above the second column, write *Where?*
- Ask Ss to tell you the activities they learned in this lesson (*dance*, *exercise*, *fish*, *play basketball*, *play cards*, *swim*). Write them in list form in the first column.
- Point to the word *Where?* in the second column. Ask: *Where can you dance in (name of your city or town)?* Write Ss' answers in the second column. Write only the names of local places, or draw a line to indicate that no place for dancing exists where Ss live.
- Continue by asking about the other activities. By talking about local places to socialize, Ss can learn more about their community.

Evaluation

- Direct Ss' attention to the lesson focus written on the board and then to the picture on page 122. Check Ss' understanding of free-time activities vocabulary by asking them to point to the activities that are listed at the top of the page. Walk around and check that Ss are pointing to the correct parts of the picture.
- Check off the lesson focus as Ss demonstrate an understanding of what they have learned in the lesson.

More Ventures, Unit 10, Lesson A	
Literacy Workbook, 15–30 min.	
Basic Workbook, 15–30 min.	
Writing worksheets 15–30 min.	www.cambridge.org/myresourceroom
Student Arcade, time varies	www.cambridge.org/venturesarcade

Unit Goals

Identify free-time activities
Describe what people like to do
Interpret information on a class flyer

2 Listen

STUDENT TK 43
CLASS CD2 TK 46

A Listen and repeat.

1. dance 2. exercise 3. fish
4. play basketball 5. play cards 6. swim

STUDENT TK 44
CLASS CD2 TK 47

B Listen and circle.

1. (a.)  b. 

2. a.  (b.) 

3. (a.)  b. 

4. a.  (b.) 

Listen again. Check your answers.

3 After you listen

Talk with a partner. Point to a picture.
Your partner says the words.

LESSON **B** Around the house

1 Vocabulary focus

Listen and repeat.

CLASS CD2 TK 48

1. cook

2. play the guitar

3. listen to music

4. watch TV

5. read magazines

6. work in the garden

2 Practice

A Read and match.

Lesson objective

- Introduce and practice vocabulary about leisure activities

Warm-up and review

- Before class. Write today's lesson focus on the board.
  Lesson B:
  More vocabulary about free-time activities
- Begin class. Books open. Write on the board: *lake*, *basketball court*, *home*, *party*, *gym*, *pool*. Point to each word in turn. Say it aloud and ask Ss to repeat after you. Define any words if needed. You can do this by drawing pictures on the board.
- Point to *free-time activities* in the lesson focus. Ask: *What free-time activities did we learn about in the last lesson?* Elicit and write on the board: *dance*, *exercise*, *fish*, *play basketball*, *play cards*, *swim*.
- Ask: *What activity can you do at the lake?* (fish, swim) Continue asking about the other places on the board.
- Ask Ss: *What other activities do you like to do in your free time?* If Ss know the names of any other activities, write them on the board. Ask Ss who say the words to convey them with gestures. If Ss don't know any other names of activities, say: *We will learn more in this lesson.*

Teaching tip

If Ss need help remembering the free-time activity vocabulary learned in Lesson A, hold up the Student's Book. Point to each activity on page 122 or 123 as you say the words.

Presentation

- Set the scene. Books open. Direct Ss' attention to the picture in Exercise **1**. Say: *This is a family. Where are they?* Elicit: *They are at their house.* Read aloud the instructions.

Class Audio CD2 track 48 Play or read the audio program (see audio script, page T-162). Listen and repeat the vocabulary along with Ss. Repeat the audio program as needed.

- Listen carefully to Ss' pronunciation and correct as needed.

Expansion activity *(student pairs)*

- Ask Ss to review the names of different rooms in a house. Write the names of the rooms on the board: *bedroom*, *kitchen*, *living room*, *bathroom*, *dining room*, *laundry room*.
- Direct Ss' attention to the picture in Exercise **1**. Write on the board:
  Where is the _____?
  She / He is in the _____.
- Ss in pairs. Say: *Ask your partner questions about the people in Exercise* **1**. Encourage Ss to use the question and answer on the board as a guide. Model the task. Say: *Where is the woman?* Elicit: *In the kitchen.*
- Ss complete the exercise in pairs. Walk around and help as needed.
- Ask several pairs to ask and answer questions about each person and where he / she is.

Teaching tip

Ss may not know the meaning of the word *garden.* Point to picture 6 in Exercise **1**. Tell Ss that the woman is working in the garden outside the house.

Practice

- Direct Ss' attention to Exercise **2A**. Read the instructions aloud.
- Focus Ss' attention on the first picture. Model the task. Ask: *What are the activities in this picture?* Elicit: *play the guitar* and *read magazines.* Hold up the Student's Book. Point to the lines connecting the first picture to the phrases *play the guitar* and *read magazines.* Say: *Match the pictures and the words.*
- Ss complete the exercise individually. Help as needed.

Literacy tip

For an alternative activity, refer literacy Ss to pages 116–117 in the *Literacy Workbook* at any time during the lesson.

Comprehension check

- Ask different Ss to point to each picture in Exercise **2A** and read the phrases that match the picture.
- Ask different Ss to read the answers written on the board. After each phrase is read, ask: *Is this correct?* Ask another S to make any corrections if needed.

LESSON B Around the house

Presentation

- Direct Ss' attention to the pictures in Exercise **2B**. Say: *These are pictures of free-time activities. What activities do you see?* Point to each activity in turn. Elicit: *watch TV*, *listen to music*, *play the guitar*, *cook*, *work in the garden*, *read magazines.* Read the names of the people and ask Ss to repeat.
- Focus Ss' attention on the words in the word bank. Say each word or phrase aloud. Ask Ss to repeat them after you. Read the instructions for Exercise **2B** aloud.

Class Audio CD2 track 49 Model the task. Say: *Listen and repeat.* Play or read the audio program for number 1 (see audio script, page T-162), and point to Pablo in the picture as you repeat. Say: *Then write.* Point to where *watch TV* has been written in the Activity column of the chart. Make sure Ss understand the task.

Class Audio CD2 track 49 Play or read the complete audio program (see audio script, page T-162). Ss listen and repeat. Encourage Ss to point to the people in the pictures as they repeat.

- Ss complete the charts individually using words from the word bank. Repeat the audio program as needed.
- Check answers with the class. Draw the charts from Exercise **2B** on the board. Ask five Ss to fill in the blanks in the charts.
- Point to each answer and ask the class: *Yes? Is this correct?* Ask other Ss to make any necessary corrections on the board.
- Read aloud the second part of the instructions for Exercise **2B**. Point to and model the example conversation.
- Call on a pair of volunteers to read the example conversation aloud for the class. Then ask the same Ss to make up a new conversation about another person in the pictures in Exercise **2B**. Indicate that Ss should ask and answer questions about all the people in the pictures.
- Ss complete the exercise in pairs. Walk around and help as needed.

Literacy tip

Be sure to give literacy Ss extra time to do Exercise **2B**. Ask them to work with a partner. Literacy Ss should be able to do this exercise with extra time and help from a classmate.

Expansion activity (student pairs)

- Before class. Prepare the following chart and give each S a copy.

Name				
What do you do in the morning?				
What do you do in the afternoon?				
What do you do in the evening?				

- Write *Saturday* on the board. Point to the word. Say it aloud. Tell Ss to talk to four other Ss in the class. They will ask the questions in the chart about what other Ss do on Saturday morning, afternoon, and evening.
- Model the activity. Ask a S the questions. Hold up the chart. Write the S's answers in short form in the chart, for example: *clean the house*, *listen to music*, *watch TV.*
- Ss complete the exercise. Walk around and help as needed.

Application

- Direct Ss' attention to Exercise **3** and read the instructions aloud. Direct Ss' attention to the picture. Tell them that one person in the picture is acting an activity, and the other S is guessing what it is.
- Model the task. Ask one S to read part A of the conversation with you. Pantomime playing the electric guitar while you read the conversation.
- Ss complete the exercise in pairs. Walk around and help as needed.
- Ask several Ss to act out leisure activities learned in this unit for the rest of the class.

Evaluation

- Direct Ss' attention to the lesson focus written on the board. Check Ss' understanding of the key vocabulary by asking them to point to the free-time activities in the pictures in Exercise **2B** on page 125: *cook*, *listen to music*, *play the guitar*, *read magazines*, *watch TV*, and *work in the garden.* Walk around and check that Ss are pointing to the correct items.
- Check off the lesson focus as Ss demonstrate an understanding of what they have learned in the lesson.

More Ventures, Unit 10, Lesson B	
Literacy Workbook, 15–30 min.	
Basic Workbook, 15–30 min.	
Writing worksheets, 15–30 min.	www.cambridge.org/myresourceroom
Student Arcade, time varies	www.cambridge.org/venturesarcade

CLASS CD2 TK 49

B Listen and repeat. Then write.

cook	listen to music	play the guitar
read magazines	watch TV	work in the garden

Name	Activity	Name	Activity
1. Pablo	*watch TV*	4. Estela	*listen to music*
2. Tom	*work in the garden*	5. Ling	*read magazines*
3. Rashid	*play the guitar*	6. Farah	*cook*

Talk with a partner. Ask and answer.

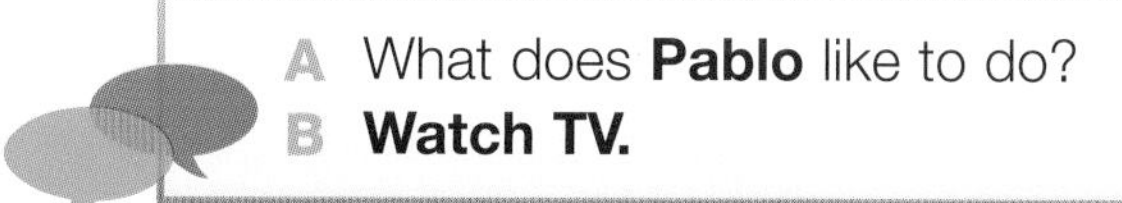

A What does **Pablo** like to do?
B **Watch TV.**

3 Communicate

Talk with a partner. Act and guess.

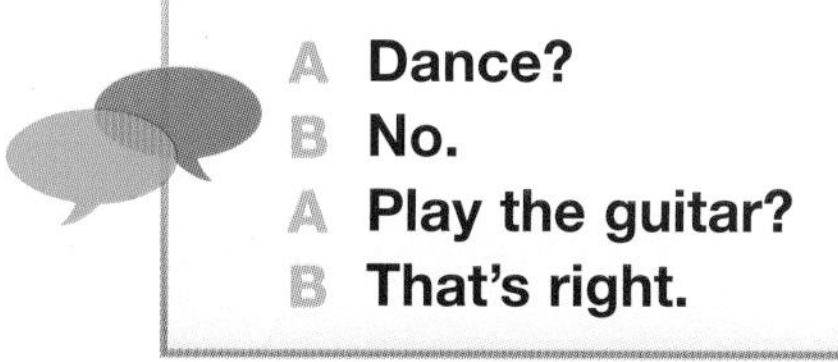

A **Dance?**
B **No.**
A **Play the guitar?**
B **That's right.**

☑ Use vocabulary for activities around the house

LESSON C I like to watch TV.

1 Grammar focus: *like to*

Questions

What	**do**	you	**like to** do?
	do	they	
	does	he	
	does	she	

Answers

I	**like**	**to** watch TV.
They	**like**	
He	**likes**	
She	**likes**	

2 Practice

A Read and circle. Then write.

1. A What do they like to do?
   B They ___like___ to play basketball.
   (like) likes

2. A What does she like to do?
   B She ___likes___ to swim.
   like (likes)

3. A What does he like to do?
   B He ___likes___ to play cards.
   like (likes)

4. A What does she like to do?
   B She ___likes___ to fish.
   like (likes)

5. A What do they like to do?
   B They ___like___ to dance.
   (like) likes

CLASS CD2 TK 50

Listen and repeat. Then practice with a partner.

Lesson objective

- Introduce and practice *like to*

Warm-up and review

- Before class. Write today's lesson focus on the board.
  Lesson C:
  Questions and answers with like to
- Begin class. Books closed. Write *like* on the board. Point to it. Say it aloud. Ask Ss to repeat after you. Draw a smiley-face on the board. Say: *like means something is good for you.* Say some things you like, such as: *I like pizza. I like ice cream. I like books.* Ask Ss: *What do you like?* Allow Ss to give one-word responses.

Teaching tip

If Ss have a difficult time thinking of what they like, ask *Yes / No* questions, such as: *Do you like English class? Do you like movies? Do you like TV?* Ss can give simple *Yes / No* responses.

Presentation

- Books open. Direct Ss' attention to the grammar chart in Exercise **1**. Read the questions and the corresponding answers aloud. Ask Ss to repeat after you.

Teaching tip

It might be helpful to point out the *s* in the third-person singular for *he likes* and *she likes.* Tell Ss to put an *s* on the verb for *he* and *she.* Then point out that the verb in the question never takes an *s.* Tell Ss that the *s* in the question form is on the word *does.*

- Ask the questions in the grammar chart about the Ss in the class. Point to two Ss and ask: *What do they like to do?* Point to a male S and ask: *What does he like to do?* Point to a female S and ask: *What does she like to do?* Ss should answer appropriately using examples they learned in Lessons A and B.

Practice

- Read aloud the instructions for Exercise **2A**. Model the task. Read aloud the example conversation in number 1. When you read Speaker A's first line, show Ss the two answer choices under the blank and ask: *"Like" or "likes"?* Elicit *like.*
- Point to where *like* has been circled and written for number 1. Say: *Circle the correct answer. Then write it in the blank.*
- Ss complete the exercise in pairs. Walk around and help as needed.
- Ask several pairs to read the conversations to the rest of the class.

Comprehension check

- Read aloud the second part of the instructions for Exercise **2A**.

Class Audio CD2 track 50 Play or read the audio program (see audio script, page T-162). Ss listen and repeat as they check their answers.

- Write the numbers *2–5* on the board. Ask volunteers to come to the board and write the answers they circled. Remind Ss to write only the words they circled, not the complete sentences. Make any necessary corrections on the board.
- Ss in pairs. Ask Ss to choose Role A or B and practice the questions and answers in Exercise **2A**. Then have Ss switch roles and practice again. Walk around and help as needed.
- Ask several pairs to read the conversations to the rest of the class.

Teaching tip

If appropriate for your class, ask the Ss why the answers on the board are correct. Ss should respond that the verb after *they* and *you* is *like* and the verb after *he* and *she* is *likes.*

Expansion activity *(student pairs)*

- Direct Ss' attention to the picture on page 122. Say: *Ask your partner questions about this picture. Use the questions and answers on page 126 as a guide.*
- Encourage Ss to point to people in the picture and ask: *What do they like to do? What does he like to do? What does she like to do?* Partners will answer appropriately about the pictures. (They like to play basketball. She likes to exercise. They like to dance. etc.)
- Ask several pairs to hold up the Student's Book and point to people in the picture. Have them ask and answer questions about the picture for the rest of the class.

LESSON C I like to watch TV.

Presentation

- Write on the board: *What _____ he like to do? What _____ she like to do? What _____ they like to do?*
- Point to the sentences. Ask Ss what words are missing. Write the missing words in the blanks (*does*, *does*, and *do*). Say the questions aloud. Ask Ss to repeat after you.
- Direct Ss' attention to Exercise **2B**. Read aloud the instructions.

Practice

- Class Audio CD2 track 51 Model the task. Say: *Listen and repeat.* Play or read the audio program for number 1 (see audio script, page T-162) and point to the man in picture number 1 as you repeat.
- Class Audio CD2 track 51 Play or read the complete audio program (see audio script, page T-162). Ss listen and repeat. Encourage Ss to point to the people in the pictures as they repeat.
- Read aloud the second part of the instructions in Exercise **2B**. Model the activity. Ask two Ss to read the example question and answer aloud.
- Ss complete the exercise in pairs, asking and answering questions about the people in the pictures. Walk around and listen to Ss' pronunciation. Write down any errors that you hear. Write the words that were pronounced incorrectly on the board. When Ss are finished, point to the words and say them aloud. Ask Ss to repeat them after you.

Comprehension check

- Ask several pairs to say the conversations for pictures *1–6* in order for the rest of the class. When a pair finishes one conversation, ask: *Is the answer correct?* Ask other Ss to make corrections if needed.

Application

- Direct Ss' attention to Exercise **3** and read the instructions aloud.
- Model the task. Ask two Ss to read the conversation aloud. Hold up the Student's Book. Point to the first line in the chart. Tell Ss to fill in the information that they hear from their classmates.
- Ss complete the exercise by talking to four different Ss in the class. Encourage Ss to stand up and walk around the room.

Teaching tip

It is helpful to encourage Ss to speak to more than one partner in the classroom. Ask Ss to find new partners periodically. This gives them a chance to practice with Ss of all abilities in the class.

Expansion activity (student pairs)

- Expand on Exercise **3** by asking Ss to talk to a new partner. Tell Ss to talk about the answers on their charts with the new partner.
- Write on the board: *What does _____ like to do? He / She likes to _____.* Tell Ss to ask their new partners the question on the board. They will ask about the names on their partner's chart.
- Model the activity. Direct Ss' attention to the example of *Vinh* in Exercise **3**. Ask a S: *What does Vinh like to do?* (He likes to play basketball.)
- Ss complete the activity in pairs. Walk around and make sure Ss are answering with the *s* added on to the verb.

Literacy tip

For an alternative activity, refer literacy Ss to pages 118–119 in the *Literacy Workbook* at any time during the lesson.

Evaluation

- Direct Ss' attention to the lesson focus written on the board. Point to different Ss in the class. Ask: *What do you like to do? What do they like to do? What does he like to do? What does she like to do?* Listen as other Ss answer the questions. Make sure they answer with the correct form of the verb.
- Check off the lesson focus as Ss demonstrate an understanding of what they have learned in the lesson.

More Ventures, Unit 10, Lesson C	
Literacy Workbook, 15–30 min. **Basic Workbook,** 15–30 min.	
Writing worksheets, 15–30 min.	www.cambridge.org/myresourceroom
Student Arcade, time varies	www.cambridge.org/venturesarcade

CLASS CD2 TK 51

B Listen and repeat.

1. exercise

2. cook

3. play cards

4. work in the garden

5. swim

6. play soccer

Talk with a partner. Ask and answer.

A What **does he** like to do?
B **He likes to exercise.**

3 Communicate

Talk with your classmates. Complete the chart.

A What do you like to do, **Vinh**?
B I like to **play basketball**.

Name	What do you like to do?
Vinh	*play basketball*
(Answers will vary.)	

LESSON **D** Reading

1 Before you read

Talk about the picture.
What do you see?

2 Read

Listen and read.

New Message

From: Lupe
To: Miriam
Subject: Call me

Hi Miriam,

I'm not working today. It's my day off. Are you busy? Come and visit me!

What do you like to do? I like to cook. I like to play cards. I like to listen to music and dance. I like to watch TV. Do you like to watch TV?

Please call me at 10:00.

See you soon!

Lupe

3 After you read

Check (✓) the answers. What does Lupe like to do?

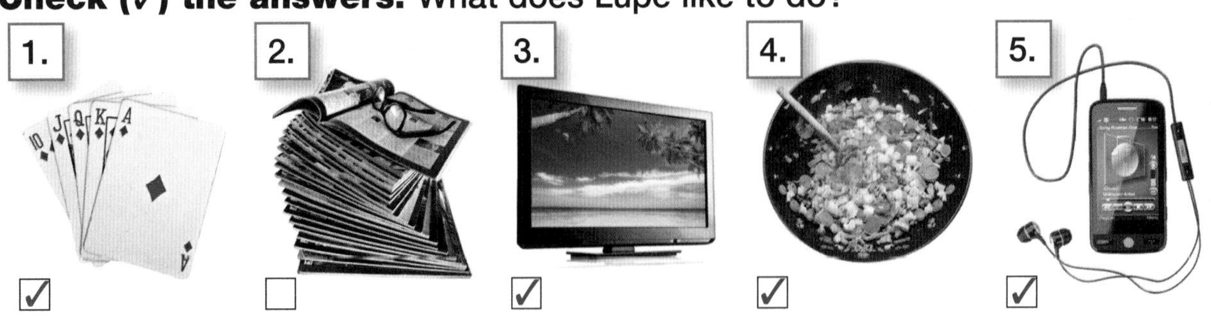

1. ☑
2. ☐
3. ☑
4. ☑
5. ☑

Lesson objectives

- Introduce and read an e-mail message about free-time activities
- Introduce and practice using new words about free-time activities

Warm-up and review

- Before class. Write today's lesson focus on the board.
  Lesson D:
  Read and discuss an e-mail message
  Learn more vocabulary about free-time activities
- Begin class. Books closed. Ask Ss to review saying the activities they like to do in their free time. Write any activities that Ss say on the board. These can include activities learned in Lessons A, B, and C and any other activities that Ss already know.
- Ask Ss who they do these activities with. Elicit short answers such as: *my mother*, *my father*, *my husband*, *my friend*, *my daughter*, *my son.*

Presentation

- Books open. Direct Ss' attention to the picture in Exercise **1**. Read the instructions aloud. Ask: *What do you see?* Elicit and write on the board any vocabulary that Ss know, such as: *computer*, *woman*, *Lupe*, *coffee*, *music.*

Teaching tip

Do not expect Ss to answer the question in complete sentences. The purpose of this exercise is to prepare Ss for the reading that follows.

Practice

- Write *e-mail* on the board. Point to the word. Say it aloud and ask Ss to repeat it after you. Ask: *Do you remember the e-mail message you read in Unit 7?* Explain to Ss that they will read another e-mail message in this lesson.
- Direct Ss' attention to Exercise **2**. Read the instructions aloud.

Class Audio CD2 track 52 Play or read the audio program and ask Ss to read along (see audio script, page T-162). Repeat the audio program as needed.

- Read aloud each sentence of the reading, and ask Ss to repeat after you. Answer any questions Ss have about new words in the reading.

Learner persistence (individual work)

Self-Study Audio CD track 45 Exercise **2** is recorded on the CD at the back of the Student's Book. Ss can listen to the CD at home for reinforcement and review and also for self-directed learning when class attendance is not possible.

Comprehension check

- Direct Ss' attention to Exercise **3** and read the instructions aloud.
- Model the task. Hold up the Student's Book. Point to the first picture. Ask Ss to identify it. Elicit: *Playing cards.* Point to the next pictures in turn. Elicit the names of the items (*magazines*, *TV*, *food*, *music player*). Focus Ss' attention on picture 1 again. Ask: *Does Lupe like to play cards?* (Yes.) Ask Ss the questions for the next four pictures. Say: *Check the boxes for the "yes" answers.*
- Ss complete the exercise individually. Walk around and help as needed.
- Ask Ss which pictures they checked. Walk around and make sure they checked Pictures 1, 3, 4, and 5.

Expansion activity (student pairs)

- Direct Ss' attention to the pictures in Exercise **3**. Write on the board: *Does Lupe like to ______? Yes, she does.* / *No, she doesn't.*
- Ss in pairs. Say: *Ask your partner the question on the board. Point to the pictures in Exercise* **3**. *Your partner will answer the questions.*
- When Ss are finished, ask them to switch roles.
- Walk around and help as needed.

Community building (whole class)

- Ask Ss if they use e-mail. Ask them who they usually send e-mails to and receive e-mails from. If appropriate for your class, encourage Ss to write e-mails to each other to practice their writing in English.

LESSON D Reading

Presentation

- Direct Ss' attention to the picture dictionary in Exercise 4. Tell Ss that they are going to learn the names of more free-time activities in English. Hold up the Student's Book. Point to each picture in turn and read aloud the words corresponding to them. Ask Ss to repeat the words after you.

Teaching tip

Ss may not understand the word *volunteer* from the illustration alone. Explain to Ss that a volunteer works without pay. Point to Picture 6. Tell Ss that the people in the picture are cleaning up because they like to help, and they won't get paid for this work.

Class Audio CD2 track 53 Play or read the audio program (see audio script, page T-162). Listen to Ss' pronunciation as they repeat the leisure activities. Correct pronunciation as needed.

Learner persistence (individual work)

Self-Study Audio CD track 46 Exercise 4A is recorded on the CD at the back of the Student's Book. Ss can listen to the CD at home for reinforcement and review. They can also listen to the CD for self-directed learning when class attendance is not possible.

Expansion activity (student pairs)

- Cut out the picture dictionary cards that correspond to this unit. Make enough copies for each pair of Ss in your class. The picture should be on the front of the card and the description of the activity on the back.
- Ss in pairs. Tell Ss to show their partner the pictures. Their partners need to identify the pictures. Then Ss can check to see if they are right by looking at the back of the picture card.
- Ask Ss to practice with these flash cards until they know all the names of the activities without looking at the words on the back of the cards.

Practice

- Direct Ss' attention to Exercise 4B. Read the instructions aloud. Model the conversation. Hold up the Student's Book and point to the first picture. Ask two Ss to read the conversation aloud.
- Ss complete the exercise in pairs, asking and answering questions about the picture dictionary pictures. Walk around and help as needed.
- Ask several pairs to ask and answer the questions for the rest of the class.

Literacy tip

For an alternative activity, refer literacy Ss to pages 120–121 in the *Literacy Workbook* at any time during the lesson.

Evaluation

- Direct Ss' attention to the first part of the lesson focus written on the board. Ask: *What does Lupe like to do?* Elicit: *cook*, *play cards*, *listen to music*, *dance*, and *watch TV.*
- Direct Ss' attention to the pictures in the picture dictionary. Ask Ss to cover the names of the activities with a piece of paper and then identify them one by one.
- Check off each part of the lesson focus as Ss demonstrate understanding of what they have learned in the lesson.

More Ventures, Unit 10, Lesson D	
Literacy Workbook, 15–30 min. **Basic Workbook,** 15–30 min.	
Picture Dictionary activities, 30–45 min. **Writing worksheets,** 15–30 min.	www.cambridge.org/myresourceroom
Student Arcade, time varies	www.cambridge.org/venturesarcade

4 Picture dictionary Free-time activities

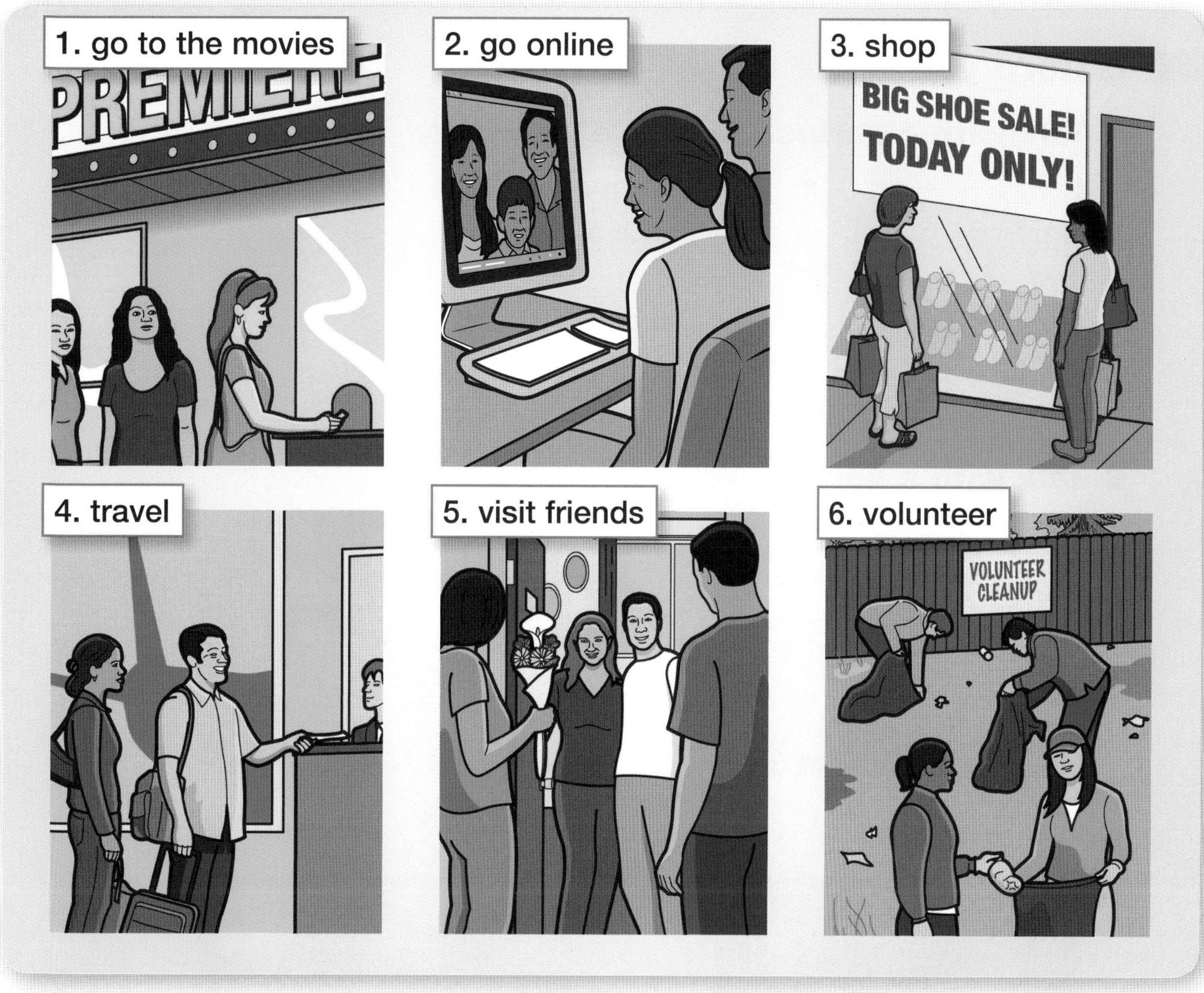

1. go to the movies
2. go online
3. shop
4. travel
5. visit friends
6. volunteer

STUDENT TK 46
CLASS CD2 TK 53

A Listen and repeat. Look at the picture dictionary.

B Talk with a partner. Point and ask. Your partner answers.

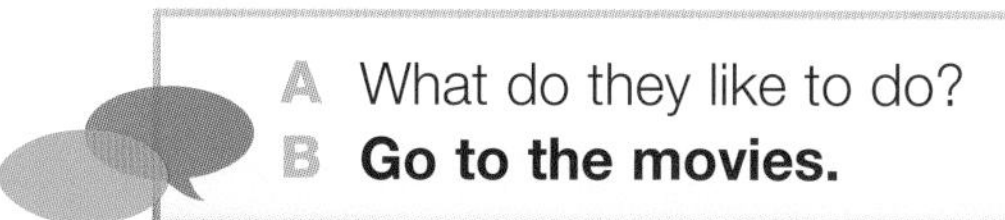

A What do they like to do?
B **Go to the movies.**

LESSON E Writing

1 Before you write

A Talk with a partner. Complete the words.

1. r _e_ _a_ d m _a_ g a z i n e s
2. p l _a_ y b _a_ s k _e_ t b a l l
3. w _a_ t c h T V
4. v _i_ s _i_ t f r i _e_ n d s
5. _e_ x _e_ r c _i_ s e
6. w _o_ r k _i_ n the g a r d _e_ n

B Talk with a partner. Write the words.

1. _exercise_

2. _read_ magazines

3. _play_ basketball

4. _work_ in the garden

5. _visit_ friends

6. _watch_ TV

Lesson objective

- Discuss and write about free-time activities

Warm-up and review

- Before class. Write today's lesson focus on the board.
  Lesson E:
  Write about free-time activities
- Begin class. Books closed. Ask Ss to recall some of the free-time activities that they have studied in the unit so far. Emphasize that they are not supposed to look in their books for the answers but should try to remember the activities. Write the activities on the board: *go to the movies*, *visit friends*, *shop*, *travel*, etc.
- Point to the activities on the board. Ask individual Ss: *Do you like to (the activity you are pointing to)?* Elicit appropriate responses.

Presentation

- Direct Ss' attention to Exercise **1A**. Read aloud the instructions.
- Point to the first item and say: *Number 1. What's the activity?* (read magazines) Ask: *What letters do we need?* (*e*, *a* and *a*) Point to where the letters are written in the blanks. Say: *Now you complete the rest of the words.*
- Ss work in pairs to complete the words. Encourage Ss to figure out the activities together.
- Write the numbers *2–6* on the board. Ask individual Ss to write the completed words from Exercise **1A** on the board. Ask different Ss: *Are the words correct?* Make corrections if needed.

Expansion activity (individual work)

- Write on the board: *I like to _____. I don't like to _____.*
- Say: *Look at the activities in Exercise* **1A**. *Make sentences about yourself. Use the words on the board.* For example: *I like to read magazines. I don't like to work in the garden.*
- Ss complete the activity individually. Walk around and help as needed.
- Ask several Ss to read their likes and dislikes to the rest of the class.

Practice

- Focus Ss' attention on Exercise **1B** and read the instructions aloud.
- Model the task. Direct Ss' attention to Picture 1. Ask: *What does he like to do?* (exercise) Say: *Now you complete the rest of the phrases. Use the words in Exercise* **1A**.
- Ss complete the exercise in pairs. Walk around and help as needed.
- Write the numbers *2–6* on the board. Ask individual Ss to write the answers on the board.
- Go over the answers. Ask: *Are these words spelled correctly?* Correct any errors if needed.

Expansion activity (student pairs)

- Write on the board: *What does he like to do? He likes to _____.*
- Direct Ss' attention to the pictures in Exercise **1B**. Say: *Ask your partner the question on the board about each picture.*
- Ss complete the exercise in pairs. Walk around and help as needed.
- Ask several pairs to ask and answer the questions for the rest of the class.

Community building (whole class)

- Brainstorm Ss' likes and dislikes of free-time activities. If any Ss have common interests, encourage them to get together and try some of these activities together on the weekends or whenever they have free time.

Literacy tip

For an alternative activity, refer literacy Ss to pages 122–123 in the *Literacy Workbook* at any time during the lesson.

LESSON E Writing

Presentation

- Write *day off* on the board. Point to the words. Say them aloud and ask Ss to repeat them after you. Ask: *What's a day off?* If Ss don't know, say: *It's a day when you don't work or go to school.*
- Hold up the Student's Book. Point to the pictures in Exercise 1B on page 130. Say: *This man's name is Brian. He likes to do different activities on his day off.*
- Direct Ss' attention to Exercise 2A and read the instructions aloud. Ask a S to read the statement *My name is Brian. Saturday is my day off.*
- Model the task. Explain that the sentences in Exercise 2A go with the pictures in Exercise 1B. Hold up the Student's Book. Point to picture 1 in Exercise 1B. Ask: *What does Brian like to do on his day off?*
- Ask a S to read the first sentence in Exercise 2A aloud. Say: *That's right. Brian likes to exercise in the morning.*
- Ss complete the exercise individually. Walk around and help as needed.

Comprehension check

- Write the numbers *2–6* on the board. Ask individual Ss to write their answers on the board. Ask: *Is this answer correct?*

Application

- Direct Ss' attention to Exercise 2B. Read the instructions aloud.
- Model the task. Tell Ss what you like to do on your day off. Hold up the Student's Book, and pretend to check off the activities as you say them. Point to the word *other.* Say: *I like to sing.* Write *sing* on the board and check it off.
- Ss complete the exercise individually. Walk around and help as needed.

Literacy tip

Literacy Ss should be able to complete this exercise with some help from a more advanced S. Ask an advanced S to read the activities to the literacy Ss to make sure that they understand the activities.

Practice

- Direct Ss' attention to the second part of Exercise 2B. Read the instructions aloud.
- Model the task. Write on the board: *I like to* ______. Say: *Remember, I like to sing.* Write *sing* in the blank. Continue with the activities you mentioned in Exercise 2B.
- Ss complete the exercise individually. Walk around and help as needed.

Application

- Direct Ss' attention to Exercise 3. Read aloud the instructions. Tell Ss to read their lists to their partners aloud. Walk around and help as needed.

Teaching tip

This exercise asks Ss to work together to share their writing. Encourage Ss to peer-correct each other's writing if necessary. Say: *Help your partner with any mistakes. Then your partner will help you.*

- Ask several Ss to read their sentences aloud for the whole class.

Expansion activity *(whole group)*

- Dictation. Books closed. Ask Ss to take out a piece of paper and write the numbers *1–5* on it. Dictate the following sentences: *1. I like to volunteer. 2. He likes to go to the movies. 3. She likes to exercise. 4. I like to cook. 5. They like to swim.*
- Ask Ss to write their sentences on the board. Ask other Ss: *Are the sentences correct?* Different Ss can correct any errors if needed.

Evaluation

- Direct Ss' attention to the lesson focus written on the board.
- Ask different Ss to come to the board and write sentences about leisure activities that they enjoy. They should use the form *I like to* ______.
- Check off the lesson focus as Ss demonstrate understanding of what they have learned in the lesson.

More Ventures, Unit 10, Lesson E	
Literacy Workbook, 15–30 min.	
Basic Workbook, 15–30 min.	
Writing worksheets, 15–30 min.	www.cambridge.org/myresourceroom

2 Write

A Complete the sentences. Look at 1B.

My name is Brian.

Saturday is my day off.

1. I like to ___exercise___ in the morning.
2. I like to ___read___ magazines, too.
3. I like to ___play___ basketball with my son in the afternoon.
4. I also like to ___work___ in the garden.
5. I like to ___visit___ friends in the evening.
6. I like to ___watch___ TV at night.

B Check (✓). What do you like to do on your day off?

- ☐ cook
- ☐ dance
- ☐ exercise
- ☐ fish
- ☐ go to the movies
- ☐ play cards
- ☐ shop
- ☐ swim
- ☐ volunteer
- ☐ other: ___(Answers will vary.)___

Write about yourself.

My Day Off

My name is ___(Answers will vary.)___.

_______________ is my day off.

I like to _______________.

I like to _______________.

I like to _______________.

I like to _______________.

3 After you write

Talk with a partner. Share your writing.

LESSON F Another view

1 Life-skills reading

Valley Senior Center
Evening Classes

Guitar class
Learn to play the guitar.
September 3 to November 21
Monday and Wednesday
7:00 p.m. to 9:00 p.m.
Room 101
$100.00

A Read the sentences. Look at the class description. Fill in the answer.

1. This description is for ____.
   - Ⓐ a guitar class
   - Ⓑ an exercise class
   - Ⓒ an ESL class
2. The class is in Room ____.
   - Ⓐ 100
   - Ⓑ 101
   - Ⓒ 901
3. The class is in the ____.
   - Ⓐ morning
   - Ⓑ afternoon
   - Ⓒ evening
4. The class is ____.
   - Ⓐ $10.00
   - Ⓑ $100.00
   - Ⓒ $101.00

B Talk with a partner.

What are your classes?

Lesson objectives

- Practice reading a class description
- Review unit vocabulary and grammar
- Complete the self-assessment

Warm-up and review

- Before class. Write today's lesson focus on the board.
  Lesson F:
  Read and answer questions about a class description
  Talk about free-time activities
  Complete the self-assessment
- Begin class. Books closed. Write the words *class description* on the board. Point to the words. Say them aloud and ask Ss to repeat. Ask: *What kinds of classes are there?* Elicit appropriate responses, such as: *English classes, music classes, sports classes.*

Teaching tip
If your school has a catalog with class descriptions in it, bring it to class to show Ss a real-life example.

- Ask: *Are you taking any other classes?* If any Ss say *yes*, ask them what classes they are taking. If you have Ss with children, ask if the children are taking any classes after school. If any Ss say *yes*, ask them to say the names of the classes.

Presentation

- Books open. Direct Ss' attention to the class description in Exercise **1A**.
- Hold up the Student's Book. Point to the class description. Ask questions about the class:
  What kind of class is this? (A guitar class.)
  Where is the class? (Valley Senior Center.)
  When is the class? (September 3 to November 21.)
  What day is the class? (Monday and Wednesday.)
  What time is the class? (7:00 p.m. to 9:00 p.m.)

Teaching tip
Elicit the meaning of senior center. Explain that a senior citizen is someone over the age of 65 or 70.

Practice

- Read aloud the instructions in Exercise **1A**. This task helps prepare Ss for standardized-type tests they may have to take.
- Write the first item on the board along with the three answer choices labeled *a*, *b*, and *c*.
- Read the item and answer choices aloud and then point to the class description. Ask Ss: *What is this class for?* Show Ss where to find the information. Elicit: *a guitar class.*
- Point to the three answer choices on the board. Ask Ss: *a*, *b*, or *c*? (a) Fill in the letter *a* and tell Ss: *Fill in.* Make sure Ss understand the task.
- Have Ss individually scan for and fill in the answers.

Comprehension check

- Go over the answers to Exercise **1A** with the class. Make sure that Ss followed directions and filled in their answers. Ask Ss to point to the information in the class description.

Application

- Read the instructions aloud for Exercise **1B**.
- Model the task. Hold up the Student's Book. Point to the class description. Ask: *Do you like this guitar class?* Point to various Ss to answer. Then ask: *What are your classes?* Elicit appropriate responses from Ss.
- Ss ask and answer the question in pairs.

Expansion activity *(individual work)*

- Ask Ss to write a description for an imaginary class in their notebooks. Tell them to model their class description after the one in Exercise **1A**. Encourage them to change the information in their description to make the class different. Remind Ss of the classes they brainstormed at the beginning of the lesson.
- Ask several Ss to write their class descriptions on the board. Encourage Ss to ask questions about the class using the question words written on the board.

Community building *(whole group)*

- If possible, bring several copies of a local continuing education course catalog to your class. Tell Ss about courses they can take that don't require a lot of English, such as art, music, and dance courses. Tell Ss that this is a great way to meet other people and practice English outside of class.

LESSON F Another view

Practice

- Direct Ss' attention to Exercise 2A and read the instructions aloud.
- Model the task. Point to the first picture and ask: *What is this?* Elicit: *guitar.* Ask: *What's the activity?* (Play the guitar.) Point to the line connecting the picture to the word *play.*
- Tell Ss: *Match the pictures and the words.*
- Ss complete the task in pairs. Help as needed.
- Go over the answers to Exercise 2A with the class. Ask Ss to say aloud the full verb phrase for each picture.
- Write the numbers *2–8* on the board. Ask individual Ss to come to the board to write their answers. Then ask different Ss to complete each verb phrase on the board.
- Ask: *Are the answers correct?* Have other Ss correct any errors on the board.

Expansion activity (whole group)

- Before class. Make copies of the following chart for each S in your class:

Do you like to . . .						
Name	*play the guitar?*	*watch TV?*	*work in the garden?*	*read magazines?*	*go to the movies?*	*play basketball?*

- Write on the board: *Yes, I do. / No, I don't.* Tell Ss to use these answers as guidelines for this activity.
- Ask Ss to stand up and talk to four other Ss. Ask them to choose Ss they are not usually partners with.
- Tell Ss to write the names of the people they speak with in the chart as well as the answers these Ss give them for each question. Point to the answers on the board to remind Ss of the correct form and help as needed.

Practice

- Direct Ss' attention to Exercise 2B. Read the instructions aloud.
- Write *inside* and *outside* on the board. Point to each word. Say it aloud. Ask Ss to repeat the words after you. Say: *We are inside now.* Point to a window or in the direction of the outdoors. Say: *That's outside.*
- Ask: *What else do you do inside?* Elicit: *watch TV, cook, play the guitar*, etc. Ask: *What do you do outside?* Elicit: *play basketball, work in the garden*, etc.
- Model the activity. Hold up the Student's Book. Point to the chart in Exercise 2B. Ask: *Do you cook inside the house?* (Yes.) Ask: *Do you cook outside the house?* Elicit *Yes / No* responses. Point to the check marks in both columns of the chart.
- Ss complete the activity in pairs. Walk around and help as needed.
- Go over the answers to Exercise 2B with the class. Ask questions about Exercise 2B. Ask about each activity: *Can you _____ inside the house? Can you _____ outside the house?*
- If Ss disagree, ask them to explain their opinions. For example, you can cook inside the house and outside at a picnic.
- Reproduce the chart in Exercise 2B on the board. Ask different Ss to check the columns for each activity. Ss compare their own charts to the one on the board.

Literacy tip

For an alternative activity, refer literacy Ss to pages 124–125 in the *Literacy Workbook* at any time during the lesson.

Evaluation

- Before asking Ss to turn to the self-assessment on page 145, do a quick review of the unit. Have Ss turn to Lesson A. Ask the class to talk about what they remember about this lesson. Prompt Ss, if necessary, with questions, for example: *What words are on this page? What do you see in the picture?* Continue in this manner to review each lesson quickly.
- **Self-assessment** Read the instructions for Exercise 3. Ask Ss to turn to the self-assessment page and complete the unit self-assessment.
- If Ss are ready, administer the unit test on pages T-196–T-198 of this Teacher's Edition (or on the Assessment Audio CD / CD-ROM).
- If Ss are ready, administer the final test on pages T-199–T-202 of this Teacher's Edition (or on the Assessment Audio CD / CD-ROM).

More Ventures, Unit 10, Lesson F	
Literacy Workbook, 15–30 min.	
Basic Workbook, 15–30 min.	
Writing worksheets, 15–30 min.	www.cambridge.org/myresourceroom

2 Fun with vocabulary

A Talk with a partner. Read and match.

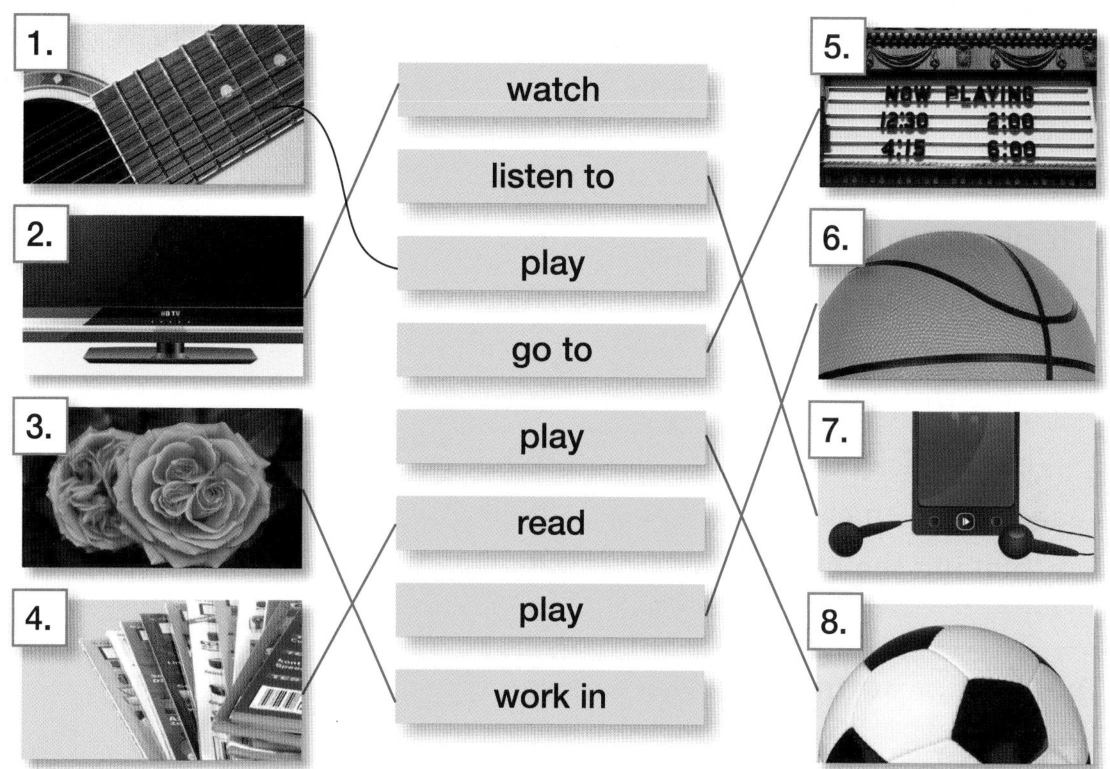

B Talk with a partner. Complete the chart.

	Inside the house	Outside the house
cook	✓	✓
fish		✓
dance	✓	✓
shop		✓
swim		✓
watch TV	✓	

3 Wrap up

Complete the **Self-assessment** on page 145.

Review

1 Listening

CLASS CD2 TK 54

Read. Then listen and circle.

1. What is Marco doing?
   (a.) washing the car
   b. playing the guitar
2. What does he like to do?
   a. wash the car
   (b.) play the guitar
3. What is Ricky doing?
   a. making lunch
   (b.) making the bed
4. What is Fred doing?
   (a.) reading magazines
   b. watching TV
5. What does Tina like to do?
   (a.) cook
   b. exercise
6. What does she like to do on the weekend?
   a. fish
   (b.) dance

Talk with a partner. Ask and answer.

2 Vocabulary

Write. Complete the story.

bedroom	kitchen	playing	watching	work

Sunday at Home

Today is Sunday. My son is watching (1) TV in the living room. My daughter is playing (2) the guitar in her bedroom (3). My wife is in the kitchen (4). She likes to cook. I am in the garden. I like to work (5) in the garden. Sunday is our favorite day of the week. We like to relax.

Lesson objectives
- Review vocabulary and grammar from Units 9 and 10
- Review pronunciation of *a*, *e*, *i*, *o*, and *u*

Warm-up and review

- Before class. Write today's lesson focus on the board.
  Review unit:
  Review vocabulary and grammar from Units 9 and 10.
  Review pronunciation of a, e, i, o, and u.
- Begin class. Books closed. Draw a simple floor plan of a house on the board. Include a bedroom, kitchen, living room, dining room, and laundry room.
- Ask a S to come to the board. Say: *Draw Rosa. She is in the living room.* Encourage the S to draw a stick figure in the living room by pointing to that room on the board. Write *Rosa* under the stick figure.
- Ask other Ss to draw people in the other rooms. Use the names *Ali*, *Sara*, *Mike*, and *Sally* or other names that you choose. Write the names under the stick figures.
- Point to the people in the house and ask questions. For example, point to Rosa. Ask: *Where is she?* (In the living room.) Ask: *What's she doing?* Elicit an appropriate response, such as: *She's watching TV.* Encourage the Ss to make up activities for the stick figures.
- Continue asking about the other people in the house. Ss can invent answers about activities in the house.

Practice

- Books open. Direct Ss' attention to Exercise **1** and read the instructions aloud.
- Ask individual Ss to read the questions and answers aloud. Say: *Now listen to the conversations. Circle the correct answers.*

Class Audio CD2 track 54 Model the task. Play or read the first conversation on the audio program (see audio script, page T-163). Point to the two answer choices in number 1 and ask: *Is Marco washing the car or playing the guitar?* (washing the car) Point to where the answer *a* has been circled.

Class Audio CD2 track 54 Play or read the complete audio program (see audio script, page T-163). Ss listen and circle the correct answers. Repeat the audio program as needed.

- Check answers with the class. Read each question aloud and call on different Ss to answer.

Teaching tip

You may need to play the audio program several times in order to give Ss a chance to extract the information they need. Then, to check comprehension and to help Ss who may be struggling, play the audio program again and ask Ss to repeat the parts of the conversation that contain the answers to the questions.

- Read aloud the second part of the instructions for Exercise **1**. Ss complete the exercise in pairs. Walk around and help as needed.
- Ask several pairs to ask and answer the questions for the rest of the class.

Multilevel tip (small groups)

If you have any Ss who are struggling in class, put them in a group with more advanced Ss who like to help others in the class. In this way, struggling Ss will have the help of someone who knows the target language better than they do.

Practice

- Direct Ss' attention to Exercise **2**. Point to the title of the story and ask Ss: *What is the title of this story?* (Sunday at Home)
- Direct Ss' attention to the words in the word bank. Say each word aloud. Ask Ss to repeat them after you.
- Read aloud the instructions in Exercise **2**. Ask a S to read the first and second sentences in the story aloud. Say: *Use the words from the word bank to complete the story.*
- Ss read the story and fill in the blanks individually. Walk around and help as needed.
- Write the numbers *1–5* on the board. Ask Ss to come up to the board to write the answers.
- Ask several Ss to read different sentences of the story aloud using the words on the board. Ask: *Are these words correct?* Ask different Ss to correct any errors.

Expansion activity *(individual work, student pairs)*

- Tell Ss: *Write this story again. Use information about you. What do you like to do on Sunday?* Elicit appropriate responses.

Teaching tip

If some of your Ss work on Sundays, ask them to change the day in the title to reflect a day when they don't have to work. If they work every day, ask them to write about a morning or afternoon when they have free time.

- Ss complete the story individually. Walk around and help as needed.
- Ask Ss to read their stories to a partner. Tell the partners to check the stories for errors, and help correct the errors.
- Ask several Ss to read their stories to the rest of the class.

Review

Warm-up and review

- Books closed. Ask Ss to brainstorm free-time activities that they learned in Unit 10. Write them on the board.
- Ask a S to stand up. Ask: *What do you like to do in your free time?* Elicit an appropriate response, such as: *I like to cook.* Ask another S: *What does (student's name) like to do?* Elicit: *He / She likes to cook.*
- Continue by asking other Ss what they like to do in their free time.

Practice

- Direct Ss' attention to Exercise **3A**. Read the instructions aloud.
- Model the task. Write *they*, *he*, and *she* on the board. Point to *they.* Ask: *Is it "they is" or "they are"?* (they are) Continue by asking about *she* and *he.* (he is / she is)
- Direct Ss' attention to question number 1. Ask two Ss to read the question and answer aloud.
- Ss complete the exercise individually. Walk around and help as needed.
- Check answers to Exercise **3A** with the class. Ask different pairs of Ss to read the questions and answers aloud. After each question, ask: *Is that correct?* Ask different Ss to make corrections if needed.
- Direct Ss' attention to Exercise **3B**. Read the instructions aloud.
- Model the task. Ask two Ss to read the example question and answer aloud. Ask: *Is it "does" or "do"?* (does) Hold up the Student's Book. Point to where *does* has been written for number 1. Ask: *Why is it "does" and not "do"?* Elicit: *Because we use "does" with "he" and "she."* Ask: *When do we use "do"?* Elicit: *Use "do" with "I" or "you."*
- Ss complete the exercise individually.
- Check answers to Exercise **3B** with the class. Ask different pairs of Ss to read the questions and answers aloud. After each question and answer, ask: *Is that correct?* Different Ss can make corrections if needed.

Presentation

- Direct Ss' attention to the second part of the lesson focus written on the board.
- Ask: *What are the vowels in English?* (a, e, i, o, u) Write the vowels on the board.
- Say each vowel aloud while pointing to it. Ask Ss to repeat after you. Say: *These letters each have two sounds.* Ask Ss to say the two sounds for each letter.

Practice

Class Audio CD2 track 55 Direct Ss' attention to Exercise **4A** and read the instructions aloud. Play or read the audio program (see audio script, page T-163). Ss listen to examples of the two sounds for each vowel.

Class Audio CD2 track 56 Direct Ss' attention to Exercise **4B** and read aloud the instructions. Play or read the audio program (see audio script, page T-163). Ss listen and repeat what they hear.

- Read aloud the second part of the instructions for Exercise **4B**. Model the task. Point to the charts in the exercise and tell one S: *Say a word.* After that S says any word in the chart, tell his or her partner: *Point to the word.*
- Ss complete the task in pairs. Walk around and help as needed.

Expansion activity (whole group)

- Draw nine vertical lines on the board, making 10 columns. Write the vowels twice, so that the headings of the columns will be like this: *a*, *a*, *e*, *e*, *i*, *i*, *o*, *o*, *u*, *u*.
- Write the example words from Exercise **4A** in each corresponding column.
- Ask Ss to brainstorm more words that would fit in each column. For example: *say*, *cat*, *need*, *red*, *drive*, *fix*, *go*, *Tom*, *tune*, *cut.*

  Option Ask Ss to look up words in Units 9 and 10 that fit the categories.

Evaluation

- Direct Ss' attention to the lesson focus written on the board.
- Ask individual Ss questions similar to the ones in Exercise **3B**. Ask real questions about Ss in the class. Make sure Ss answer the questions correctly.
- Write on the board: *name*, *at*, *read*, *red*, *five*, *six*, *phone*, *on*, *June*, *bus.* Call on individual Ss as you point to one of the words, and ask them to say the word. Listen carefully to Ss' pronunciation and provide help and correction as needed.
- Check off each part of the lesson focus as Ss demonstrate an understanding of what they have learned in the lesson.

3 Grammar

A Complete the sentences. Use *is* or *are*.

1. A What ___*are*___ they doing?
   B Drying the dishes.
2. A What ___*is*___ she doing?
   B Taking out the trash.
3. A What ___*is*___ he doing?
   B Washing the clothes.
4. A What ___*are*___ they doing?
   B Getting the mail.

B Read and circle. Then write.

1. A What ___*does*___ Pai like to do?
   do / (does)
   B He ___*likes to*___ listen to music.
   like to / (likes to)
2. A What ___*do*___ Vance and Anh like to do?
   (do) / does
   B They ___*like to*___ read magazines.
   (like to) / likes to
3. A What ___*do*___ you like to do?
   (do) / does
   B I ___*like to*___ travel.
   (like to) / likes to

4 Pronunciation

A Listen to the two sounds of *a, e, i, o,* and *u*.

CLASS CD2 TK 55

a		e		i		o		u	
name	at	read	red	five	six	phone	on	June	bus

B Listen and repeat.

CLASS CD2 TK 56

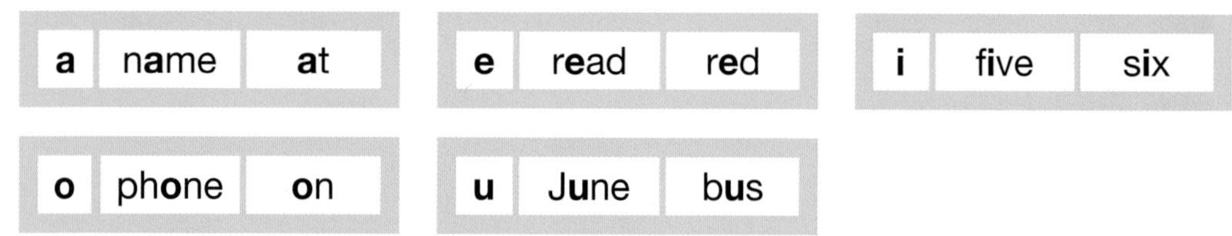

Talk with a partner. Say a word. Your partner points. Take turns.

Self-assessments

Overview

Each unit of *Ventures Basic* Student's Book ends with a self-assessment. Self-assessments allow students to reflect on what they have learned and to decide whether they need more review of the material.

How self-assessments help students

- It is not possible for English language teachers to teach students all the English they need to know. Therefore, it is important that teachers help students develop strategies for learning and for measuring their learning. One important strategy is self-assessment. With self-assessment, students become aware of their own learning and focus on their own performance. Being able to self-assess is important for developing learner autonomy. This autonomy will equip students for lifelong learning.
- Self-assessment allows students to participate in the assessment process. Responsibility for learning shifts from the teacher to the students as self-assessment makes the students more aware of their role in learning and monitoring their own performance.
- Self-assessment can also contribute to learner persistence. Learners will continue to attend classes when they have verification that learning has taken place. They can measure this learning when they complete the self-assessment checklists.

How self-assessments help teachers

- Teachers can use the results of the self-assessments to identify areas that need further instruction or review. They can use the results to meet with students and discuss items that have been mastered as well as those that need further study.
- The information on the self-assessment forms can also be used at the beginning of the unit to identify and discuss the learning objectives of the unit. In this way, students will have a clear understanding of the learning goals. If they know what the learning objectives are, they can better monitor their own progress. This results in greater learner gains, which is gratifying to both students and teachers.

Self-assessment in *Ventures*

- Each self-assessment asks students to check the words they have learned and the skills and functions they feel they have mastered. Students then decide if they are ready to take the unit test to confirm this acquisition of unit language. The self-assessments are in checklist form, making it easier for lower-level students to check off how they feel they are progressing.
- If students feel they need additional study for a particular unit, the *Ventures* series provides additional practice in the Workbook.
- The Online Teacher's Resource Room contains the same self-assessments that are found in the Student's Book. Each unit's self-assessment can be printed, distributed to, and completed by the student after each unit, and placed in his or her learner portfolio. It can also be given to students to keep as a personal record of their progress.

UNIT 1 Personal information

A Vocabulary Check (✓) the words you know.

☐ area code	☐ January	☐ July
☐ country	☐ February	☐ August
☐ first name	☐ March	☐ September
☐ ID card	☐ April	☐ October
☐ last name	☐ May	☐ November
☐ phone number	☐ June	☐ December

B Skills Check (✓) *Yes* or *No*.

	Yes	No
I can use ***my***, ***your***, ***his***, and ***her***: *What's **your** name? **My** name is Maria.*		
I can read about personal information.		
I can write about myself.		
I can read an ID card.		

C What's next? Choose one.

☐ I am ready for the unit test.

☐ I need more practice with ______________________________ .

UNIT 2 At school

A Vocabulary Check (✓) the words you know.

☐ book	☐ dictionary	☐ pen
☐ chair	☐ eraser	☐ pencil
☐ computer	☐ notebook	☐ ruler
☐ desk	☐ paper	☐ stapler

B Skills Check (✓) *Yes* or *No*.

	Yes	No
I can use ***in***, ***on***, and ***under***: *Where's my pencil?* ***In*** *the desk.* ***On*** *the desk.* ***Under*** *the desk.*		
I can read a note.		
I can write about school supplies.		
I can read a class schedule.		

C What's next? Choose one.

☐ I am ready for the unit test.

☐ I need more practice with ______________________________ .

UNIT 3 Friends and family

A Vocabulary Check (✓) the words you know.

☐ aunt	☐ grandfather	☐ sister
☐ brother	☐ grandmother	☐ son
☐ daughter	☐ husband	☐ uncle
☐ father	☐ mother	☐ wife

B Skills Check (✓) *Yes* or *No*.

	Yes	No
I can ask and answer questions with ***Do you have . . . ?***: ***Do you have** a sister?* ***Yes, I do. No, I don't.***		
I can read about a family.		
I can write about my family.		
I can read a housing application.		

C What's next? Choose one.

☐ I am ready for the unit test.

☐ I need more practice with ______________________________ .

UNIT 4 Health

A Vocabulary Check (✓) the words you know.

☐ arm	☐ foot	☐ leg
☐ cold	☐ hand	☐ sore throat
☐ eye	☐ head	☐ stomach
☐ fever	☐ headache	☐ toothache

B Skills Check (✓) *Yes* or *No*.

	Yes	No
I can use singular and plural nouns: ***one eye***, ***two eyes***		
I can read about health problems.		
I can complete a form.		
I can read a medicine label.		

C What's next? Choose one.

☐ I am ready for the unit test.

☐ I need more practice with ______________________________ .

UNIT 5 Around town

A **Vocabulary** Check (✓) the words you know.

☐ bank	☐ library	☐ restaurant
☐ gas station	☐ movie theater	☐ school
☐ hospital	☐ pharmacy	☐ street
☐ laundromat	☐ post office	☐ supermarket

B **Skills** Check (✓) *Yes* or *No*.

	Yes	No
I can use ***on***, ***next to***, ***across from***, and ***between***: *Where's the school?* ***Next to*** *the bank.*		
I can read a notice about a new library.		
I can write about the buildings on a street.		
I can read a map.		

C **What's next?** Choose one.

☐ I am ready for the unit test.

☐ I need more practice with ______________________ .

UNIT 6 Time

A Vocabulary Check (✓) the words you know.

☐ appointment	☐ class	☐ meeting
☐ at midnight	☐ in the afternoon	☐ movie
☐ at night	☐ in the evening	☐ party
☐ at noon	☐ in the morning	☐ TV show

B Skills Check (✓) *Yes* or *No*.

	Yes	No
I can ask and answer *yes* / *no* questions with ***be***: ***Is*** *your class at 11:00?* ***Yes, it is. No, it isn't.***		
I can read about a schedule.		
I can write about my schedule.		
I can read an invitation.		

C What's next? Choose one.

☐ I am ready for the unit test.

☐ I need more practice with ______________________ .

UNIT 7 Shopping

A Vocabulary Check (✓) the words you know.

☐ blouse	☐ raincoat	☐ socks
☐ dress	☐ shirt	☐ sweater
☐ jacket	☐ shoes	☐ tie
☐ pants	☐ skirt	☐ T-shirt

B Skills Check (✓) *Yes* or *No*.

	Yes	No
I can ask questions with ***How much***: ***How much is*** *the shirt?* ***How much are*** *the shoes?*		
I can read an e-mail.		
I can write a shopping list.		
I can read a receipt.		

C What's next? Choose one.

☐ I am ready for the unit test.

☐ I need more practice with ______________________________ .

UNIT 8 Work

A Vocabulary Check (✓) the words you know.

☐ answer the phone	☐ custodian	☐ salesperson
☐ cashier	☐ fix cars	☐ sell clothes
☐ clean buildings	☐ mechanic	☐ serve food
☐ count money	☐ receptionist	☐ server

B Skills Check (✓) *Yes* or *No*.

	Yes	No
I can ask and answer questions with ***does***: ***Does*** *he* ***sell*** *clothes?* ***Yes,*** *he* ***does. No,*** *he* ***doesn't.***		
I can read an article about an employee.		
I can write about jobs.		
I can read a help-wanted ad.		

C What's next? Choose one.

☐ I am ready for the unit test.

☐ I need more practice with ______________________________ .

UNIT 9 Daily living

A **Vocabulary** Check (✓) the words you know.

☐ cut the grass	☐ get the mail	☐ walk the dog
☐ do homework	☐ make lunch	☐ wash the car
☐ do the laundry	☐ make the bed	☐ wash the dishes
☐ dry the dishes	☐ take out the trash	☐ water the grass

B **Skills** Check (✓) *Yes* or *No*.

	Yes	**No**
I can ask and answer questions with ***What***: ***What is** he **doing**? **What are** they **doing**?* ***Making lunch.***		
I can read an e-mail about what people are doing.		
I can write about what people are doing.		
I can read a work order.		

C **What's next?** Choose one.

☐ I am ready for the unit test.

☐ I need more practice with _______________________________ .

UNIT 10 Free time

A Vocabulary Check (✓) the words you know.

☐ cook	☐ listen to music	☐ read magazines
☐ dance	☐ play basketball	☐ swim
☐ exercise	☐ play cards	☐ watch TV
☐ fish	☐ play the guitar	☐ work in the garden

B Skills Check (✓) *Yes* or *No*.

	Yes	No
I can ask and answer questions with ***like to***: *What* ***do*** *you* ***like to*** *do? I* ***like to*** *swim.*		
I can read an e-mail from a friend.		
I can write about what I like to do.		
I can read a course description.		

C What's next? Choose one.

☐ I am ready for the unit test.

☐ I need more practice with __________________________ .

Reference

Possessive adjectives

Questions

What's	my	phone number?
	your	
	his	
	her	
	its	
	our	
	your	
	their	

Answers

Your	phone number is 555-3348.
My	
His	
Her	
Its	
Your	
Our	
Their	

Present of *be*

***Yes / No* questions**

Am	I	from Somalia?
Are	you	
Is	he	
Is	she	
Is	it	
Are	we	
Are	you	
Are	they	

Short answers

Yes,	you	are.
	I	am.
	he	is.
	she	is.
	it	is.
	you	are.
	we	are.
	they	are.

No,	you aren't.
	I'm not.
	he isn't.
	she isn't.
	it isn't.
	you aren't.
	we aren't.
	they aren't.

Contractions

I'm	=	I am
You're	=	You are
He's	=	He is
She's	=	She is
It's	=	It is
We're	=	We are
You're	=	You are
They're	=	They are

aren't	=	are not
isn't	=	is not

Simple present

Yes / No questions

Do	I	sell clothes?
Do	you	
Does	he	
Does	she	
Does	it	
Do	we	
Do	you	
Do	they	

Short answers

Yes,	you	do.
	I	do.
	he	does.
	she	does.
	it	does.
	you	do.
	we	do.
	they	do.

No,	you	don't.
	I	don't.
	he	doesn't.
	she	doesn't.
	it	doesn't.
	you	don't.
	we	don't.
	they	don't.

don't = do not
doesn't = does not

Present continuous

Questions with *What*

What	am	I	doing?
	are	you	
	is	he	
	is	she	
	is	it	
	are	we	
	are	you	
	are	they	

Short answers

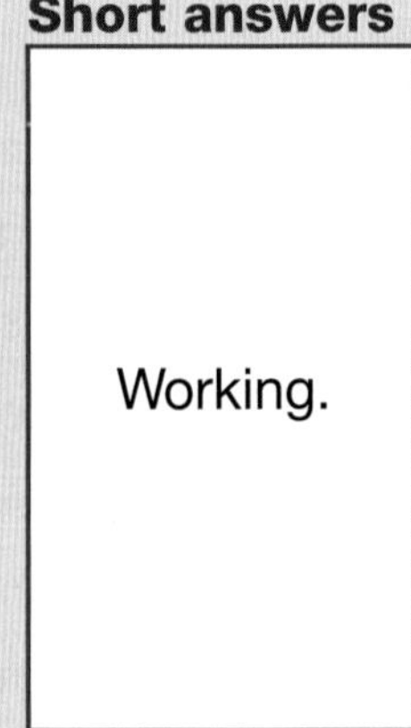

Working.

Simple present of *like to* + verb

Questions with *What*

What	do	I	like to do?
	do	you	
	does	he	
	does	she	
	does	it	
	do	we	
	do	you	
	do	they	

Answers

You	like	to swim.
I	like	
He	likes	
She	likes	
It	likes	
You	like	
We	like	
They	like	

***Yes / No* questions**

Do	I	like to swim?
Do	you	
Does	he	
Does	she	
Does	it	
Do	we	
Do	you	
Do	they	

Short answers

Yes,	you	do.
	I	do.
	he	does.
	she	does.
	it	does.
	you	do.
	we	do.
	they	do.

No,	you	don't.
	I	don't.
	he	doesn't.
	she	doesn't.
	it	doesn't.
	you	don't.
	we	don't.
	they	don't.

Simple present of *have*

Yes / No questions

Do	I	have a sister?
Do	you	
Does	he	
Does	she	
Do	we	
Do	you	
Do	they	

Short answers

Yes,	you	do.
	I	do.
	he	does.
	she	does.
	you	do.
	we	do.
	they	do.

No,	you	don't.
	I	don't.
	he	doesn't.
	she	doesn't.
	you	don't.
	we	don't.
	they	don't.

Affirmative statements

I	have	a sister.
You	have	
He	has	
She	has	
We	have	
You	have	
They	have	

Negative statements

I	don't	have	a sister.
You	don't		
He	doesn't		
She	doesn't		
We	don't		
You	don't		
They	don't		

Projects

Overview

The *Ventures* projects are optional material to be used at the completion of a unit. There is one project per unit, and most of the projects can be completed in one class period.

The Online Teacher's Resource Room contains the same projects that are found on pages T-150–T-154. Each unit's project can be printed and distributed to students after each unit. Projects are valuable activities because they extend students' learning into a real-world context. They work within the unit topic, but they also go beyond the Student's Book.

These projects are designed to be fun and practical, with the goal of helping students become more independent while learning to live in a new culture and speak a new language.

Project set-up and materials

Projects may be done in class as a group activity or outside of class, individually.

Some projects will need the teacher to gather simple materials to be used in class. For example, some require large poster paper or authentic materials such as copies of a local newspaper. In order to complete other projects, students will need access to a computer that is linked to the Internet.

Skills learned through the projects

Students learn different skills through these projects. For example, half the projects involve use of the Internet. Students search for information using key words. This is an essential skill that most students will need to use in English. In addition, the projects encourage students to practice other essential life skills, such as working collaboratively to make a poster or a booklet, looking up information on community resources, and making charts or maps to present information.

Community building and learner persistence

Ventures projects help build community inside and outside the classroom as students work together, using materials such as local newspapers and telephone directories to find information. Building community, in turn, helps to promote learner persistence. As students apply essential life skills, they will become more confident in their English skills and will be more motivated to come to class to learn additional skills that will help them in daily life.

UNIT 1 Class list

A **Make a chart.**

Write the names of three students in your class.

B **Talk to the students.**

Ask these questions. Write the answers.

1. What's your first name?
2. What's your last name?
3. What's your phone number?

First name	*Last name*	*Phone number*
Patricio	*Cano*	*708-555-6737*
Lien	*Tran*	*708-555-2986*
Phillip	*Thomas*	*708-555-8227*

C **Share your information.**

Make a class booklet.

UNIT 2 Shop for school supplies

A **Use the Internet.**

1. Shop for school supplies near your home.

Keywords school supplies (your city)

2. Find a store.
3. Click on the store.

B **Make a chart.**

Write the name, address, and phone number of the store.

Name	*Address*	*Phone number*
Grady's Office Supplies	*1865 Mesa Drive*	*555-2984*

C **Share your information.**

Show your chart to the class. Talk about the stores.

UNIT 3 Family chart

A Make a family chart.

On the left, write the names of three students in your class. Across the top, write the words for family members.

B Talk to the students.

Ask these questions. Check (✓) the answers.

1. Do you have a brother?
2. Do you have a sister?
3. Do you have a husband?
4. Do you have a wife?
5. Do you have a son?
6. Do you have a daughter?

Name	Brother	Sister	Husband	Wife	Son	Daughter
Trong	✓			✓	✓	✓
Hannah	✓	✓	✓			
Nasser				✓		✓

C Share your information.

Show your chart to the class. Talk about the family members.

UNIT 4 Find a health clinic

A Use the Internet.

1. Find a health clinic near your home.

Keywords health clinics (your city)

2. Click on the health clinic.

B Make a chart.

Write the name, address, and phone number of the health clinic.

Name	Address	Phone number
People's Health Clinic	600 Hill Street	555-2381

C Share your information.

Show your chart to the class. Talk about the clinic.

UNIT 5 Community map

A **Think of a street near your school.**

Write the name of the street. Write the names of five places on the street.

B **Draw a map of the street.**

Draw the places on your map. Write the names on the map.

Main Street Library | City Adult School | Simon's Supermarket

Main Street

United Bank | Main Street Post Office

C **Share your information.**

Put your map on the wall. Talk about your map.

UNIT 6 Library hours

A **Use the Internet.**

1. Find a library near your home.

Keywords public libraries | (your city)

2. Click on the library.
3. Find the hours for the library.

B **Make a chart.**

Write the name, address, and hours of the library.

Name	*Address*	*Hours*
Millwood Branch Library	*640 Anderson Lane*	*10:00 a.m. to 7:00 p.m.*

C **Share your information.**

Show your chart to the class. Talk about the library.

UNIT 7 A shopping center

A Use the Internet.

1. Find a shopping center near your home.

Keywords shopping centers (your city)

2. Click on the shopping center.

B Make a chart.

Write the name and address of the shopping center.

Name	Address
Greenfield Mall	12080 Highway 49

C Share your information.

Show your chart to the class.
Talk about the shopping center.

UNIT 8 Find a job

A Make a list.

Write three jobs you want.

1.	receptionist
2.	teacher's aide
3.	mechanic

B Make a chart.

Read the help-wanted ads in the newspaper.
Cut out one ad.
Write the name of the job, the place, and the phone number.

Job	Place	Phone number
receptionist	Caldwell Industries, Inc.	555-8273

C Share your information.

Find a picture of the job.
Read the ad to the class.
Make a class poster with the ad and the picture.

UNIT 9 Class survey

A Make a chart.

Write the names of three students in your class. Write four chores.

B Talk to the students.

Ask questions like these. Check (✓) the answers.

1. Do you get the mail?
2. Do you take out the trash?
3. Do you do the laundry?
4. Do you wash the dishes?

Name	Get the mail	Take out the trash	Do the laundry	Wash the dishes
Stacy	✓			✓
Park	✓	✓	✓	
Aiko				✓

C Share your information.

Show your chart to the class. Talk about your classmates' chores.

UNIT 10 A movie theater

A Use the Internet.

1. Find a movie theater near your home.

Keywords [movie theaters] [(your city)]

2. Click on the movie theater.

B Make a chart.

Write the name, address, and phone number of the movie theater. Write the name of a movie.

Name	Address	Phone number	Movie
Plaza Cinema	87 Stone Road	555-7865	Avatar

C Share your information.

Show your chart to the class. Talk about the theater and the movie.

Class audio script

Welcome

Page 3, Exercise 2A – CD1, Track 2

A, B, C, D, E, F, G, H, I, J, K, L, M, N, O, P, Q, R, S, T, U, V, W, X, Y, Z

Page 3, Exercise 2B – CD1, Track 3

1. Hello, my name is Anita. A-N-I-T-A.
2. My name is Daniel. D-A-N-I-E-L.
3. I'm Peizhi. P-E-I-Z-H-I.
4. My name is Yuri. Y-U-R-I.
5. Hi, I'm Franco. F-R-A-N-C-O.
6. Hi, my name is Lee. L-E-E.
7. Hello, my name is Hakim. H-A-K-I-M.
8. Hi there. My name is Karla. K-A-R-L-A.

Page 4, Exercise 3A – CD1, Track 4

1. Look.
2. Listen.
3. Point.
4. Repeat.
5. Talk.
6. Write.
7. Read.
8. Circle.
9. Match.

Page 5, Exercise 4A – CD1, Track 5

One, two, three, four, five, six, seven, eight, nine, ten, eleven, twelve, thirteen, fourteen, fifteen, sixteen, seventeen, eighteen, nineteen, twenty

Page 5, Exercise 4B – CD1, Track 6

1. six
2. eighteen
3. five
4. three
5. twelve
6. eleven
7. fifteen
8. nine

Unit 1: Personal information

Page 6, Exercise 1B – CD1, Track 7

Area code, country, first name, ID card, last name, phone number

Page 7, Exercise 2A – CD1, Track 8

1. area code
2. country
3. first name
4. ID card
5. last name
6. phone number

Page 7, Exercise 2B – CD1, Track 9

1. **A** What's your area code?
   B 201.
2. **A** What's your phone number?
   B 555-5983.
3. **A** What's your first name?
   B Glen.
4. **A** What's your last name?
   B Reyna.

Page 8, Exercise 1 – CD1, Track 10

1. the United States
2. Mexico
3. Haiti
4. Brazil
5. Russia
6. Somalia
7. Vietnam
8. China

Page 9, Exercise 2B – CD1, Track 11

1. **A** Where is Ivan from?
   B Russia.
2. **A** Where is Asad from?
   B Somalia.
3. **A** Where is Eduardo from?
   B Mexico.
4. **A** Where is Elsa from?
   B The United States.
5. **A** Where is Luisa from?
   B Brazil.
6. **A** Where is Jun-Ming from?
   B China.

Page 10, Exercise 2A – CD1, Track 12

1. **A** What's your name?
   B My name is Nancy.
2. **A** What's his name?
   B His name is Chin.
3. **A** What's her name?
   B Her name is Alima.
4. **A** What's your name?
   B My name is Vincent.

Page 11, Exercise 2B – CD1, Track 13

1. **A** What's his first name?
   B Jack.
2. **A** What's his last name?
   B Lee.
3. **A** What's his area code?
   B 203.
4. **A** What's his phone number?
   B 555-9687.
5. **A** What's her area code?
   B 415.
6. **A** What's her phone number?
   B 555-3702.
7. **A** What's her last name?
   B Garza.
8. **A** What's her first name?
   B Sara.

Page 12, Exercise 2 – CD1, Track 14

Welcome!

Meet our new student. His first name is Ernesto. His last name is Delgado. He is from Mexico. Welcome, Ernesto Delgado!

Page 13, Exercise 4A – CD1, Track 15

1. January
2. February
3. March
4. April
5. May
6. June
7. July
8. August
9. September
10. October
11. November
12. December

Unit 2: At school

Page 18, Exercise 1B – CD1, Track 16

A book, a chair, a computer, a desk, a notebook, a pencil

Page 19, Exercise 2A – CD1, Track 17

1. a book
2. a chair
3. a computer
4. a desk
5. a notebook
6. a pencil

Page 19, Exercise 2B – CD1, Track 18

1. A What do you need?
   B A pencil.
   A Here. Take this one.
2. A What do you need?
   B A notebook.
   A Here. Take this one.
3. A What do you need?
   B A book.
   A Here. Take this one.
4. A What do you need?
   B A chair.
   A Here. Take this one.

Page 20, Exercise 1 – CD1, Track 19

1. a dictionary
2. paper
3. a pen
4. an eraser
5. a stapler
6. a ruler

Page 21, Exercise 2B – CD1, Track 20

1. A What do you need, Carla?
   B A dictionary.
   A Here you are.
2. A What do you need, Daw?
   B An eraser.
   A Here you are.
3. A What do you need, Stefan?
   B A ruler.
   A Here you are.
4. A What do you need, Felicia?
   B Paper.
   A Here you are.
5. A What do you need, Kim?
   B A pen.
   A Here you are.
6. A What do you need, Pablo?
   B A stapler.
   A Here you are.

Page 22, Exercise 2A – CD1, Track 21

1. A Where's my pencil?
   B In the desk.
2. A Where's my notebook?
   B On the desk.
3. A Where's my pen?
   B On the floor.
4. A Where's my dictionary?
   B Under the table.
5. A Where's my ruler?
   B On the table.
6. A Where's my paper?
   B Under the desk.

Page 24, Exercise 2 – CD1, Track 22

Sue,

It's Monday, your first day of English class! You need a pencil, eraser, notebook, and dictionary. The pencil is in the desk. The eraser is on the desk. The notebook is on my computer. And the dictionary is under the chair. Have fun at school!

Mom

Page 25, Exercise 4A – CD1, Track 23

1. Monday
2. Tuesday
3. Wednesday
4. Thursday
5. Friday
6. Saturday
7. Sunday

Review: Units 1 and 2

Page 30, Exercise 1 – CD1, Track 24

1. A Welcome to class. What's your name?
   B My name is Hassan.
   A Your first name?
   B Yes.
2. A And what's your last name?
   B My last name is Ali.
3. A Where are you from, Hassan?
   B Somalia.
4. A And when's your birthday?
   B In August.
5. A What do you need, Hassan?
   B A notebook.
   A The notebook is on the desk.
6. A Ms. Garcia?
   B Yes, Hassan? What do you need?
   A Paper.
   B The paper is in the notebook.

Page 31, Exercise 4A – CD1, Track 25

/eɪ/ name
/oʊ/ phone

Page 31, Exercise 4B – CD1, Track 26

/eɪ/ name /oʊ/ phone
/eɪ/ day /oʊ/ code
/eɪ/ say /oʊ/ note

Page 31, Exercise 4C – CD1, Track 27

1. say
2. code
3. name
4. phone
5. day

Unit 3: Friends and family

Page 32, Exercise 1B – CD1, Track 28

Daughter, father, grandfather, grandmother, mother, son

Page 33, Exercise 2A – CD1, Track 29

1. daughter
2. father
3. grandfather
4. grandmother
5. mother
6. son

Page 33, Exercise 2B – CD1, Track 30

1. A Who's that?
 B The grandmother.
2. A Who's that?
 B The daughter.
3. A Who's that?
 B The father.
4. A Who's that?
 B The grandfather.

Page 34, Exercise 1 – CD1, Track 31

1. husband
2. wife
3. uncle
4. aunt
5. brother
6. sister

Page 35, Exercise 2B – CD1, Track 32

1. A Who is Vera?
 B Sam's aunt.
2. A Who is Mike?
 B Sam's uncle.
3. A Who is Sophie?
 B Sam's sister.
4. A Who is Susan?
 B Dave's wife.
5. A Who is Sam?
 B Sophie's brother.
6. A Who is Dave?
 B Susan's husband.

Page 36, Exercise 2A – CD1, Track 33

1. A Do you have a brother?
 B Yes, I do.
2. A Do you have a sister?
 B No, we don't.
3. A Do you have a son?
 B Yes, I do.
4. A Do you have a daughter?
 B Yes, we do.
5. A Do you have a wife?
 B No, I don't.

Page 37, Exercise 2B – CD1, Track 34

1. A Do you have a sister?
 B Yes, I do.
 A What's her name?
 B Diana.
2. A Do you have a brother?
 B No, I don't.
3. A Do you have a husband?
 B Yes, I do.
 A What's his name?
 B Ken.
4. A Do you have a son?
 B Yes, we do.
 A What's his name?
 B Danny.
5. A Do you have a daughter?
 B No, we don't.
6. A Do you have a grandmother?
 B Yes, I do.
 A What's her name?
 B Rose.

Page 38, Exercise 2 – CD1, Track 35

My Family

My name is Gloria. This is my family. This is my mother. Her name is Natalia. It is her birthday. This is my father. His name is Enrico. This is my husband, Luis. We have one daughter. Her name is Lisa. We have one son. His name is Tony. I love my family!

Page 39, Exercise 4A – CD1, Track 36

1. baby
2. girl
3. boy
4. teenager
5. woman
6. man

Unit 4: Health

Page 44, Exercise 1B – CD1, Track 37

Doctor, doctor's office, medicine, nurse, patient

Page 45, Exercise 2A – CD1, Track 38

1. doctor
2. doctor's office
3. medicine
4. nurse
5. patient

Page 45, Exercise 2B – CD1, Track 39

1. A What's the matter?
 B I need a nurse.
2. A What's the matter?
 B I need a doctor.
3. A What's the matter?
 B I need a nurse.
4. A What's the matter?
 B I need some medicine.

Page 46, Exercise 1 – CD1, Track 40

1. head
2. hand
3. arm
4. stomach
5. leg
6. foot

Page 47, Exercise 2B – CD1, Track 41

1. A What hurts?
 B My hand.
2. A What hurts?
 B My head.
3. A What hurts?
 B My leg.
4. A What hurts?
 B My stomach.
5. A What hurts?
 B My arm.
6. A What hurts?
 B My foot.

Page 48, Exercise 2A – CD1, Track 42

1. A What hurts?
 B My hands.
2. A What hurts?
 B My eyes.
3. A What hurts?
 B My arm.
4. A What hurts?
 B My foot.
5. A What hurts?
 B My legs.
6. A What hurts?
 B My hand.

Page 49, Exercise 2B – CD1, Track 43

1. A What hurts?
 B My legs.
 A Oh, I'm sorry.
2. A What hurts?
 B My hand.
 A Oh, I'm sorry.
3. A What hurts?
 B My stomach.
 A Oh, I'm sorry.
4. A What hurts?
 B My feet.
 A Oh, I'm sorry.

5. A What hurts?
   B My eyes.
   A Oh, I'm sorry.
6. A What hurts?
   B My head.
   A Oh, I'm sorry.

Page 50, Exercise 2 – CD1, Track 44

At the Doctor's Office

Tony and Mario are at the doctor's office. They are patients. Tony's leg hurts. His head hurts, too. He has a headache. Mario's arm hurts. His hands hurt, too. Tony and Mario are not happy. It is not a good day.

Page 51, Exercise 4A – CD1, Track 45

1. a cold
2. a fever
3. a headache
4. a sore throat
5. a stomachache
6. a toothache

Review: Units 3 and 4

Page 56, Exercise 1 – CD1, Track 46

1. A Tom, who is Sonya?
   B My aunt.
2. A Tom, do you have a brother?
   B Yes, I do. His name is David.
3. A Ray, do you have a wife?
   B Yes, I do. Her name is Tina.
4. A Barbara, do you have a son?
   B Yes, I do. His name is Jay.
5. A What's the matter?
   B My head hurts.
   A Oh, I'm sorry.
6. A What's the matter?
   B My foot hurts.
   A Oh, I'm sorry.

Page 57, Exercise 4A – CD1, Track 47

/iː/ read
/aɪ/ five
/uː/ June

Page 57, Exercise 4B – CD1, Track 48

/iː/ read	/aɪ/ write
/iː/ need	/uː/ June
/aɪ/ five	/uː/ rule

Page 57, Exercise 4C – CD1, Track 49

1. write
2. June
3. need
4. read
5. five

Unit 5: Around town

Page 58, Exercise 1B – CD1, Track 50

Bank, library, restaurant, school, street, supermarket

Page 59, Exercise 2A – CD1, Track 51

1. bank
2. library
3. restaurant
4. school
5. street
6. supermarket

Page 59, Exercise 2B – CD1, Track 52

1. A Where's the school?
   B The school? It's on Main Street.
   A Thanks.
2. A Where's the restaurant?
   B The restaurant? I don't know.
   A OK. Thank you.
3. A Where's the library?
   B The library's on Market Street.
   A Thanks a lot.
4. A Where's the supermarket?
   B Sorry, I don't know.
   A Thanks, anyway.

Page 60, Exercise 1 – CD1, Track 53

1. pharmacy
2. hospital
3. laundromat
4. post office
5. movie theater
6. gas station

Page 61, Exercise 2B – CD1, Track 54

1. A Where's Minh?
   B At the movie theater.
2. A Where's Alan?
   B At the hospital.
3. A Where's Mr. Lopez?
   B At the pharmacy.
4. A Where's Paula?
   B At the laundromat.
5. A Where's Jackie?
   B At the post office.
6. A Where's Isabel?
   B At the gas station.

Page 62, Exercise 2A – CD1, Track 55

1. A Where's the pharmacy?
   B Between the restaurant and the supermarket.
2. A Where's the supermarket?
   B On Main Street.
3. A Where's the restaurant?
   B Next to the pharmacy.
4. A Where's the bakery?
   B Across from the restaurant.
5. A Where's the police station?
   B Next to the bakery.

Page 63, Exercise 2B – CD1, Track 56

1. A Excuse me. Where's the bank?
   B Next to the supermarket.
   A Thanks.
2. A Excuse me. Where's the restaurant?
   B Across from the bank.
   A Thanks.
3. A Excuse me. Where's the bank?
   B Between the pharmacy and the supermarket.
   A Thanks.
4. A Excuse me. Where's the police station?
   B On Park Street.
   A Thanks.
5. A Excuse me. Where's the bakery?
   B Next to the restaurant.
   A Thanks.

6. **A** Excuse me. Where's the supermarket?
   B Across from the bakery.
   A Thanks.

Page 64, Exercise 2 – CD1, Track 57

Notice from Riverside Library

Come and visit Riverside Library. The new library opens today. The library is on Main Street. It is across from Riverside Adult School. It is next to K and P Supermarket. It is between K and P Supermarket and Rosie's Restaurant. The library is open from 9:00 to 5:00, Monday, Wednesday, and Friday.

Page 65, Exercise 4A – CD1, Track 58

1. by bicycle
2. by bus
3. by car
4. by taxi
5. by train
6. on foot

Unit 6: Time

Page 70, Exercise 1B – CD2, Track 2

Seven o'clock, nine o'clock, ten o'clock, ten-thirty, two-thirty, six-thirty

Page 71, Exercise 2A – CD2, Track 3

1. seven o'clock 4. ten-thirty
2. nine o'clock 5. two-thirty
3. ten o'clock 6. six-thirty

Page 71, Exercise 2B – CD2, Track 4

1. **A** What time is it?
   B It's nine o'clock.
2. **A** Excuse me. What time is it?
   B It's ten-thirty.
3. **A** What time is it?
   B It's two-thirty.
4. **A** Excuse me. What time is it?
   B It's ten o'clock.

Page 72, Exercise 1 – CD2, Track 5

1. appointment 4. movie
2. meeting 5. party
3. class 6. TV show

Page 73, Exercise 2B – CD2, Track 6

1. **A** What time is the appointment?
   B At one-thirty on Friday.
2. **A** What time is the class?
   B At eight-thirty on Friday.
3. **A** What time is the TV show?
   B At four-thirty on Friday.
4. **A** What time is the meeting?
   B At three o'clock on Saturday.
5. **A** What time is the movie?
   B At nine o'clock on Saturday.
6. **A** What time is the party?
   B At five o'clock on Saturday.

Page 74, Exercise 2A – CD2, Track 7

1. **A** Is your class at eleven o'clock?
   B Yes, it is.
2. **A** Is your appointment at twelve-thirty?
   B No, it isn't.
3. **A** Is your concert at eight o'clock?
   B No, it isn't.
4. **A** Is your movie at six o'clock?
   B Yes, it is.
5. **A** Is your party at four o'clock?
   B Yes, it is.
6. **A** Is your TV show at seven-thirty?
   B No, it isn't.

Page 76, Exercise 2 – CD2, Track 8

Teresa's Day

Teresa is busy today. Her meeting with her friend Joan is at 10:00 in the morning. Her doctor's appointment is at 1:00 in the afternoon. Her favorite TV show is at 4:30. Her class is at 6:30 in the evening. Her uncle's birthday party is also at 6:30. Oh, no! What will she do?

Page 77, Exercise 4A – CD2, Track 9

1. in the morning
2. in the afternoon
3. in the evening
4. at noon
5. at night
6. at midnight

Review: Units 5 and 6

Page 82, Exercise 1 – CD2, Track 10

1. **A** When is the meeting with Mr. Johnson?
   B On Friday.
2. **A** Is the meeting at two-thirty?
   B No, it isn't. It's at ten-thirty.
3. **A** Is your appointment at two o'clock?
   B Yes, It is.
4. **A** Excuse me. Where's the school?
   B Across from the bank.
   A Thanks.
5. **A** Where are you?
   B At the movie theater.
   A Next to the supermarket?
   B Right.
6. **A** What time is the movie?
   B Seven-thirty.

Page 83, Exercise 4A – CD2, Track 11

/æ/ at
/ɒ/ on

Page 83, Exercise 4B – CD2, Track 12

/æ/ at /ɒ/ on
/æ/ class /ɒ/ clock
/æ/ map /ɒ/ not

Page 83, Exercise 4C – CD2, Track 13

1. not
2. clock
3. at
4. class
5. on

Unit 7: Shopping

Page 84, Exercise 1B – CD2, Track 14

A dress, pants, a shirt, shoes, socks, a T-shirt

Page 85, Exercise 2A – CD2, Track 15

1. a dress
2. pants
3. a shirt
4. shoes
5. socks
6. a T-shirt

Page 85, Exercise 2B – CD2, Track 16

1. A How much is the shirt?
   B The shirt? Nineteen dollars.
2. A How much are the socks?
   B The socks? One ninety-nine.
3. A How much is the dress?
   B The dress? Thirty-nine ninety-nine.
4. A How much are the pants?
   B The pants? Twenty-four ninety-nine.

Page 86, Exercise 1 – CD2, Track 17

1. a tie
2. a blouse
3. a sweater
4. a skirt
5. a jacket
6. a raincoat

Page 87, Exercise 2B – CD2, Track 18

1. A How much is the tie?
   B The tie is nine ninety-nine.
2. A How much is the raincoat?
   B The raincoat is twenty-six ninety-five.
3. A How much is the skirt?
   B The skirt is thirty-five ninety-five.
4. A How much is the sweater?
   B The sweater is thirty-nine ninety-nine.
5. A How much is the jacket?
   B The jacket is forty-eight ninety-nine.
6. A How much is the blouse?
   B The blouse is twenty-five ninety-five.

Page 88, Exercise 2A – CD2, Track 19

1. A How much are the pants?
   B Twenty-four ninety-nine.
2. A How much is the skirt?
   B Eighteen ninety-nine.
3. A How much is the raincoat?
   B Sixteen ninety-five.
4. A How much are the shoes?
   B Fifty-eight ninety-nine.
5. A How much is the sweater?
   B Thirty-one ninety-nine.
6. A How much are the socks?
   B Five ninety-five.

Page 89, Exercise 2B – CD2, Track 20

1. A How much is the T-shirt?
   B Two dollars.
   A Two dollars? Thanks.
2. A How much are the shoes?
   B Three dollars.
   A Three dollars? Thanks.
3. A How much is the jacket?
   B Eight dollars.
   A Eight dollars? Thanks.
4. A How much is the sweater?
   B Four dollars.
   A Four dollars? Thanks.
5. A How much is the raincoat?
   B Five dollars.
   A Five dollars? Thanks.
6. A How much are the pants?
   B Six dollars.
   A Six dollars? Thanks.
7. A How much are the socks?
   B One dollar.
   A One dollar? Thanks.
8. A How much is the blouse?
   B Seven dollars.
   A Seven dollars? Thanks.

Page 90, Exercise 2 – CD2, Track 21

Hi Patty,

This morning, Samuel and I are going to The Clothes Place. Samuel needs blue pants. He needs a tie, too. I need a red dress and black shoes. Dresses are on sale. They're $49.99. Shoes are on sale, too. They're $34.99. That's good.

Call you later,

Rose

Page 91, Exercise 4A – CD2, Track 22

1. black
2. white
3. yellow
4. orange
5. brown
6. green
7. blue
8. purple
9. pink
10. red

Unit 8: Work

Page 96, Exercise 1B – CD2, Track 23

Cashier, custodian, mechanic, receptionist, salesperson, server

Page 97, Exercise 2A – CD2, Track 24

1. cashier
2. custodian
3. mechanic
4. receptionist
5. salesperson
6. server

Page 97, Exercise 2B – CD2, Track 25

1. A What does he do?
   B He's a server.
2. A What does she do?
   B She's a receptionist.
3. A What's his job?
   B He's a custodian.
4. A What's her job?
   B She's a mechanic.

Page 98, Exercise 1 – CD2, Track 26

1. She answers the phone.
2. She counts money.
3. He fixes cars.
4. He cleans buildings.
5. She sells clothes.
6. He serves food.

Page 99, Exercise 2B – CD2, Track 27

1. A What does Sandra do?
   B She counts money.
2. A What does Stephanie do?
   B She serves food.
3. A What does Alba do?
   B She answers the phone.

4. **A** What does Oscar do?
   B He sells clothes.
5. **A** What does Tim do?
   B He cleans buildings.
6. **A** What does Ahmad do?
   B He fixes cars.

Page 100, Exercise 2A – CD2, Track 28

1. **A** Does he serve food?
   B No, he doesn't.
2. **A** Does he clean buildings?
   B Yes, he does.
3. **A** Does she answer the phone?
   B Yes, she does.
4. **A** Does he sell clothes?
   B Yes, he does.
5. **A** Does she fix cars?
   B No, she doesn't.

Page 101, Exercise 2B – CD2, Track 29

1. **A** Does he sell clothes?
   B No, he doesn't.
2. **A** Does he fix cars?
   B No, he doesn't.
3. **A** Does he clean buildings?
   B No, he doesn't.
4. **A** Does he serve food?
   B No, he doesn't.
5. **A** Does he count money?
   B No, he doesn't.
6. **A** Does he answer the phone?
   B Yes, he does.

Page 102, Exercise 2 – CD2, Track 30

Employee of the Month: Sara Lopez

Congratulations, Sara Lopez – Employee of the Month! Sara is a salesperson. She sells clothes. Sara's whole family works here at Shop Smart. Her father is a custodian, and her mother is a receptionist. Her Uncle Eduardo is a server. He serves food. Her sister Lucy is a cashier. She counts money. Her brother Leo fixes cars. He's a mechanic. Everybody in the store knows the Lopez family!

Page 103, Exercise 4A – CD2, Track 31

1. bus driver
2. homemaker
3. painter
4. plumber
5. teacher's aide
6. truck driver

Review: Units 7 and 8

Page 108, Exercise 1 – CD2, Track 32

1. **A** Chul, what's your job?
   B I'm a cashier at City Café.
2. **A** What do you do, Chul?
   B I count money.
3. **A** Luz, what's your job?
   B I'm a receptionist at Shop Smart.
4. **A** What do you do, Luz?
   B I answer phones.
5. **A** Look! Pants are on sale.
   B What color are the pants?
   A They're blue.
6. **A** Excuse me. How much are the pants?
   B They're nineteen ninety-nine.
   A Nineteen ninety-nine? Thanks.

Page 109, Exercise 4A – CD2, Track 33

/e/ red
/ɪ/ six
/ʌ/ bus

Page 109, Exercise 4B – CD2, Track 34

/e/ red	/ɪ/ his
/e/ when	/ʌ/ bus
/ɪ/ six	/ʌ/ much

Page 109, Exercise 4C – CD2, Track 35

1. red
2. much
3. his
4. six
5. when

Unit 9: Daily living

Page 110, Exercise 1B – CD2, Track 36

Doing homework, doing the laundry, drying the dishes, making lunch, making the bed, washing the dishes

Page 111, Exercise 2A – CD2, Track 37

1. doing homework
2. doing the laundry
3. drying the dishes
4. making lunch
5. making the bed
6. washing the dishes

Page 111, Exercise 2B – CD2, Track 38

1. **A** What's she doing?
   B She's doing homework.
2. **A** What's he doing?
   B He's washing the dishes.
3. **A** What's she doing?
   B She's making the bed.
4. **A** What's he doing?
   B He's making lunch.

Page 112, Exercise 1 – CD2, Track 39

1. cutting the grass
2. getting the mail
3. taking out the trash
4. walking the dog
5. washing the car
6. watering the grass

Page 113, Exercise 2B – CD2, Track 40

1. **A** What is Mrs. Navarro doing?
   B Watering the grass.
2. **A** What is Mr. Navarro doing?
   B Cutting the grass.
3. **A** What is Roberto doing?
   B Washing the car.
4. **A** What is Diego doing?
   B Taking out the trash.
5. **A** What is Norma doing?
   B Getting the mail.
6. **A** What is Rita doing?
   B Walking the dog.

Page 114, Exercise 2A – CD2, Track 41

1. A What are they doing?
   B Making dinner.
   A What is he doing?
   B Washing the dishes.
2. A What are they doing?
   B Making the bed.
   A What is he doing?
   B Taking out the trash.
3. A What is he doing?
   B Washing the car.
   A What is she doing?
   B Watering the grass.

Page 115, Exercise 2B – CD2, Track 42

1. A What are they doing?
   B Getting the mail.
2. A What is he doing?
   B Making lunch.
3. A What are they doing?
   B Cutting the grass.
4. A What is she doing?
   B Doing the laundry.
5. A What is she doing?
   B Drying the dishes.
6. A What are they doing?
   B Taking out the trash.

Page 116, Exercise 2 – CD2, Track 43

Dear Susie,

It's after dinner. My family is working in the kitchen. My daughter Li is washing the dishes. My daughter Mei is drying the dishes. My husband and Tao are taking out the trash. Where is my oldest son? He isn't in the kitchen. He is sleeping in the living room! I am not happy.

I need help. What can I do?

Huan

Page 117, Exercise 4A – CD2, Track 44

1. bathroom
2. bedroom
3. living room
4. laundry room
5. kitchen
6. dining room

Unit 10: Free time

Page 122, Exercise 1B – CD2, Track 45

Dance, exercise, fish, play basketball, play cards, swim

Page 123, Exercise 2A – CD2, Track 46

1. dance
2. exercise
3. fish
4. play basketball
5. play cards
6. swim

Page 123, Exercise 2B – CD2, Track 47

1. A Do you like to dance?
   B Yes, we do.
2. A Do you like to play cards?
   B Yes, we do.
3. A What do you like to do?
   B I like to fish.
4. A What do you like to do?
   B I like to swim.

Page 124, Exercise 1 – CD2, Track 48

1. cook
2. play the guitar
3. listen to music
4. watch TV
5. read magazines
6. work in the garden

Page 125, Exercise 2B – CD2, Track 49

1. A What does Pablo like to do?
   B Watch TV.
2. A What does Tom like to do?
   B Work in the garden.
3. A What does Rashid like to do?
   B Play the guitar.
4. A What does Estela like to do?
   B Listen to music.
5. A What does Ling like to do?
   B Read magazines.
6. A What does Farah like to do?
   B Cook.

Page 126, Exercise 2A – CD2, Track 50

1. A What do they like to do?
   B They like to play basketball.
2. A What does she like to do?
   B She likes to swim.
3. A What does he like to do?
   B He likes to play cards.
4. A What does she like to do?
   B She likes to fish.
5. A What do they like to do?
   B They like to dance.

Page 127, Exercise 2B – CD2, Track 51

1. A What does he like to do?
   B He likes to exercise.
2. A What does he like to do?
   B He likes to cook.
3. A What do they like to do?
   B They like to play cards.
4. A What does she like to do?
   B She likes to work in the garden.
5. A What does he like to do?
   B He likes to swim.
6. A What do they like to do?
   B They like to play soccer.

Page 128, Exercise 2 – CD2, Track 52

Hi Miriam,

I'm not working today. It's my day off. Are you busy? Come and visit me!

What do you like to do? I like to cook. I like to play cards. I like to listen to music and dance. I like to watch TV. Do you like to watch TV?

Please call me at 10:00.

See you soon!

Lupe

Page 129, Exercise 4A – CD2, Track 53

1. go to the movies
2. go online
3. shop
4. travel
5. visit friends
6. volunteer

Review: Units 9 and 10

Page 134, Exercise 1 – CD2, Track 54

1. A What are you doing, Marco?
   B Washing the car.
   A It's your day off! You need to relax.
2. A Marco, what do you like to do?
   B I like to play the guitar.
3. A Ricky, are you busy?
   B Yes. I'm making the bed.
4. A Fred, what are you doing?
   B I'm reading magazines in the living room.
5. A What do you like to do, Tina?
   B I like to cook.
6. A Tina, what do you like to do on the weekend?
   B I like to dance.

Page 135, Exercise 4A – CD2, Track 55

/eɪ/ name	/ɪ/ six
/æ/ at	/oʊ/ phone
/iː/ read	/ɒ/ on
/e/ red	/uː/ June
/aɪ/ five	/ʌ/ bus

Page 135, Exercise 4B – CD2, Track 56

/eɪ/ name	/ɪ/ six
/æ/ at	/oʊ/ phone
/iː/ read	/ɒ/ on
/e/ red	/uː/ June
/aɪ/ five	/ʌ/ bus

Tests

Overview

The unit tests, midterm test, and final test help teachers assess students' mastery of the material in the *Ventures Basic* Student's Book.

- Each of the ten unit tests covers one unit.
- The midterm test covers Units 1–5.
- The final test covers Units 6–10.
- Each test assesses listening, grammar, reading, and writing, with real-life documents incorporated into the reading and writing sections.

Students' performance on the tests helps to determine what has been successfully learned and what may need more attention. Successful completion of a test can also give students a sense of accomplishment.

Getting ready for a test

- Plan to give a unit test shortly after students have completed a unit and have had time for a review. The midterm should follow completion of Unit 5 and the review lesson for Units 5 and 6. The final test should follow completion of Unit 10 and the review lesson for Units 9 and 10. Tell students when the test will be given. Encourage students to study together and to ask you for help if needed.
- Explain the purpose of the test and how students' scores will be used.
- Prepare one test for each student. The tests may be photocopied from the Teacher's Edition, starting on page T-165, or printed from the Assessment Audio CD / CD-ROM.
- Schedule approximately 30 minutes for each unit test and 1 hour for the midterm and final tests. Allow more time if needed.
- Locate the audio program for each test's listening section on the Assessment Audio CD / CD-ROM. The CD is a hybrid. It will work in both a stereo and a computer CD-ROM drive.

Giving a test

- During the test, have students use a pencil and an eraser. Tell students to put away their Student's Books and dictionaries before the test.
- Hand out one copy of the test to each student.
- Encourage students to take a few minutes to look through the test without answering any of the items. Go through the instructions to make sure students understand them.
- Tell students that approximately 5 minutes of the unit test (10 minutes of the midterm and final tests) will be used for the listening section.
- When playing the listening section of the test, you may choose to pause or repeat the audio program if you feel that students require more time to answer. The audio script appears in the Teacher's Edition on page T-203. The script can also be printed from the Assessment Audio CD / CD-ROM and read aloud in class.

Scoring

- You can collect the tests and grade them on your own. Alternatively, you can have students correct their own tests by going over the answers in class or by having students exchange tests with a partner and correcting each other's answers. The answer key is located in the Teacher's Edition on page T-205. It can also be printed from the Assessment Audio CD / CD-ROM.
- Each test has a total score of 100 points. Each unit test has five sections worth 20 points each. The midterm and final tests have eight sections worth 10 or 15 points each.

Track list for test audio program

Track 1: Introduction
Track 2: Unit 1 Test
Track 3: Unit 2 Test
Track 4: Unit 3 Test
Track 5: Unit 4 Test
Track 6: Unit 5 Test
Track 7: Midterm Test, Section A
Track 8: Midterm Test, Section B
Track 9: Unit 6 Test
Track 10: Unit 7 Test
Track 11: Unit 8 Test
Track 12: Unit 9 Test
Track 13: Unit 10 Test
Track 14: Final Test, Section A
Track 15: Final Test, Section B

Name: ______________________

Date: ______________________

Score: ____________

TEST UNIT 1 Personal information

A Listening

TRACK 2

Listen and circle.

1. a. 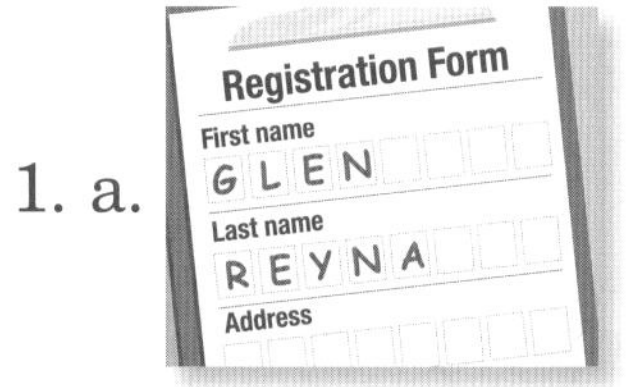

Registration Form
First name
GLEN
Last name
REYNA
Address

b.

Class Sign Up

First name	Last name
Pilar	Mendez

2. a. 

b. 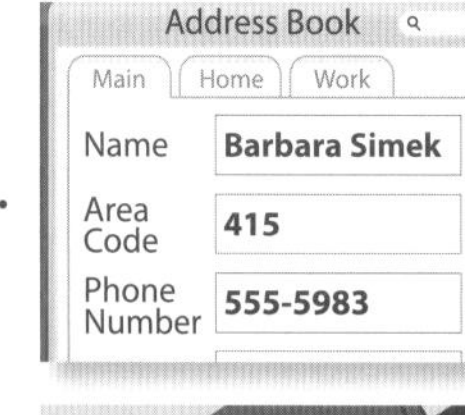

Address Book
Main | Home | Work

Name	Barbara Simek
Area Code	415
Phone Number	555-5983

3. a. 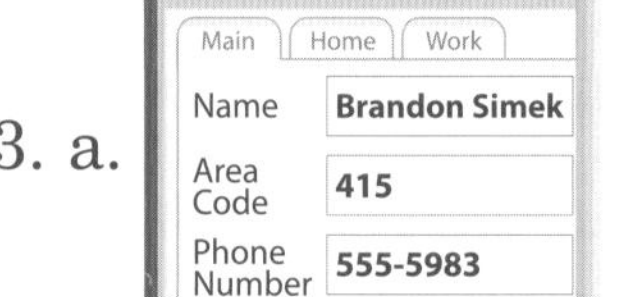

Address Book
Main | Home | Work

Name	Brandon Simek
Area Code	415
Phone Number	555-5983

b. 

4. a.

July

1	2	3	4	5	6	7
8	9	10	11	12	13	14
15	16	17	18	19	20	21
22	23	24	25	26	27	28
29	30	31				

b. 

June

					1	2
3	4	5	6	7	8	9
10	11	12	13	14	15	16
17	18	19	20	21	22	23
24	25	26	27	28	29	30

5. a. 

China

b. 

Somalia

B Vocabulary

Read and write.

Name	Country
1. Ivan	
2. Asad	
3. Eduardo	

Name	Country
4. Elsa	
5. Luisa	
6. Jun-Ming	

Name: ______________________

Date: ______________________

C Grammar

Read and circle. Then write.

1. **A** What's her name?

   B ______________ name is Luisa.
   Her His

2. **A** What's my area code?

   B ______________ area code is 415.
   Your My

3. **A** What's his last name?

   B ______________ last name is Delgado.
   Her His

4. **A** ______________ your name?
   What What's

   B My name is Nancy.

5. **A** What's your name?

   B ______________ name is Angela.
   My Your

D Reading

A New Student

Meet our new student. Her first name is Ling. Her last name is Lee. She is from China. Her birthday is in May. Welcome, Ling!

Read the sentences. Circle *Yes* or *No*.

1. Her name is Ling Chin.	Yes	No
2. Her first name is Chin.	Yes	No
3. Her last name is Lee.	Yes	No
4. She is from China.	Yes	No
5. Her birthday is in March.	Yes	No

Name: ______________________

Date: ______________________

E Writing

Read the ID card. Then complete the sentences.

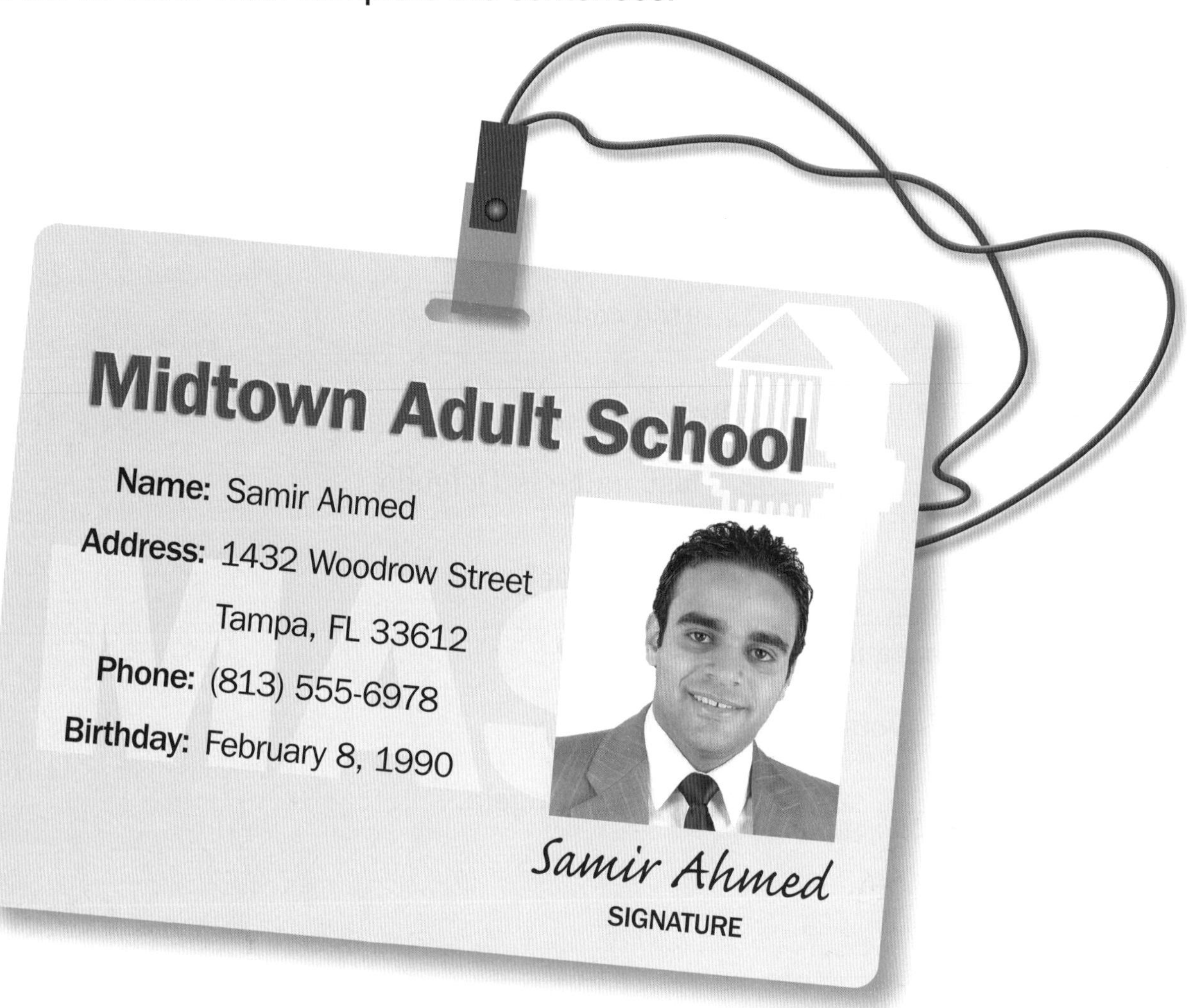

1. His first name is ______________________.
2. His last name is ______________________.
3. His area code is ______________________.
4. His telephone number is ______________________.
5. His birthday is in ______________________.

Name: ____________________

Date: ____________________

Score: ____________________

TEST UNIT 2 At school

A Listening

Listen and circle.

TRACK 3

1. a.  b. 

2. a.  b. 

3. a.  b. 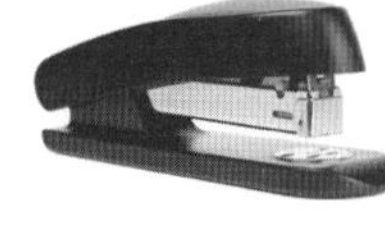

4. a. 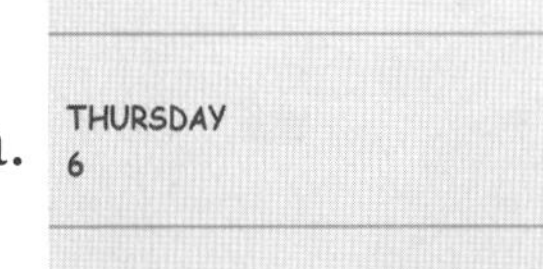

b. 

5. a. 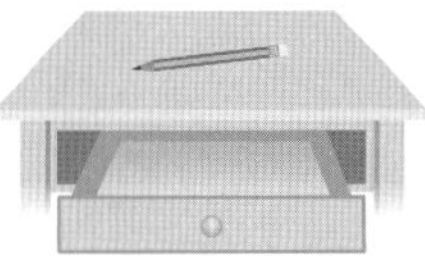 b. 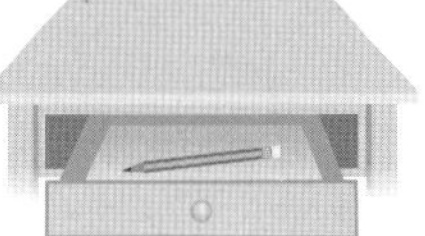

B Vocabulary

Read and match.

1. 

2. 

3.

dictionary

Friday

computer

Tuesday

desk

4. 

5. 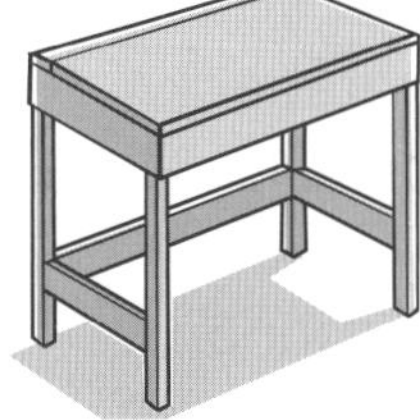

Name: ______________________

Date: ______________________

C Grammar

Read the sentences. Choose *in*, *on*, or *under*.

1. The dictionary is in / on / under the floor.
2. The paper is in / on / under the desk.
3. The chair is in / on / under the notebook.
4. The pencil is in / on / under the desk.
5. The notebook is in / on / under the eraser.

D Reading

Welcome to Community Adult School!

Your teacher is Ms. Angela Delgado.
Your first day of class is Tuesday.
Your class is in Room 203.
For class, you need:
- a notebook
- a pencil
- an eraser
- a dictionary

Read the sentences. Circle *Yes* or *No*.

1. The teacher is Mr. Delgado.	Yes	No
2. The first day of class is Tuesday.	Yes	No
3. The class is in Room 302.	Yes	No
4. You need a pencil.	Yes	No
5. You need a ruler.	Yes	No

Name: ______________________________

Date: ______________________

E Writing

Look at the picture. Complete the letter to Carla.

chair	desk	dictionary	floor	notebook

Carla,

You need a dictionary. It's on the _______________(1). You need a stapler. It's on the _______________(2). You need an eraser. It's on the _______________(3). You need a ruler. It's in the _______________(4). You need a notebook. It's under the _______________(5). Have fun at school!

Love,

Mom

Name: ____________________

Date: ____________________

Score: ____________________

TEST

UNIT 3 Friends and family

A Listening

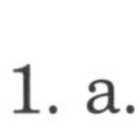

TRACK 4

Listen and circle.

1. a.  b. 

4. a.   b. 

2. a.  b. 

5. a.  b. 

3. a.  b. 

B Vocabulary

Look at the picture. Read and match.

1. Ramona is	Ramona's grandmother.
2. Pilar is	Pilar's husband.
3. Hugo is	Geraldo's daughter.
4. Magdalena is	Ramona's mother.
5. Geraldo is	Geraldo's father.

Name: ______________________

Date: ______________________

C Grammar

Read and circle. Then write.

1. **A** Do you have a brother?

   B Yes, we ______________.
   do don't

2. **A** Do you have a grandfather?

   B Yes, I ______________.
   do don't

3. **A** Do you have a daughter?

   B No, I ______________.
   do don't

4. **A** Do you have a wife?

   B Yes, I ______________.
   do don't

5. **A** Do you have a son?

   B No, we ______________.
   do don't

D Reading

About My Family

My name is Ken. I have a nice family. I have a daughter. Her name is Cindy. I have a son, Danny. I have a wife. Her name is Felicia. I have a brother, too. His name is Mark. Mark has a wife. Her name is Diana. I love my family!

Read the sentences. Circle *Yes* or *No*.

1. Cindy is Ken's daughter.	Yes	No
2. Ken is Danny's father.	Yes	No
3. Felicia is Ken's husband.	Yes	No
4. Ken and Mark are brothers.	Yes	No
5. Mark is Felicia's husband.	Yes	No

Name: ______________________

Date: ______________________

E Writing

Look at the picture. Complete the story.

daughter   family   husband   sister   son

My name is Carla. This is my ______(1)______. His name is Roberto. This is my ______(2)______, Alfredo. This is my ______(3)______. Her name is Inez. This is my ______(4)______, Gabriela. I love my ______(5)______!

Name: ____________________

Date: ____________________

Score: ____________________

TEST UNIT 4 Health

A Listening

Listen and circle.

TRACK 5

1. a.  b. 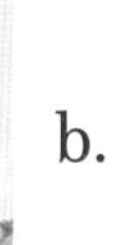 

4. a. 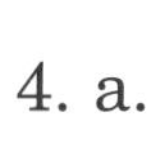 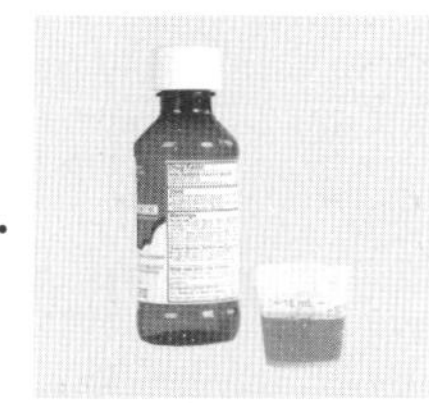 b.  

2. a. 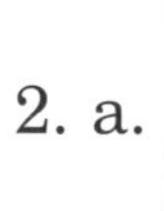 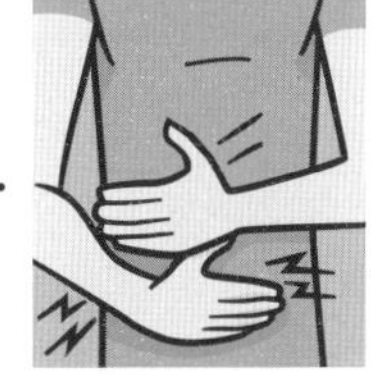 b. 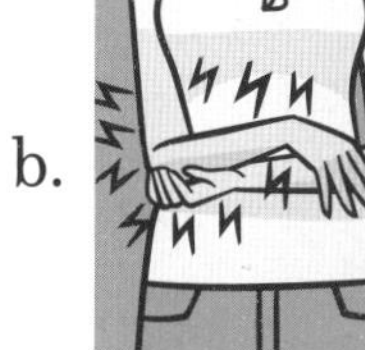

5. a. 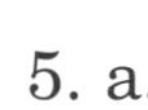  b.  

3. a. 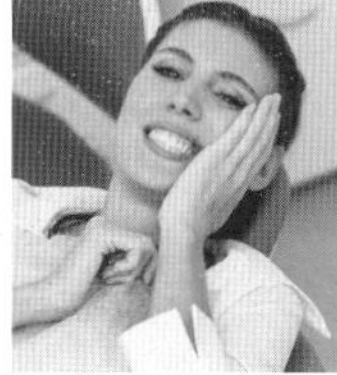 b. 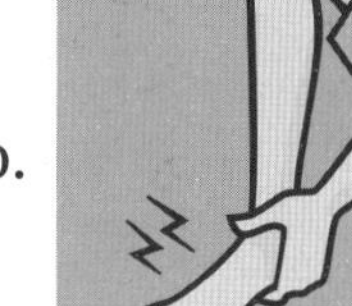

B Vocabulary

Read and match.

1.  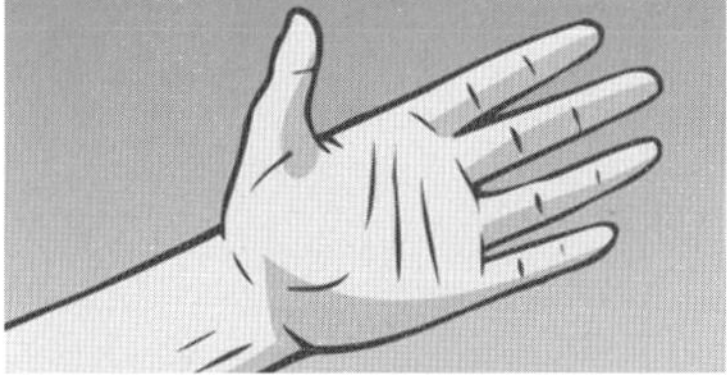

2. 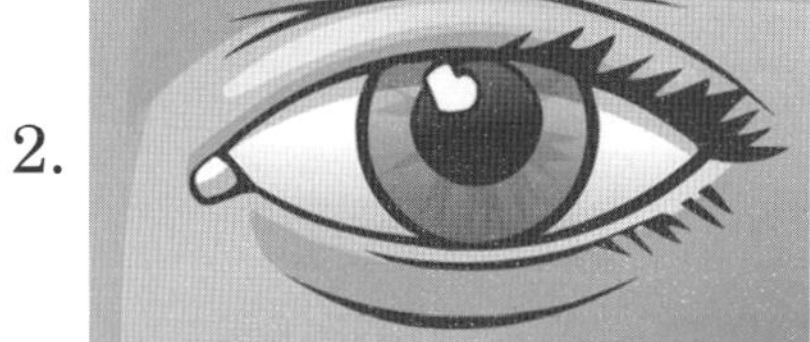

3. 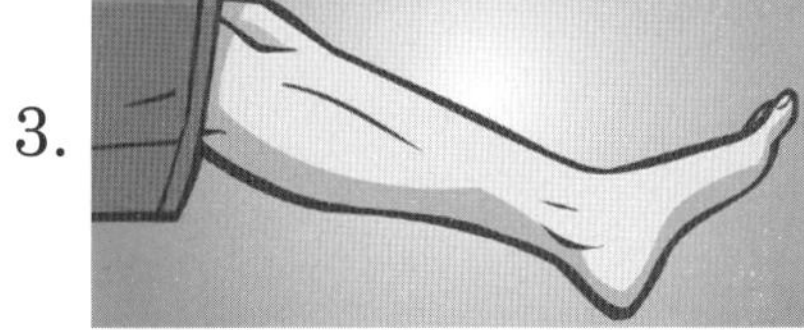

leg

foot

hand

eye

arm

4. 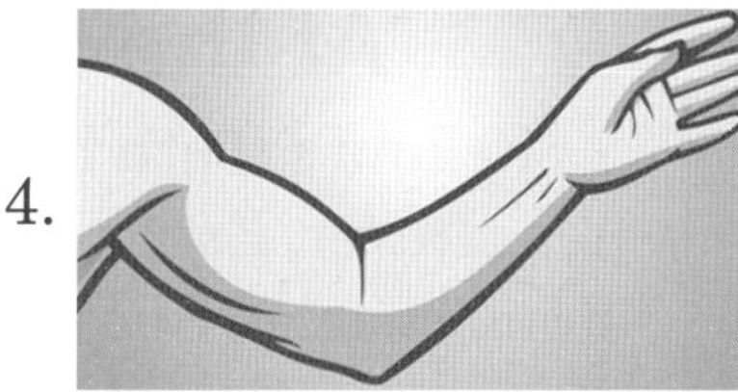

5.  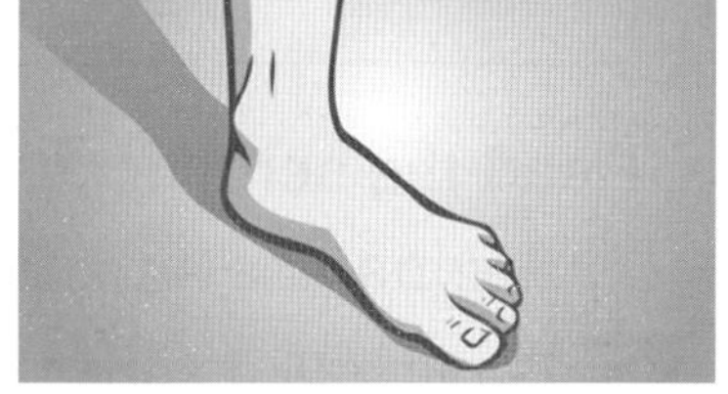

Name: ____________________

Date: ____________________

C Grammar

Read and circle. Then write.

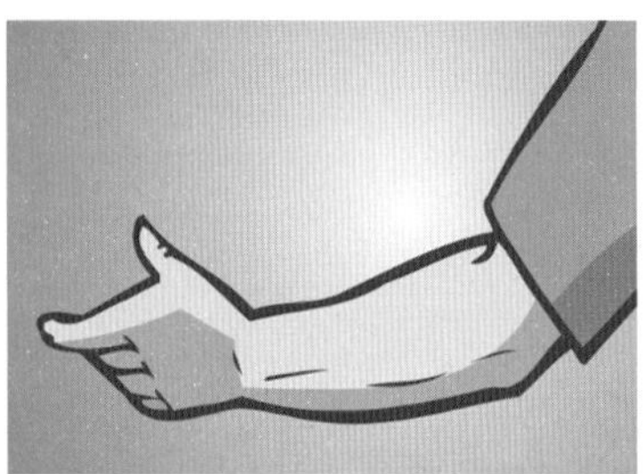

1. **A** What hurts?

   B My ______________.
   arm arms

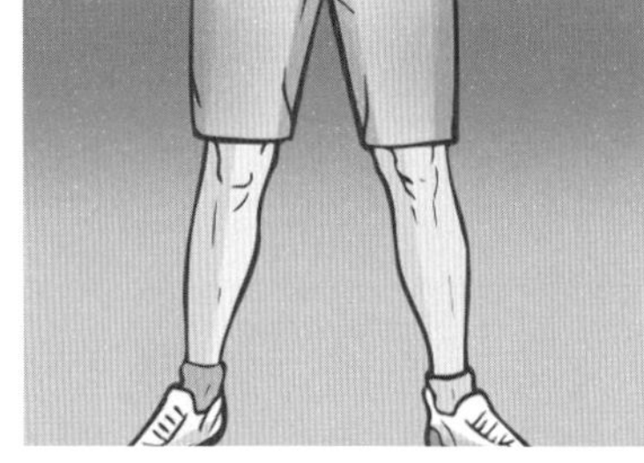

2. **A** What hurts?

   B My ______________.
   leg legs

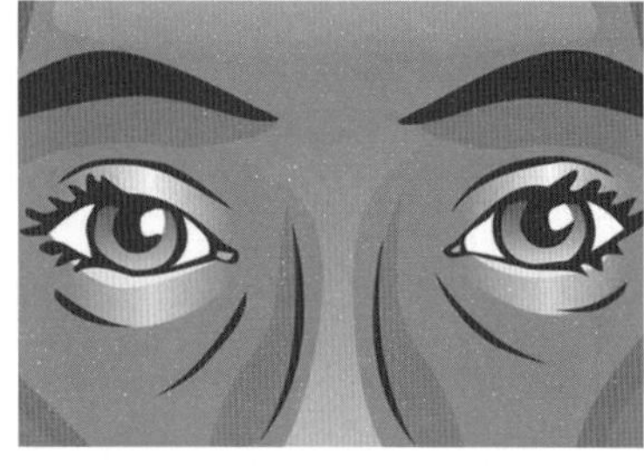

3. **A** What hurts?

   B My ______________.
   eye eyes

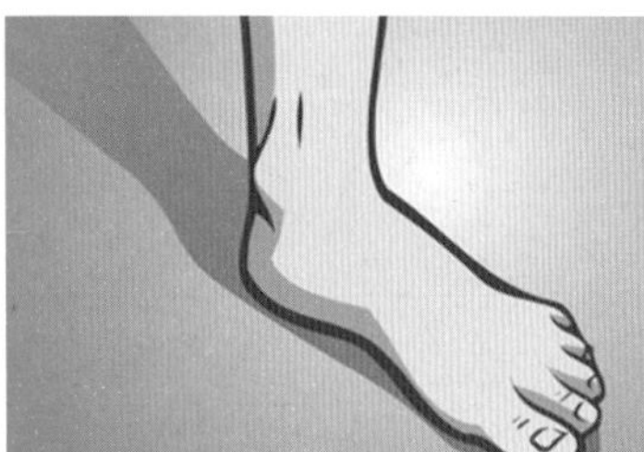

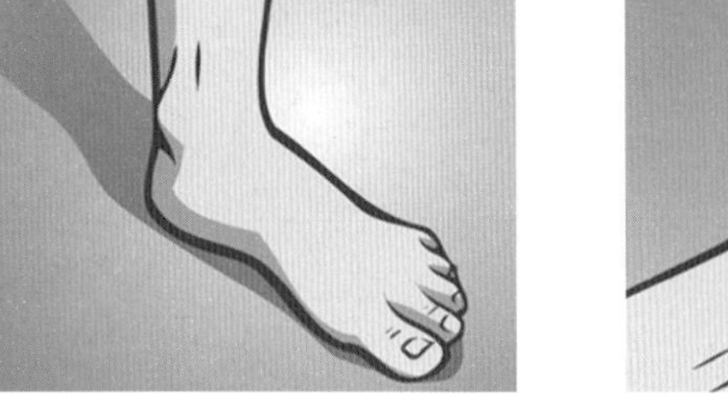

4. **A** What hurts?

   B My ______________.
   foot feet

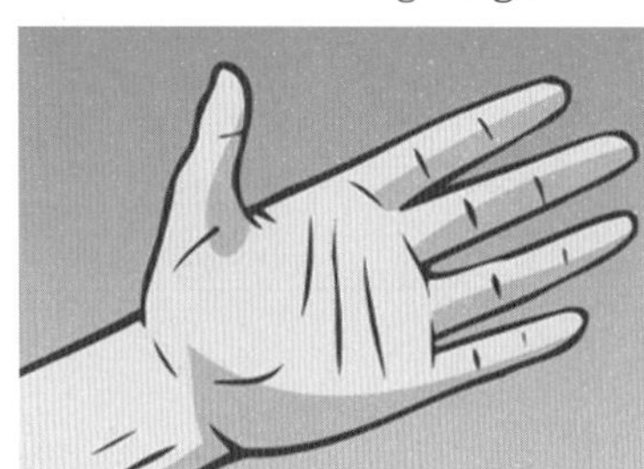

5. **A** What hurts?

   B My ______________.
   hand hands

D Reading

At the Doctor's Office

Regina's tooth hurts. Isaac's throat hurts. Joe has a fever. Esperanza has a cold. James has a stomachache. Sue's head hurts. It's not a good day at the doctor's office!

Read the sentences. Circle *Yes* or *No*.

1. Regina has a toothache.	Yes	No
2. Isaac has a sore throat.	Yes	No
3. Esperanza has a fever.	Yes	No
4. James has a toothache.	Yes	No
5. Sue has a headache.	Yes	No

Name: ____________________

Date: ____________________

E Writing

Look at the picture. Then complete the patient sign-in sheet.

cold	fever	sore throat	stomachache	toothache

Patient Sign-In Sheet

Name of Patient:	Reason for Visit:
Matt	I have a ____________.
Ella	I have a ____________.
Stefano	I have a ____________.
Reyna	I have a ____________.
Minh	I have a ____________.

Name: ____________________

Date: ____________________

Score: ____________________

TEST UNIT 5 Around town

A Listening

TRACK 6

Listen and circle.

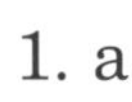

1. a. 

b. 

2. a. 

b. 

3. a. 

b. 

4. a. 

b. 

5. a. 
b. 

B Vocabulary

Read and match.

1. 

2. 

3. 

movie theater

by car

hospital

pharmacy

by train

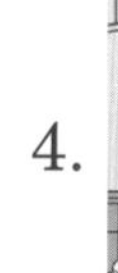

4. 

5. 

Name: ____________________

Date: ____________________

C Grammar

Look at the picture.

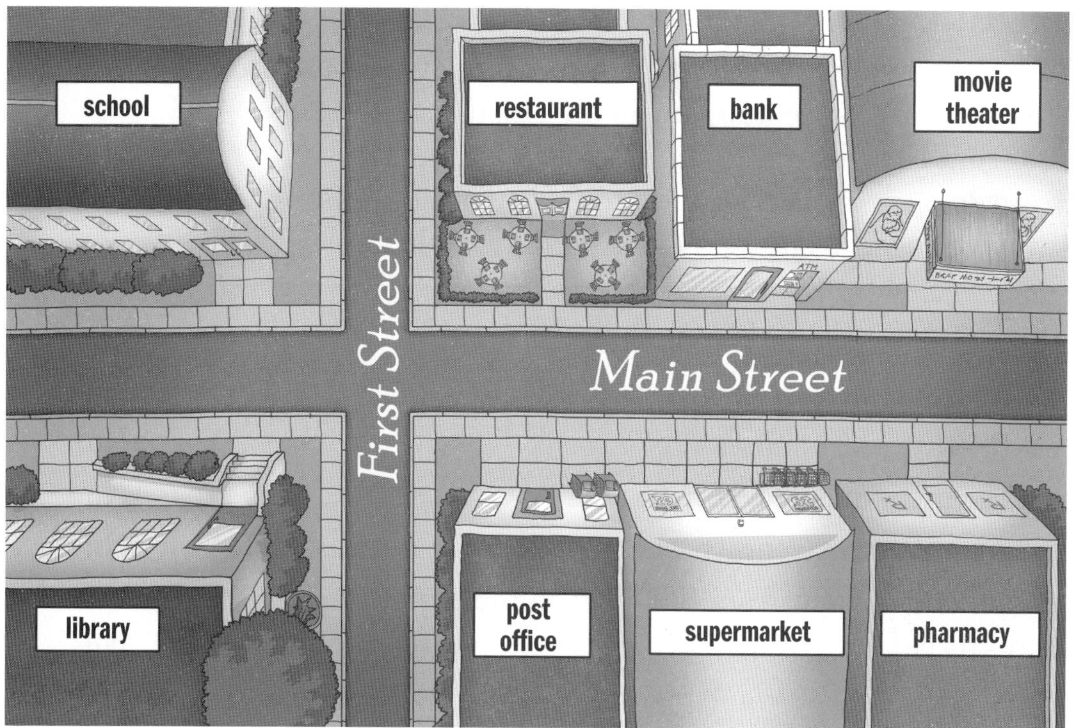

Read and circle. Then write.

1. **A** Where's the post office?

   B ____________________ the supermarket.
   Between   Next to

2. **A** Where's the school?

   B ____________________ the library.
   Next to   Across from

3. **A** Where's the pharmacy?

   B ____________________ Main Street.
   Next to   On

4. **A** Where's the supermarket?

   B ____________________ the post office and the pharmacy.
   On   Between

5. **A** Where's the bank?

   B Between the movie theater and the ____________________.
   pharmacy   restaurant

Name: ______________________

Date: ______________________

D Reading

> ### Notice from Enrico's Restaurant
> Come and visit Enrico's Restaurant. The new restaurant opens today. Enrico's Restaurant is on Third Street. It is across from the library. It is next to the bank. The restaurant is open from 8:00 a.m. to 9:00 p.m., Monday, Tuesday, Wednesday, Thursday, and Friday. Welcome!

Read the sentences. Circle *Yes* or *No*.

1. Enrico's Restaurant is a new restaurant. Yes No
2. Enrico's Restaurant opens today. Yes No
3. The restaurant is next to Third Street. Yes No
4. The restaurant is between the library and the bank. Yes No
5. The restaurant is open from 8:00 in the morning to 9:00 at night. Yes No

E Writing

Look at the picture. Complete the sentences.

by bicycle	by bus	by taxi	by train	on foot

1. Ted gets to school ______________________
2. Sam gets to school ______________________
3. Yoko gets to school ______________________
4. Martin gets to school ______________________
5. Katia gets to school ______________________

Name: ______________________

Date: ______________________

Score: ______________

MIDTERM TEST
UNITS 1–5

A Listening

TRACK 7

Listen and circle.

1. a.  b. 

2. a. 

b. 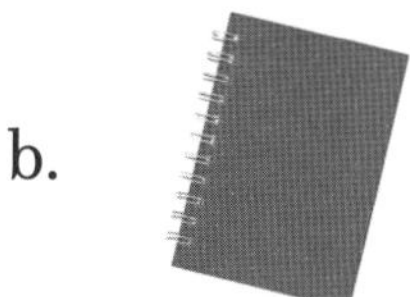

3. a.  b.

4. a. 

b. 

5. a. 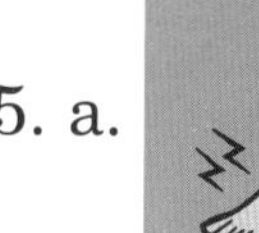 b. 

B Listening

TRACK 8

Listen and circle the answer.

1. a. Anita. b. Brazil.
2. a. My arm. b. Kim.
3. a. A patient. b. A pen.
4. a. On the desk. b. The United States.
5. a. Natalia's brother. b. By train.

C Vocabulary

Read and match.

1. 

2.

3. 

paper

headache

woman

school

car

4. 

5. 

Name: ______________________

Date: ______________________

D Grammar

Read and match. Write the letter.

1. Where's my pencil? ____
2. Who is Vincent? ____
3. Do you have a son? ____
4. What hurts? ____
5. Where's the library? ____

a. Yes, I do.
b. On First Street.
c. On the desk.
d. My son.
e. My hand.

E Reading

For relief of headaches and toothaches

20 tablets
Do not use after February 2016.

Read the sentences. Look at the label. Circle *Yes* or *No*.

1. This medicine is for headaches. Yes No
2. This medicine is for stomachaches. Yes No
3. This medicine is for toothaches. Yes No
4. Use after February 2016. Yes No
5. The name of the pharmacy is PPC. Yes No

Name: ______________________

Date: ______________________

F Reading

City Property Management
38 North Pine Street
Lancaster, PA 17111
(717) 555-4498

HOUSING APPLICATION

DIRECTIONS: Complete the form. Please print.

What is your name? *Ivan Mendoza*

Who will live with you in the house?

Name	Relationship
Elsa Mendoza	*wife*
Eduardo Mendoza	*father*
Ernesto Mendoza	*son*
Rosa Mendoza	*daughter*
Luisa Mendoza	*daughter*

Read the questions. Look at the housing application. Circle the answers.

1. Who is Elsa Mendoza?
   a. Ivan's wife   b. Ivan's husband
2. Who is Ivan's father?
   a. Ernesto   b. Eduardo
3. Who is Rosa Mendoza?
   a. Ivan's sister   b. Ivan's daughter
4. Who is Ernesto's sister?
   a. Luisa   b. Elsa
5. Who is Luisa's grandfather?
   a. Ivan   b. Eduardo

Name: ______________________

Date: ______________________

G Writing

Write the missing letters.

1. J a ___ u a ___ y
2. T u ___ ___ d a y
3. U n ___ t e d S t a t e ___
4. l ___ b r a ___ y
5. h ___ s p ___ t a l

H Writing

Complete the note.

eye	mother	needs	November	office

_______________ 15, 2013
(1)

Dear Mr. Garza,

I am Chi's _______________ (2). He is at the doctor's _______________ (3) today. His _______________ (4) hurts. He _______________ (5) medicine.

Thank you,

Mrs. Tran

Name: ______________________

Date: ______________________

Score: ______________________

TEST UNIT 6 Time

A Listening

TRACK 9

Listen and circle.

1. a. 

b. 2:30

4. a. 

b. 3 6:30 Tuesday

2. a. 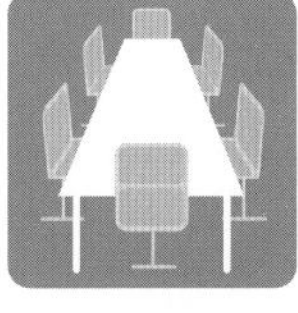 b. 

5. a.  b. 

3. a. 

b. 10:00

B Vocabulary

Read and match.

1. 

2. 

3. 

midnight

class

TV show

party

movie

4. 

5. 

Name: ______________________________

Date: ____________________

C Grammar

Read and circle. Then write.

1. **A** Is your appointment at 10:00?

   B ________________, it isn't.
   No Yes

2. **A** Is your class at 1:00?

   B ________________, it is.
   No Yes

3. **A** Is your concert at night?

   B No, ________________.
   it is it isn't

4. **A** Is your TV show at 5:00?

   B Yes, ________________.
   it is it isn't

5. **A** Is your party in the afternoon?

   B ________________, it is.
   No Yes

D Reading

It's a party!

Vincent is 40!

When: Friday, May 6
What time: 7:00 p.m.
Where: Jack's apartment

581 Spring Street
Apt. 5

RSVP: 555-3107

Read the sentences. Look at the invitation. Circle *Yes* or *No*.

1. It's Vincent's birthday party. Yes No
2. The party is for Jack. Yes No
3. The party is in the morning. Yes No
4. The party is at seven o'clock. Yes No
5. The party is at Jack's apartment. Yes No

Name: ____________________

Date: ____________________

E Writing

Complete the story.

afternoon	appointment	at	birthday	busy

Asad is busy today. His doctor's ________ (1) is at 8:00 a.m. His meeting with his friend Glen is at 10:30 a.m. His class is at 2:00 in the ________ (2). His meeting with his teacher is ________ (3) 4:00 p.m. His wife's ________ (4) party is at 6:00 p.m. He needs to go shopping! Asad is very ________ (5) today!

Name: ______________________

Date: ______________

Score: __________

TEST UNIT 7 Shopping

A Listening

Listen and circle.

TRACK 10

1. a.  b. 

4. a. 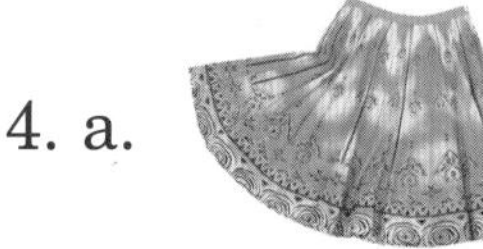 b. 

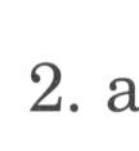

2. a.  b. 

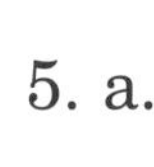

5. a.  b. 

3. a.  b. 

B Vocabulary

Read and match.

1. 

2. 

3. 

socks

sweater

blouse

skirt

tie

4. 

5. 

Name: ____________________

Date: ____________________

C Grammar

Read and circle. Then write.

1. How much ______________ the brown shoes?
   is are
2. How much ______________ the jacket?
   is are
3. How much ______________ the black dress?
   is are
4. How much ______________ the blue pants?
   is are
5. How much ______________ the skirt?
   is are

D Reading

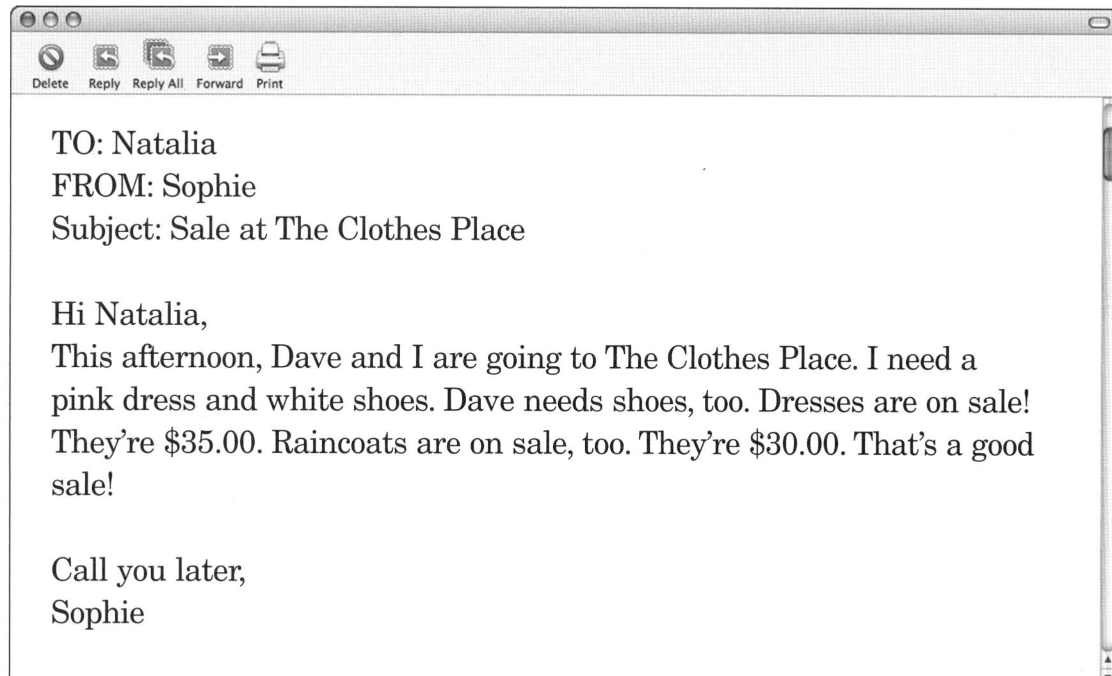

TO: Natalia
FROM: Sophie
Subject: Sale at The Clothes Place

Hi Natalia,
This afternoon, Dave and I are going to The Clothes Place. I need a pink dress and white shoes. Dave needs shoes, too. Dresses are on sale! They're $35.00. Raincoats are on sale, too. They're $30.00. That's a good sale!

Call you later,
Sophie

Read the sentences. Circle *Yes* or *No*.

1. Natalia and Dave are going to The Clothes Place today. Yes No
2. Sophie needs a pink dress. Yes No
3. Dave and Sophie need shoes. Yes No
4. Dresses are $30.00. Yes No
5. Raincoats are $30.00. Yes No

Name: ____________________

Date: ____________________

E Writing

Complete the story.

are	black	blouse	children	tie

Sheila and her ______(1)______ are going to The Clothes Place today. Her son needs a shirt and a ______(2)______. Her daughter needs a ______(3)______ and a ______(4)______ skirt. Her children need shoes. Shoes ______(5)______ on sale. They're $20.00!

Name: ______________________

Date: ______________________

Score: ______________

TEST UNIT 8 Work

A Listening

TRACK 11

Listen and circle.

1. a.  b. 
4. a.  b. 
2. a. 

b. 
5. a.  b. 
3. a. 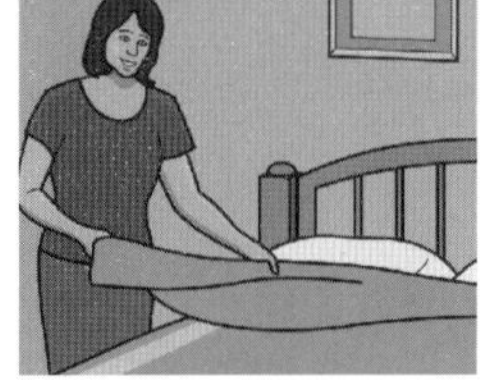 b. 

B Vocabulary

Read and match.

1. A server	sells clothes.
2. A custodian	serves food.
3. A mechanic	answers the phone.
4. A salesperson	cleans buildings.
5. A receptionist	fixes cars.

C Reading

Dear Aunt Kayla,

How are you? We are all well. We have new jobs! Allen is a mechanic. Sandra is a custodian. She doesn't work in the evening. Alba sells clothes at Shop Smart. I paint houses in the morning, and I go to school in the evening. We are busy! Write soon.

Love,
Brenda

Name: ______________________________

Date: ____________________

Read the sentences. Circle *Yes* or *No*.

1. Kayla fixes cars. Yes No
2. Sandra works in the evening. Yes No
3. Alba is a salesperson. Yes No
4. Brenda is a painter. Yes No
5. Allen is a student in the evening. Yes No

D Grammar

Read and circle. Then write.

1. 

A Does she serve food?

B No, she ________________.
does doesn't

2. 

A Does she answer the phone?

B Yes, she ________________.
does doesn't

3. 

A Does she fix cars?

B No, she ________________.
does doesn't

4. 

A Does he count money?

B ________________, he doesn't.
Yes No

5. 

A Does he clean buildings?

B ________________, he does.
Yes No

Name: ______________________

Date: ______________________

E Writing

Complete the story.

answers	clothes	homemaker	job	serves

Stephanie cleans her apartment. She takes the ______________ (1) to the laundromat. She goes to the supermarket. She ______________ (2) food to her family. She ______________ (3) the phone. What's her ______________ (4)? She's a ______________ (5)!

Name: ____________________

Date: ____________________

Score: ____________________

TEST UNIT 9 Daily living

A Listening

TRACK 12

Listen and circle.

1. a. 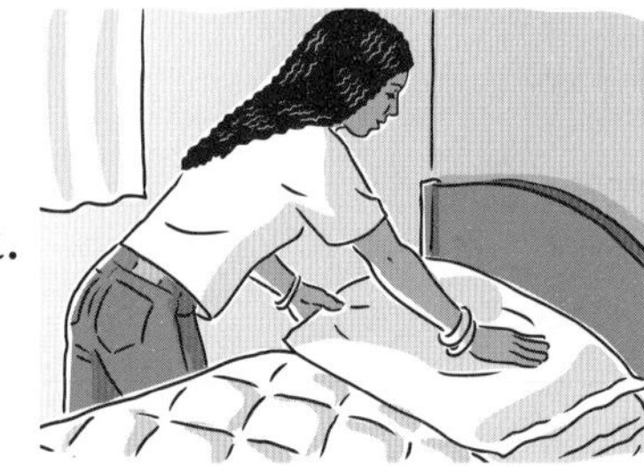 b. 

2. a.  b. 

3. a.  b. 

4. a.  b. 

5. a.  b. 

Name: ______________________

Date: ______________________

B Vocabulary

Read and match.

1. making	the mail
2. doing	the grass
3. walking	the laundry
4. getting	the bed
5. cutting	the dog

C Grammar

Read and circle. Then write.

1. What ______________ he doing?
   is are

2. ______________ out the trash.
   Cutting Taking

3. What ______________ they doing?
   is are

4. ______________ lunch.
   Making Washing

5. What ______________ Norma doing?
   is are

Name: ____________________

Date: ____________________

D Reading

TO: Felicia
FROM: Rita
Subject: My family

Felicia,
I have a cold today! My family is helping me. My daughter Kim is making the bed. My son is washing the dishes. My daughter Lynn is making lunch. My husband is doing the laundry. I have a wonderful family!

Talk to you soon,
Rita

Read the sentences. Circle *Yes* or *No*.

1. Rita has a cold. Yes No
2. Kim is in the bathroom. Yes No
3. Her son is in the kitchen. Yes No
4. Lynn is in the bedroom. Yes No
5. Her husband is in the laundry room. Yes No

E Writing

Complete the words.

do homework	take out the trash	water the grass
make lunch	wash the car	

1. w a ___ ___ t h e c ___ ___
2. ___ o ___ o m ___ w o ___ k
3. t ___ k ___ o u ___ t h e t r ___ s h
4. w ___ ___ er t h e ___ r a s ___
5. ___ ___ k e ___ ___ n c h

Name: ______________________

Date: ______________

Score: ________

TEST
UNIT 10 Free time

A Listening

Listen and circle.

TRACK 13

1. a.  b. 

4. a.   b. 

2. a. 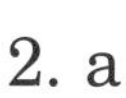  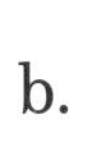 b. 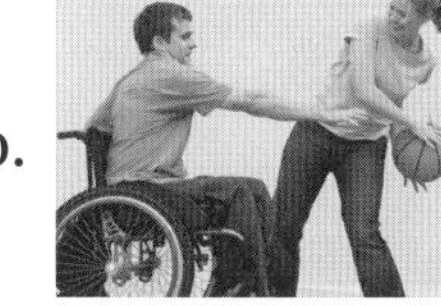

5. a.  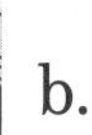 b. 

3. a.  b. 

B Vocabulary

Read and match.

1. 

2. 

3. 

He likes to shop.

He likes to work in the garden.

He likes to go to the movies.

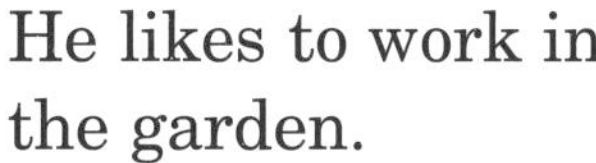

He likes to exercise.

He likes to visit friends.

4. 

5. 

Name: ______________________

Date: ______________________

C Grammar

Read and circle. Then write.

1. She ______________ to cook.
   like likes

2. What ______________ they like to do?
   do does

3. Fred ______________ to play soccer.
   like likes

4. What ______________ Tina like to do?
   do does

5. They ______________ to volunteer.
   like likes

D Reading

Valley Community Center

Morning Classes

Dance class

Learn to dance!

January 18 to March 20
Tuesday and Thursday
10:00 a.m. to 12:00 p.m.
Room 12

$50.00

Read the sentences. Look at the course description. Circle the answers.

1. This is for ______________.
   a. a music class b. a dance class

2. The class is in Room ______________.
   a. 12 b. 120

3. The class is in the ______________.
   a. morning b. evening

4. The class is ______________.
   a. $5.00 b. $50.00

5. Students in this class like to ______________.
   a. exercise b. read magazines

Name: ______________________

Date: ______________________

E Writing

Complete the story.

cook	guitar	like	likes	listen

Today is Sunday. My wife is in the kitchen. She likes to ______(1)______. My son is in his bedroom. He likes to ______(2)______ to music. My daughter ______(3)______ to play the ______(4)______. I ______(5)______ to work in the garden. We like Sunday!

Name: ______________________

Date: ______________________

Score: ______________________

FINAL TEST
UNITS 6–10

A Listening

Listen and circle.

TRACK 14

1. a.  b. 

2. a.  b. 

3. a. 

b. 

4. a.  b. 

5. a.  b. 

B Listening

Listen and circle the answer.

TRACK 15

1. a. At 5:00. b. It's 12:00.
2. a. Yes, she is. b. No, she doesn't.
3. a. Getting the mail. b. Receptionist.
4. a. He's a painter. b. A red jacket.
5. a. Yes, it is. b. No, I don't.

C Vocabulary

Read and match.

1. 

2. 

3. 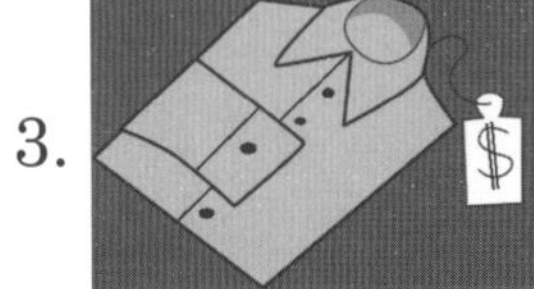

shoes

shirt

plumber

bus driver

cashier

4. 

5. 

Name: ______________________________

Date: ____________________

D Grammar

Read and match. Write the letter.

1. What color are the pants? ____	a. Yes, we do.
2. What do you like to do? ____	b. Washing the car.
3. Does he fix cars? ____	c. Blue.
4. What's he doing? ____	d. Yes, he does.
5. Do you like to swim? ____	e. Cook.

E Reading

Our Saturday

My family is busy on Saturday. My husband is a salesperson. He sells clothes in the morning. My daughter listens to music. She doesn't like to do her homework. My son takes out the trash. Then he plays basketball. I shop in the afternoon. We watch our favorite TV show at 8:00.

Read the sentences. Circle *Yes* or *No*.

1. She shops in the afternoon.	Yes	No
2. Her husband does chores in the morning.	Yes	No
3. Her daughter listens to music.	Yes	No
4. Her son plays cards.	Yes	No
5. They watch TV at 7:00.	Yes	No

Name: ______________________

Date: ______________

F Reading

Miriam's Shopping List		
Name	Clothing	Price
Farah	*black skirt*	*$20.00*
Rashid	*blue sweater*	*$15.00*
Asad	*brown shoes*	*$45.00*
Miriam	*white raincoat*	*$50.00*
Alima	*green dress*	*$35.00*

Read the questions. Look at Miriam's shopping list. Circle the answers.

1. How much is the blue sweater?
   a. $10.00 b. $15.00
2. Who needs a white raincoat?
   a. Rashid b. Miriam
3. The black skirt is ____.
   a. $20.00 b. $30.00
4. Rashid needs ____.
   a. brown shoes b. a blue sweater
5. How much is the green dress?
   a. $35.00 b. $25.00

G Writing

Write the missing letters.

1. o ____ a ____ g e
2. a p ____ o i n ____ m e n t
3. c ____ s t o d ____ a n
4. ____ e c ____ a n i c
5. p u ____ p ____ e

Name: ______________________

Date: ______________________

H Writing

Complete the story.

aide	busy	cashier	money	visit

Dear Grandmother,

Hi! How are you?

We are ________________(1)! Alex has a new job! He's a teacher's ________________(2). He likes the school and the teacher. I'm a ________________(3) at The Clothes Place. I count ________________(4). I like my job, too.

We like to ________________(5) friends on Sunday. Sunday is our day off!

Love,

Tina

Tests audio script

This audio script contains the listening portions of the *Ventures Basic* unit tests, midterm test, and final test. A customizable copy is available on the Assessment Audio CD/CD-ROM. You can play the audio program using the Assessment Audio CD/CD-ROM in a computer or a stereo, or you can read the script aloud.

Unit 1: Personal information

Track 2

A Listening

1. **A** What's your last name?
   B Mendez.
2. **A** What's her phone number?
   B 555-5983.
3. **A** What's your area code?
   B 415.
4. **A** When's his birthday?
   B In July.
5. **A** Where is Asad from?
   B He's from Somalia.

Unit 2: At school

Track 3

A Listening

1. **A** What do you need?
   B A pencil.
2. **A** What do you need, Luisa?
   B A ruler.
3. **A** Where's my stapler?
   B Here. Take this one.
   A Thanks.
4. **A** What day is it?
   B Tuesday.
5. **A** Where's my pencil?
   B On the desk.

Unit 3: Friends and family

Track 4

A Listening

1. **A** Who's that?
   B The father.
2. **A** Who is Luis?
   B Rose's brother.
3. **A** Do you have a daughter?
   B Yes, I do.
4. **A** Do you have a baby?
   B Yes, I do.
   A What's her name?
   B Marie.
5. **A** Show me the woman.
   B Here's the woman.

Unit 4: Health

Track 5

A Listening

1. **A** What's the matter?
   B My head hurts.
2. **A** What hurts?
   B My stomach hurts.
3. **A** What hurts?
   B My foot.
   A Oh, I'm sorry.
4. **A** What's the matter?
   B I need some medicine.
5. **A** What's the matter?
   B My hand hurts.

Unit 5: Around town

Track 6

A Listening

1. **A** Where's the bank?
   B The bank? It's next to the supermarket.
2. **A** Excuse me. Where's the movie theater?
   B The movie theater? Sorry, I don't know.
3. **A** Where's Kim?
   B At the hospital.
4. **A** Where are you?
   B At the restaurant.
5. **A** How do you get to school?
   B By bus.

Midterm Test Units 1–5

Track 7

A Listening

1. **A** Who's that?
   B My son.
2. **A** Where's my notebook?
   B I don't know.
3. **A** Do you have a sister?
   B Yes, I do.
4. **A** Where's the bank?
   B Next to the school.
5. **A** What's the matter?
   B My stomach hurts.

Track 8

B Listening

1. What's her name?
2. What hurts?
3. What do you need?
4. Where is he from?
5. Who is Franco?

Unit 6: Time

Track 9

A Listening

1. **A** What time is it?
   B It's two-thirty.
2. **A** What time is your meeting?
   B At five o'clock on Monday.
3. **A** What time is your class?
   B At seven o'clock in the morning.
4. **A** What time is your TV show?
   B At eight o'clock on Thursday.
5. **A** Is your concert at noon?
   B Yes, it is.

Unit 7: Shopping

Track 10

A Listening

1. **A** How much are the pants?
   B The pants? Twenty-five dollars.
2. **A** How much is the raincoat?
   B It's twenty-two dollars.
3. **A** How much is the blue dress?
   B The blue dress? It's fifteen dollars.
4. **A** How much is the shirt?
   B The shirt? It's eighteen dollars.
5. **A** How much is the orange jacket?

B $89.99.
A $89.99? Thank you.

Unit 8: Work

Track 11

A Listening

1. A What does she do?
   B She's a cashier.
2. A What's his job?
   B He's a truck driver.
3. A What does she do?
   B She's a homemaker.
4. A What's your job?
   B I'm a salesperson.
5. A What do you do?
   B I'm a plumber.

Unit 9: Daily living

Track 12

A Listening

1. A What's she doing?
   B She's doing homework.
2. A What are they doing?
   B Making lunch.
3. A What is he doing?
   B Taking out the trash.
4. A What's Mrs. Lee doing?
   B Watering the grass.
5. A What's he doing?
   B He's washing the car.

Unit 10: Free time

Track 13

A Listening

1. A What does he like to do?
   B He likes to fish.
2. A What does she like to do?
   B She likes to exercise.
3. A What do they like to do?
   B Dance.
4. A What does Paul like to do?
   B He likes to play basketball.
5. A Do you like to read magazines?
   B Yes, I do.

Final Test Units 6-10

Track 14

A Listening

1. A What color is her skirt?
   B Red.
2. A What's she doing?
   B Drying the dishes.
3. A How much is this T-shirt?
   B Nine dollars.
4. A What does she like to do?
   B Shop.
5. A What does he do?
   B He's a server.

Track 15

B Listening

1. A What time is it?
2. A Does she serve food?
3. A What is she doing?
4. A What's his job?
5. A Is your TV show at seven o'clock?

Tests answer key

Each unit test item is 4 points. Unit test sections have five items; therefore, each section is worth 20 points, for a total of 100 points per unit test.

Unit 1: Personal information

A Listening

1. b 2. b 3. a 4. a 5. b

B Vocabulary

1. Russia
2. Somalia
3. Mexico
4. the United States
5. Brazil
6. China

C Grammar

1. Her 3. His 5. My
2. Your 4. What's

D Reading

1. No 3. Yes 5. No
2. No 4. Yes

E Writing

1. Samir 4. 555-6978
2. Ahmed 5. February
3. 813

Unit 2: At school

A Listening

1. b 2. a 3. b 4. b 5. a

B Vocabulary

1. computer 4. Friday
2. Tuesday 5. desk
3. dictionary

C Grammar

1. on 4. in
2. on 5. under
3. under

D Reading

1. No 3. No 5. No
2. Yes 4. Yes

E Writing

1. chair 4. notebook
2. dictionary 5. floor
3. desk

Unit 3: Friends and family

A Listening

1. b 2. a 3. b 4. a 5. a

B Vocabulary

1. Ramona is Geraldo's daughter.
2. Pilar is Ramona's mother.
3. Hugo is Geraldo's father.
4. Magdalena is Ramona's grandmother.
5. Geraldo is Pilar's husband.

C Grammar

1. do 3. don't 5. don't
2. do 4. do

D Reading

1. Yes 3. No 5. No
2. Yes 4. Yes

E Writing

1. husband 4. sister
2. son 5. family
3. daughter

Unit 4: Health

A Listening

1. a 2. a 3. b 4. a 5. b

B Vocabulary

1. hand 4. arm
2. eye 5. foot
3. leg

C Grammar

1. arm 4. foot
2. legs 5. hand
3. eyes

D Reading

1. Yes 3. No 5. Yes
2. Yes 4. No

E Writing

1. sore throat 4. cold
2. toothache 5. stomachache
3. fever

Unit 5: Around town

A Listening

1. a 2. a 3. b 4. b 5. a

B Vocabulary

1. pharmacy
2. by train
3. movie theater
4. hospital
5. by car

C Grammar

1. Next to 4. Between
2. Across from 5. restaurant
3. On

D Reading

1. Yes 3. No 5. Yes
2. Yes 4. No

E Writing

1. by bus 4. by bicycle
2. on foot 5. by train
3. by taxi

Midterm Test Units 1–5

A Listening

(2 points per item)

1. a 2. b 3. a 4. a 5. b

B Listening

(3 points per item)

1. a 2. a 3. b 4. b 5. a

C Vocabulary

(2 points per item)

1. school 4. car
2. woman 5. headache
3. paper

D Grammar

(3 points per item)

1. c 2. d 3. a 4. e 5. b

E Reading

(2 points per item)

1. Yes 4. No
2. No 5. Yes
3. Yes

F Reading

(3 points per item)

1. a 2. b 3. b 4. a 5. b

G Writing

(2 points per item)

1. n r (January)
2. e s (Tuesday)
3. i s (United States)
4. i r (library)
5. o i (hospital)

H Writing
(3 points per item)
1. November 4. eye
2. mother 5. needs
3. office

Unit 6: Time

A Listening
1. b 2. a 3. a 4. a 5. b

B Vocabulary
1. TV show 4. class
2. movie 5. party
3. midnight

C Grammar
1. No 3. it isn't 5. Yes
2. Yes 4. it is

D Reading
1. Yes 3. No 5. Yes
2. No 4. Yes

E Writing
1. appointment 4. birthday
2. afternoon 5. busy
3. at

Unit 7: Shopping

A Listening
1. a 2. a 3. b 4. b 5. a

B Vocabulary
1. blouse 4. sweater
2. tie 5. skirt
3. socks

C Grammar
1. are 3. is 5. is
2. is 4. are

D Reading
1. No 3. Yes 5. Yes
2. Yes 4. No

E Writing
1. children 4. black
2. tie 5. are
3. blouse

Unit 8: Work

A Listening
1. b 2. b 3. a 4. b 5. a

B Vocabulary
1. A server serves food.
2. A custodian cleans buildings.
3. A mechanic fixes cars.
4. A salesperson sells clothes.
5. A receptionist answers the phone.

C Reading
1. No 3. Yes 5. No
2. No 4. Yes

D Grammar
1. doesn't 4. No
2. does 5. Yes
3. doesn't

E Writing
1. clothes 4. job
2. serves 5. homemaker
3. answers

Unit 9: Daily living

A Listening
1. b 2. a 3. b 4. b 5. a

B Vocabulary
1. making the bed
2. doing the laundry
3. walking the dog
4. getting the mail
5. cutting the grass

C Grammar
1. is 4. Making
2. Taking 5. is
3. are

D Reading
1. Yes 3. Yes 5. Yes
2. No 4. No

E Writing
1. wash the car
2. do homework
3. take out the trash
4. water the grass
5. make lunch

Unit 10: Free time

A Listening
1. a 2. b 3. b 4. b 5. a

B Vocabulary
1. He likes to go to the movies.
2. He likes to visit friends.
3. He likes to shop.
4. He likes to exercise.
5. He likes to work in the garden.

C Grammar
1. likes 4. does
2. do 5. like
3. likes

D Reading
1. b 2. a 3. a 4. b 5. a

E Writing
1. cook 4. guitar
2. listen 5. like
3. likes

Final Test Units 6–10

A Listening
(2 points per item)
1. a 2. b 3. b 4. a 5. b

B Listening
(3 points per item)
1. b 2. b 3. a 4. a 5. a

C Vocabulary
(2 points per item)
1. bus driver 4. plumber
2. cashier 5. shoes
3. shirt

D Grammar
(3 points per item)
1. c 2. e 3. d 4. b 5. a

E Reading
(2 points per item)
1. Yes 4. No
2. No 5. No
3. Yes

F Reading
(3 points per item)
1. b 2. b 3. a 4. b 5. a

G Writing
(2 points per item)
1. r n (orange)
2. p t (appointment)
3. u i (custodian)
4. m h (mechanic)
5. r l (purple)

H Writing
(3 points per item)
1. busy 4. money
2. aide 5. visit
3. cashier

Online Teacher's Resource Room

Overview

The Online Teacher's Resource Room (www.cambridge.org/myresourceroom) is an additional resource for teachers using the *Ventures Basic* Student's Book. The Online Teacher's Resource Room provides reproducible, supplementary materials for use during in-class assessment, whole-class activities, and group work. It provides more than 200 pages of additional material.

What's included in the Online Teacher's Resource Room:

- The **self-assessments** from the *Ventures Basic* Student's Book. Each unit self-assessment can be printed out, completed by students, and saved as a portfolio assessment tool.
- The **projects** from the *Ventures Basic* Teacher's Edition. Unit projects extend students' learning into a real-world context. They work within the unit topic, but they also go beyond the Student's Book.
- Reproducible **Alphabet and Number Cards**, in both large and small formats. These can be used to introduce letters and numbers to literacy students and to offer foundational practice in letter and number recognition.
- Reproducible **Writing Worksheets**. These offer preliterate, nonliterate, and semiliterate students the opportunity for further practice in recognizing and forming letters and numbers.
- Reproducible **Picture Dictionary Cards**, in both large and small formats. The Picture Dictionary Cards display each vocabulary item from the *Ventures Basic* Student's Book Picture dictionary pages. In addition, there are **Picture Dictionary Worksheets** and **Picture Dictionary Card Indexes**. The Picture Dictionary Cards and Worksheets offer additional unit-by-unit practice of all the vocabulary introduced on the Picture dictionary, Lesson D, Reading pages.
- **Real-life Documents**. Forms and documents introduced in *Ventures Basic* Student's Book can be reproduced and completed by students to reinforce necessary life skills.
- A **vocabulary list**. All key vocabulary in *Ventures Basic* Student's Book is listed alphabetically, with first occurrence page numbers included for easy reference.
- A **certificate of completion**. To recognize students for satisfactory completion of *Ventures Basic*, a printable certificate is included.

Additional resources include:

- A **placement test** that helps place students into the appropriate level of *Ventures*.
- A **Career and Educational Pathways solution** that helps students identify their educational and career goals.
- The ***Canadian Teacher's Guide***, a valuable tool for teachers using the *Ventures* series in Canada. With an easy-to-use format and clear and simple explanations, it shows teachers how to adapt *Ventures* Student's Books for a Canadian setting.
- The ***Multilevel Lesson Planner***. This invaluable part of the *Ventures* series helps instructors who manage a single classroom in which students use different levels of *Ventures* Student's Books.
- Reproducible ***Civics Worksheets*** for use alongside the *Ventures* series.
- **Audio scripts** for both the *Ventures Basic* class audio program and the Workbook audio program. These audio scripts can be used by teachers who don't have classroom access to a CD player or computer.
- A variety of national and state **correlations** meant to be used as a guide to developing or aligning your program's curriculum with *Ventures*.

Games

Overview

Games provide practice and reinforcement of skills, but in a fun and engaging manner. Students love to play games. Games raise motivation and enjoyment for learning. They can be used as a warm-up, practice, or review activity. The games described below can be adjusted and adapted to the skill level of the class.

1. Stand By

Skills: speaking, listening, writing
Objective: to practice asking and answering questions
Preparation: Write the question and answers on the board. Prepare grids.

- Write a question on the board, for example: *How do you get to work?*
- Write possible answers (*by bus, by car . . .*) scattered on the board or taped around the room.
- Ss copy the question and write their answer on the grid.
- When Ss have finished writing, they stand next to the answer that corresponds to their own answer.
- Then Ss mingle with the rest of the class, asking the initial question and recording each S's name and response on the grid.
- The questions can be made easier or more difficult, depending on the level of the Ss.

Sample Grid:

Question:	
Student's Name	Answer

2. Match the Leader

Skills: speaking, listening, writing
Objective: to practice giving and following directions
Preparation: Prepare grids with boxes – 3x3, 3x4, or 3x5. Number the boxes in the grid.

- Ss form groups of four or five and choose one S as leader.
- Provide the leader with a list of review words/items (for example, vocabulary words or telephone numbers).
- The leader selects an item from the list and tells the group where to write/draw that item on their grids. (For example, *Write "pen" in box number 3.*)
- The leader enters the item in the same box on his/her own grid (behind an opened file folder so Ss can't see).
- The leader continues until the grid is full.
- The leader then shows his/her grid to the group to use to check their own grids.

3. Round Table

Skills: speaking, listening, writing
Objective: to review vocabulary from a unit
Preparation: none

- Ss form groups of four or five. Each group has a blank sheet of paper.
- Announce the topic, usually the current unit topic.
- The first S says a word related to the topic, writes the word on the paper, and passes the paper to S2.
- S2 says a new word related to the topic, enters the word on the paper, and passes the paper to S3, who continues the process.
- Ss can ask for help from teammates when they cannot think of a new word or need help with spelling.
- The paper continues around the table until no one can think of another related word.
- Have Group 1 read its first word. If no other group has that word, Group 1 receives three points. If any other group has that word, Group 1 receives one point. Group 1 continues through its list, one word at a time.
- The other groups mark off the words on their lists and record one point for each word read.
- When Group 1 finishes, Group 2 reads only words that have not already been mentioned. Again, if other groups have the word, they each score one point; if no other group has the word, Group 2 scores three points.
- Continue until all groups have accounted for all their words.

4. Bingo

Skills: listening, writing
Objective: to review vocabulary
Preparation: Bingo grids (3x3, 3x4, 4x4 . . .)

- Select enough words to fill a Bingo grid. Read and spell each new word and use it in a sentence.

- Ss write each word randomly on their grids. Literacy Ss may need to copy the words from the board.
- When the grids are filled, play Bingo. Call the words by saying the word, spelling the word, or holding up examples of the items.
- The S who shouts "Bingo" first calls the next game.

5. Picture It

Skill: speaking
Objective: to review vocabulary
Preparation: sets of vocabulary cards (one per group)

- Ss form groups of three or four. Give each group one set of vocabulary cards.
- One S chooses a card but does not tell the group members the word.
- On a piece of paper, this S draws a picture or pictures representing the word. Point out that the S drawing the picture cannot talk or make gestures.
- The other Ss try to guess the word, using the drawings as clues.
- Ss take turns choosing and drawing words until all words are chosen.

Adaptation: Instead of drawing the words, Ss can act out the words for group members to guess.

6. Prediction Bingo

Skills: reading or listening
Objective: to develop the prereading or prelistening strategy of predicting
Preparation: Bingo grids (3x3, 3x4, 4x4 . . .)

- Provide Ss with the title or topic of a selection to be read or heard from an audio recording.
- In each square of the Bingo grid, Ss enter a word related to that topic that they think will appear in the reading or audio.
- Ss listen to the audio or read the text. When they hear or see a word that is on their Bingo grid, they circle it.
- Ss discuss their choices, both correct and incorrect.

7. Disappearing Dialog

Skills: speaking, listening, reading, writing
Objective: to practice learning dialogs
Preparation: none

- Write a dialog on the board.
- Go over the dialog with the whole class, then have selected groups say the dialog.
- Next, have Ss practice the dialog in pairs.
- Erase one word from each line of the dialog each time pairs practice, until all words are gone.
- Have volunteers recite the dialog without support from words on the board.
- Then have Ss add words back to the board until all words are again in place.

8. Moving Dialog

Skills: speaking, listening
Objective: to practice using dialogs
Preparation: none

- Ss stand in two lines (*A* and *B*), facing each other as partners.
- Ss in line *A* have one side of a simple conversation. Ss in line *B* have the other side. At a signal, Ss in line *A* begin the dialog, with Ss in line *B* responding.
- When Ss have completed the dialog, Ss in line *A* move one person to the left and practice the dialog again with a new partner.
- Ss at the end of the line will move to the beginning of the line to find their new partners.

Adaptation: This exchange may be a simple question and answer (**A:** *What is your name?* **B:** *My name is* _____.) for lower-level Ss.

9. Hear Ye, Hear Ye

Skills: listening or reading
Objective: to refine listening skills
Preparation: a reading text or an audio clip; a file card with a word or phrase from the clip on it (one word or phrase for each S or, if not enough words, use the same word multiple times)

- Select an audio clip or a reading segment.
- Provide each S with a file card containing a word or phrase that occurs one or more times in the clip or reading segment.
- Play or read the segment.
- Ss listen, paying particular attention for their word or phrase. They raise, then lower, their file card each time they hear the word. Alternatively, Ss can stand up or sit down when they hear their word.

Multilevel classroom management

All classrooms are multilevel in some sense. No two students will ever be exactly the same. Learners vary in demographic factors such as culture and ethnicity, personal factors such as a willingness to take risks and differing learning styles, and experiential factors such as background knowledge and previous education. With all these differences, it will always be a challenge to provide useful learning activities for all members of the class. Yet there are some techniques that make working with a multilevel class more manageable.

1. Group work is one of the best ways of working with a multilevel class. Some tasks, such as watching a video, going on a field trip, or describing a picture, can be performed as a whole group. What will change in a multilevel class is the level of expectation of responses following the shared experience. Other tasks can be performed as a whole group, but the tasks are adapted for the students' levels. This could include interviews with varying difficulty of questions or a project such as a class newspaper, where students of differing levels contribute through activities appropriate to their abilities.

   Smaller, homogeneous groups allow students of the same level the opportunity to work together on activities such as a problem-solving task or a group writing activity. Smaller, heterogeneous groups are good for board games or jigsaw activities where the difficulty of the material can be controlled. In *Ventures Basic,* the picture cards on the Online Teacher's Resource Room are excellent resources for working with heterogeneous or homogeneous groups. Ideas for how to use the picture cards are also online.

2. Varying the materials or activities is another method of addressing the issue of multiple levels in the classroom. Literacy students who are not yet able to do tasks that require them to read and write can work on related pages in the Literacy Workbook or with the Writing Worksheets found on the Online Teacher's Resource Room, while other students complete the activities in the Student's Book.

3. Self-access centers are another kind of classroom management technique. These centers would be located in corners of the classroom and would provide opportunities for learners to work at varying levels. By providing a variety of materials, which can be color-coded for levels of difficulty, students have the opportunity to make choices as to the level they feel comfortable working on. Students can self-correct with answer keys. In this way, students are working toward more learner autonomy, which is a valuable assistant in a multilevel classroom and a good start toward promoting lifelong learning skills.

4. Computer-assisted learning, using computers located within the classroom, can provide self-directed learning through software programs geared to a student's individual ability. Most programs provide immediate feedback to students to correct errors and build in a level of difficulty as a student progresses. Groups of students of like ability can rotate their time on the computer, working in pairs, or students can work individually at their own level.

A multilevel classroom, while challenging to the teacher, should offer each learner appropriate levels of instruction according to the learner's abilities, interests, needs, and experiences, and it should be designed to maximize each learner's educational gains. Good management techniques call for the teacher to provide a mixture of whole class, small group, and individual activities, create a learner-centered class by establishing self-access materials, use computers, and incorporate variety in the difficulty of the tasks and materials given to each student.

Authors' acknowledgments

The authors would like to acknowledge and thank focus group participants and reviewers for their insightful comments, as well as Cambridge University Press editorial, marketing, and production staffs, whose thorough research and attention to detail have resulted in a quality product.

The publishers would also like to extend their particular thanks to the following reviewers and consultants for their valuable insights and suggestions:

Kit Bell, LAUSD division of Adult and Career Education, Los Angeles, CA; **Bethany Bogage**, San Diego Community College District, San Diego, CA; **Leslie Keaton Boyd**, Dallas ISD, Dallas, TX; **Barbara Brodsky**, Teaching Work Readiness English for Refugees – Lutheran Family Services, Omaha, NE; **Jessica Buchsbaum**, City College of San Francisco, San Francisco, CA; **Helen Butner**, University of the Fraser Valley, British Columbia, Canada; **Sharon Churchill Roe**, Acadia University, Wolfville, NS, Canada; **Lisa Dolehide**, San Mateo Adult School, San Mateo, CA; **Yadira M. Dominguez**, Dallas ISD, Dallas, TX; **Donna M. Douglas**, College of DuPage, Glen Ellyn, IL; **Latarsha Dykes**, Broward Collge, Pembroke Pines, FL; **Megan L. Ernst**, Glendale Community College, Glendale, CA; **Megan Esler**, Portland Community College, Portland, OR; **Jennifer Fadden**, Fairfax County Public Schools, Fairfax, VA; **Fotine Fahouris**, College of Marin, Kentfield, CA; **Lynn Francis, M.A, M.S.**, San Diego Community College, San Diego, CA; **Danielle Gines**, Tarrant County College, Arlington, TX; **Katherine Hayne**, College of Marin, Kentfield, CA; **Armenuhi Hovhannes**, City College of San Francisco, San Francisco, CA; **Fayne B. Johnson**; **Martha L. Koranda**, College of DuPage, Glen Ellyn, IL; **Daphne Lagios**, San Mateo Adult School, San Mateo, CA; **Judy Langelier**, School District of Palm Beach County, Wellington, FL; **Janet Les**, Chilliwack Community Services, Chilliwack, British Columbia, Canada; **Keila Louzada**, Northern Virginia Community College, Sterling, VA; **Karen Mauer**, Fort Worth ISD, Fort Worth, TX; **Silvana Mehner**, Northern Virginia Community College, Sterling, VA; **Astrid T. Mendez-Gines,** Tarrant County College, Arlington, TX; **Beverly A. Miller**, Houston Community College, Houston, TX; **José Montes, MS. Ed.**, The English Center, Miami-Dade County Public Schools, Miami, FL; **Suzi Monti**, Community College of Baltimore County, Baltimore, MD; **Irina Morgunova**, Roxbury Community College, Roxbury Crossing, MA; **Julia Morgunova**, Roxbury Community College, Roxbury Crossing, MA; **Susan Otero**, Fairfax County Public Schools, Fairfax, VA; **Sergei Paromchik**, Hillsborough County Public Schools, Tampa, FL; **Pearl W. Pigott**, Houston Community College, Houston, TX; **Marlene Ramirez**, The English Center, Miami-Dade County Public Schools, Miami, FL; **Cory Rayala**, Harbor Service Center, LAUSD, Los Angeles, CA; **Catherine M. Rifkin**, Florida State College at Jacksonville, Jacksonville, FL; **Danette Roe**, Evans Community Adult School, Los Angeles, CA; **Maria Roy**, Kilgore College, Kilgore, TX; **Jill Shalongo**, Glendale Community College, Glendale, CA, and Sierra Linda High School, Phoenix, AZ; **Laurel Owensby Slater**, San Diego Community College District, San Diego, CA; **Rheba Smith**, San Diego Community College District, San Diego, CA; **Jennifer Snyder**, Portland Community College, Portland, OR; **Mary K. Solberg**, Metropolitan Community College, Omaha, NE; **Rosanne Vitola**, Austin Community College, Austin, TX

Ventures Basic Student's Book

Illustration credits

Kenneth Batelman: 20, 68
Travis Foster: 4, 49, 55, 61, 98, 124, 125 (b)
Chuck Gonzales: 40, 46, 47, 57, 100, 101, 112 (t), 113, 126, 130
Colin Hayes: 103, 117, 129
Pamela Hobbs: 9, 48, 112 (b)
Rod Hunt: 60 (b), 99, 125 (t)
Victor Kulihin: 77, 91
Frank Montagna: 10, 52, 109, 115
Jason O'Malley: 22 (t), 26, 72, 87, 90 (b)
Greg Paprocki: 21, 34, 35, 89, 114
Q2A Media Services: 2, 8, 22 (b), 23, 24 (t, b #3), 25, 37, 60 (t #6, b #4), 61 (#3, #6), 62 (b), 63 (#4), 64 (t), 71, 92, 116 (t, b #1, #3)
Monika Roe: 7, 31, 36, 86, 88, 89
Phil Williams: 60 (t), 63

Photography credits

Cover front (tl) Andrew Zarivny/Shutterstock, (tr) Stuart Monk/Shutterstock, (r) Gary D Ercole/Photolibrary/Getty Images, (cr) Sam Kolich; (br) Nathan Maxfield/iStockphoto, (c) Monkey Business Images/Shutterstock, (bl) Alistair Forrester Shankie/iStockphoto, (cl) ML Harris/Iconica/Getty Images, (l) Mark Lewis/Digital Vision/Getty Images, back (tc) cloki/Shutterstock, (br) gualtiero boffi/Shutterstock, **3** (b) ©Jupiterimages/Thinkstock, **4** (br) ©Jack Hollingsworth/Thinkstock, **5** (b) ©zhu difeng/Shutterstock, **11** (tl) ©leungchopan/Shutterstock, (tr) ©Andres Rodriguez/Fotolia, **14** (c) ©Maridav/Fotolia, **16** (cr) ©Ebtikar/Shutterstock, **19** (tl) ©f9photos/Shutterstock, (tr) ©Julia Ivantsova/Shutterstock, (tcl) ©Christopher Elwell/Shutterstock, (tcr) ©zirconicusso/Fotolia, (l) ©Alfonso de Tom-s/Fotolia, (r) ©f9photos/Shutterstock, (bl) ©Christopher Elwell/Shutterstock, (br) ©Tr1sha/Shutterstock, **20** (tl) ©magicoven/Shutterstock, (cl) ©Lipskiy/Shutterstock, (bl) ©Luminis/Shutterstock, (tr) ©sagir/Shutterstock, (cr) ©Michael D Brown/Shutterstock, (br) ©CrackerClips Stock Media/Shutterstock, **24** (tl) ©George Kerrigan, (bl) ©George Kerrigan, (br) ©George Kerrigan, **39** (tl) ©aslysun/Shutterstock, (tc) ©iofoto/Shutterstock, (tr) ©Monkey Business/Fotolia, (bl) ©AISPIX by Image Source/Shutterstock, (bc) ©lev dolgachov/Shutterstock, (br) ©Monkey Business Images/Shutterstock, **45** (tl) ©Cheryl Casey/Shutterstock, (tr) ©Nobilior/Fotolia, (tcl) ©Yuri Arcurs/Fotolia, (tcr) ©Getty Images/Thinkstock, (l) ©Nobilior/Fotolia, (r) ©Yuri Arcurs/Fotolia, (bl) ©karamysh/Shutterstock, (br) ©Getty Images/Thinkstock, **46** (tc) ©Nicholas Piccillo/Shutterstock, **47** (br) ©Jamie Grill/Tetra Images/Corbis, **48** (tl) ©micro10x/Shutterstock, (bl) ©micro10x/Shutterstock, (tc) ©photobank.ch/Shutterstock, (bc) ©photobank.ch/Shutterstock, (tr) ©Igor Normann/Shutterstock, (br) ©Igor Normann/Shutterstock, **51** (tl) ©kaarsten/Shutterstock, (tc) ©Noam Armonn/Shutterstock, (tr) ©kurhan/Shutterstock, (bl) ©bjsites/Shutterstock, (bc) ©Dragos Iliescu/Shutterstock, (br) ©Ice Tea Media/Alamy, **59** (tl) ©Steve Shepard/iStockphoto, (tr) ©Cynthia Farmer/iStockphoto, (tcl) ©Fuse/Getty Images, (tcr) ©Jim West/Alamy, (l) ©Cynthia Farmer/iStockphoto, (r) ©i love images/Alamy, (bl) ©Fuse/Getty Images, (br) ©Steve Shepard/iStockphoto, **61** (br) ©Image Source/Corbis, **63** (bl) ©Mika Heittola/Shutterstock, (br) ©Supri Suharjoto/Shutterstock, **65** (tl) ©Blend Images/Alamy, (tc) ©Johnny Habell/Shutterstock, (tr) ©Miramiska/Shutterstock, (br) ©Stephen Coburn/Shutterstock, (bc) ©Joan Barnett Lee/ZUMA Press/Corbis, (bl) ©beyond/Corbis, **69** (tl) ©mch67/Fotolia, (cl) ©aleksandar kamasi/Fotolia, (bl) ©Africa Studio/Fotolia, (tr) ©fstop123/iStockphoto, (cr) ©Margaret M Stewart/Shutterstock, (br) ©mikie11/Shutterstock, **71** (br) ©Andres Rodriguez/Fotolia, **85** (tl) ©kedrov/Shutterstock, (tr) ©Karkas/Shutterstock, (tcl) ©zhaoyan/Shutterstock, (tcr) ©Brooke Becker/Shutterstock, (cl) ©Olga Popova/Shutterstock, (cr) ©discpicture/Shutterstock, (bl) ©Karkas/Shutterstock, (bc) ©Alexander Kalina/Shutterstock, (br) ©WavebreakMediaMicro/Fotolia, **86** (tl) ©mallivan/Fotolia, (tc) ©Karkas/Shutterstock, (tr) ©Pakhnyushcha/Shutterstock, (bl) ©Ruslan Kudrin/Shutterstock, (bc) ©coloss/iStockphoto, (br) © Hemera Technologies/Getty Images/Thinkstock, **87** (tl) ©terekhov igor/Shutterstock, (tc) ©Saime Deniz Tuyel Dogan/iStockphoto, (tr) ©Karkas/Shutterstock, (bl) ©ElnurShutterstock, (bc) ©mates/Shutterstock, (br) ©kedrovShutterstock, **95** (tl) ©Karkas/Shutterstock, (tcl) ©Coloss/Shutterstock, (cl) ©Karkas/Shutterstock, (bcl) ©kedrov/Shutterstock, (bl) ©sagir/Shutterstock, (tcr) ©Pakhnyushcha/Shutterstock, (tr) ©K. Miri Photography/Shutterstock, (bcr) ©Karkas/Shutterstock, (cr) ©sommthink/Shutterstock, (bc) ©Suslik1983/Shutterstock, (br) ©oksix/Fotolia, **97** (tl) ©kurhan/Shutterstock, (tr) ©Kadmy/Fotolia, (tcl) ©auremar/Fotolia, (tcr) ©pressmaster/Fotolia, (l) ©sjlocke/iStockphoto, (r) ©Eliza Snow/iStockphoto, (bl) ©Tyler Olson/Fotolia, (br) ©pressmaster/Fotolia, **101** (tr) ©Wavebreak Media/Thinkstock, **107** (tl) ©Robert Wilson/Fotolia, (l) ©Adisa/Shutterstock, (bl) ©Tetra Images/Alamy, (tr) ©Scanrail/Fotolia, (r) ©Quang Ho/Shutterstock, (br) ©Galushko Sergey/Shutterstock, **111** (tl) ©Piti Tan/Shutterstock, (tr) ©Monkey Business Images/Shutterstock, (tcl) ©Monkey Business Images/Shutterstock, (tcr) ©Jupiterimages/Getty Images/Thinkstock, (l) ©Ryan McVay/Thinkstock, (r) ©Piti Tan/Shutterstock, (bl) ©RubberBall/Alamy, (br) ©Fancy/Alamy, **113** (br) ©Image Source/Getty Images, **123** (tl) ©PhotoInc/iStockphoto, (tr) ©Huntstock/Thinkstock, (tcl) ©Cultura/Lost Horizon Images /Getty Images, (tcr) ©kocis202/Fotolia, (l) ©big_tau/Fotolia, (r) ©Kzenon/Shutterstock, (bl) ©Mircea BEZERGHEANU/Shutterstock, (br) ©bogdanhoda/Shutterstock, **124** (tl) ©Sophie Louise Davis/Shutterstock, (tc) ©MY - Music/Alamy, (tr) ©OJO Images Ltd/Alamy, (bl) ©Levent Konuk/Shutterstock, (bc) ©Steve Heap/Shutterstock, (br) ©Yi Lu/Viewstock/Corbis, **127** (tl) ©Catherine Yeulet/iStockphoto, (tc) ©siamionau pavel/Shutterstock, (tr) ©Jupiterimages/Getty Images/Thinkstock, (bl) ©ferkelraggae/Fotolia, (bc) ©AISPIX by Image Source/Shutterstock, (br) ©Monteverde/Alamy, **128** (bl) ©Artkot/Shutterstock, (bcl) ©Deniz Thetis/Fotolia, (bc) ©Dmitry Ersler/Fotolia, (bcr) ©illustrez-vous/Fotolia, (br) ©Maxx-Studio/Shutterstock, **133** (tl) ©ilposeidone/Fotolia, (tcl) ©Nicemonkey/Shutterstock, (bcl) ©Design Pics/Thinkstock, (br) ©Krokodyl/Fotolia, (tr) ©Patricia Marroquin/Shutterstock, (tcr) ©Ar_nas Gabalis/Fotolia, (bcr) ©Balu/Shutterstock, (br) ©mirpic/Fotolia

Ventures Basic Teacher's Edition tests

Illustration credits

John Batten: T-168 (b) 3, 5; T-171 (b); T-180 (b) 3; T-193, 1a, 2a-b, 3b
Kevin Brown: T-169; T-175, 1, 2, 3
Travis Foster: T-190, 1a-b
Chuck Gonzales: T-171 (t) 4a; T-174 (t) 2a-b, 3b; T-180 (t) 5a; T-190, 4b; T-196 (t) 4b, 5a-b
Paul Hampson: T-174 (b); T-175, 4, 5; T-196 (b) 5
Ben Hasler: T-177 (b) 1, 3, 4; T-187 (b) 2
Colin Hayes: T-177, 5a-b; T-180 (t) 5b; T-190, 2a-b, 3a, 5a; T-196 (t) 4a
Pamela Hobbs: T-165 (b)
Kim Johnson: T-199 (b) 1, 4
Victor Kulihin: T-184 (t) 2b, 5a-b
Frank Montagna: T-174 (t) 1b, 5a-b; T-180 (b) 5; T-184 (b) 2, 4, 5; T-191; T-196 (b) 2; T-199 (t) 3b, (b) 3, 5
Scott Mooney: T-173; T-179; T-196 (b) 1, 3, 4
Jason O'Malley: T-168 (t) 5a-b; T-184 (t) 2a, (b) 1
Q2A Media Services: T-168 (t) 4a-b; T-184 (t) 1a-b, 3a-b, (b) 3; T-199 (t) 3a
Monika Roe: T-165 (t) 1a-b, 2a-b, 3a-b; T-180 (t) 1a, 2a
William Waitzman: T-170; T-176; T-187 (b) 1, 3-5; T-199 (b) 2
Phil Williams: T-177 (t) 1a-b, 2a, 3b, 4a; T-178

Photography credits

T-166 (br) szefei/Shutterstock, **T-167** (c) Ebtikar/Shutterstock, **T-168** (bc) Luminis/Shutterstock, (bcl) Christopher Elwell/Shutterstock, (bl) Kitch Bain/Shutterstock, (c) sagir/Shutterstock, (cl) magicoven/Shutterstock, (tc) Julia Ivantsova/Shutterstock , (tcl) f9photos/Shutterstock, **T-171** (cr) lev dolgachov/Shutterstock, (r) Monkey Business Images/Shutterstock, (tr) AISPIX by Image Source/Shutterstock, **T-174** (bl) Ice Tea Media/Alamy, (tc) Cheryl Casey/Shutterstock, (tl) Jamie Grill/Tetra Images/Corbis, (tr) Yuri Arcurs/Fotolia, **T-177** (bcl) Steve Shepard/iStockphoto, (bl) Craig Lovell/Eagle Visions Photography/Alamy, (br) Car Culture ® Collection/Getty Images, (cl) Fuse/Getty Images, (tr) Jim West/Alamy, T-180: (bl) Erik Isakson/Tetra Images/Corbis, (br) Peter38/Shutterstock, (cl) zirconicusso/Fotolia, (l) Julia Ivantsova/Shutterstock, (tcl) karamysh/Shutterstock, (tcr) Cynthia Farmer/iStockphoto, (tr) Alfonso de Tomçs/Fotolia, **T-187** (bcl) Karkas/Shutterstock, (bl) kedrov/Shutterstock, (cl) mates/Shutterstock, (cr) coloss/iStockphoto, (l) Saime Deniz Tuyel Dogan/iStockphoto, (r) Pakhnyushcha/Shutterstock, (tcl) Olga Popova/Shutterstock, (tcr) Karkas/Shutterstock, (tl) Karkas/Shutterstock, (tr) kedrov/Shutterstock, **T-190** (bcl) auremar/Fotolia, (r) Jeroen van den Broek/Shutterstock, (tcr) Kadmy/Fotolia, **T-193** (bcl) Elenathewise/Fotolia, (bcr) Ned Frisk/Blend Images/Alamy, (bl) Hemera/Thinkstock, (br) Echo/Cultura/Getty Images, (cl) katja kodba/Shutterstock, (tr) Piti Tan/Shutterstock, **T-196** (bcl) PhotoInc/iStockphoto, (bl) Catherine Yeulet/iStockphoto, (cl) Huntstock/Thinkstock, (l) kocis202/Fotolia, (tcl) Kzenon/Shutterstock, (tl) big_tau/Fotolia, **T-199** (cl) Monkey Business Images/Shutterstock, (cr) Eliza Snow/iStockphoto, (l) Digital Vision/Thinkstock, (r) Kadmy/Fotolia, (tcl) Saime Deniz Tuyel Dogan/iStockphoto, (tcr) pressmaster/Fotolia, (tl) Karkas/Shutterstock, (tr) Piti Tan/Shutterstock

Assessment Audio CD / CD-ROM

What is the Assessment Audio CD / CD-ROM?

- The Assessment Audio CD / CD-ROM contains the unit, midterm, and final tests (in both .pdf and customizable Word formats). In addition, it includes audio scripts, answer keys, instructions for administering tests, and the test audio for the listening portions.
- The complete test audio can also be played using a conventional CD player.

Audio CD tracks:

Track 1:	Introduction
Track 2:	Unit 1 Test
Track 3:	Unit 2 Test
Track 4:	Unit 3 Test
Track 5:	Unit 4 Test
Track 6:	Unit 5 Test
Track 7:	Midterm Test, Section A
Track 8:	Midterm Test, Section B
Track 9:	Unit 6 Test
Track 10:	Unit 7 Test
Track 11:	Unit 8 Test
Track 12:	Unit 9 Test
Track 13:	Unit 10 Test
Track 14:	Final Test, Section A
Track 15:	Final Test, Section B

To access the assessment materials (including test audio):

Windows XP, Vista, 7

- Insert the disc into a CD-ROM drive on your computer.
- If Autorun is enabled, the application will start automatically.
- If Autorun is disabled, open My Computer. Right-click the CD-ROM icon and then select "Open"or "Explore." Double-click "Cambridge-University-Press."

Mac OS X

- Insert the disc into a CD-ROM drive on your computer.
- Double-click the CD-ROM icon on the desktop to launch the application. Double-click the Audio CD icon to access the audio via iTunes.

System requirements:

- Sound card. Speakers or headphones.
- Media player.
- PDF reader. Word processor.

Windows XP, Vista, 7

- 400 MHz processor speed
- 128 MB RAM

Mac OS X

- 300 MHz processor speed
- 64 MB RAM

Support:

If you experience difficulties with this audio CD / CD-ROM, please visit: www.cambridge.org/esl/support